What's in the Bible for . . .™

Mothers

Judy Bodmer

CARTOONS BY

Reverend Fun

(Dennis "Max" Hengeveld)
Dennis is a graphic designer for Gospel Films and the author of *Has Anybody Seen My Locust?* His cartoons can be seen worldwide at
.reverendfun.com

P. O. Box 4123, Lancaster, Pennsylvania 17604

To schedule author appearances, write:

Author Appearances
Starburst Publishers
P.O. Box 4123
Lancaster, Pennsylvania 17604
(717) 293-0939

www.starburstpublishers.com

CREDITS:
Cover design by David Marty Design
Text design and composition by John Reinhardt Book Design
Illustrations by Bruce Burkhart and Melissa A. Burkhart
Cartoons by Dennis "Max" Hengeveld

Unless otherwise noted, or paraphrased by the author, all Scripture quotations are from the New International Version of The Holy Bible.

To the best of its ability, Starburst Publishers® has strived to find the source of all material. If there has been an oversight, please contact us, and we will make any correction deemed necessary in future printings. We also declare that to the best of our knowledge all material (quoted or not) contained herein is accurate, and we shall not be held liable for the same.

First Printing, March 2000

ISBN: 1-892016-26-5
Library of Congress Number 99-69038
Printed in the United States of America

READ THESE PAGES BEFORE YOU READ THIS BOOK . . .

Welcome to the *What's in the Bible for . . .* series. This series is the result of a belief that no matter who you are—teenager or senior, pastor or plumber—the Bible is the most important book for you to read and understand.

You could open up to the first page of the Bible and start plowing through, but let's be honest. Doing so can be a little overwhelming. Don't worry. This book combines bullet points, expert quotes, sidebar help, and cartoon humor so your time in the Bible will be enjoyable and meaningful. Have fun as you learn the Word!

On this page and the next you'll find information about the *What's in the Bible for . . .* and *God's Word for the Biblically-Inept* series. Please note the "Title Code" of each book. This code along with page numbers is used throughout each series, allowing easy reference from one book to another.

What's in the Bible for . . .™ Mothers

Judy Bodmer — TITLE CODE: WBFM

Is home schooling a good idea? Is it okay to work? At what age should I start treating my children like responsible adults? What is the most important thing I can teach my children? If you are asking these questions and need help answering them, *What's in the Bible for . . . Mothers* is especially for you! Simple and user-friendly, this motherhood manual offers hope and instruction for today's mothers by jumping into the lives of mothers in the Bible (e.g., Naomi, Elizabeth, and Mary) and by exploring biblical principles that are essential to being a nurturing mother. (trade paper) ISBN 1892016265 **$16.95**

What's in the Bible for . . .™ Women

Georgia Curtis Ling — TITLE CODE: WBFW

What does the Bible have to say to women? Women of all ages will find biblical insight on topics that are meaningful to them in four sections: Wisdom for the Journey; Family Ties; Bread, Breadwinners, and Bread Makers; and Fellowship and Community Involvement. This book uses illustrations, bullet points, chapter summaries, and icons to make understanding God's Word easier than ever!
(trade paper) ISBN 1892016109 **$16.95**

What's in the Bible for . . .™ Teens

Mark and Jeanette Littleton — TITLE CODE: WBFT

This is a book that teens will love! *What's in the Bible for . . . Teens* contains topical Bible themes that parallel the challenges and pressures of today's adolescents. Learn about Bible Prophecy, God's plan for relationships, and Peer Pressure in a conversational and fun tone. Helpful and eye-catching "WWJD?" icons, illustrations and sidebars included. (trade paper) ISBN 1892016052 **$16.95**

For Purchasing Information, see page 350 • Learn more at **www.biblicallyinept.com**

IT'S THE BIBLE MADE EASY!

The *God's Word for the Biblically-Inept*™ series is already a best-seller with over 100,000 books sold! Designed to make reading the Bible easy, educational, and fun, this series of verse-by-verse Bible studies, topical studies, and overviews mixes scholarly information from experts with helpful icons, illustrations, sidebars, and time lines. It's the Bible made easy!

God's Word for the Biblically-Inept™ Series

The Bible by Larry Richards	ISBN 0914984551	**GWBI**	**$16.95**
Daniel by Daymond R. Duck	ISBN 0914984489	**GWDN**	**$16.95**
Genesis by Joyce Gibson	ISBN 1892016125	**GWGN**	**$16.95**
Health & Nutrition by Kathleen O'Bannon Baldinger	ISBN 0914984055	**GWHN**	**$16.95**
Life of Christ, Volume 1, by Robert C. Girard	ISBN 1892016230	**GWLC**	**$16.95**
Men of the Bible by D. Larry Miller	ISBN 1892016079	**GWMB**	**$16.95**
Prophecies of the Bible by Daymond R. Duck	ISBN 1892016222	**GWPB**	**$16.95**
Revelation by Daymond R. Duck	ISBN 0914984985	**GWRV**	**$16.95**
Women of the Bible by Kathy Collard Miller	ISBN 0914984063	**GWWB**	**$16.95**

New Titles Are Coming!

Starburst Publishers will continue expanding the *What's in the Bible for . . .* and *God's Word for the Biblically-Inept* series. Look for these future titles:

- **What's in the Bible for . . . Couples**
- **What's in the Bible for . . . Leaders**
- **Romans—God's Word for the Biblically-Inept**
- **Life of Christ, Volume 2—God's Word for the Biblically-Inept**
- **John—God's Word for the Biblically-Inept**
- **Mark—God's Word for the Biblically-Inept**

For Purchasing Information, see page 350 • Learn more at **www.biblicallyinept.com**

CHAPTERS AT A GLANCE

PART TWO: GIVING BIRTH

PART THREE: RAISING UP

ILLUSTRATIONS

For a preview of the icons in this book, check out the sidebar in this Introduction!

INTRODUCTION

WHAT'S IN THIS CHAPTER

Here We Go

Welcome to *What's in the Bible for . . .™ Mothers*!

When I was asked to write this book, my first thought was there isn't enough information in the Bible to write a whole book about being a mom. But I was wrong. The Bible has a lot to say on this important topic.

My second thought was whatever it did have to say would not apply to us today. I was wrong about that, too. During my research I was constantly surprised how timeless the Scriptures are as I looked at such subjects as the role of women in society, working outside of the home, home schooling, abortion, miscarriage, discipline, setting priorities, letting go, the empty nest, grandmothers, and mothers-in-law. I now have a new appreciation for the Bible and how God views me, a woman and a mother. I hope through the pages of this REVOLUTIONARY COMMENTARY™ you too will discover how precious your task is and how valuable you are in God's great plan of raising up godly children.

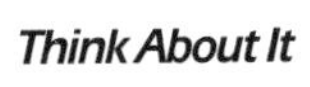

Why Look to the Bible?

Being a mother can be scary. When we leave the hospital we carry with us not only a new life, but a lot of responsibility and fear of living up to the task. Many of us turn to professionals like Spock, Dobson, or Brazelton for information on how to handle each stage of parenting, infancy, the terrible twos, toilet training, or a rebellious child. But how many of us turn to the Bible?

Why don't we? If God created us, then who better than God to lay out a plan for our lives? And what better way to communicate that plan than through the written word. Maybe you don't

believe that the Bible is a communication from God, but Jesus called the Scripture the *"word of God"* (John 10:34). It is full of wisdom and timely advice directly from the one who designed the family.

What Others are Saying:

Charles Colson: At its simplest level, if God is God and cannot err, and if the Scriptures are God's Word, then it has to be **infallible**. An infallible God cannot err. Scripture, which comes from God, by definition has to be infallible.

infallible: *absolutely trustworthy*

Norman Geisler: [The Bible] was written in two major languages (Hebrew and Greek) over a period of about sixteen hundred years (c. 1500 B.C.–A.D. 100). It covers hundreds of different topics by authors from widely diverse backgrounds (kings, shepherds, doctor, tax collector, fishermen). Yet in spite of all of this, the Bible is one book with one message: people are sinners, but God loves us and Christ died and rose for us so that we can be forgiven (John 3:16; Romans 5:8; 10:9, 10).

KEY POINT

Children are God's gift and a sign of his favor.

2 Timothy 3:16–17 All scripture is **God-breathed** and is useful for teaching, rebuking, correcting, and training in righteousness, so that the man of God may be thoroughly equipped for every good work.

God-breathed: *God's active involvement in writing the Scripture*

GO TO:

2 Peter 1:20–21 (God-breathed)

2 Timothy 2:21 (good work)

Advice on Being a Mom

The Bible is a valuable resource for every area of life, including parenting. God created the family as the foundation for raising godly children who would pass along their faith to their children who would then pass along their faith to their children.

Instead of boring us with long lists of dos and don'ts, the Bible uses the examples of women like Eve, Sarah, Hannah, and Mary to teach us the joy and heartbreak that we all have in common whether we lived centuries ago or today. These women struggled with infertility, childbirth, rebellious children, sacrifice, and death. Sometimes they took things into their own hands suffering the consequences. Yes, there is much we can learn from the mothers of the Bible and from the wisdom of God.

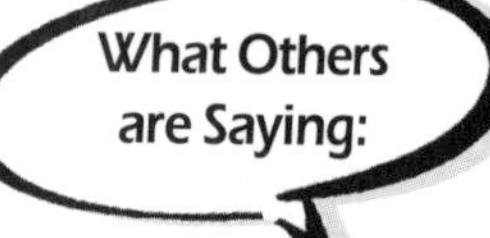

James Boice: Regular meals are necessary for us to be healthy and alert. On occasion we may miss a meal, but we can't do that too often. In the same way we must regularly study God's Word if we are to become spiritually strong.

How to Use *What's in the Bible for . . .*™ *Mothers*

- Sit down with this book and your Bible.
- Say a prayer that God will open your heart to the message he has for you.
- Start the book at chapter 1.
- Use the sidebar loaded with icons and helpful information to get a knowledge boost.
- At the end of each chapter answer the Study Questions and review the Chapter Wrap-Up.
- Then go to the next chapter.

If you like to hop, skip, and jump, go ahead. The book is laid out in a carefully planned order, but if you are yearning for answers to a specific need, go ahead and play leapfrog, but I hope you return to those chapters you skipped. You may think a given chapter doesn't apply to you, but try reading it anyway. Odds are, you'll be pleasantly surprised as you find gems of truth specifically for you. Even if you don't use the information now, it may be a great resource later.

Why Use the New International Version (NIV)?

I want this book to be easy to read and understand; that's why I chose to use the New International Version (NIV) of the Bible. It is a scholarly translation that accurately expresses the original Bible in clear and contemporary English. But don't worry if you don't own a copy of an NIV Bible, the one you have will work fine.

The Features

This book contains a variety of special features that can help you learn. They're illustrated in the outside column of this introduction and in the following sample page. Here they are again, with a brief explanation of each.

Sections and Icons	*What's It For?*
What's in This Chapter	*the most important points of the chapter*
Here We Go	*a short introduction to the chapter*
Bible Quote	*an important quote from the Bible*
The Big Picture	*summary of a long passage from the Bible*
Commentary	*my thoughts on the Bible verse(s)*

Study Questions

CHAPTER WRAP-UP

JUDY'S

BOOKSHELF

Sections and Icons	*What's It For?*
What Others Are Saying	*quotes from experts that agree and sometimes even disagree with my position*
Go To	*other Bible verses to explore and to clarify (underlined in text)*
What?	*the meaning of a word (bold in text)*
Think about It	*questions or statements that will make you think*
Remember This	*important points to remember*
Examples from the Bible	*other places in the Bible that illustrate the point*
Key Point	*main point of each section*
Warning	*strong recommendations to keep you on track*
Build Your Marriage	*advice on strengthening your marriage*
For Single Moms	*thoughts for single women*
Lighten Up	*a funny anecdote or humorous saying*
From Judy's Heart	*thoughts on being a mom that come straight from my heart to yours*
Study Questions	*questions for discussion and/or Bible study*
Chapter Wrap-Up	*the important points of chapter revisited*

A Word about Words

As you read *What's in the Bible for . . .™ Mothers*, you'll notice some interchangeable words: Scripture, Scriptures, Word, Word of God, God's Word, etc. All of these terms mean the same thing and come under the broad heading of "the Bible."

In most cases the phrase "*the Scriptures*" in the New Testament refers to the Old Testament. Peter indicated that the writings of the apostle Paul were quickly accepted in the early church as equal to "*the other scriptures*" (2 Peter 3:16). Both Testaments consistently demonstrate the belief that is expressed in 2 Timothy 3:16, "*all scripture is God-breathed.*"

One Final Tip

Open your heart to the message of each chapter. Allow God to work in your life and mold you into the mother you always wanted to be. Discover, along with me, that the Bible is rich with advice, encouragement, and even laughter. I hope you will be as blessed as I have been in my search of what the Bible has to say to mothers.

Here's a Sample Page!

Bible Quote: This is where you'll read a quote from the Bible.

James 1:5 If any of you lacks wisdom, he should ask God, who gives generously to all without finding fault, and it will be given to him.

Commentary: This is where you'll read commentary about the biblical quote.

Decisions, Decisions: In or Out?

James, the brother of Jesus, is writing to the new believers who were scattered about the Roman world (see GWBI, pages 213–214) when they fled from persecution. James knows that godly wisdom is a great gift. He gives a simple plan to get it: need wisdom, ask for it. God will give it to us.

Up 'til now we've concentrated on finding the wind sails of your drifting marriage and overcoming marital lems. But you may be the reader who is shaking her head, thinking that I just don't understand what you're going through. You can't take the abuse any longer; you've forgiven the **infidelity** time after time; and in order for you and your children to survive, you see no alternative but divorce.

"What?": When you see a word in bold, go to the sidebar for a definition.

infidelity: sexual unfaithfulness of a spouse

So let me make this clear: in no way am I saying to allow your husband to abuse you or your children. If the abuse continues, get out and seek professional ... keep the a... Do not only dam... not physical a... ren's

"Go To": When you see a word or phrase that's underlined, go to the sidebar for a biblical cross-reference.

When you feel you've depleted all of your options, continue to ask God for wisdom in order to have the knowledge to make the right decisions. Wise women seek God. God is the <u>source</u> of wisdom and wisdom is found in Christ and the Word.

GO TO:

Psalm 111:10 (source)

REMEMBER THIS

Gary Chapman, Ph.D.: Is there hope for women who suffer physical abuse from their husbands? Does reality living offer any genuine hope? I believe the answer to those questions is yes.[6]

What Others are Saying:

Give It Away

You don't have to be a farmer to understand what the Apostle Paul wrote to the Corinthian church (see illustration, page 143). A picture is worth a thousand words, and Paul is painting masterpiece. He reminds us of what any smart farmer knows in order to produce a bountiful harvest, he has to plan for it.

What Others Are Saying: This is where you'll read what an expert has to say about the subject at hand.

MONEY, MONEY, MONEY • 5

127

Feature with icon in the sidebar: Thoughout the book you will see sections of text with corresponding icons in the sidebar. See the chart on pages xiii–xiv for a description of all the features in this book.

Part One

BEING BLESSED

REVEREND FUN

"Abraham and I are not interested in a condo community . . . we need a place that would be nice for raising children."

1 GOD HAD A PLAN

WHAT'S IN THIS CHAPTER

- The Oldest Profession—Motherhood
- An Old-Fashioned Word—Marriage
- Children—a Burden or a Blessing?
- Families—Are They Passé?

Here We Go

In our modern era of women's rights, working mothers, high divorce rates, and single parenting, it's hard to imagine that the Bible has much to say that would apply to mothers today. Most of us carry around the notion that during biblical times women were nothing but **chattel** to be bought and sold at the whim of a man. But you will be surprised, for women, in particularly mothers, are treated with deep respect in the Old Testament.

chattel: *a slave or piece of property*

With the birth of Christ, motherhood was elevated to an even higher plane. The respect and freedoms we have today, we owe directly to the spread of the teachings of Jesus in the New Testament. Believe it or not, wherever the Gospel has gone women's and children's lives have improved.

In the following pages we'll examine these teachings and learn from some outstanding (and not-so-outstanding) examples, like Mary the mother of Jesus; Hannah, who gave her son to the service of the Lord; and Rebekah, who showed partiality for one son over the other. We'll laugh a little and cry a little and, at the end, be really glad someone calls us "Mother."

☞ GO TO:

Exodus 20:12; 21:15, 17 (respect)

Exodus 20:8; Leviticus 19:30 (Sabbaths)

THE OLDEST PROFESSION—MOTHERHOOD

> **Leviticus 19:3** Each of you must **respect** his mother and father, and you must observe my **Sabbaths**. I am the LORD your God.

respect: *to be held in reverence*

Sabbaths: *seventh day of the week (Saturday)*

Nothing but a Form of Slavery

The treatment of women in today's Middle East has left us with the impression that this is the way women were treated in biblical times. On the nightly news we see pictures of darkly shrouded figures completely covered except for their eyes. We read stories of how the women in Iran have been forced to abandon their careers and how they are treated like slaves by their husbands, and we assume that's the way it was in the Old Testament times.

But is this true? Were women treated like this? Were they hidden away never to be seen or heard from? Let's look at what the Bible has to say.

☞ **GO TO:**

Exodus 24:28; Deuteronomy 4:13 (Ten Commandments)

Proverbs: *truths about human behavior*

reverence: *to hold in awe*

EXAMPLES FROM THE BIBLE

The Old Testament is full of Scripture commanding the respect of children for both mother and father. In fact, this is such a basic principle that it's one of the Ten Commandments (see GBWI, page 29). In the book of **Proverbs** the duty of **reverence**, love, and obedience of sons to their mothers is emphasized over and over.

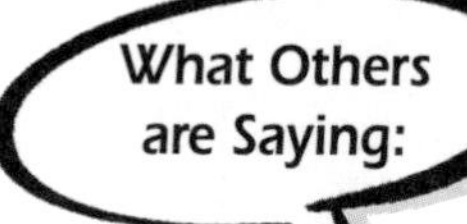

Dr. Henry Cloud and Dr. John Townsend: Mothering is the most significant, demanding, and underpaid profession around. . . . We strongly believe that God ordained the specialness and importance of mothering: "Honor your mother and your father" is a recurring theme throughout the entire Bible.[1]

> **Genesis 1:28, 31** God blessed them and said to them, "Be fruitful and increase in number, fill the earth and subdue it. Rule over the fish of the sea and the birds of the air and over every living creature that moves on the ground.". . . . God saw all that he had made and it was very good.

☞ **GO TO:**

Genesis 17:6 (be fruitful)

Genesis 6:1; Acts 17:26 (fill the earth)

Psalm 115:16 (rule over)

Genesis 1:4, 10, 12, 18, 21, 25 (very good)

Equality in the Garden

In the story of the Garden of Eden, Eve is as important as Adam is. In fact, the Scripture clearly states that they were given equal responsibility. He didn't give this command to just Adam, but to *them*, Adam and Eve. Their roles changed after the Fall, but their status didn't change.

EXAMPLES FROM THE BIBLE

Other examples of prominent women are Sarah (Genesis 12–23), Rebekah (Genesis 24–28), Miriam (Exodus 15:20), and Deborah (Judges 4–5). Abraham listened carefully to Sarah's advice in Genesis 16 when she suggested that her maidservant provide him with a son. Later, God tells Abraham to listen to Sarah again, in Genesis 21:11–12, because she will be the mother of a great nation through Isaac. Jacob's chief counselor was his mother, Rebekah (Genesis 28:7). Miriam, Moses' sister, led the women in Exodus 15:20. In Judges 4:4, it clearly states that Deborah was leading the nation of Israel. God spoke to the leaders of Judah through the **prophetess** Huldah (2 Kings 22:14) even though the prophets Jeremiah and Zephaniah were alive. The biblical stories wouldn't be the same without Leah and Rachel, Delilah, Bathsheba, Ruth and Naomi, Hannah, and Esther. Women of the Old Testament played prominent roles in the formation of the **Hebrew nation**.

☞ **GO TO:**

Genesis 29–35:19 (Leah and Rachel)

Judges 16 (Delilah)

2 Samuel 11–12:24 (Bathsheba)

Ruth (Ruth and Naomi)

prophetess: *a woman who spoke for God*

Hebrew nation: *the nation of Israel*

Women were listed in the lineage of Jesus Christ. This was considered to be the highest honor that could be bestowed upon an Israelite. Another example of the importance placed on women in the Bible.

What Others are Saying:

Beverly LaHaye: Genesis 1:27 says that God "created" man, but Genesis 2:22 tells us that God "fashioned" the woman. This word comes from the Hebrew root word meaning "to build" or "to design". God had a special blueprint and design for woman, so he fashioned her into what he wanted her to be. Could it possibly be that God took extra care in making woman, so she could be a fairer sex and a feminine beauty? She was designed to complement the man, not to replace him.[2]

Dr. Deborah Newman: Most women accept the subtle messages the world tells us about what we need to be as women—young, sexy, rich, powerful. Others of us try to measure ourselves by certain roles we see outlined in the Bible—submissive, gentle, hospitable. But there is so much more God wants us to experience as women.[3]

☞ **GO TO:**

1 Samuel 1 (Hannah)

Esther (Esther)

Matthew 1:1–17; Luke 3:28–38 (lineage)

Parent's Dictionary

Family Planning: the art of spacing your children the proper distance apart to keep you on the edge of financial disaster

Full name: what you call your child when you're mad at him

Show-off: a child who is more talented than yours

disciple: a follower of Jesus

> **John 19:26–27** When Jesus saw his mother there, and the **disciple** whom he loved standing nearby, he said to his mother, "Dear woman, here is your son," and to the disciple, "Here is your mother." From that time on, this disciple took her into his home.

Ave Maria—a Child Is Born

☞ **GO TO:**

Luke 10:38 (visiting)

John 4:7–26 (forgiving)

Luke 7:11–15 (caring)

Mark 5:21–34 (healing)

With the birth of Jesus, a new era dawned for women. For 2,000 years Mary has been honored and even worshiped.

But she wasn't the only woman whom Jesus treated with respect. Throughout the New Testament he is shown visiting women in their homes, forgiving their sins, caring for the widows, and healing women of their ailments.

His final act on the cross was seeing to the care of his mother. He asked one of his disciples, John "the beloved," to take his mother into his home and treat her as if she were his own.

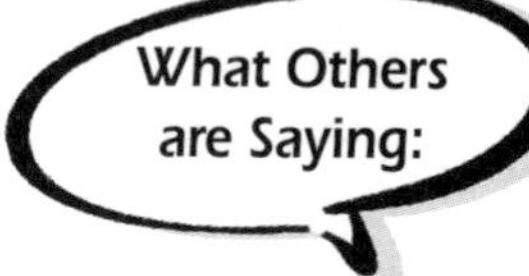

Henry E. Dosker: The birth of Christ lifted motherhood to the highest possible plane and idealized it for all time. . . . What woman is today, what she is in particular in her motherhood, she owes wholly to the position in which the Scriptures have placed her.[4]

philosophy: a Greek word meaning rational investigation of a principle or truth

human tradition: man-made rules

> **Colossians 2:8** See to it that no one takes you captive through hollow and deceptive **philosophy**, which depends on **human tradition** and the basic principles of this world rather than on Christ.

☞ **GO TO:**

Galatians 4:3; Colossians 2:20 (philosophy)

Where Have All the Mothers Gone?

Mothers today face a mixed reaction from the world. On one hand there is a special day set aside to honor mothers. Yet women who have more than two children often face rude remarks from thoughtless people who think that having any more than two is contributing to overpopulation. Working mothers feel guilty about leaving their children in day care and stay-at-home moms feel looked down upon as not fulfilling their potential. At social get-togethers, women are asked if they work and if their answer is no, the conversation may end as if they have nothing of interest to add.

The media portrays professional moms as women who keep perfect homes, have children with only minor problems, and have husbands who are as disposable as diapers. Their hair is always perfect, meals magically appear after a few minutes spent in the kitchen, no one ever worries about bills, and the car always starts.

Problems are fixed in half-hour or hour segments. Sometimes it's dished up with humor, but it always looks easy from our living room couch. Donna Reed and June Cleaver may be gone, but they've been replaced by characters just as unreal. If we try to live up to them or let the world pressure us into conforming to its rules, we will be unhappy.

Each of us must make our decisions based on God's will, for our families and ourselves. Only then will we find the peace we're seeking.

What Others are Saying:

Mary Whelchel: If you are sure of God's direction for you in the working world, then your role there is just as sacred, just as important to God, and of just as much service to him as anything else you could do. It is not second best; it is not the alternative for those who have never sensed a call into a public ministry. It is full-time Christian service![5]

Mother's Day

On the second Sunday of every May, the English-speaking world stops and honors its mothers. Hallmark stores and florist shops rake in big bucks. Children write poems and make plaster casts of their hands. Breakfast is served to Mom in bed, and someone else, for a change, prepares dinner.

> We have Ann Jarvis to thank for coming up with the idea for this special day. After the death of her mother, she brought a group together on the second Sunday of May to honor her memory. The first Mother's Day was celebrated on May 10, 1908, at Andrews Church in Philadelphia. Two years later the governor of West Virginia officially set aside the second Sunday in May to honor all mothers.

Herbert Lockyer: The influence of mothers is without comparison or competition. The church, nations, governments, society depend upon our mothers for their stability. Within the home, mother is the reigning queen. Thus when home life is decadent, every phase of life lacks wholesomeness. . . . We do well to honor mothers, who are the prime kingdom-builders, chief soul-moulders, conspicuous character-constructors, and the foremost recruiting agents for the eternal realms above.[6]

AN OLD-FASHIONED WORD—MARRIAGE

Now that we've looked at what the Bible has to say about motherhood, it's time to look at what it says about marriage. God's original plan was for a man and woman to form a stable, lifelong union. Into that environment children would be born. These children would be taught by their parents to follow his ways. When they grew up, they would form stable unions and bear children who would also follow the teachings of the Bible, and so on and on until the earth would be filled with his followers.

☞ **GO TO:**

Psalm 33:20; 121:2 (helper)

helper: *counterpart, aid*

one flesh: *one person*

shame: *to feel disgraced*

> **Genesis 2:18; 2:21–25** The Lord God said, "It is not good for the man to be alone. I will make a **helper** suitable for him." . . . So the Lord God caused the man to fall into a deep sleep; and while he was sleeping, he took one of the man's ribs and closed up the place with flesh. Then the Lord God made a woman from the rib he had taken out of the man, and he brought her to the man. The man said, "This is now bone of my bones and flesh of my flesh; she shall be called 'woman,' for she was taken out of man." For this reason a man will leave his father and mother and be united to his wife, and they will become **one flesh**. The man and his wife were both naked, and they felt no **shame**.

KEY POINT

The term *one flesh* strongly implies that from the beginning God intended for a man to be the husband of one wife and the marriage would be a lifetime commitment.

Wake Up, Adam!

Motherhood under God's original plan begins with a rather old-fashioned word called marriage. The very first marriage is spelled out in a dramatic way here in these verses of Genesis.

Can you imagine Adam's surprise after he awoke from his afternoon nap to find another creature that looked, talked, and walked similarly, but was oh, so much better looking?

Up to that point Adam had experienced complete mastery of his existence. He could go to bed when he pleased, watch all the football games on Sunday, leave his socks on the floor, and squeeze the toothpaste tube in the middle. There was no one to nag him or to backseat drive or give him unwanted advice.

But there was also no one there to cuddle with when he went to bed at night or to tell him what a great dad he was or to talk over the problems of tending the garden. He was lonely.

Oh sure, he had God; in fact, he had a perfect relationship with him, unmarred by sin. But it wasn't enough. God recognized that man needed companionship and so he created woman.

For Single Moms—Many of you who are reading this are single moms. Some, through no fault of your own, find yourselves divorced; others have been widowed, and some have had a child out of wedlock. This book is designed to celebrate motherhood, not to make you feel guilty. We live under a new **covenant** and serve a God of **forgiveness**. He can take you from where you are and create something wonderful. Let him be your husband and the father of your children.

covenant: *an agreement between man and God*

forgiveness: *the wiping away of sins*

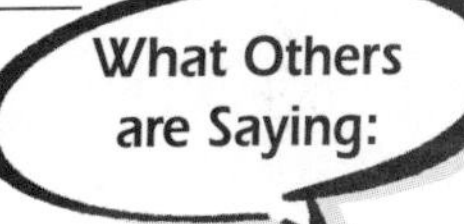

Dr. William Sears and Martha Sears, R.N: Acknowledging God as the cornerstone of your marriage is not just a nice, pious thought or a tip that may make your marriage work better; it is an absolute necessity for a healthy marriage. Throughout many years of counseling parents, we have seen that couples who acknowledge this triangle weather the storms of marriage crises more successfully than those going at it alone.[7]

> **Deuteronomy 7:3–6** Do not intermarry with [the **Canaanites**]. Do not give your daughters to their sons or take their daughters for your sons, for they will turn your sons away from following me to serve other gods, and the LORD's anger will burn against you and will quickly destroy you. This is what you are to do to them: Break down their **altars**, smash their sacred stones, cut down their **Asherah poles** and burn their **idols** in the fire. For you are a people holy to the LORD your God. The LORD your God has chosen you out of all the peoples on the face of the earth to be his people, his treasured possession.

Canaanites: *an ancient tribe that lived in the land of Palestine*

altars: *an elevated place where religious rites are performed*

Asherah poles: *symbol of the fertility goddess Asherah*

idols: *anything that is worshiped other than God*

Love Makes the World Go Round

These words may seem harsh to us today, because marriage between a believer and a nonbeliever doesn't seem like such a big deal to us now. But at that time God needed a people who were separate from the rest of the world. He knew that if the Israelites

☞ **GO TO:**

Deuteronomy 16:21; Judges 6:25 (Asherah poles)

Mosaic Law: the ancient laws that were handed down by Moses

intermarried they would slowly turn from him and follow the gods of their mates. The **Mosaic Law** clearly stated that an Israelite was not to marry a Canaanite. The punishment for breaking this law was often death.

Think About It

Of course, today we aren't put to death if we marry a nonbeliever or someone from another faith, but the consequences can still be severe. Many women suffer because their husbands are not believers. Others have walked away from the church in order to keep unity in the family, or have been drawn away by the gods of this world. We think in our naiveté that the believer will bring the unbeliever to the Lord, and that can happen. Often, though, just like the history of the Bible shows, it's another story.

> **Genesis 24:58** So they called Rebekah and asked her, "Will you go with this man?" "I will go," she said.

Here Comes the Bride

Can you imagine knowing at the age of ten or twelve whom you were going to marry? Not only would you know, but your intended would probably be a relative you played with while growing up. That's how it was for the Israelites.

The parents arranged marriages carefully, for several reasons. One, it was a way to ensure that the marriage was within the faith. Two, it was a way of keeping the wealth within the family. Three, it assured that your family knew who his parents were. And four, it helped keep peace in the family in that the bride went to live with her husband's family, and it was her responsibility to fit in.

This doesn't mean that the bride and groom never had a say in the matter. As you can clearly see from this scripture, Rebekah was asked.

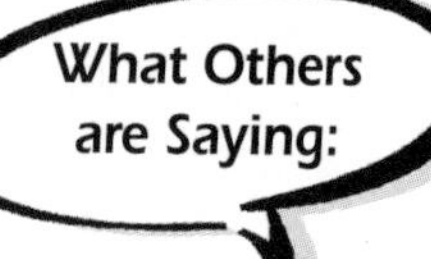

Herbert Lockyer: Marrying "sight unseen" is a most dangerous venture, but in this case it was successful because "the angel of the Lord" had directed the events leading up to the union. When Rebekah saw the handsome, mild-mannered and meditative Isaac, her heart went out to him. As for Isaac, a man of forty, and some twenty years older than Rebekah, he instantly loved the most beautiful woman he beheld, and she remained his only love.[8]

T. J. Bach: Home, sweet home—where each lives for the other, and all live for God.[9]

What Others are Saying:

Genesis 24:67 Isaac brought her into the <u>tent</u> of his mother Sarah, and he married Rebekah. So she became his wife, and he loved her; and Isaac was comforted after his mother's death.

GO TO:

Psalm 19:4–5 (tent)

I Have to Marry Whom?

As horrifying as it may sound to us today, love was not the primary reason for marriage in biblical times. Marriages then were more likely to be based on considerations of religion, parentage, wealth, and children. There are a few examples of couples falling in love before marriage, but from this scripture it is clear that love was expected to begin on the wedding day.

EXAMPLES FROM THE BIBLE

The greatest example in the Bible of romantic love was that of Jacob for Rachel. He worked seven years to earn the right to marry her and then was tricked into marrying her sister. He then had to work another seven years in order to "earn" his true love, Rachel (see GWWB, page 67).

Alexander Whyte: A sweeter chapter was never written than the twenty-fourth of Genesis. . . . The picture of aged Abraham swearing his most trusty servant about a bride for his son Isaac; that servant's journey to Padan-aram in the far east; Rebekah, first at the well, and then in her mother's house; and then her first sight of her future husband—that long chapter is a perfect gem of ancient authorship.[10]

What Others are Saying:

Genesis 29:18–20 Jacob was in love with Rachel and said, "I'll work for you seven years in return for your younger daughter Rachel." Laban said, "It's better that I give her to you than to some other man. Stay here with me." So Jacob served seven years to get Rachel, but they seemed like only a few days to him because of his love for her.

☞ GO TO:

Genesis 34:12 (sum of money)

Think About It

What Others are Saying:

righteous: morally upright

betrothal: engagement

☞ GO TO:

Deuteronomy 20:7 (military duty)

Old-Fashioned Prenuptial Agreements

Before a man could become engaged, he had to pay a sum of money, or, as in the case of Jacob, work for the prospective father-in-law for several years. This was not the same as buying a slave. It was to compensate the bride's family for the loss of a valuable asset.

Today we have prenuptial agreements that protect the wealth of one or both marriage partners in case of divorce. In biblical times this exchange of money or labor bound the couple together in engagement.

Reader's Digest Illustrated Dictionary of Bible Life & Times: The bridegroom . . . paid a price to the bride's father to compensate for the loss of his daughter. This gift was kept for her in case her husband died or abandoned her. The payment of the bride price also made the union legal.[11]

> **Matthew 1:18–19** This is how the birth of Jesus Christ came about: His mother Mary was pledged to be married to Joseph, but before they came together, she was found to be with child through the Holy Spirit. Because Joseph her husband was a **righteous** man and did not want to expose her to public disgrace, he had in mind to divorce her quietly.

Promises, Promises

Becoming engaged was serious business, and not to be entered into lightly.

The **betrothal** took place before two witnesses and the couple exchanged rings. The length of the engagement varied, but it usually lasted one year. During this time the young man prepared a place in his father's house for his new bride, and the young woman's mother helped prepare her daughter for married life. The groom paid a bride-price, and the bride was asked to supply a dowry. This would help the young couple set up their own home.

This was such an important period that during the engagement period, the bridegroom was exempt from military duty. Death and divorce were the only events that could break an engagement.

Reader's Digest Illustrated Dictionary of Bible Life & Times: To signify that the families of both the bride and bridegroom had an interest in seeing the marriage preserved, each put up a financial stake. The bridegroom's family made a present, called the bride-price, to the woman's parents to compensate them for the loss of their daughter's services, or the bridegroom might substitute a term of labor for cash or goods. . . . The bride's family made a larger gift—the dowry—to the woman to bring to her marriage. In the case of divorce, the wife may have been allowed to take back the dowry, which could have included money, jewelry, clothing, household goods, slaves, and land. The families often used a written contract to spell out the terms of the marriage.[12]

What Others are Saying:

> **John 2:1–2** On the third day a wedding took place at Cana in Galilee. Jesus' mother was there, and Jesus and his disciples had also been invited to the wedding.

We're Going to the Chapel

Here Jesus is celebrating with his mother and his closest friends at the marriage of a friend or relative.

He could have been out healing the sick, preaching to the masses, taunting the Pharisees and Sadducees, but instead he's having a good time. This shows how important people were to him.

He's putting his stamp of approval on a marriage of two people he cared about.

Think About It

When you exchanged your wedding vows before God, he was there celebrating right along with you just like Jesus celebrated with this couple. God cares about your marriage because he cares about you and your children.

Something Old, Something New, Something Borrowed, Something Blue

Every nation and race of people observes wedding customs that are handed down from generation to generation. The Israelites were no exception.

On the day of the wedding the groom and his friends dressed in their finest clothes and danced their way to the home of the bride where she waited anxiously with her bridesmaids.

☞ **GO TO:**

Matthew 25:1–10 (bridesmaids)

Wedding Feast

Pictured here is a typical wedding feast much like the one Jesus would have attended.

The party then danced their way back to the groom's home. While everyone partied outside, the couple entered the groom's home and the marriage was consummated.

Afterwards, the celebrating began in earnest, with a great feast at the husband's home (see illustration above). The wedding could go on for a week or more, depending upon the wealth of the family.

Think About It

God's plan for marriage was so well preserved that the customs from Old Testament times to New Testament times did not change that much. Jesus only referred to marriage a few times, and each time his comments were directed toward preserving God's original plan.

***Pharisees:** a Jewish sect that believed in the strict observance of the Law*

GO TO:

Deuteronomy 24:1–4 (every reason)

Genesis 1:27; 2:24 (male and female)

Matthew 19:3–6 Some **Pharisees** came to him to test him. They asked, "Is it lawful for a man to divorce his wife for any and every reason?" "Haven't you read," he replied, "that at the beginning the Creator 'made them male and female,' and said, 'For this reason a man will leave his father and mother and be united to his wife, and the two will become one flesh'? So they are no longer two, but one. Therefore what God has joined together, let man not separate."

What Did Jesus Say about Marriage?

Jesus spoke about marriage after being challenged by the Pharisees. At that time, there were two schools of thought regarding divorce.

One view was held by the school of Shammai. They believed that the only reason for divorce was marital unfaithfulness. The other view was held by the school of Hillel. They said that a man could divorce his wife for doing anything that displeased him.

> **Matthew 19:7–9** "Why then," they asked, "did Moses command that a man give his wife a certificate of divorce and send her away?" Jesus replied, "Moses permitted you to divorce your wives because your hearts were **hard**. But it was not this way from the beginning. I tell you that anyone who divorces his wife, except for marital unfaithfulness, and marries another woman commits adultery."

☞ **GO TO:**

Deuteronomy 24:1–4 (divorce)

Mark 10:5 (hearts were hard)

hard: *completely lacking understanding*

Jesus Takes a Stand for Marriage

In these verses Jesus clearly states that from the beginning God did not plan for divorce. It was only because of the hard hearts of man that it was permitted, and then for only one reason—adultery. Jesus clearly takes the side of those who believed there was only one reason for divorce.

KEY POINT

God's original plan for marriage was that it be "until death us do part."

Think About It

Divorce was never part of God's original plan. It destroys the family and thus undermines the ability of everyone involved to become wholly whom God intended. Divorce was, however, permitted under certain circumstances, not because God's plan was flawed, but because of man's hard heart.

With This Ring, I Thee Wed

Marriage customs today are as varied as there are people getting married. But still there are some constants. There is a ring, and vows of one type or another are recited before witnesses. Afterwards there is a celebration and often a honeymoon. The new couple then sets up their own household.

Most states require a wedding license and a three-day waiting period before a couple can marry, but there is no official preparation period. This is changing, as more and more churches and communities are banding together to require engaged couples to undergo some sort of premarital counseling.

Weddings can cost thousands of dollars or only a few hundred, but the parents of the bride traditionally are the ones who pay for them. Whereas weddings used to take place in churches or at city hall, now they can take place anywhere—jumping out of an airplane, underwater, riding a roller coaster, or on top of a mountain.

What has changed most dramatically in the past few years is the custom of a bride taking her husband's name. These days, the bride may choose to keep her own name, or combine names by hyphenating her name with that of her new husband.

Invite your husband out to dinner. Take your wedding pictures with you. Go over each one and relive the highlights of the days leading up to the event, the things that went wrong during the wedding, and the love you shared for each other.

CHILDREN—A BURDEN OR A BLESSING?

Now that we've looked at motherhood and marriage, it's time to examine what the Bible has to say about children.

According to Census Bureau projections, by the year 2010 approximately 72 percent of all households will be childless.[13]

An aging population explains some of this; some of it is because there are fewer young adults forming new families. But there is another, more disturbing trend. More and more couples are deciding to go childless.

In biblical times, that would have been unthinkable.

> **Genesis 30:1** Rachel . . . said to Jacob, "Give me children, or I'll die!"

Give Me Children or Give Me Death

Rachel's outburst may seem a little extreme, but in biblical times having children was considered the highest possible blessing for a woman and being childless the worst possible fate. Barren women were scorned and their husbands were forced to take new wives in order to assure that their **lineage** would continue.

lineage: *line of descendants*

Beth Spring: As crises go, after all, infertility doesn't compare with the death of a loved one, a fractured relationship, alcoholism, or adultery. Or does it? Even infertile couples can wonder, "Are we just being selfish about wanting children? Some people don't have jobs, don't have homes, and go hungry. We are blessed beyond measure, yet we mourn our childlessness. It seems much too minor a complaint to bring to a busy pastor or counselor." Yet their pain continues, and it is real.[14]

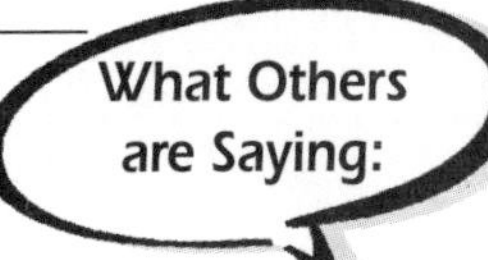

> **Genesis 9:7** Be fruitful and increase in number; multiply on the earth and increase upon it."

☞ **GO TO:**

Genesis 1:28; Genesis 9:1–2 (multiply)

John 1:41; 4:25 (Messiah)

Messiah: *the promised deliverer of the Jewish people*

Fill the Earth

You don't disobey direct orders from God, and he made it clear that Adam and Eve were to multiply and fill the earth with their descendants. This was part of his plan to prepare the way for the **Messiah.**

John MacArthur: Parenthood is God's gift to us. This is true even in a fallen world, infected with the curse of sin. In the midst of all that's evil, children are tokens of God's loving-kindness. They are living proof that God's mercy extends to fallen, sinful creatures.[15]

What Others are Saying:

The story of Adam and Eve as told to Bill Cosby by a five-year-old girl:

"God made Adam and Adam made Eve and they had a snake. And this snake told them to have apples for dinner, but God didn't want 'em to have dinner, so He got mad and gave 'em a punishment."

"And what was that punishment?"

"That Eve had a whole mess o' babies."[16]

> **Psalm 127:3–5 Sons** are a heritage from the LORD, children a reward from him. Like arrows in the hands of a warrior are sons born in one's youth. Blessed is the man whose **quiver** is full of them. They will not be put to shame when they contend with their enemies in the gate.

sons: *in the broadest general sense; children*

quiver: *arrow case*

☞ **GO TO:**

Numbers 27:8–11 (heritage)

A Blessing from God

KEY POINT

Children are God's gift and a sign of his favor.

Having many children while young was a blessing because these children came of age about the same time their parents were declining in age and strength. In a world where the family had to provide its own protection against enemies, a small army of sons and daughters was a great blessing.

> **Genesis 15:2–3** But Abram said, "O Sovereign LORD, what can you give me since I remain childless and the one who will inherit my estate is **Eliezer of Damascus**?" And Abram said, "You have given me no children; so a servant in my household will be my heir."

Eliezer of Damascus: *a servant acquired on the journey from Haran*

☞ **GO TO:**

Genesis 24:2 (Eliezer of Damascus)

A Necessity

Children were not only needed for protection, but were also the basis for the family.

Wealth was accumulated in hopes of handing it down to children who then would hand it down to their children. With no one to inherit, the family died out.

KEY POINT

In the New Testament, the inheritance that Jesus gives is salvation (Hebrews 9:15).

Today with our small family units, it's hard to understand this situation, but remember that the family provided everything. A roof over your head, food on the table, retirement in your old age.

It was very much like a business with many levels of management. Every member was important, but with no children, disaster would follow.

What Others are Saying:

John MacArthur: An old Chinese proverb says, "One generation plants the trees and another gets the shade." . . . In spiritual terms, we derive shade from our parents' and grandparents' ethical standard, their perceptions of right and wrong, their sense of moral duty, and above all, their spiritual commitment. Their ideals determined the kind of civilization we inherited from them, and our generation's ideal will likewise shape tomorrow's culture for our kids. . . . Are we planting the right kind of shade trees or are we leaving our children totally exposed?[17]

When I was in my early twenties, I sat in a college classroom and listened to a favorite professor tell the class that the world was dying of overpopulation. He predicted that, within twenty years, great famines would sweep across the world because farmers would not be able to keep up with the pace of this huge explosion of humanity.

FROM JUDY'S HEART

I was scared. What could I possibly do to save the world from this horrible calamity? The answer seemed to be clear—limit my own family to two. That was the responsible thing to do.

Now, almost thirty years later, I have two children, but the world has not been overrun with people. Some remote countries are experiencing famines, but they have been caused by droughts, political strife, strict caste systems, and transportation problems, not overpopulation.

We have not run out of food. The farmers in this country grow so much that the federal government pays them to not grow certain crops. Surplus cheese, flour, and canned goods are purchased by the government and stored in warehouses in order to help the farmer survive this overabundance of food. It is then distributed through local school lunch programs and other federal feeding programs. But much of it goes to waste.

I look at my two grown sons and am sorry I listened to that professor. Instead I wish I'd had more faith in God.

FAMILIES—ARE THEY PASSÉ?

Families today are different than in Old Testament times.

When we marry, we set up separate homes, raise our children, and when they marry they leave and set up their own homes. Only rarely does a family take in a grandparent. And it's considered somewhat abnormal for children to live at home after they marry.

But in biblical times the term "family" meant "household." It included the male head, his parents, one or more wives, the wives of his sons, his unmarried daughters, his grandchildren, slaves, and servants.

Genesis 46:26–27 All those who went to Egypt with Jacob—those who were his direct descendants, not counting his sons' wives—numbered sixty-six persons. With the two sons who had been born to Joseph in Egypt, the members of Jacob's family, which went to Egypt, were **seventy** in all.

☞ **GO TO:**

Genesis 27–33 (Jacob)

Deuteronomy 10:22 (seventy)

seventy: *an ideal family number*

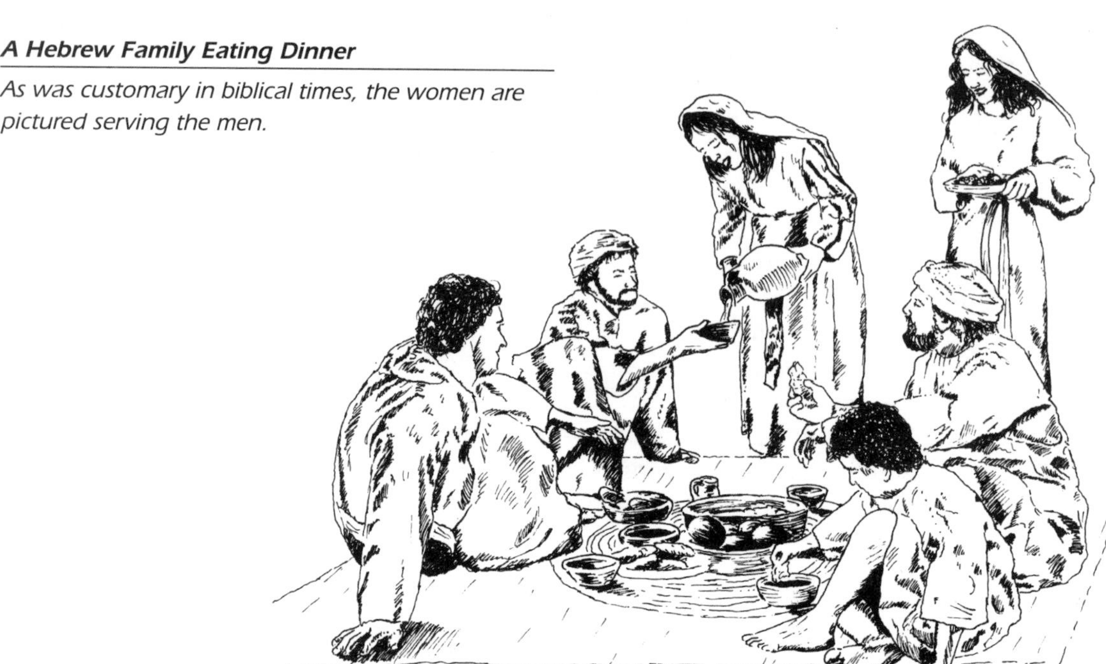

A Hebrew Family Eating Dinner

As was customary in biblical times, the women are pictured serving the men.

A Big Family

As you can see this was a very large family and did not even count Jacob's sons' wives. The number sixty-six is arrived at by subtracting the two sons of Judah who had died and Joseph's two sons who were in Egypt. A Hebrew dinner was quite an affair (see illustration above).

What Others are Saying:

John MacArthur: The only real values that can save the family are rooted in Scripture—they are biblical values, not just family values.[18]

Don't take your extended family for granted. It's evident from studying the Scripture that strong families create strong foundations.

GO TO:

Malachi 2:15 (united)

Matthew 19:5; Mark 10:7–8; 1 Corinthians 6:16; Ephesians 5:31 (one flesh)

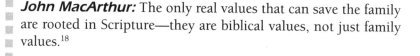

Genesis 2:24 For this reason a man will leave his father and mother and be united to his wife, and they will become one flesh.

The Husband of One Wife

It is clear that from the beginning God's plan was for **monogamy**. He knew that any other arrangement would only bring strife and jealousy.

Can you imagine trying to share your husband with another woman? What about your kitchen? The bathroom? The disciplining of your children?

It would take superhumans to pull it off.

monogamy: *marriage between one man and one woman*

> **Genesis 1:27** So God created **man** in his own **image**, in the image of God he created him; **male** and **female** he created them.

man: *human being*

image: *reflection in a mirror*

male: *male of the species*

female: *female of the species*

Different Species?

The book *Men Are From Mars, Women Are From Venus* was on the best-seller list for months. The author, John Gray, had discovered something new.

Men and women are different!

This was so astounding that people ran out and bought his book, making Mr. Gray a wealthy man.

But is his theory new? The answer lies in this scripture. God's image is most clearly reflected in male and female; not just in man, not just in woman, but in man and woman. God put some of his attributes into men and he put others into women. Only when the two come together do they reflect God's image.

Of course, sin has marred that reflection, but still there is nothing else on earth that compares to it.

KEY POINT

Together the man and woman were to form an inseparable union, of which "one flesh" is both a sign and an expression.

Children who are raised by two parents, one male, one female, more clearly see the image of God. He shares both attributes equally. In Genesis it says, "*So God created man in his own image, in the image of God he created him; male and female he created them*" (Genesis 1:27).

Sit down with your husband and talk about how you are different from one another. Instead of seeing your differences as problems to overcome, look at them as something to celebrate.

Luci Shaw: There are womanly images of God in the Bible. Very often they're passed over or ignored because they don't fit our traditional way of picturing God. But God is the mother hen who wants to gather us like little chicks. God is the nurturer, the comforter, the builder. God is the woman who searches for the lost coin and rejoices when she finds it. The very idea of the family of God points to God's motherly characteristics, for what's a family without a mother? . . . Jesus said, "Let the little children come to me, and do not hinder them, for the kingdom of God belongs to such as these" (Mark 10:14). Such closeness, intimacy, warmth, and provision are typical of mothers.[19]

> **Genesis 4:19** Lamech married two women, one named Adah and the other Zillah.

The Truth about Polygamy

GO TO:

Genesis 4:19–24; 6:5 (polygamy)

polygamy: *having more than one spouse*

This is the first example of **polygamy** recorded in the Old Testament. It's interesting to note that Lamech was the son of Cain, who killed his brother Abel. Lamech, like his father, was a murderer. He bragged about killing other men. If he was so callous about murder, you can see how easy it would be for him to break one of God's other commandments.

Polygamy is against the law in the United States. Only a few extremist groups practice it. But what about the proliferation of divorce? Could this be a form of polygamy?

> **Exodus 20:12** "Honor your father and your mother, so that you may live long in the land the LORD your God is giving you."

A Promise Made—the Fifth Commandment

Many of us have lost sight of this great commandment. Today, psychologists, authors, movies, television, and other media carry the strong message that the personal problems we face today are not our fault—they come from our childhood. They are our parents' fault. Many have been taught to despise their parents for these remembered slights, mistakes, and transgressions.

The word "honor" would leave a bad taste in their mouths, and yet this scripture makes it quite clear that if we want things to go well for us, if we want long lives, we should honor our parents.

Notice also that it says "mother and father." They are given equal status here. They are a united front, the basis of every family. We are to honor them equally.

But what does "honor" mean? It means the opposite of mocking and despising. It means we should fear, give reverence, obey, and support them. Note it doesn't add "if you feel like it," or "only if they treated you well," or "only if they live in the same town as you."

Proverbs 30:17 (mocking and despising)

Leviticus 19:3 (fear)

Hebrews 12:9 (give reverence)

Nelson's Illustrated Bible Dictionary: God established parents as the authority figures in the family unit. Children often get their first impressions about God from their parents. Parents who walk in the Spirit, honestly desiring to follow the guidelines of the Scriptures, will set better examples for their children. And children who want to please God will respect their parents, regardless of pressure from the world and their peers.[20]

GO TO:

Ephesians 6:1–3; Matthew 21:29 (obey)

Matthew 15:4–6 (support)

Exodus 20:14 "You shall not commit adultery."

The Sanctity of Marriage Preserved—the Seventh Commandment

This commandment secures the home. It forbids adultery, which is the cause of much sorrow in every society.

If this commandment were obeyed, then more marriages would stay together and more children would be raised in two-parent homes. Teenage drug and alcohol abuse would decline, teenage pregnancy would decrease, and women on welfare would be almost unheard of.

Seventy percent of couples who divorce do so because they have met someone else.[21]

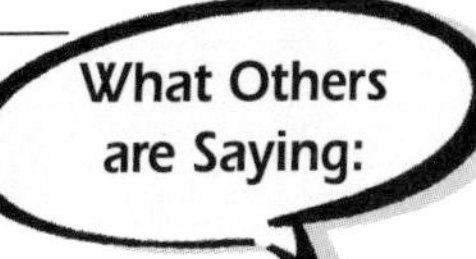

Dave Veerman: In our culture sex has been overrated and undervalued. Sex is not the "ultimate" in any sense of the word, but because of the continual media bombardment, we can begin to believe this myth. Many Christian young people, saving themselves for marriage, have expected far too much from sex; so marriage becomes a letdown and they harbor doubts about themselves and their spouses.[22]

covet: *desire wrongfully*

> **Exodus 20:17** "You shall not **covet** your neighbor's house. You shall not covet your neighbor's wife, or his manservant or maidservant, his ox or donkey, or anything that belongs to your neighbor."

Wanting What Isn't Yours—the Tenth Commandment

This is the only commandment that deals with the inner heart, for that is where sin first begins. If not controlled, coveting can lead to taking. The taking of any of these items would destroy or severely damage another family.

Think About It

When we start to compare what we have to what others have, it can lead directly to our unhappiness.

No matter how much we have, someone will always have more. No matter how clean our home, someone else's will be cleaner. No matter how talented our children, someone else's will be more talented.

Learning to appreciate what we have begins with thanking God for his blessings every day.

the Law: *the first five books of the Jewish Scriptures (Old Testament)*

When we are coveting, we are saying to God, "I'm not happy with what you have given me. I want more."

What Others are Saying:

Max Lucado: Regardless of what you've done, it's not too late. Regardless of how far you've fallen, it's not too late. It doesn't matter how low the mistake is, it's not too late to dig down, pull out that mistake and then let it go—and be free. What makes a Christian a Christian is not perfection but forgiveness.[23]

the smallest letter: *an iota in Greek, yodh in Hebrew*

☞ GO TO:

Psalm 119:73 (the smallest letter)

> **Matthew 5:17–20** "Do not think that I have come to abolish **the Law** or the Prophets; I have not come to abolish them but to fulfill them. I tell you the truth, until heaven and earth disappear, not **the smallest let-**

ter, not the least stroke of a pen, will by any means disappear from the Law until everything is accomplished. Anyone who breaks one of the least of these commandments and teaches others to do the same will be called least in the kingdom of heaven, but whoever practices and teaches these commands will be called great in the kingdom of heaven."

☞ **GO TO:**

James 2:10 (breaks)

What Exactly Did Jesus Teach about the Family?

You might be surprised to discover that Jesus said very little about the family. Commentators believe that's because God's original plan as set forth in the Old Testament was still valid. Jesus states in this scripture that he came *"not to abolish the law but to fulfill it."* When he looked around, he saw that the family unit was secure, but that individual hearts were what needed changing.

Think About It

Can you imagine coming up with ten rules for a whole nation to govern itself by?

They would fit on one piece of paper and could be posted in every public place and every private home. They could easily be memorized and taught from one generation to another.

That's what God did with the Ten Commandments. They were the very foundation of the Israelite nation, and the family was such an important part of that foundation that three of the Commandments pertain directly to it.

What Others are Saying:

R. C. Sproul: I believe that we are required to believe, to trust, and to obey every word that comes from the mouth of God. If the Bible comes from the mouth of God, it imposes this obligation on us to believe everything in it.[24]

What's Tearing the Family Apart Today?

The two biggest dangers to families today are migration and divorce.

Migration tears families away from grandparents, aunts and uncles, cousins, and family traditions. Families move to where the jobs are and find loneliness and strangers there. There's no one who cares if you don't go to church. There's no one to look to for sound advice. There are new influences that lure us away from the things our parents taught.

Divorce is shredding the American family. In 1993 approximately 1.2 million divorces were granted.[25] According to one study, many of these were for vague reasons like inability to communicate or immaturity, not for reasons you might expect, like drug and alcohol use or physical abuse.

There are no winners in a divorce, but the biggest losers are the children. Too many of them are growing up without a mother or father. A long-term study showed that, even twenty-five years after a divorce, the majority of children blamed their inability to hold down a job or maintain a relationship on the breakup of their families. Divorce can throw women and children into poverty and men into deep, clinical depression that can last for years. Children of divorce are more likely to abuse drugs, commit crimes, or get pregnant out of wedlock. Stepfamilies carry with them their own set of problems, with the majority of sexual and physical abuse taking place in these environments.

When God said in Malachi, *"I hate divorce,"* he knew the heartache it would cause not just for the couple, but also for generations to come.

He meant for children to grow up with one set of parents who would teach them the right way to live so that they could go out and pass those values on to the next generation. When that basic unit fails, our whole society loses.

For Single Moms—If you are already divorced, then consider this a new beginning. Be all God wants you to be so that you will be the best you can be for your children.

If you are considering divorce, then reconsider. Get counseling, read books, find a support group. Keep looking until you find the solution to your marital unhappiness. Your children deserve that, you deserve that, and someday you'll be really glad you stayed.

What Others are Saying:

John MacArthur: Many people today would happily carve out the tombstone for the family. In his 1971 book, *The Death of the Family*, British psychiatrist Dr. David Cooper suggested that it is time to do away with the family completely. A similar suggestion was made in Kate Millet's 1970 feminist manifesto, *Sexual Politics*. She claimed that families, along with all patriarchal structures, must go because they are nothing more than tools for the oppression and enslavement of women.[26]

Study Questions

1. What was God's original intention for Adam and Eve?
2. What does the term "one flesh" mean?
3. How did an engagement in biblical times differ from today?
4. Why were children considered such a blessing?
5. What does it mean to honor your father and mother?
6. What are the two most harmful trends in our society for the family, and why?

CHAPTER WRAP-UP

- Before the Fall of man, Eve and Adam shared the same responsibilities. After the Fall, they were still considered equals, but their roles changed. Adam was to toil and Eve was to bear children.
- God's original plan was for one man to be united with one woman for life and for them, together, to bring up children to know and love the Lord.
- God created marriage as the foundation for raising up generation after generation of godly children. Man altered that plan by allowing polygamy and divorce. Neither were part of God's plan.
- Children today may sometimes be considered a burden by American society, but in God's economy they are of great value. The Jewish people of the Old and New Testaments considered having many children to be a sign of God's blessing.
- Families were necessary for survival in biblical times. When a man married, he brought his bride home to live with his family, which might include his parents, grandparents, single sisters, slaves, and servants.

These are my favorite books on love and marriage.

- *The Gift of Sex: A Christian Guide to Sexual Fulfillment*, Clifford and Joyce Penner, Word Publishing. My husband and I read each chapter aloud to one another and then discussed it.

- *When Love Dies: How to Save a Hopeless Marriage,* Judy Bodmer, Word Publishing. This is my personal story of how God rekindled my love for my husband.
- *What Husbands Wish Their Wives Knew about Men*, Patrick M. Morley, Zondervan. A Christian look at how men are different than women. You will learn a lot about your husband that you didn't know.
- *Love Is a Decision,* Gary Smalley, Word Books. A classic every married couple should read.
- *Torn Asunder,* Dave Carder, Moody Press. A book for those who have had an extramarital affair. Great advice on healing.

2 TRAGEDY IN THE GARDEN

WHAT'S IN THIS CHAPTER

- Childbirth, Curse or Blessing?
- A Deep Desire for Children
- The Curse of Being a Woman

Here We Go

In the last chapter we looked at God's original plan for families. Marriage was to be between one man and one woman. This union would draw them so close, physically, emotionally, and spiritually, that they would become one flesh. Children were to be born into this solid foundation. They were to be raised to worship and serve God by two loving parents who reflected God's image. But something tragic happened, and nothing has been the same since.

CHILDBIRTH, CURSE OR BLESSING?

Genesis 2:15–17 The LORD God took the man and put him in the Garden of Eden to work it and take care of it. And the LORD God commanded the man, "You are free to eat from any tree in the garden; but you must not eat from the tree of the knowledge of good and evil, for when you eat of it you will surely die."

Don't Eat It

Before Eve was created God gave Adam the responsibility to work and take care of the Garden of Eden. He asked only one thing, that he not eat of the Tree of the Knowledge of Good and Evil (see GWHN, page 4). Then God warns Adam that if he does there will be a severe consequence: "you will surely die." Seems simple and straightforward. Why in the world would Adam do anything else?

Whenever I make a dessert, I place it in my refrigerator or cookie jar. The reason? Out of sight, out of mind. For once I see it, I want it. It doesn't matter that I've just had dinner and am not at all hungry, or that I'm on a diet, or that I really don't even like it. Just knowing it's there and that I shouldn't have a piece makes it irresistible. The more I try not to think about it, the more I think about it. And so I understand the temptation Adam and Eve experienced after God gave them everything, yet said, "Don't eat this."

☞ **GO TO:**

Numbers 21:5–6; Deuteronomy 8:15; Jeremiah 8:17; Matthew 3:7; Luke 10:19 (serpent)

serpent: *a crawling reptile or snake*

Genesis 3:1–5 Now the **serpent** was more crafty than any of the wild animals the LORD God had made. He said to the woman, "Did God really say, 'You must not eat from any tree in the garden'?" The woman said to the serpent, "We may eat fruit from the trees in the garden, but God did say, 'You must not eat fruit from the tree that is in the middle of the garden, and you must not touch it, or you will die.'" "You will not surely die," the serpent said to the woman. "For God knows that when you eat of it your eyes will be opened, and you will be like God, knowing good and evil."

Tempting Words

Satan in the guise of the serpent whispered in Eve's ear, "Is that what God really said?" He planted doubt in her heart. But give Eve credit, she knew what God had said and she recited it to him.

Her next error, though, was to listen again. For Satan was crafty and he knew that once Eve started listening to him, he could plant even more doubts. He said, "Surely you won't die. God's just trying to keep you from being equal to him. He just doesn't want you to be all-knowing, like he is."

With that, Eve made her next big mistake. She turned and looked at the fruit.

Liz Curtis Higgs: Why Eve and not Adam? I wonder. Was she in the wrong place at the wrong time, or did the serpent go looking for her? And why, oh, why didn't she realize that if none of the other animals talked, this one shouldn't either?[1]

How Satan Works in Our Lives

Blinds us	2 Corinthians 4:4
Pressures conformity	Ephesians 2:2
Attacks ruthlessly	1 Peter 5:8
Strikes while we are weak, questions our identity, misquotes Scripture, appeals to our pride, shortcuts God's plan	Matthew 4:1–11
Appears attractive	2 Corinthians 11:14
Lies	John 8:44
Questions God's words	Genesis 3:1–13
Inspires false teachers	1 Timothy 4:1–4
Raises up false prophets	Matthew 24:24
Lives among Christians	Matthew 13:24–30; 13:36–43
Inspires jealousy, selfishness	James 3:15–16
Takes our possessions; takes our health	Job 1:6–12; 2:4–6

> **Genesis 3:6–7** When the woman saw that the fruit of the tree was good for food and pleasing to the eye, and also desirable for gaining wisdom, she took some and ate it. She also gave some to her husband, who was with her, and he ate it. Then the eyes of both of them were **opened**, and they realized they were **naked**; so they sewed fig leaves together and made coverings for themselves.

opened: *opening of the senses, particularly the eyes*

naked: *without clothing*

☞ GO TO:

Genesis 9:21–27 (naked)

Oops! She Didn't Mean to Do It

When Eve turned and looked at the fruit, she was hooked, for it was beautiful. All the other fruits and vegetables they had been eating paled in comparison. And when she thought about how it might make her wiser, like God, she was sure no harm would come of her taking some. She quickly plucked a piece and ate, and then just as quickly gave some to her husband who was standing nearby (see GWWB, page 10).

EXAMPLES FROM THE BIBLE

Eve often gets the blame for eating the forbidden fruit, but Adam could have spoken up. He could've stopped her, but for some reason he didn't. He let her do what he knew God had forbidden. Perhaps he was just as tempted. Letting Eve do it was his way of seeing what would happen.

It's also interesting to note that nothing happened after Eve ate. It was only after Adam ate that their eyes were opened.

They felt ashamed at their nakedness for the very first time. Up until that point they must've been like small children who think nothing of toddling around without their diapers. Now they felt self-conscious, so they went and covered themselves. We human beings have been hiding ever since, both from God and from each other. We hide not only our naked bodies, but our naked souls as well.

What Others are Saying:

Eugenia Price: God made women in such a way that they wield a singular kind of mysterious influence over the lives their lives touch. . . . God backs up my thinking in the book of Genesis. In the otherwise tightly written narrative of chapter three which tells of our first parents in the Garden of Eden, almost six complete verses are given over to the first attack by the tempter on the first woman. The wily one went straight to Eve, and the entire basic problem of human nature, the right to one's self, sprang into being through a woman! He didn't approach Adam. He approached Eve. . . . Adam ate because Eve talked him into it.[2]

Think About It

What would have happened to Eve if Adam had refused to eat of the fruit? Would she alone have been banned from the Garden? Would God have created another woman for Adam? Or was he considered guilty because he did not stop her from eating of the fruit?

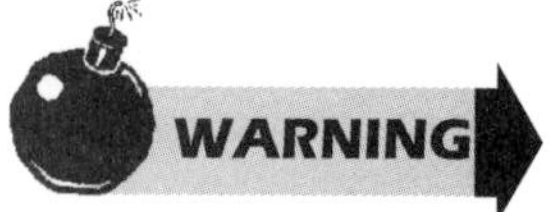

It's easy to place the blame for our sins on someone else. It's much harder to take responsibility.

> **Genesis 3: 8–13** Then the man and his wife heard the sound of the LORD God as he was walking in the garden in the cool of the day, and they hid from the LORD God among the trees of the garden. But the LORD God called to the man, "Where are you?" He answered, "I heard you in the garden, and I was afraid because I was naked; so I hid." And he said, "Who told you that you were naked? Have you eaten from the tree that I commanded you not to eat from?" The man said, "The woman you put here with me—she gave me some fruit from the tree, and I ate it." Then the LORD God said to the woman, "What is this you have done?" The woman said, "The serpent deceived me, and I ate."

GO TO:

Leviticus 26:12; Deuteronomy 23:14 (walking)

Romans 7:11 (deceived)

It's Satan's Fault

"She did it." "No, he did it." "No, it was her fault."

We hear these words almost every day from our children, so it's interesting to see the blame shifting going on in these verses.

Adam blames God and Eve. "It was that woman you gave me, it's all her fault." Eve blames the serpent. Neither takes responsibility.

Sound familiar? No one likes to admit they've sinned. It takes a strong person to own up to his or her own mistakes, and it's a quality that we need to teach our children, over and over and over.

H. V. Morton: The words of the first Adam are like the words of a rather sneaky little boy caught out by the headmaster and blames another—She gave me of the tree and I did eat.[3]

My husband left this morning without kissing me good-bye. When I realized this, I felt hurt and then angry at his thoughtlessness. Then it dawned on me. I hadn't kissed him good-bye, either. I should've made a point of giving him a big hug and a long kiss, but instead I had my head buried in the newspaper. At that point, I shifted my thinking from blaming him to taking responsibility for my own actions. You can do this too and when you do, it will lead to a much healthier and happier relationship.

> **Genesis 3:16** To the woman he said, "I will greatly increase your pains in **childbearing**; with pain you will give birth to children."

☞ **GO TO:**

Psalm 48:6; Isaiah 13:8; Matthew 24:8 (childbearing)

childbearing: *giving birth*

Consequences for Disobedience

Before the Fall, Eve had everything. She was coequal with her husband and she had unrestricted access to God. Her life was one of ease. Everything she wanted and needed had been provided. She had beauty and brains. She had Adam's love and companionship. She played a significant role in tending to the Garden of Eden.

After the Fall, her life changed dramatically. The consequences were more severe than this translation states. Commentaries make it clear that in the original language God said he would multiply her sorrows in every aspect of childbearing and then he'd multiply those sorrows by even more sorrows.

That means that every aspect of our femaleness from **menses** to menopause is affected by the Fall. No other creature has as much trouble during conception and childbirth. No other animal suffers **malaise**, nausea, and vomiting during pregnancy. Nothing physiologically explains all the suffering we experience, except the Fall.

menses: *the menstrual cycle*

malaise: *general weakness*

For Single Moms—It can be difficult to overcome the blame game when you're a single mom. It can seem as if the whole world conspires against you and your children. Don't blame others for your predicament. Instead, take an active role in overcoming your circumstances.

What Others are Saying:

Kathy Collard Miller: Adam and Eve thought they would become god-like. Instead, because they believed Satan's lie, they are held in the bondage of pain in childbirth and in the curse of hard work. God rebukes Adam for not discouraging Eve from eating the fruit, and Adam receives the consequences. The same Hebrew word "issaabon" is used for the "pain" Eve will experience and the "painful" toil Adam will suffer.[4]

☞ **GO TO:**

Genesis 4:7 (desire)

> **Genesis 3:16** "Your desire will be for your husband, and he will rule over you."

A Change of Roles

From this point on, women have been cursed with this desire for their husbands. The word "desire" comes from the Greek word "teshuwqah" and it is not a positive term. It means a longing for in such a way that would consume the person. Our longing for our husbands has taken the place of our longing for God. We look to men to fulfill us.

But men are sinners, just like we are, and they will disappoint us. For after the Fall, they, instead of looking to their wives for fulfillment, looked to their jobs. This is our curse. We marry thinking we've found our Prince Charming, only to discover that he's a man with clay feet, and he's not always very charming after all! Today, women file for six out of every ten divorces.[5] Is it because of their disappointment in their husbands?

The role of woman changed, too. She became subject to her husband's rule. Her domestic duties included tending the flocks, spinning the wool, and making clothing. She ground the grain, baked the bread, prepared the meals, drew water for household use and for the camels of guests. She frequently entertained. Most importantly she raised up the children and trained them, her sons until age three, her daughters until they married.

Think About It

It's interesting that the role of women hasn't dramatically changed in all this time. There are some exceptions, as we move into a new millennium, but they are that, exceptions.

What Others are Saying:

NIV Study Bible: Her sexual attraction for the man, and his headship over her, will become intimate aspects of her life in which she experiences trouble and anguish rather than **unalloyed** joy and blessing.[6]

unalloyed: *pure*

For Single Moms—It's awfully easy in our society to believe that the answer to all our problems is a man. Don't get caught up in that lie. Put all your energies into raising your children. If God has a man in mind for you, it will happen. If not, be content. Build your life on his foundation.

☞ GO TO:

Numbers 35:33; Psalm 106:39; Isaiah 24:5 (cursed)

Genesis 29:32; 31:42; Exodus 3:7 (painful toil)

Job 31:40; Isaiah 5:6; Hebrews 6:8 (thorns and thistles)

> **Genesis 3:17–19** To Adam he said, "Because you listened to your wife and ate from the tree about which I commanded you, 'You must not eat of it,' Cursed is the ground because of you; through painful toil you will eat of it all the days of your life. It will produce thorns and thistles for you, and you will eat the plants of the field. By the sweat of your brow you will eat your food until you return to the ground, since from it you were taken; for dust you are and to dust you will return."

The Role of Every Father

Adam's life, up to this point, had been one of leisure. Afterwards, things changed for him, too. Instead of sharing responsibilities with Eve, he became the one who was responsible. He became the provider, the teacher, the protector, and the leader of the family—roles men have not always handled well.

Think About It

As women we often look upon men's role with envy, but single moms know that this responsibility can weigh heavily. There is no one there to help with the discipline. There is no one there to carry the burden when a child is sick. And there is no one there to just unload on when things get tough or the worries seem overwhelming.

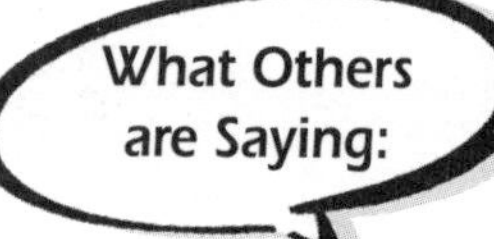

Paul D. Gardner: Adam set the scene for humanity. It is a scene in which the true origins of mankind as unique in God's creation are clearly revealed, but it is also a scene in which the one who was given so much dominion by the Creator tried to deny his dependence on God. In that denial, in that sin, Adam set his sights on a life that would try to ignore and even deny God. In that sin man set himself up in the place of God. Through Adam sin entered the world and brought upon the whole of creation God's judgment curse.[7]

A DEEP DESIRE FOR CHILDREN

The desire for children beats deeply in the heart of most women. At an early age, we play with dolls and pretend to be mommies. We practice rocking and holding and bathing and burping. No one has to urge us; it comes naturally. It's the way God made us from the very beginning.

But with that longing comes the consequences of Eve's original sin—pain.

Genesis 29:32–34 Leah became pregnant and gave birth to a son. She named him Reuben, for she said, "It is because the LORD has seen my misery. Surely my husband will love me now." She conceived again, and when she gave birth to a son she said, "Because the LORD heard that I am not loved, he gave me this one too." So she named him Simeon. Again she conceived, and when she gave birth to a son she said, "Now at last my husband will become attached to me, because I have borne him three sons." So he was named Levi.

Unrealistic Expectations

KEY POINT

It's God's desire for us to have children, but only for the right reasons.

Children can bring great joy, but when we begin to look to them to provide our emotional needs, we will be disappointed.

Here Leah believes that if she has children, her husband will love her. With each child she faces disappointment, for her husband loves only Rachel.

Rachel on the other hand, has her own reasons to be jealous and unhappy. She fears that her husband will love her sister more because Leah is bearing him children.

GO TO:

Genesis 30:1 (jealous)

Today women get pregnant for a variety of reasons. Some like Leah, in hopes that their marriage will improve. Others, in hopes of being loved for the first time or to replace an aborted child. A recent study showed that 15 percent of teenage pregnancies are planned.[8] These young girls hope that getting pregnant will make them feel better about themselves or make their lovers stay, or that it will get them the attention they crave.

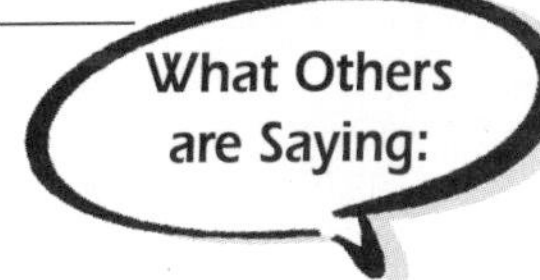

Dr. Laura Schlessinger: Procreation has little to do with your needs; it has everything to do with the child's needs. When you look at making a baby solely from the vantage point of healing yourself, identifying yourself, solidifying yourself in a precarious relationship, or entertaining yourself in an otherwise ho-hum existence, you're terribly disappointed, and the children ultimately pay the price.[9]

There's a time when you have to explain to your children why they're born, and it's a marvelous thing if you can give them a positive reason.

You know you're really a mom when:

- You only have the chance to shave one leg at a time.
- You hope ketchup *is* a vegetable, because it's the only one your child will eat.
- You hide in the bathroom to be alone.

☞ **GO TO:**

Romans 8:15 (fear)

> **1 John 4:18** There is no fear in love. But perfect love drives out fear, because fear has to do with punishment. The one who fears is not made perfect in love.

Fears during Pregnancy

Fear is a common feeling for women who are pregnant. Following are some of the most common ones.

"What If I Lose the Baby?" Miscarriage happens once in every five pregnancies. It most commonly occurs in the first trimester. Even if you've miscarried before, the chance that it will happen again does not go up.

"A Baby Will Wreck My Life." A baby will definitely change your life. If you're worried about a certain area, now is the time to make plans. Talk with your husband, your boss, or your doctor. Arrange child care ahead of time or look at your budget to see if you can quit your job or go part-time.

"I Won't Have a Say in How My Baby Is Born." Take charge of your delivery by reading as much reliable medical material as you can find. Don't feel you have to follow a friend's advice, or go by trendy new methods you read about in women's magazines. Find a medical professional whom you can trust, and then follow his or her advice. And don't be afraid to change doctors if you really feel your needs aren't being met.

Today there are many options available for the whole family to participate, from in-home delivery to hospital rooms. Be prepared for last-minute changes, just in case something goes wrong.

"Will the Baby Be Normal?" Ninety-seven percent of all babies are born perfectly normal. Prenatal tests can rule out many problems, but you need to take care of yourself. Get regular checkups, eat right, exercise, avoid alcoholic beverages and coffee, and follow the advice of your obstetrician closely.

KEY POINT

If this list of fears isn't enough, you'll make some up of your own, for it's in every woman's very nature to worry!

"My Body Will Never Be the Same." A normal weight gain for women during pregnancy is thirty pounds. Of that seven and one-half are baby, ten are increased fluids, five and one-half are for the uterus, breasts, and placenta, and seven are extra stores of baby fat which will be needed while nursing the baby. Your body may never be quite the same again, but controlling your weight gain during pregnancy will help.

If you do gain a little too much, then beware of the diet treadmill. It's better to carry a few extra pounds than to gain and lose and gain and lose.

What Others are Saying:

Gwen Shamblin: Studies show that we are fatter than ever. And it seems that the more weight-obsessed we are, the less we lose and the more we revile the pudgy, the plump, the rotund, the fat, and the morbidly obese. The billion-dollar weight-loss industry is a dizzying carousel of promises, hardly ever fulfilled.[10]

One mother had an abortion after a prenatal test revealed there was a chance the baby could be born with Down's syndrome. Another mother's prenatal screening also showed a chance that her child would be born abnormal. She decided to carry the baby to term, and he turned out to be perfectly normal. Which woman made the right decision? What if the second child had been born with a handicap?

Share your fears with your husband. He may have fears of his own. Together you can work through them and support one another. Praying together for each other will not only bring you closer to God, but to each other.

> **Psalm 34:4–5** I sought the LORD, and he answered me; he delivered me from all my fears. Those who look to him are radiant; their faces are never covered with shame.

"Will Labor Hurt?"

Take a childbirth class to help you and your husband prepare for the labor. Learn as much as you can about what to expect and what you can do to help yourself. There are many options available. Again, learn what they are, and then you choose what's right for you.

KEY POINT

Give your troubles to God; he will be up all night anyway.

"Will I Be a Good Mom?"

Some women decide not to have children because they fear they won't make good moms. If this is your first child, look at it as if you're facing a new job. You don't always know what to expect there, either. Read books, take classes, develop friendships with new moms, pick out an older woman whom you admire and follow her example. Finally, trust your own instincts. Yes, you will make some mistakes, but as long as you're willing to learn and rely on others for help, you will be fine.

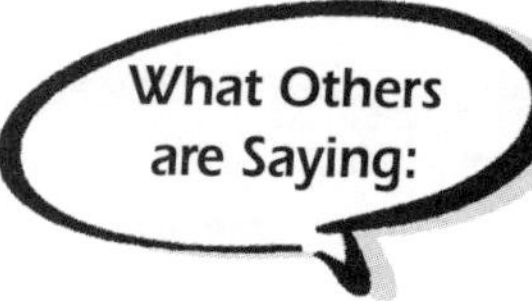

Anne Tyler: I remember leaving the hospital thinking, "Wait, are they going to let me just walk off with him? I don't know beans about babies."[11]

Think About It

Here are some other common worries that pregnant women have:

- That the water will break in public
- That they won't realize they're in labor
- That they will lose control during labor
- That, afterwards, they'll have stretch marks and looser vaginal muscles

FROM JUDY'S HEART

I was twenty-five when I first got pregnant. It was a surprise, for I had not planned it. In fact, my husband and I had pretty much decided that we didn't want children. They would get in the way of our careers. Besides, this world was a mess, and we weren't sure we wanted to bring children into it.

But God had other plans. The first signs were nausea and heartburn—all the time. Since I seemed to be still having a menstrual cycle the doctor decided I must be having gallbladder problems, but he'd do a pregnancy check just to be safe. Pregnant? Me? I had been using an IUD for six years. There was no way I could be pregnant!

But I was.

Along with the announcement came a complication, for, you see, because I was bleeding, the doctor feared I would lose this child. He felt that removing the IUD would be too dangerous. The first four months were crucial. If I made it past month four, then I probably would be okay.

I went home from that visit a changed person. Not only was I pregnant, but I knew I wanted the baby, desperately. I turned to God for the first time in a long time and begged him to save the baby that was growing in my belly.

The next two months were not easy. My husband had to bear

the brunt of most of my impatience and anger. For the first time in my twenty-five years, I faced a situation that was out of my control, and I was scared.

The bleeding didn't stop and I was confined to bed. Each day seemed like a lifetime. My doctor finally referred me to another doctor who said the IUD had to come out. Frightened, and not knowing what else to do, I put myself in his hands.

It worked. The bleeding stopped, and six months later I gave birth to a perfect baby boy. Since then, I've experienced the peace that comes with knowing Christ on a personal basis. Now, I understand how he holds me in his loving arms and goes through my troubles with me, but back then I felt alone and lost and anxious about everything.

If you are frightened about anything, turn it over to him. He will be there for you.

Luke 2:4–6 So Joseph also went up from the town of Nazareth in Galilee to Judea, to Bethlehem the town of David, because he belonged to the house and line of David. He went there to register with Mary, who was pledged to be married to him and was expecting a child.

Think about Mary

Mary traveled to Bethlehem on a donkey. For approximately seventy miles (see illustration, page 42) she endured cold, dust, heat, tired aching muscles, swollen ankles, and, if she chose to walk instead of ride, probably sore feet.

She must've been close to her due date, so that means she was nine months pregnant. Remember how you felt then? How every task was harder because your belly was so big? What do you think her fears were?

What Others are Saying:

Janette Oke: Bethlehem . . . had reason for pride. It was from Bethlehem that King David and his line had come. It was a tiny town among the fields grazed by sheep, and the true Jews looked to it with respect. Had not their mighty king been born there? . . . And had not the great God of Israel promised that of David's line, and in his town, a new king would one day be born?[12]

Mary's Journey

Pictured is a map showing the route Mary and Joseph traveled from Bethlehem to Egypt and then Egypt to Nazareth.

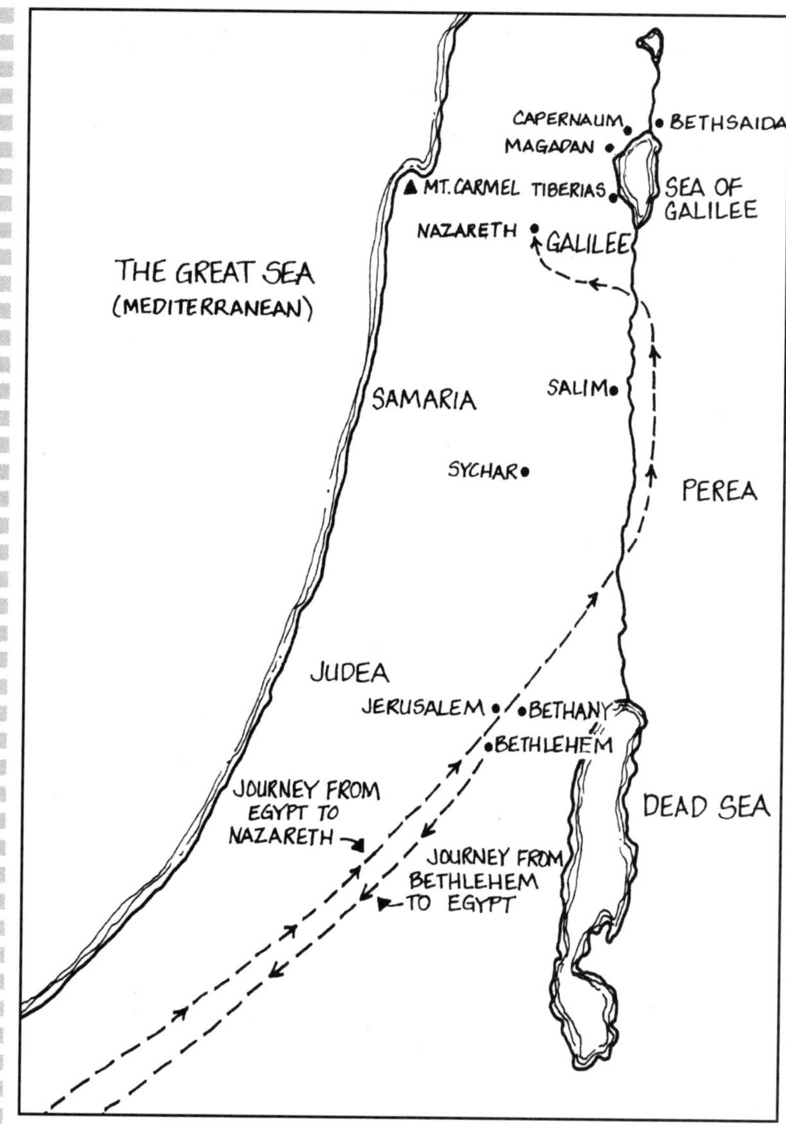

Psalm 33:20–22 We wait in hope for the LORD; he is our help and our shield. In him our hearts rejoice, for we trust in his holy name. May your unfailing love rest upon us, O LORD, even as we put our hope in you.

The Best Source of Strength

Perhaps Mary was able to endure all she experienced because she sought the Lord and he delivered her from all her fears. If you are fearful, turn to God. He is your help and your shield.

☞ **GO TO:**

Psalm 3:3; Ephesians 6:16 (shield)

Psalm 4:7 (hearts)

Psalm 5:11 (holy name)

THE CURSE OF BEING A WOMAN

> **Genesis 3:16** I will greatly increase your pains in **childbearing**.

childbearing: *every aspect of the reproductive system*

Pain upon Pain

The desire for children has to come from God, because if it didn't, there would be no way any of us would go through with it. From the moment we hit menses, we enter a crazy world of emotional roller coasters and physical challenges that would deter most men.

> **Leviticus 15:19** When a woman has her regular flow of blood, the impurity of her monthly period will last seven days, and anyone who touches her will be **unclean** till evening.

GO TO:

Leviticus 12:2 (seven days)

2 Samuel 11:4 (unclean)

unclean: *religious impurity*

The Monthly Curse

It's interesting to note that this normal cycle is often referred to as "the curse." During biblical times a woman was considered ceremonially unclean during that time and could not go to the temple or the area surrounding it until she became "clean" again. To become clean in this instance meant washing her hands or waiting until after dark.

Today, our monthly period, at the least, is an inconvenience. However, some women experience severe pain and wild mood swings associated with the hormonal fluctuations.

What Others are Saying:

Jean Lush: Dramatic hormonal changes can occur during each monthly cycle, as well as throughout most of a woman's adult life. Is it any wonder that many of us experience life as sailing the ocean in a sailboat—calm and serene with gentle swells one day, then hurricane gales and tidal waves the next? Sometimes we wonder if we'll ever survive.[13]

Barbara Johnson tells this story: A lady picked up several items at a discount store. When she finally got up to the checker, she learned that one of her items had no price tag. Imagine her embarrassment when the checker got on the intercom and boomed out for all the store to hear: "PRICE CHECK ON LANE THIRTEEN. TAMPAX. SUPERSIZE."

That was bad enough, but somebody at the rear of the store apparently misunderstood the word "Tampax" for "THUMBTACK." In a businesslike tone, a voice boomed back over the intercom: "DO YOU WANT THE KIND YOU PUSH IN WITH YOUR THUMB OR THE KIND YOU POUND IN WITH A HAMMER?"[14]

> **2 Kings 4:17** But the woman became pregnant, and the next year about that same time she gave birth to a son, just as Elisha had told her.

Nine Months of Heartburn

Some women say they've never felt better than when they were pregnant. Most of us experience nausea, vomiting, and a deep malaise for at least the first four months of our pregnancies. After that there are bouts of each of these symptoms. Some women throw up every morning for nine months; others can't hold food down at all. As the fetus grows and develops, it can press against inner organs causing water retention, swollen ankles and hands, frequent urination, and cracked ribs. All of these are part of a normal pregnancy.

writhe: *to twist*

> **Isaiah 13:8** Terror will seize them, pain and anguish will grip them; they will **writhe** like a woman in labor.

That's Why They Call It Labor

This verse pretty much captures it. Luckily the pain ebbs and flows, making it a little more bearable. It's a wonder any of us ever goes through it again.

What Others are Saying:

Chandran Devanesen:

Seasons
I thank Thee for Pain,
The sister of joy.
I thank Thee for sorrow,
The twin of happiness.
Pain, Joy, Sorrow, Happiness.
Four angels at work on the Well of Love.

Pain and Sorrow dig it deep with aches.
Joy and Happiness fill it up with tears that come with smiles.
For the seasons of emotion in my heart,
I thank Thee, O Lord.[15]

The Loss of a Dream

The Hebrew word for miscarriage is "shakol," and it means "to bereave." A woman who miscarries feels the loss keenly, and today, with ultrasound images that so clearly show the developing fetus, it can be even more devastating. The American Medical Association reports that women who miscarry are more than two and one-half times more likely to suffer from a major depression in the six months following the loss. The emotional toll, including sleep disorders and suicidal thoughts, is similar to that of a woman whose baby dies after birth.

A woman who experiences a miscarriage should expect to go through the normal cycle of bereavement—denial, anger, bargaining, depression, acceptance, and hope. A year would not be an unreasonable period of time to expect to take to recover from this tragedy.

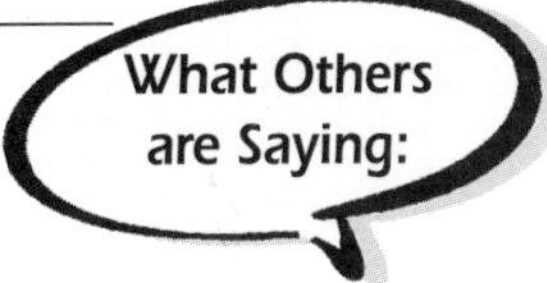

Melissa Sexson Hanson: I guess I never really understood what the Bible meant when it said that "joy comes in the morning" (Psalm 30:5, NKJV) until I lost my children through miscarriage. Now I believe that this text not only refers to that glorious Resurrection day, when I will be reunited with my little ones, but it also is a promise for today, describing the wonderful gift God offers to all during the darkest hour of grief. Just as the sun banishes the blackness of night, so God's infinite love shines the brightest—when mourning breaks.[16]

Your husband goes through all of these phases right along with you. Talk openly to him about your mood swings and reassure him that he's not the cause.

Exodus 21:22–26 "If men who are fighting hit a pregnant woman and . . . there is serious injury, you are to take life for life, eye for eye, tooth for tooth, hand for hand, foot for foot, burn for burn, wound for wound, bruise for bruise."

Murder of an Unborn Baby

The conception of a child in biblical times was such a blessing that the killing of an unborn child was considered a capital offense, punishable by death. The devaluing of human life, combined with an easy **believe-ism** in God, has led this country to adopt a new set of values. Our Supreme Court ruled in 1973 that a woman had the right to kill her unborn baby up to the ninth month with no legal consequences at all.

believe-ism: *shallow knowledge*

Think About It

Since *Roe v. Wade* thirty-eight million abortions have occurred. What if one of those children grew up and discovered the cure for cancer or danced on Broadway or saved your child from drowning in a pool? At the time, the killing of a small fetus can seem insignificant, like the killing of the runt in a puppy litter. But each of these souls would have become an adult. Our world is much poorer without having known them.

STDs

The Bible doesn't mention sexually transmitted diseases (STDs). Perhaps they were unknown then because of the strict laws against sex outside of marriage. Perhaps those laws were a warning of what would happen if any society allowed perverted sex to enter our world.

The first STD showed up in the mid-1700s. To the English, syphilis was known as the French Disease; to the French, it was the English Disease! Before World War II there were four known STDs. Currently there are over fifty-five.

Today forty-five million Americans now have genital herpes, and an estimated fifty-five million more may be living with another of the twenty STDs that have been identified. Viruses such as hepatitis C, hepatitis B, and human papilloma virus can be fatal. Chlamydia and gonorrhea can cause infertility, chronic pelvic pain, and potentially fatal tubal pregnancies, if left untreated.[17]

Think About It

Venereal diseases represent what some public health experts have called this country's "Silent Epidemic." At least one in four and possibly as many as one in two Americans will contract a venereal disease, yet many Americans have never heard of many of the highly contagious ones and most don't even believe they are at risk.

Genesis 17:17 Abraham fell facedown; he **laughed** and said to himself, "Will a son be born to a man a hundred years old? Will Sarah bear a child at the age of ninety?"

☞ **GO TO:**

Genesis 18:12; Romans 4:19–21 (laughed)

Genesis 18:11, 13; 23:1 (age of ninety)

laughed: *temporarily disbelieved*

You're Kidding—Aren't You?

Abraham laughed when he was told Sarah would have a son. I mean, who wouldn't laugh? Sarah was ninety years old. Menstrual cycles, hot flashes, and those feelings of being crazy that are associated with menopause would have been far behind her, and good riddance!

Menopause is the final stage of the reproductive cycle that falls under the "pain in childbearing" that God cursed all of womankind with. If we live long enough, all of us will go through some or all of these symptoms.

In the early forties, the ovaries slowly start to shut down and we begin to experience irregular periods. This process can last up to ten years, but usually between the ages of forty-nine and fifty-one the ovaries quit working altogether. As the hormones produced by the body begin to wane, the following symptoms appear: insomnia, vaginal changes, urinary incontinence, mood swings, irritability, and anxiety.

Some women breeze through this period, but some require hormone replacement. If any of these symptoms are troubling you, you might want to read reliable medical literature and talk about it with your doctor so you can make an informed decision.

Jean Lush: Menopause is the final transition between youth and maturity. Many of us who have suffered from years of emotional upheaval due to hormonal problems can say, "Soon, very soon, it will be over."[18]

Study Questions

1. God said to Eve, "Your desire will be for your husband." Explain how that affects us today.
2. What was Eve's role in the Garden before the Fall? What was it after?
3. What did God mean when he said, "I will greatly increase your pains in childbearing"?
4. Explain why getting pregnant for the wrong reasons will only bring unhappiness.

5. What steps can you take to allay your fears during a pregnancy?
6. Why was the taking of an unborn baby's life considered a capital offense in Old Testament times?

CHAPTER WRAP-UP

- When Eve sinned in the Garden, it affected every aspect of our femaleness. It also changed our role. Instead of sharing the same role with Adam, we are now, with a few exceptions, relegated to the household chores.
- We have an abnormal desire for our husbands. We think they will provide for all our needs, but because they are sinners, like us, they continue to disappoint.
- Deep within the heart of most every woman is the desire for a child. But mixed with that desire is fear, another consequence of the Fall.
- Women experience pain in childbirth that can't totally be explained physiologically. From menses to menopause, we suffer from one degree to another.

JUDY'S BOOKSHELF

- *Meditations for the Expectant Mother,* Helen Good Brenneman, Herald Press. An inspiring book of poems and essays that I loan to all my expectant friends and relatives.
- *When Mourning Breaks,* Melissa Sexson Hanson, Morehouse Publishing. A collection of inspirational essays for women coping with miscarriage.

3 BE FRUITFUL AND MULTIPLY

WHAT'S IN THIS CHAPTER

- The Problem of Infertility
- Choosing to Go Childless
- Children without Fathers

Here We Go

In biblical times, every woman hoped to have babies, lots of babies, for this was seen as a special blessing from God—especially if they were sons. If she did have many children, she was revered by her husband, regarded highly by her neighbors, and held up to her children and grandchildren as someone very special.

A barren woman was someone to be pitied. Even if she was rich and her husband loved her very much, it wasn't enough. She was leered at and made fun of. Her husband could divorce her or he could take a second wife, because children were essential to the survival of the family. Is it any wonder that being barren was the greatest fear of every Hebrew woman?

And yet, five of the greatest women in the Bible were barren for a time. Let's look at their lives and see what we can learn from them.

THE PROBLEM OF INFERTILITY

1 Samuel 1:4–8 Whenever the day came for Elkanah to sacrifice, he would give portions of the meat to his wife Peninnah and to all her sons and daughters. But to **Hannah** he gave a double portion because he loved her, and the LORD had closed her womb. And because the LORD had closed her womb, her rival kept provoking her in order to irritate her. This went on year after year. Whenever Hannah went up to the house of the LORD, her rival **provoked** her till she wept and would not eat. Elkanah her husband would say to her, "Hannah, why are you weeping? Why don't you eat? Why are you **downhearted**? Don't I mean more to you than ten sons?"

☞ **GO TO:**

Ezekiel 20:40; John 8:56; Hebrews 11:39–40; 10:11–18 (sacrifice)

sacrifice: *payment for sin*

Hannah: *"gracious"*

provoked: *irritated to anger*

downhearted: *having a broken heart*

Lin Yutang: Of all the rights of women, the greatest is to be a mother.[1]

Hannah's Problem

Hannah was the favored wife of her husband, but that wasn't enough. She wanted children. Her heart ached with the desire for a son, yet year after year she was unable to conceive. To make matters worse her husband's other wife, Peninnah, taunted her until she was in tears. She was so devastated that even her husband could not console her (see GWWB, page 129).

Think About It

God closed Hannah's womb for a purpose. If you too have a prayer that seems like it's being ignored, remember Hannah and the good that came out of what seemed like a hopeless situation. Trust what God is doing in your life.

☞ GO TO:

Genesis 28:20–22; Psalm 132:2–5 (vow)

vow: *a solemn pledge to perform a specified act*

> **1 Samuel 1:10–11** In bitterness of soul Hannah wept much and prayed to the LORD. And she made a **vow**, saying, "O LORD Almighty, if you will only look upon your servant's misery and remember me, and not forget your servant but give her a son, then I will give him to the LORD for all the days of his life, and no razor will ever be used on his head."

Hannah's Vow

Hannah was in such misery that she vowed to God that, if he would grant her a son, she would give the boy up to the service of the Lord, not just for the normal period of **Nazirite** (Nazarite) service (about twenty-five to fifty days), but for *"all the days of his life."*

Hannah's prayer is a cry from the depths of her soul, an example for many of us who flippantly ask for the more superficial things we want and then wonder why God doesn't grant the desires of our heart.

☞ GO TO:

Numbers 6:1–21 (Nazirite)

Nazirite: *a religious devotee who has taken strict vows*

Think About It

What Hannah promised God is almost incomprehensible to most of us. How many of us would be willing to give up the one thing we want most in order to get it? Hannah was indeed a woman to be admired.

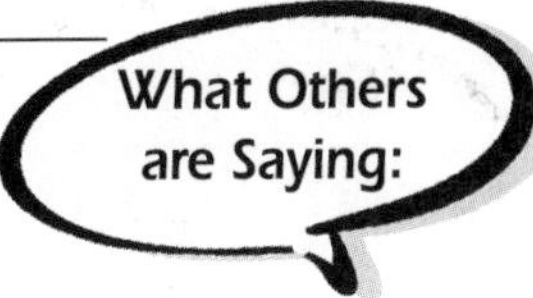

Kathy McReynolds: This was no simple dedication. This vow meant that she was surrendering her privilege to raise him in her home. He would become a Nazirite, wholly devoted to the service of the Lord. This was an incredible promise made by Hannah. She would offer the Lord her only son, giving up her heart's desire to raise and nurture a child.[2]

What a Mother Knows

- When you hear the toilet flush and the words "Uh-oh," it's already too late.
- Always look in the oven before you turn it on.
- Cats throw up twice their body weight.

> **1 Samuel 1:17–18** Eli [the priest, said], "Go in peace, and may the God of Israel grant you what you have asked of him." She said, "May your servant find favor in your eyes." Then she went her way and ate something, and her face was no longer downcast.

GO TO:

Numbers 6:26; 1 Samuel 20:42; 2 Kings 5:19 (peace)

Psalm 20:3–5 (grant)

Genesis 18:3 (favor)

Peace at Last

After her anguished prayer, Hannah arose and was blessed by the priest. Immediately she felt better and was able to eat.

Do you take your desires to the Lord? How many times do you anguish about something to yourself or to your neighbor or to your husband, never turning to the Lord for the answer? Maybe you're missing out on a "peace that passes all understanding."

What Others are Saying:

Cheri Fuller: Prayer isn't a secondary thing; it's the most important thing we can do for our children and ourselves, and it will dispense the most blessings. If all that we do as mothers flows out of the fountain of prayer, we will experience grace, joy, and rest in the heart of the Father. It doesn't mean we won't have difficulties, but we will be able to face them with more energy and confidence.[3]

> **1 Samuel 1:19–20** Early the next morning they arose and worshiped before the LORD and then went back to their home at Ramah. Elkanah lay with Hannah his wife, and the LORD remembered her. So in the course of time Hannah conceived and gave birth to a son. She named him **Samuel**, saying, "Because I asked the LORD for him."

☞ **GO TO:**

1 Samuel; 2 Samuel; Jeremiah 15:1; Hebrews 11:32 (Samuel)

Samuel: *"heard of God"*

Another Answered Prayer!

There must have been great rejoicing when Hannah discovered she was pregnant. But in the back of her mind, she had to remember her vow to God to give the child up to him.

Think About It

God had closed Hannah's womb for a reason. If Hannah hadn't been desperate for a son, she might not have made her vow to God, and Israel would never have known its most renowned prophet—Samuel.

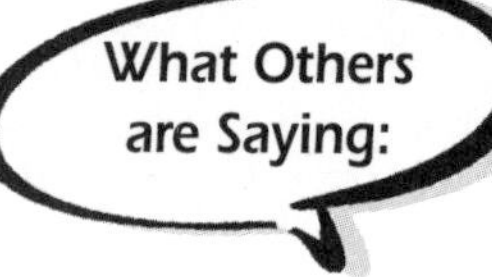

Kathy McReynolds: Hannah's life, though mentioned only in the first two chapters of 1 Samuel, speaks loudly. She stands, to this day, as a supreme example of devotion and sacrifice and she teaches us what true commitment to the LORD of the universe really means.[4]

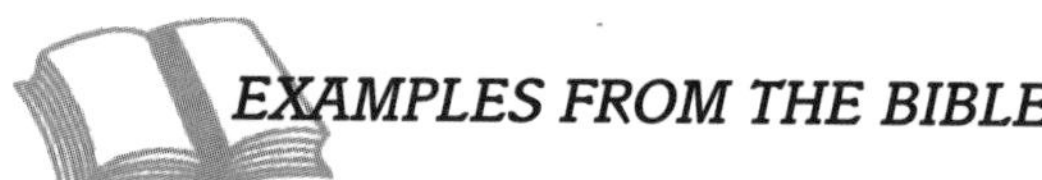

EXAMPLES FROM THE BIBLE

God used Samuel to establish rule by a king in Israel. Samuel anointed both Saul and David, Israel's first two kings.

Sarai: *"contentious"*

Abram: *"the father of a multitude"*

maidservant: *a female slave*

☞ **GO TO:**

Genesis 20:14; 30:7; Leviticus 19:20; 1 Samuel 25:41 (maidservant)

Genesis 15:4–5 (stars)

> **Genesis 16:1–2** Now **Sarai**, **Abram**'s wife, had borne him no children. But she had an Egyptian **maidservant** named Hagar; so she said to Abram, "The LORD has kept me from having children. Go, sleep with my maidservant; perhaps I can build a family through her."

Desperate Times Call for Desperate Measures

God had promised Abram (whose name God later changed to Abraham) that his descendants would be as numerous as the stars. That meant he needed to father at least one child.

But year after year went by and still there was no heir. When Sarai (whose name God later changed to Sarah) was seventy-five, she panicked and took matters into her own hands. She gave Abram her maidservant, and they produced a child (see GWWB, page 27).

When God doesn't answer our prayers right away, it's tempting to answer them ourselves.

We pray for a new car and then go into debt to buy it. We want happiness in our marriage, and then leave our husbands in order to find it. We rush ahead of God, then turn to him to fix the mess we create.

We all can learn from Sarai (Sarah). Wait patiently and trust God, for his ways are not our ways, and his timing is always perfect.

Genesis 18:10–14 Then the LORD said, "I will surely return to you about this time next year, and **Sarah** your wife will have a son." Now Sarah was listening at the entrance to the tent, which was behind him. Abraham and Sarah were already old and well advanced in years, and Sarah was past the age of childbearing. So Sarah laughed to herself as she thought, "After I am worn out and my master is old, will I now have this pleasure?" Then the LORD said to Abraham, "Why did Sarah laugh and say, 'Will I really have a child, now that I am old?' Is anything too hard for the LORD? I will return to you at the appointed time next year and Sarah will have a son."

Sarah: *"princess"*

☞ **GO TO:**

Joshua 9:13; Isaiah 51:6; Lamentations 3:4 (worn out)

Exodus 34:10; Deuteronomy 17:8; 1 Chronicles 16:9, 12, 24; Jeremiah 32:27 (hard)

No Laughing Matter

Can you blame Sarah for laughing?

She was ninety years old when she overheard a conversation that said she would be having a baby. Even if it was straight from God's mouth, such a thing was impossible. Her womb was dead; she was well past menopause.

But God gently reminds both Abraham and Sarah that nothing is impossible with him.

Why do you think God made Abraham and Sarah wait so long for their baby? Why didn't he give them their son when they were young and could really enjoy him? Why didn't he give them twelve sons?

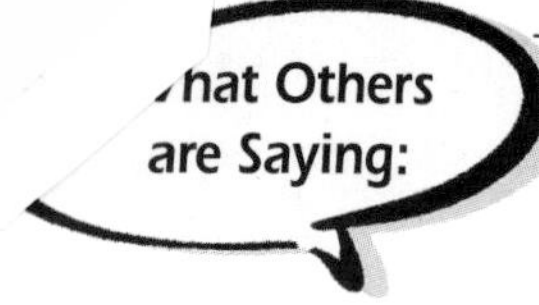

J. Alec Motyer: [Sarah's] laughter in Genesis 18:12 betrayed a doubting spirit but she laughed with open delight [Genesis 21:6] when the Lord proved that nothing is too hard for him. . . . Sarah's experience provides a case study of the spiritual dimensions of childlessness and fertility which remains as the Word of God even in our medically sophisticated age.[5]

KEY POINT

Faith does not refuse to face reality, but looks beyond all difficulties to God and his promises.

☞ **GO TO:**

Genesis 21–27 (Isaac)

Isaac: *"laughter"*

> **Genesis 21:1–3, 6–7** Now the LORD was gracious to Sarah as he had said, and the LORD did for Sarah what he had promised. Sarah became pregnant and bore a son to Abraham in his old age, at the very time God had promised him. Abraham gave the name **Isaac** to the son Sarah bore him. . . . Sarah said, "God has brought me laughter, and everyone who hears about this will laugh with me." And she added, "Who would have said to Abraham that Sarah would nurse children? Yet I have borne him a son in his old age."

A Miraculous Birth

And so Sarah and Abraham are given their long-promised child. Sarah calls him Isaac, which means "laughter." I'm sure there was much rejoicing and laughter from the day he was born, for his birth was a miracle.

fruit of the Spirit: *love, joy, peace, patience, kindness, goodness, faithfulness, gentleness, and self-control*

What Others are Saying:

Janette Oke: Great faith in God means humility, obedience, and growth. Its results are not necessarily success, good health, popularity, prestige, or financial blessing; its most obvious result is the **fruit of the Spirit** [Galatians 5:22–23]. Our faith, then, should not be measured by what we have but by what we are.[6]

Think About It

If you are facing an impossible situation and yet you feel you are fully following God's will, then take hope from Sarah. Even if you doubt, God will be faithful to his promise to you.

Sometimes God's behavior seems strange to us because we are merely human. Only he knows his full purpose.

Genesis 29:1–35 Jacob travels to the home of his mother's brother, Laban, in search of a wife. There he meets beautiful Rachel and offers to work for Laban for seven years in exchange for her hand in marriage. Laban tricks Jacob and on his wedding day substitutes his older daughter, Leah, who has weak eyes. Jacob is furious at being cheated. Laban then agrees that he can have Rachel after Leah's **bridal week** is up, if Jacob will agree to work for him another seven years. Because Jacob loves Rachel, he agrees.

GO TO:

2 Samuel 3:39 (weak)

bridal week: *a traditional wedding feast that lasted one week*

Jacob Loves Rachel!

Can you imagine this scenario? A handsome young stranger moves into your family's tent (see illustration below) and wants your hand in marriage. Your father agrees to it, but you have to wait seven years. During that time you get to know your intended, and even though this isn't exactly made clear in this scripture, very likely fall in love with him.

There is great anticipation as you approach your wedding day.

Then at the last minute, you are tricked! Your big sister gets your man, instead of you.

EXAMPLES FROM THE BIBLE

Laban did a great disservice to these two girls. From the beginning, his trickery set them up for an unhappy lifetime of trying to live together and share a husband (see GWWB, page 67).

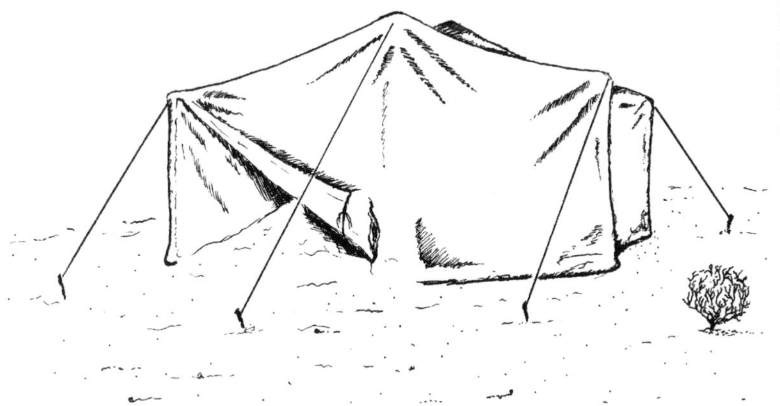

Bedouin Tent

Laban and his family might have lived in a tent that looked like this one.

GO TO:

Leviticus 18:18 (jealous)

Genesis 29:31; 30:1–2 When the LORD saw that Leah was not loved, he opened her womb, but Rachel was barren. . . . When Rachel saw that she was not bearing Jacob any children, she became jealous of her sister. So she said to Jacob, "Give me children, or I'll die!" Jacob became angry with her and said, "Am I in the place of God, who has kept you from having children?"

Shifting the Blame

Rachel's heart filled with jealousy, and she grew angry. She yelled at her husband, blaming him for not giving her what she wanted.

Doesn't that sound familiar? Isn't that what we do when we don't get what we want? We blame someone else, and often that someone else is our husband.

In this case God had closed Rachel's womb, but Rachel's anger was toward her husband.

Think About It

If Rachel had been patient and waited upon God's timing, do you think God would have answered her prayer more quickly?

Grow Your Marriage

Are you angry with your husband for not giving you something you think you need? Is it a larger home, more children, a different job, more income so you can quit your job, or private school for the kids?

Look to God to provide your needs, whatever they might be, and if he doesn't seem to answer your prayers as quickly as you'd like him to, remember Rachel.

What Others are Saying:

J. Alec Motyer: Under a sometimes hard exterior beat a tender heart and fittingly it was Rachel whom Jeremiah heard weeping for her exiled children (Jeremiah 31:15) and whose tears reached their full intensity over the world's savage counterattack against the divine plan of salvation (Matthew 2:17–18).[7]

EXAMPLES FROM THE BIBLE

Leah, though she was unloved by her husband, became the mother of six sons.

In this life she never got what she wanted. But in history she is honored. Jesus' genealogy can be traced directly to her, an honor that every Hebrew mother would have desired.

Looking for our fulfillment here on earth from anything other than God has a good chance of leading to disappointment.

Genesis 25:21 Isaac prayed to the LORD on behalf of his wife, because she was <u>barren</u>. The LORD answered his prayer, and his wife Rebekah became pregnant.

☞ **GO TO:**

Genesis 11:30 (barren)

Isaac Loves Rebekah!

Rebekah must have been aware of the promise made to her father-in-law that he would be the father of many nations, and so it must have bewildered everyone when she remained childless for the first nineteen years of her marriage to Isaac.

It says here that she became pregnant after her husband prayed, but it's hard to believe that he hadn't prayed many, many times before this. He must've begged God for a son.

What was so special about this one time? There is no answer to that question except to remember that we should never give up praying for what we believe is God's will for our lives (see GWWB, page 45).

Joan H. Young: Even those of us who love the Lord sometimes have trouble with the idea that a God who is omniscient—who knows everything—needs to be asked for things in prayer. . . . Probably the best reason for us to pray, even though God knows what we need, is because Jesus did it.[8]

If you are barren like Rebekah, begin today to ask others to pray for you—your husband, your pastor, friends, relatives, prayer partners. Join or form a group to meet just for the purpose of prayer.

Luke 1:5–7 In the time of Herod king of Judea there was a priest named Zechariah, who belonged to the priestly division of Abijah; his wife Elizabeth was also a descendant of Aaron. Both of them were **<u>upright</u>** in the sight of God, observing all the Lord's commandments and regulations **blamelessly**. But they had no children, because Elizabeth was barren, and they were both well along in years.

☞ **GO TO:**

Matthew 9:13; 25:37; Acts 3:14 (upright)

upright: *innocent*

blamelessly: *faultlessly*

Elizabeth, Another Late Bloomer

Elizabeth, the mother of John the Baptist, was another great woman of the Bible who remained barren well into her old age.

Her neighbors may have whispered behind her back that there had to be something in her life that was displeasing to the Lord. Otherwise she would have had a child.

But, we can see that both she and her husband were godly people. Again, God had something special in mind (see GWWB, page 293).

Think About It

Waiting is something no one likes to do. We want what we want and we want it now!

But it seems that in God's economy, when you have to wait for something, it always turns out to be something really, really special.

If you are waiting for that something right now, try to take on this attitude. It will make the wait easier.

This can be a difficult time for your husband too. Sometimes blame and guilt can become a part of your relationship. If you find you are struggling with this issue, seek a good Christian counselor.

What Others are Saying:

Beth Spring: In all the Bible's teachings about marriage, there is no suggestion that children are essential. They are a wonderful gift and blessing, and they are the usual result of a man and woman committing their lives to one another in marriage. In the desolation of your infertility, you may want to dust off the marriage vows you said to one another and contemplate the meaning of "In sickness and in health; for richer or for poorer."[9]

seclusion: *to conceal entirely, to keep hidden*

disgrace: *reproach, taunt*

> **Luke 1:24–25** After this his wife Elizabeth became pregnant and for five months remained in **seclusion**. "The Lord has done this for me," she said. "In these days he has shown his favor and taken away my **disgrace** among the people."

☞ GO TO:

Genesis 30:1; 1 Samuel 1:6–10 (disgrace)

Good Things Just Keep Coming to Those Who Wait

Most of us would have immediately run to our neighbors with the good news that God had answered our prayers. We would have flaunted it in front of those who had been talking behind our backs and making little snide comments to our faces.

Elizabeth chose another way. She hid herself for five months. Perhaps it was to give thanks to the Lord for what he had done; perhaps she just wanted to make sure the pregnancy was going to work out before she made the big announcement.

Whatever the reason, she's a good example for all of us to follow.

FROM JUDY'S HEART

I can empathize with Elizabeth. Within the last three years I have developed migraine headaches. They were so bad at one point that I was having one almost every day. At first, well-meaning friends gave me all sorts of advice. "See your doctor." "Drink more coffee." "Drink less coffee." "Take vitamin E." "See a chiropractor." "Acupuncture helped my Uncle Joe."

I'm sure Elizabeth was receiving similar advice. "Sleep on your left side." "Search your life for sin." "Go to the synagogue more often." "Drink the milk of a spotted goat." When nothing seemed to work, she probably wanted to avoid her friends, because when nothing seems to help, everyone gets frustrated and they start to look at you like, what's really wrong with you?

The hardest people to face were the ones who prayed for me. Faithfully they prayed, week in and week out, for my headaches to go away. With each prayer came hope that this time it would work. But when a day or two would go by and I'd have another headache, I had to give them the bad news, "No, it didn't work." Their faces would fall, and I'd feel terrible.

Slowly I stopped telling anyone about my problem and hoped no one would ask. In the meantime, my headaches have gotten better, but are not gone entirely. If tomorrow my headaches would stop, I hope I would follow Elizabeth's example and keep it to myself for a while, to savor the answering of my prayer, but also to make sure it was real before I flaunted it all over the neighborhood.

As Mark Twain once said, "Familiarity breeds contempt—and children."

Esther 2:7 Mordecai had a cousin named Hadassah, whom he had brought up because she had neither father nor mother. This girl, who was also known as Esther, was lovely in form and features, and Mordecai had taken her as his own daughter when her father and mother died.

Taking Matters into Your Own Hands—Adoption

Although being barren was a mark of shame, one solution, adoption, was rarely used in the Old Testament. In fact, there is no Hebrew word that describes the process of adoption. The only people who practiced it were foreigners, or Jews heavily influenced by them.

What Others are Saying:

Beth Spring: Adoption is not a "Band-Aid," and it should not be pushed on a couple hastily. It is a major life decision that is quite different from becoming pregnant and having a child. Both partners need to be enthusiastic about adoption as a positive way to build their family. They should not consider it "second best."[10]

☞ **GO TO:**

Acts 4:28; Romans 8:29–30; 1 Corinthians 2:7; Ephesians 1:11 (predestined)

predestined: *determined in advance*

adopted: *to have taken a child of other parents as one's own*

Ephesians 1:4–5 For he chose us in him before the creation of the world to be holy and blameless in his sight. In love he **predestined** us to be **adopted** as his sons through Jesus Christ, in accordance with his pleasure and will.

Adoption of Another Kind

According to historians, the Romans of New Testament times had strict rules about adoption. Roman law required that the adopter be a male and childless. The one to be adopted had to be an independent adult, able to agree to be adopted. In the eyes of the law, the adopted one became a new creature; he was regarded as being born again into a new family.

This is what happens when we accept Jesus as our Lord and Savior. When we are old enough to know what we are doing, we let go of our past, and become new creations. We are born again into the family of God.

☞ **GO TO:**

Genesis 12:4; 16:16 (ten years)

Genesis 16:1–4 Now Sarai, Abram's wife, had borne him no children. But she had an Egyptian maidservant named Hagar; so she said to Abram, "The LORD has kept me from having children. Go, sleep with my maidservant; perhaps I can build a family through her." Abram agreed to what Sarai said. So after Abram had been living in Canaan ten years, Sarai his wife took her Egyptian maidservant Hagar and gave her to her husband to be his wife. He slept with Hagar, and she conceived.

This Substitute Wives Thing Is Just a Bad Idea!

Surrogate mothers are not something new. Sarai was so desperate for a child that she gave her maidservant to her husband to bear him a son. A few years later, Rachel and Leah did the same thing.

Was this a good solution? Not in the case of Sarai, for her maidservant grew to despise her. The four sons that Rachel and Leah's maidservants bore Jacob are named among the twelve tribes of Israel, but that household knew no peace either. Remember that these sons of maidservants were among the brothers who sold their brother Joseph into slavery.

Think About It

Some time has passed since God had made his promise that Sarai and Abram would have children. It is obvious that Sarai was blaming God for not fulfilling his promise. Examine your own life and ask if you're blaming God for something.

> **Genesis 30:14–15** During wheat harvest, Reuben went out into the fields and found some plants [see illustration, page 62], which he brought to his mother Leah. Rachel said to Leah, "Please give me some of your son's **mandrakes**." But she said to her, "Wasn't it enough that you took away my husband? Will you take my son's mandrakes too?"
>
> "Very well," Rachel said, "he can sleep with you tonight in return for your son's mandrakes."

☞ **GO TO:**

Song of Songs 7:13 (mandrakes)

mandrakes: *thought to be an aphrodisiac*

Love Potion #9

After giving her maidservant to her husband, Rachel tried an even more extreme measure—the mandrake. She was desperate to have a child and so she resorted to magic, but it didn't work. In the meantime, her sister, Leah, gave birth to two more sons while Rachel continued to wait.

What Is a Mandrake?

A fruit-producing plant with dark green leaves and small bluish-purple flowers, the mandrake is a relative of the potato family, which grew abundantly throughout Palestine and the Mediterranean region.

The yellow fruit of the mandrake was small, sweet-tasting, and

A Mandrake Plant

Mandrake plants are valued in the East because they are thought to stimulate fruitfulness in women.

fragrant. It had narcotic qualities and may have been used medicinally. The fruit of the mandrake was also referred to as the "love apple" and was considered a love potion.

Its forked roots resembled the lower part of a human body and was thought to induce pregnancy when eaten.

Think About It

We may scoff at Rachel because she didn't trust God, but when a woman is desperate to have a baby she will try anything. Today we may not use mandrakes, but we turn to other solutions—computer-generated charts, which show exact moment of ovulation; in vitro fertilization; fertility drugs; and adoption. Are these solutions any more wrong than Rachel's mandrakes?

> **Psalm 33:20–22**
> We wait in hope for the LORD;
> he is our help and our shield.
> In him our hearts rejoice,
> for we trust in his holy name.
> May your unfailing love rest upon us, O LORD,
> even as we put our hope in you.

The Ticking of Our Biological Clocks

The pressure to reproduce was not just a biblical thing. It's also a very modern urge.

Since the founding of this nation, women have been encouraged to have babies. In the seventeenth century, barren women were hunted as witches or heretics. In the eighteenth century, infertility could be used as grounds for divorce. In the nineteenth century, it was condemned as an un-American activity.[11]

In the twenty-first century, a childless woman may not be called a heretic, but she may still feel that stigma of not bearing children.

And, even though they may be putting it off until they are older, most women today still want children.

KEY POINT

Today one out of every ten women is infertile.[12]

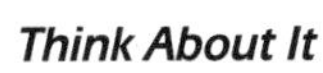

If you are one of these women, you may be feeling despair, frustration, and bitterness. You may even have dreams of kidnapping a child, or thoughts of suicide, or the feeling that you are on the verge of a nervous breakdown. None of these feelings are uncommon.

The desire to have children is deep within most of us, and it seems so unfair, feeling you have been somehow singled out. Don't be afraid to express your anger toward God. He will understand, and he will hear your cries.

For Single Moms—Many single women are so upset about being childless that they are tempted to take matters into their own hands. They think about adoption or having a child out of wedlock. As a single mom, you are in a special position to talk with such women about the struggles of single motherhood and thus to help them make informed decisions.

> **Psalm 25:16–18** Turn to me and be gracious to me, for I am lonely and afflicted. The troubles of my heart have multiplied; free me from my anguish. Look upon my affliction and my distress.

Baby, Baby, Baby

The solutions for infertility today are not that dissimilar from the ones found in the Bible. Modern science has added some new twists, the ethics of which we'll probably be debating forever, but such is the desire for children. It's planted deep within each one of us. Many of you can identify with Rachel's cry to her husband, *"Give me children or I will die."*

What Others are Saying:

Evelyn Christenson: My husband and I were attending Bible college. We were doing everything we were supposed to do, yet I was losing baby after baby after baby. I was heartbroken. But God led me to Romans 8:28, which has become my philosophy: "*We know that in all things God works for the good of those who love him.*" From God's perspective, the physical problems in my life were not meaningless. . . . Pain and suffering will come to all of us sooner or later. We are not exempt from them because we love God. But in our pain and suffering, God still uses us and draws us closer to him.[13]

What Others are Saying:

Ruth Bell Graham: The doctors told us that there would be little chance of our ever having children. Bill took it hardest—he felt that he had let me down. Bless him—as if he could help it. If possible I loved him all the more. And of course I pretended I didn't care. . . . Somehow it's easier to drink the bitter when it's God's hand that holds the cup. . . . Though He knows the uncontrollable longing, He knows too that I want nothing that He doesn't want for me.[14]

fool: *one who lacks wisdom*

Proverbs 12:15 The way of a **fool** seems right to him, but a wise man listens to advice.

Doctor, Can You Help Me?

Modern medicine now offers technology that can help couples become parents, but is that what God wants for you?

Be sure that you gather all the information you need before you leap into a decision that may thrust you into debt, result in a multiple birth, or bring a child into your home that you cannot handle. Talk to your pastor, your doctor, nurses, and other health care professionals. Spend time on your knees seeking God's will before you barrel ahead and make a mistake that you will have to live with the rest of your life.

In Vitro Fertilization

In 1999, five thousand women will have been impregnated with donor eggs. The cost for each try could be as much as fifteen thousand dollars, but only about 39 percent of those will result in a live birth.[15]

Only you and your husband can decide if a child is worth this expense. Health insurance often does not cover these services. Find out before you get into debt.

There are many discussions about the morality of some of the choices that are now available for producing a baby. No one can tell you what is right and wrong in your circumstances. You must seek the will of the Lord. When you think you know what it is, then test it by asking for confirmation from someone older and wiser than you. Do not let your emotions get in the way of making the right decision.

Think About It

Ten Ways to Make a Baby

1. The woman can have her egg fertilized by a donor's sperm.
2. The woman can use a donor's egg fertilized by her partner's sperm.
3. The woman can carry an embryo made of a donor's egg that has been fertilized by another donor's sperm.
4. The woman can receive donated embryos from a family that has successfully completed in vitro fertilization and has donated extra embryos.
5. If the woman's eggs and uterus aren't functioning, her partner's sperm can be injected into another woman to fertilize her eggs. The "surrogate" mother carries the baby.
6. The woman's eggs can be retrieved and inseminated with her partner's sperm, then transferred to the uterus of another woman who is a "gestational surrogate."
7. The couple can use donor eggs and donor sperm, creating an embryo that is placed in the uterus of a gestational surrogate. None of these three people is genetically related to the child, and the birth is essentially an adoption.
8. Eggs from two different donors can be fertilized and the embryos transferred to the woman. If twins are born, the children could have different genetic mothers.
9. In the near future, they may be able to use donor eggs that have been altered to include the woman's genetic material.
10. Of course, there's still old-fashioned conception, involving a man and a woman and privacy.[16]

Take a Pill and Call Me in the Morning

The use of fertility drugs could be an answer, but the multiple-birth rate among those who use them is higher than among the general population. The neonatal costs following multiple births are high, as are the health risks to the mother and the babies. For example, the Chukwu octuplets' births cost more than $2 million.

Desperately Seeking Baby

I think it's interesting that today the ideal adoption is thought of as something that you do when a child is an infant. Yet, in biblical times, adoptions were done at an age when the child knew what was happening and could agree to the arrangement.

The cost of adopting an infant can run as high as thirty thousand dollars. The wait can take as long as eight years. Consider this: there are one hundred couples waiting for each healthy, white infant that is available for adoption.[17] Private adoptions are becoming more and more popular. Check into all of the options available before you give up.

Society Magazine: Adoption, whatever the age or circumstances of the child, is not a simple solution to any problem. It always carries its own complications. . . . When adoptive families come to grief, it is often from a disparity in expectations; either the parents expected something the child cannot deliver or the child delivers something the parents did not expect.[18]

CHOOSING TO GO CHILDLESS

> **Deuteronomy 7:14–15** You will be blessed more than any other people; none of your men or women will be childless, nor any of your livestock without young.

The Fewer the Better?

Children have been an American tradition for over two hundred years. It used to be that the larger the family, the better. Now, with families becoming smaller and smaller, there is a newer trend.

According to the U.S. Census Bureau, 19 percent of all couples are choosing to remain childless. That's up from ten percent just a decade ago.[19] The reasons?

- They're too busy pursuing careers.
- They fear children will take away the time they now use for travel, hobbies, and volunteer work.
- They believe that children will interfere with the intimacy they now enjoy.
- Children would only make them feel old.
- They believe the world is overcrowded, or that there really is no future for another generation.
- And last on the list is the cost. According to a recent report in *U.S. News and World Report,* it now costs $210,000 for a middle-income family to raise a child.[20]

If you look closely at these reasons you will see they are all **temporal**. God says, "*Do not store up for yourselves treasures on earth, where moth and rust destroy, and where thieves break in and steal. But store up for yourselves treasures in heaven, where moth and rust do not destroy, and where thieves do not break in and steal*" (Matthew 6:19–21). Children are just such treasures.

temporal: *things of this world*

- Children can be fun and will teach you the word "joy."
- They will keep you young.
- Children help you mature as a human being and as a follower of Jesus Christ. They teach you selflessness, patience, kindness, and love.
- They are likely to be there for you in your old age.
- They may give you grandchildren.
- Their accomplishments will make you prouder than anything you will do yourself.

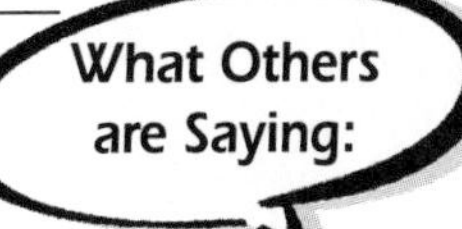

Mary Howitt: God sends children for another purpose than merely to keep up the race—to enlarge our hearts, to make us unselfish, and full of kindly sympathies and affections.[21]

CHILDREN WITHOUT FATHERS

Hosea 5:7 They are unfaithful to the LORD; they give birth to **illegitimate** children.

illegitimate: *born of parents who are not married*

☞ **GO TO:**

Deuteronomy 23:2 (bastards)

Hebrews 12:7 (discipline)

paternal: *from the father*

Fathers Need Not Apply?

In biblical times children born out of wedlock (bastards) were excluded from public worship, had no claim to their **paternal** inheritance, or the right to the same discipline as the legitimate children.

Today there is hardly any shame associated with having children out of wedlock. Many unwed mothers are opting to keep their children instead of giving them up for adoption. Celebrities, like Madonna, Jody Foster, and Farrah Fawcett, are choosing to have children without a husband. They flaunt their choice in front of the whole world, spreading the message to young, impressionable minds that this is an admirable and even good choice for women today.

But, according to the Bible, a child raised without the discipline of a father is something to be pitied.

Today there are 6.6 million children under the age of eighteen living with a never-married parent. Of these, 69 percent live in poverty, and that's just the beginning of their problems. They are more likely to have psychological problems, abuse drugs and alcohol, and fail in school. Seventy percent of kids in state reform institutions grew up without their fathers.

Fathers are not expendable. They are part of God's plan for the nurturing of healthy children. It's only in our sin-filled world that we consider it to be a good choice to raise a child without a father.

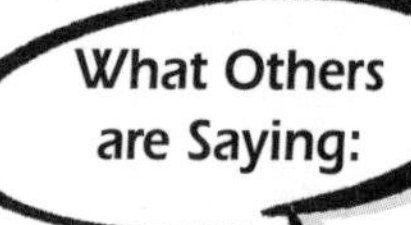

Wade Horn: Fathers parent differently than mothers do. For example, we know mothers tend to be more verbal with their children and fathers much more physical. Particularly with boys, fathers engage in rough-and-tumble play. What we're discovering is that this serves as practice for boys to develop control over their aggression. So, it's a combination of the father's tendency to challenge achievement combined with the mother's typical nurturing that creates happy kids. Now, fathers play an extra role when it comes to daughters. They give girls the experience of having a relation with a man who shows that the definition of love is "I care more about you than myself." That's important, because when girls start looking for mates, if they have the expectation that a man should be like Dad, they will be more likely to hold out for that positive model.[22]

Study Questions

1. What was the vow that Hannah made to God? Discuss whether or not you would have done the same thing in her place.
2. Why was Sarah's pregnancy such a miracle? Discuss why God made Sarah and Abraham wait so long.
3. Discuss Rachel and Leah's needs and how they went about getting them filled.
4. Why did Sarah give her maidservant to Abraham? What were the consequences?
5. Why was Elizabeth barren?
6. Discuss the pros and cons of in vitro fertilization, fertility drugs, and adoption.
7. What would a couple that chooses to go childless miss out on?
8. What role does a father play in the raising of children?

CHAPTER WRAP-UP

- Infertility is a problem that women have faced since the beginning of time. From these examples in biblical times, it seems clear that it is God who is in charge of opening and closing wombs, yet many women seek their answer somewhere else. They blame their husbands; they rush ahead and try to answer their own prayers; they reach for magic potions; and they grow jealous of other women.
- Today one out of ten women face infertility. Modern science has developed many answers—in vitro fertilization, fertility drugs, surrogate mothers—but they are not always the best answers. A wise woman seeks the face of God and the wisdom of others before she takes a course that may lead to disaster.
- Choosing to go childless is not in God's original plan. We miss out on his incredible blessing and the opportunity to develop into mature Christians.
- Trying to raise a child without a father is also not in God's plan. Children who are raised without fathers are more likely to abuse drugs and alcohol, get in trouble with the law, get pregnant out of wedlock, and live in poverty.

JUDY'S  BOOKSHELF

- *As Silver Refined,* Kay Arthur, WaterBrook Press. A look at disappointments in life and how we can cope.
- *Disappointment with God,* Philip Yancey, Zondervan. Yancey asks the hard questions about God and unanswered prayer.
- *In the Grip of Grace,* Max Lucado, Word Publishing. Lucado examines the meaning of grace in our day-to-day lives.

4 THE MIRACULOUS CONCEPTION OF JESUS

WHAT'S IN THIS CHAPTER

- Mary Was a Virgin
- The Prophecy of the Virgin Birth
- Jesus' Genealogy
- The Conception of Jesus
- Mary's Visit to Elizabeth
- Traveling to Bethlehem

Here We Go

Do you think God looked down on Earth one day and chose Mary, or had he been keeping an eye on her all her life?

Did he watch as she took her first steps, said her first words, and quarreled with her brothers and sisters? Was he there when she fell and scraped her knee, when her doll broke and she cried, and when she told a fib to her teacher?

We think Mary was special, and that's why God chose her to be the mother of Jesus. But from the scripture there is no evidence of that, and so I like to think she was just a normal teenage girl. Perhaps she had acne and argued with her mother about what she wore and daydreamed of how it would be to be grown up and married.

Mary was ordinary until the moment she was chosen by God to bear his son. She became extraordinary through her humility and her obedience.

A Sunday school class was studying the Ten Commandments. They were ready to discuss the last one. The teacher asked if anyone could tell her what it was. Susie raised her hand, stood tall, and quoted, "Thou shall not take the covers off thy neighbor's wife."

MARY WAS A VIRGIN

Deuteronomy 22:13–19 If a man takes a wife and, after lying with her, dislikes her and slanders her and gives her a bad name, saying, "I married this woman, but when I approached her, I did not find proof of her

☞ **GO TO:**

Deuteronomy 21:19 (elders)

Leviticus 21:13 (virgin)

slandered: *falsely accused*

cloth: *bedclothes*

elders: *city judges*

a hundred shekels: *twice the bride-price*

virgin: *a woman who had not had sexual relations with a man*

consummated: *completed by sexual intercourse*

hymen: *membrane partially closing the vagina*

virginity," then the girl's father and mother shall bring proof that she was a virgin to the town elders at the gate. The girl's father will say to the elders, "I gave my daughter in marriage to this man, but he dislikes her. Now he has **slandered** her and said, 'I did not find your daughter to be a virgin.' But here is the proof of my daughter's virginity." Then her parents shall display the **cloth** before the **elders** of the town, and the elders shall take the man and punish him. They shall fine him **a hundred shekels** of silver and give them to the girl's father, because this man has given an Israelite **virgin** a bad name. She shall continue to be his wife; he must not divorce her as long as he lives.

Loss of Face

Virginity was such an important matter in biblical times that part of the wedding ritual was to save the bedclothes from the night the marriage was **consummated** to prove that the bride was a virgin. If the female had never experienced intercourse before, her **hymen** would break and there would be spots of blood on the bedclothes. This then could be offered to the city judges as proof in case the husband decided he didn't like her after all and wanted to divorce her.

What Others are Saying:

Reader's Digest Illustrated Dictionary of Bible Life & Times: Women who were promised in marriage were expected to be virgins, and the parents of the bride were sometimes required to offer evidence of her virginity.[1]

☞ **GO TO:**

Deuteronomy 13:5; 17:7; 1 Corinthians 5:13 (purge)

promiscuous: *morally wicked*

purge: *eliminate*

Mary: *"bitterness"*

Deuteronomy 22:20–21 If, however, the charge is true and no proof of the girl's virginity can be found, she shall be brought to the door of her father's house and there the men of her town shall stone her to death. She has done a disgraceful thing in Israel by being **promiscuous** while still in her father's house. You must **purge** the evil from among you.

Loss of Life

Wow! This seems harsh to our twenty-first-century ears. But that is the rule that **Mary** grew up with. She knew that if she weren't a virgin on her wedding night and her husband brought this charge, she could be stoned to death.

Her parents shared the responsibility to make sure that she kept herself pure and chaste. It also was their responsibility to defend her honor when she was wrongly accused.

Ponder for a moment how different our society would be if these rules applied today. Would casual sex be so accepted? Would our TV shows and movies be so full of infidelity? What would happen to the divorce rate?

Think About It

> **Exodus 22:16–17** "If a man **seduces** a virgin who is not pledged to be married and sleeps with her, he must pay the bride-price, and she shall be his wife. If her father absolutely refuses to give her to him, he must still pay the **bride-price** for virgins."

seduces: *entices*

bride-price: *dowry*

☞ **GO TO:**

Genesis 24:53 (bride-price)

Loss of Value

The loss of a young woman's virginity also resulted in the loss of income for the family. Her value to a perspective husband was greatly reduced. Therefore, if she had sexual relations with a man who was not her husband, he was expected to pay the bride-price whether he married her or not.

> **Matthew 1:18–19** His mother Mary was pledged to be married to **Joseph**, but before they came together, she was found to be with child through the Holy Spirit. Because Joseph her husband was a righteous man and did not want to expose her to public disgrace, he had in mind to divorce her quietly.

☞ **GO TO:**

Luke 1:26–27 (pledged)

Joseph: *"the Lord added"*

Cause of Divorce

From this scripture we can see that Joseph could have made the charges that his fiancée was not a virgin and he could have exposed her to public ridicule, but not wishing to do this, he determined to divorce her quietly.

Knowing fully the consequences of being pregnant before marriage, I'm sure that Mary suffered many anguished days and sleepless nights. How could she explain this pregnancy to the man she was pledged to marry? How could he ever understand? There would be the public outcry, but also the humiliation of her family. The consequences of her unexplainable pregnancy were many and severe.

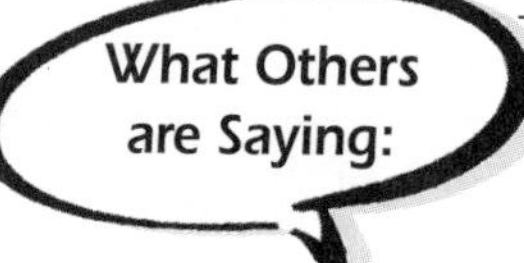

Janette Oke: As a good Jew, Joseph would have shown his religious zeal if he had denounced Mary. Scripture seems to indicate a short but difficult struggle between his legal conscience and his loving concern. God intervened and Joseph listened. That in itself shows Joseph's open-hearted relationship to the Father.[2]

NIV Study Bible: [Joseph] would sign the necessary legal papers, but not have her stoned.[3]

It's so easy to get on our "spiritual high horse" and judge others. Joseph is a good example of someone who waited and listened before he destroyed his relationship with Mary.

THE PROPHECY OF THE VIRGIN BIRTH

Immanuel: *"God with us"*

> **Matthew 1:23** "The virgin will be with child and will give birth to a son, and they will call him **Immanuel**"—which means, "God with us."

Not Your Traditional Birth Announcement

What would you think if you received a birth announcement for a child who wouldn't be born for thousands of years, or even for nine months? You would think the person who'd given it to you was nuts—unless, of course, he was an angel.

Why were Mary and Joseph so willing to listen to this prophecy and believe it? Probably from birth they had been told of the prophecy in Isaiah that a virgin would give birth to the Messiah. Every generation expected it to happen. Every young girl hoped it would happen to her. Mary and Joseph must've felt humbled at being the chosen ones (see GWBI, page 165).

What Others are Saying:

Kathy Collard Miller: [Mary's] surprise at her selection shows her humility.[4]

Mary was chosen for a special purpose because she had a close, personal relationship with the Lord. She spent time on her knees in prayer, not just asking for things, but seeking to know God. She wanted his will for her life.

Are you ready for God's call? Do you have the kind of relationship with him that will prepare you to obey even though what God asks seems impossible?

It's easy to get caught up in all the things we do for the Lord and forget that none of those things matter to him. What he wants most is a relationship with us.

JESUS' GENEALOGY

> **Isaiah 11:1** A shoot will come up from the **stump of Jesse**; from his roots a **Branch** will bear fruit.

GO TO:

Isaiah 11:10; 1 Samuel 16:1–17:20 (Jesse)

Jesse: *David's father*

stump of Jesse: *David's dynasty*

Branch: *Messiah*

Messiah: *the one anointed by God to deliver his people and establish his kingdom on earth*

David Was His Great-Great-Great-Great . . . Well, You Get the Idea

The eleventh chapter of Isaiah promises that through the line of David a **Messiah** would come. The Spirit of the Lord will rest on him and he will be wise and understanding, powerful, righteous, and will bring justice to the poor (see GWRV, page 77).

One of the criteria for choosing Mary was that she had to be a descendant of David. Note the differences and the similarities between the genealogies listed in Matthew 1:1–17 and Luke 3:23–38 (see illustration, page 76). Scholars believe that one of these (Matthew's) was Joseph's lineage and the other (Luke's) was Mary's. They both were descended from David through two different branches of the family.

KEY POINT

Jesus was the Messiah.

What Others are Saying:

Kathy McReynolds: It is clear . . . that Jesus was a descendant of David and rightful heir to his throne.[5]

Think About It

Was the New Testament written by a single person or a group who were trying to "fool us" into believing that Jesus was who he said he was? If so, they did a terrible job. These two lists alone would prove that these two separate authors wrote the account in Matthew and the account in Luke without consulting each other. That is strong proof that these writings are authentic.

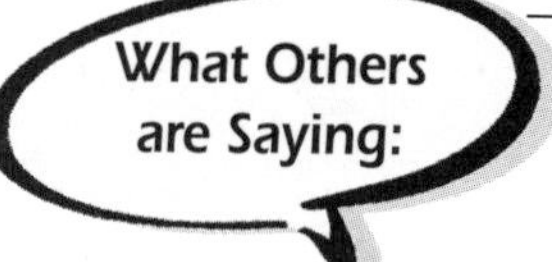

Nelson's Illustrated Bible Dictionary: Attempts have been made to explain how such different results can be arrived at by persons using the same sources of information, but no firm conclusions have emerged. Some writers suggest that both lists came from Joseph, but were compiled separately by different methods. Others believe that Matthew's list furnished a legal or "official" descent through the house of Joseph, while Luke's record actually reflected Mary's side of the family, since she herself probably was descended from David [Luke 1:27; 2:4]. The absence of Mary's name from Luke's list argues against that theory, which would actually suit Matthew's genealogy better, since Mary is mentioned in it along with four other women.[6]

Jesus' Genealogy

This chart shows how Jesus was descended from David through both Joseph, his father, and Mary, his mother.

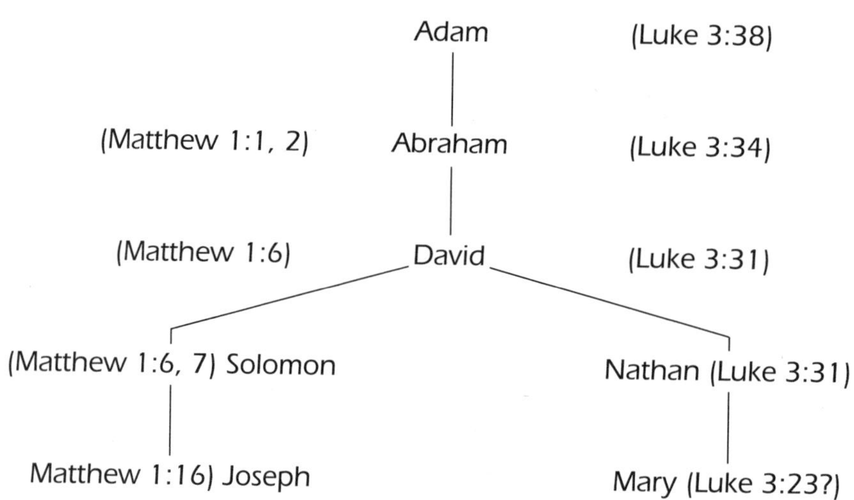

SOURCE: *Nelson's Complete Book of Bible Maps and Charts*, copyright 1993 Thomas Nelson.

THE CONCEPTION OF JESUS

Matthew 1:18–25 This is how the birth of Jesus Christ came about: His mother Mary was **pledged** to be married to Joseph, but before they came together, she was found to be with child through the **Holy Spirit**. Because Joseph her husband was a **righteous** man and did not want to expose her to public disgrace, he had in mind to divorce her quietly. But after he had considered this, an angel of the Lord appeared to him in a dream and said, "Joseph son of David, do not be afraid to take Mary home as your wife, because what is conceived in her is from the Holy Spirit. She will give birth to a son, and you are to give him the name Jesus, because he will save his people from their sins."

All this took place to fulfill what the Lord had said through the prophet: "The virgin will be with child and will give birth to a son, and they will call him Immanuel"—which means, "God with us."

When Joseph woke up, he did what the angel of the Lord had commanded him and took Mary home as his wife. But he had no union with her until she gave birth to a son. And he gave him the name Jesus.

pledged: *engaged*

Holy Spirit: *third person of the trinity; energy of God*

righteous: *zealous in keeping the law*

What a Guy!

You can tell that Joseph was more than just a nice guy. He had every reason to be upset. Most of us at this time in our courtship have put our betrothed on a pedestal, and we can only see the good things about them. Even the bad things we turn into positives. But this particular bad thing could not be turned into a positive. Joseph had been betrayed by his beloved Mary. She was not who he thought she was. In fact, she was even worse, a whore. And possibly a liar, too. Who could believe the outlandish story she was telling? Surely it was to cover up her sin.

Then the Lord appears to him in a dream and confirms everything that Mary has told him. Dear sweet Joseph; he not only goes ahead with the marriage, but puts aside his "rights" until the baby is born.

☞ **GO TO:**

Daniel 8:16 (Gabriel)

Gabriel: *"strength of God"*

What Others are Saying:

Janette Oke: God had told Joseph, through the angel **Gabriel**, that this child was special indeed. A lesser man might have sought some recognition for his role, but we have no reason to think that Joseph did.[7]

The Holy Spirit has many functions. He is the power by which Christians are brought to faith and helped to understand their walk with God. He brings a person to new birth: *"Flesh gives birth to flesh, but the Spirit gives birth to spirit"* (John 3:6); *"The Spirit gives life; the flesh counts for nothing"* (John 6:63). The Holy Spirit is called the Helper, whom Jesus promised to the disciples after his ascension. The triune family of Father, Son, and Holy Spirit are unified in ministering to believers (John 14:16, 26). It is through the Helper that Father and Son abide with the disciples (John 15:26).

Grow Your Marriage

Do you suppose Joseph and Mary's relationship was strained during these early months? They were living together as husband and wife and yet were not able to truly be together. Did Joseph resent this? Or do you think they were able to talk about it?

Are there some areas in your marriage that are causing turmoil, but you are unwilling to bring the subject up? Good communication begins with courage to share even in the face of rejection.

Luke 1:26–28 God sent the angel Gabriel to Nazareth, a town in Galilee, to a virgin pledged to be married to a man named Joseph, a descendant of David. The virgin's name was Mary. The angel went to her and said, "**Greetings**, you who are highly favored! The Lord is with you."

greetings: ave *in the Latin; thus,* Ave Maria

An Unexpected Messenger

Our museums and old Bibles are full of pictures of angels. They are usually of white human beings dressed in long flowing white robes with halos or a glow around their heads, and with two huge wings on their backs. But there is no biblical basis for this picture.

What Mary saw that night was probably a being in human form (see illustration, page 79). There most likely were no wings and no halo, but there may have been something about him that caused her to be fearful.

☞ GO TO:

Genesis 18:2; Daniel 10:18; Zechariah 2:1 (human form)

Judges 13:6; Matthew 28:3–4; Luke 24:4 (fearful)

Angels were known only to visit godly people—Abraham, Moses, David, Daniel, Jesus, Peter, and Paul. The angels' role was to take care of them in times of trouble. They guided and instructed these people, and sometimes also provided their needs for food and water.

Gabriel's job was to communicate special messages to God's servants.

What Others are Saying:

Nelson's Illustrated Bible Dictionary: [An angel is a] member of an order of heavenly beings who are superior to man in power and intelligence. By nature angels are spiritual beings [Hebrews 1:14]. Their nature is superior to human nature [Hebrews 2:7], and they have superhuman power and knowledge [2 Samuel 14:17, 20; 2 Peter 2:11]. They are not, however, all-powerful and all-knowing [Psalm 103:20; 2 Thessalonians 1:7].[8]

Think About It

Angels are a popular subject for books, movies, and television series. Are they more acceptable to an unbelieving world than Jesus is? If so, why do you think this is? What is the message that most of these shows carry? Do they ever mention Jesus?

The Annunciation

Pictured here is an artist's rendition of Gabriel's birth announcement to Mary (also known as the Annunciation).

Luke 1:29–38 Mary was greatly troubled at his words and wondered what kind of greeting this might be. But the angel said to her, "Do not be afraid, Mary, you have found favor with God. You will be with child and give birth to a son, and you are to give him the name Jesus. He will be great and will be called the Son of the Most High. The Lord God will give him the throne of his father David, and he will reign over the house of Jacob forever; his kingdom will never end."

"How will this be," Mary asked the angel, "since I am a virgin?"

The angel answered, "The Holy Spirit will come upon you, and the power of the Most High will **overshadow** you. So the holy one to be born will be called the Son of God. Even Elizabeth your **relative** is going to have a child in her old age, and she who was said to be barren is in her sixth month. For nothing is impossible with God."

"I am the Lord's **servant**," Mary answered. "May it be to me as you have said." Then the angel left her.

☞ **GO TO:**

Matthew 17:5; Mark 9:7; Luke 9:34; Acts 5:15 (overshadow)

Matthew 17:20 (nothing is impossible)

overshadow: *to envelop in a haze of brilliancy*

relative: *cousin, aunt, or other relative*

servant: *voluntary handmaiden*

I'm Sorry, Could You Run That by Me One More Time?

Like any red-blooded Hebrew woman would have been, Mary was afraid. After all, someone whom she didn't know was speaking to her. We don't know if she was in her bedroom or out in the fields, but we can assume that she was alone. Then he tells her this unbelievable thing, that she is to be the chosen one to carry the Messiah. Most of us would have laughed or asked to see this guy's credentials, or called the police. Mary doesn't do any of those things, because deep down inside she knew it was the truth. She only asks, "How can this be since I am a virgin?"

Read again the angel's explanation. Wouldn't you want to know more about how this was going to work? Not Mary; she just humbly bows her head and says, "I am willing, whatever God asks of me."

Think About It

Do you have the kind of relationship with God that if he were to send his messenger Gabriel to you that you would be prepared to do what he asked? Ask yourself what you can do today to become closer to God.

What Others are Saying:

Helen Good Brenneman: "I feel as though the baby I'm carrying will be a great person," an expectant mother confided to a friend. The feeling she has reminds us of the way all Hebrew mothers felt before the birth of Christ. For, according to the ancient writing of the prophets, some young woman would be honored by bringing into the world the promised Messiah. To whom would God bestow this great honor? No one knew, of course, and so all hoped. And one day, to one least expecting it, the good news came.[9]

MARY'S VISIT TO ELIZABETH

> **Luke 1:39–45** At that time Mary got ready and hurried to a town in the hill country of Judea [see illustration, page 82], where she entered Zechariah's home and greeted **Elizabeth**. When Elizabeth heard Mary's greeting, the baby leaped in her womb, and Elizabeth was filled with the Holy Spirit. In a loud voice she exclaimed: "**Blessed** are you among women, and blessed is the child you will bear! But why am I so favored, that the mother of my Lord should come to me? As soon as the sound of your greeting reached my ears, the baby in my womb leaped for joy. Blessed is she who has believed that what the Lord has said to her will be accomplished!"

Elizabeth: *a cousin or aunt of Mary's*

blessed: *honored*

Now That's a Bouncing Baby Boy

Whenever I have something important to tell, I can hardly keep it in me. I want to tell everyone, but Mary probably could not tell just anyone. She had to share it with a special someone who would truly understand. That someone was Elizabeth. (Saint Luke says the two women were of the same family. Although they are commonly described as cousins, the exact relationship is unclear.) Elizabeth knew the minute she saw her kinswoman that Mary was the special one, chosen by God, to carry the Messiah.

What happiness and rejoicing must've taken place during their visit? They probably stayed up late into the night laughing and whispering about the future of their two sons. Such high hopes they had, such dreams they planted during those glorious days!

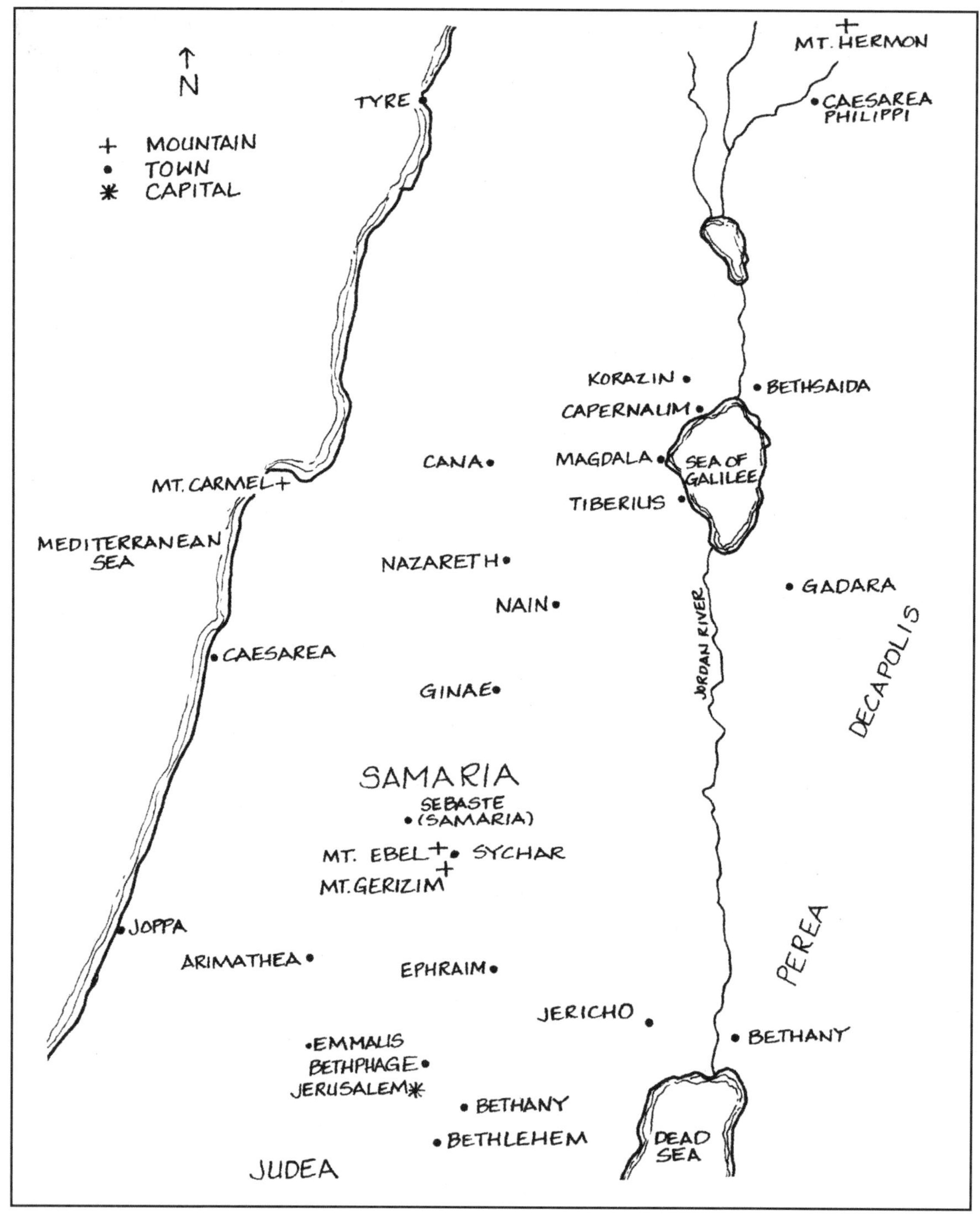

Where Jesus Lived and Traveled

Pictured here is a map of what is now Palestine. In Jesus' time, it was under Roman rule.

What Others are Saying:

Dr. William Sears and Martha Sears, R.N.: Research on fetal awareness has shown that the emotional state of the mother during the last three months of pregnancy can affect the emotional development of the baby. How a baby in the womb also senses joyful emotions is beautifully illustrated in Luke 1:44. When Mary greeted Elizabeth, the baby leaped for joy in Elizabeth's womb. Likewise, when a pregnant mother becomes anxious or stressed, levels of stress hormones cross the placenta into the baby's circulatory system and can cause the baby to be agitated as well. In other words, when mother is upset, baby is upset. Constant exposure of the baby's developing brain to stress hormones can result in an overstressed nervous system, accounting for the common statement made by parents of a hypersensitive baby, "He came wired that way."[10]

> **Psalm 139:15–16** My frame was not hidden from you when I was made in the **secret place**. When I was woven together in the depths of the earth, your eyes saw my unformed body. All the days ordained for me were written in **your book** before one of them came to be.

☞ **GO TO:**

2 Samuel 12:12 (secret place)

Psalm 56:8 (your book)

secret place: *the womb*

your book: *heavenly royal register of God's decisions*

The First Twelve Weeks of Life

What a miracle every new life is! Mary was just a few weeks along in her pregnancy and yet God knew every detail of the one whom he planted in her womb. Isn't it something that he knows us just as intimately?

What Others are Saying:

Beverly LaHaye: In the Hebrew, the words [*woven together*] mean intricately embroidered. In other words, a detail pattern of design and purpose—a human life, designed in the image of God—a personal identity—has begun! In just twelve weeks after fertilization, all the members and organs that the child will ever have are fully developed in miniature and functioning. What a miracle of life that has to be!

- At Fertilization Sex is determined
- Week 2 Occasional heart contractions
- Week 3 Foundations of brain and spinal cord established
- Week 4 Mouth is open; lung buds appear; liver is recognizable; body is ¾" long
- Week 5 Rhythmic heart contractions; stomach, esophagus, intestines are defined; arms and legs appear; face looks human

- Week 6 Skeletal system is complete; major organ systems have formed
- Week 7 Traceable brain waves; responds to touch; fingers exist; cartilage is changing into bone
- Week 12 Brain structure complete; spontaneous movements (kicking, frowning, sucking); fully developed, functioning human body (3 inches, ½ ounce); fingerprints and individualized palm and sole lines are complete[11]

Think About It

Mary was in a tough spot. She was pregnant and unmarried in a society that condemned to death such a deed. Who could possibly believe her? Wouldn't it have been tragic if Mary had chosen an abortion?

Remember that your husband is expecting along with you. Let him share your pregnancy as much as possible or as much as he desires. Invite him to go to your doctor appointments, read books together, take parenting classes, and let him help you make the decisions you now face. Don't dismiss his suggestions out of hand. Listen carefully and whenever possible follow his suggestions. Men love it when they are asked for advice.

Do you know what would have happened if it had been three wise women instead of three Wise Men who visited Mary?

They would have asked directions, arrived on time, helped deliver the baby, cleaned the stable, made a casserole, and brought practical gifts!

FROM JUDY'S HEART

When I first became pregnant, I was about as far away from God as a person can be and still claim to be a Christian. Even though I attended Sunday school and church while growing up and was baptized at eleven, I had rejected my beliefs in favor of a worldly, more scientific point of view. I even married a non-Christian without giving it a thought.

Something changed with this pregnancy. Not just in me, but in my husband. In the eighth month, my husband woke up one Sunday morning and said, "Let's go to church."

I couldn't think of a good reason not to and so we went. I reluctantly, my husband expectantly. I kept my guard up and fought the way the hymns were piercing my heart. I wanted no part of this. It was for another generation. I had other plans. The church put women into subservient roles, and I wanted liberation and equality.

We went back the following week and this time the music made me cry. The strains cutting even deeper into my heart, but I dismissed it as sentimental. Who wanted to be part of a religion that allowed bad things to happen and was so exclusive? What about the aborigines who had never heard the Gospel?

Then the unexpected happened. My husband accepted the Lord.

It must've been the shock, for in the moments and days afterward, I stopped fighting and the truth flooded into my heart.

Jesus was who he said he was and he had come to set me free and to forgive me of my sins, of which there were many. It was like going home, and the joy and peace I discovered changed my life forever.

The birth of my baby was joined by the new birth of my husband, and my rebirth. Each a miracle unto itself.

TRAVELING TO BETHLEHEM

> **Luke 2:4–5** So Joseph also went up from the town of Nazareth in Galilee to Judea, to Bethlehem the town of David, because he belonged to the house and line of David. He went there to register with Mary, who was pledged to be married to him and was expecting a child.

Another Bouncing Baby Boy!

Mary was eight or nine months pregnant when she rode a donkey to Bethlehem. Bethlehem was about a three-day trip (see illustration, page 42). Since both Mary and Joseph were from the house of David, they had to return to Bethlehem, the home of David, to register.

Philip Yancey: Jesus' hometown of Nazareth, so obscure that it did not make the list of sixty-three Galilean towns mentioned in the **Talmud**, sits on a hillside 1,300 feet above sea level. The view from a ridge allows a sweeping panorama all the way from Mt. Carmel by the ocean to the snowy peak of Mt. Hermon to the North [see illustration, page 236].[12]

Talmud: *a collection of Jewish law and tradition*

Study Questions

1. Why was it so important that Mary be a virgin?
2. What were the consequences that Mary faced if it were discovered she wasn't a virgin?
3. What was Joseph's original plan after he found out Mary was pregnant? Why did he change his mind?
4. Why is there a difference between the genealogies listed in Luke and Matthew?
5. Why do you think Mary was so willing to believe the angel Gabriel?
6. Describe the two trips that Mary made while she was pregnant. Why do you think she accompanied Joseph?

CHAPTER WRAP-UP

- In biblical times it was important to maintain your virginity, because if your husband discovered on your wedding day that you weren't a virgin he could divorce you and even have you stoned at the city gates. At the very least it would reduce your bride-price. (Most families planned on this income and without it they would suffer.)
- Every Hebrew knew the prophecy concerning the coming Messiah. He would be a direct descendant of David, and he would be born of a virgin. Every young maiden longed to be the chosen one and carry the promised Messiah.
- Jesus was a descendant of David through Mary and Joseph. The different genealogies listed in Matthew and Luke are probably because Mary and Joseph were from two different branches of the family.
- Jesus' conception was miraculous. The Holy Spirit overshadowed Mary and Jesus was conceived. She maintained her virginity until after Jesus was born.
- Mary must've had a very close relationship with God, for when the angel Gabriel appeared to her, although she was at first afraid, she willingly believed and obeyed.
- Mary traveled a great deal after she became pregnant. Her first visit was to her relative Elizabeth, who knew immediately that Mary carried the promised Messiah. Her second trip was a three-day donkey ride to Bethlehem to register along with her husband Joseph.

JUDY'S  BOOKSHELF

- *Just Like Jesus,* Max Lucado, Word Publishing. An inspirational book that will brighten your day.
- *The Jesus I Never Knew,* Philip Yancey, Zondervan. This book made me look at Jesus in a whole new light. I came away with a richer knowledge of his life and times.
- *Reflections on the Christmas Story,* Janette Oke, Bethany House. A small book that will make you think about the birth of Christ.
- *The Glorious Impossible,* Madeleine L'Engle, Simon and Schuster. A picture book for adults that recounts the glorious events surrounding the birth of Jesus.

Part Two

GIVING BIRTH

REVEREND FUN

"Hey, I think you may have put the child safety seat on a little too tightly."

5 A GLORIOUS EVENT

WHAT'S IN THIS CHAPTER

- An Exciting Time
- A Frightening Time
- Boy or Girl, Which Is Better?
- The Birth of Our Savior

Here We Go

A tiny egg unites with an even tinier sperm and life begins. Nine or so months later, a baby is born.

Each one is a miracle straight from God to this world. Each one planned before its conception to be special, to be different from everyone else.

No one of us is alike. Some of us are tall, others short. Some black, others brown. Some laugh easily, others are more serious. Some will commit horrendous crimes; others will be considered saints. Some will become kings, others servants.

The miracle is that God loves each of us from the moment we are conceived.

AN EXCITING TIME

> **Jeremiah 1:5** "Before I formed you in the womb I **knew** you, before you were born I set you apart."

☞ **GO TO:**

Genesis 18:19; Galatians 1:5 (knew)

knew: *chose*

Great Expectations

At the end of every pregnancy there comes this time of great expectation. Every day may be the day. Every hour may be the hour. Every contraction might be the beginning of the birth. The baby has been formed by God. God knew that she would have brown eyes, or that he would be skinny. Soon you will meet what God has perfectly designed. There is nothing to compare to this moment.

What Others are Saying:

Dr. William Sears and Norma Sears, R.N.: Pregnancy is an awesome time of waiting and preparing physically, emotionally, and spiritually. The most profound change ever to happen in the life of a couple is about to occur. Having a baby will change your lives in ways you would never dream possible. If this is not your first baby, you already know this. Cooperating with God in forming and shaping your child will surely drive you to your knees both in praise and **supplication**.[1]

supplication: *humble prayer*

REMEMBER THIS

You may be asking about handicapped children. What about them? Did God know that they would suffer? Why did he allow this to happen? These are tough questions and ones not easily answered here, but one thing we do know—God cares more about what's going on in the human heart than he does about outer appearance.

What Others are Saying:

Joni Earickson Tada: God deliberately chooses weak, suffering, and unlikely candidates to get His work done so that when the job is accomplished the glory goes to him and not us. . . . He screens the suffering, filtering it through fingers of love, giving us only that which works for good and which He knows will point us to him. As we grow in our faith, our way of looking at things changes. Once it seems as if the only way God could glorify Himself would be to remove our sufferings. Now it becomes clear that He can glorify Himself through our sufferings.[2]

☞ **GO TO:**

2 Peter 3:4; Galatians 6:15; Mark 10:6; Revelation 3:14 (creation)

Romans 8:19, 22 The **creation** waits in eager expectation for the Son of God to be revealed. We know that the whole creation has been groaning as in the pains of childbirth right up to the present time.

creation: *all that God has created from the beginning until today*

Think on These Things

Just as we anticipate the Second Coming of the Lord (see GWDN, page 35), we wait impatiently for the birth of each of our children. It's an anxious time, a time of preparation, a time of wonder.

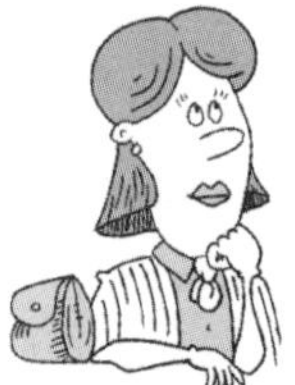
Think About It

Are you as prepared for the coming of Christ as you were for your baby? Do you anticipate his return at all? Or do you hardly think of it? How would you live your life differently if you knew that Christ was coming nine months from now?

What Others are Saying:

Janette Oke: The climax of the Christmas story might at first be thought to be the birth of the baby or the escape from Herod. But the ultimate climax is yet to come. . . . May it be an event of tremendous celebration and great rejoicing—not just for Him, but for me and for you as well.[3]

For Single Moms—As you near your due date, you may be filled with all sorts of fears. Let others help. Find a church with a support group for women without partners or a ministry for crisis pregnancies. The counseling and fellowship you receive there will help you get through this time of mixed emotions.

Psalm 139:15–16 My **frame** was not hidden from you when I was made in the secret place. When I was woven together in the depths of the earth, your eyes saw my unformed body. All the days **ordained** for me were written in your book before one of them came to be.

A Peek into the Womb

Modern technology now gives us the opportunity to peek into the womb and see what formerly was hidden. Is it a boy? Is it a girl? Is it healthy? Many of the unknowns that awaited mothers just a few years ago are no longer such a surprise.

On one hand this is good because surgeries are being performed on fetuses in the womb to correct problems before their birth. But, on the other hand, science has taken away much of the joy of learning the sex of your child at that wonderful moment of birth.

Have you thought about praying for your doctor or midwife? What about the nurses and other hospital staff? This would be a great time to cover every aspect of what you are about to experience with prayer.

A Letter to God

God,

When you found Mary for the virgin birth and you decided she would have Jesus in the manger, what I want to hear is whether there were any other finalists?

Hello God,

Brittany (age 8)[4]

KEY POINT

One thing that science will never be able to do is to predetermine how long our lives will be. This is still known only by God.

frame: *body*

ordained: *set ahead of time*

☞ GO TO:

Genesis 5:1; Exodus 32:32; Deuteronomy 17:18; Isaiah 29:11 (book)

Think About It

☞ **GO TO:**

Daniel 7:14; Matthew 4:17; 6:10; 7:21 (kingdom of heaven)

Isaiah 40:3 (voice)

repent: *make a radical change*

kingdom of heaven: *rule of God*

Matthew 3:1–3 In those days John the Baptist came, preaching in the Desert of Judea and saying, "**Repent**, for the **kingdom of heaven** is near." This is he who was spoken of through the prophet Isaiah: "A voice of one calling in the desert, 'Prepare the way for the Lord, make straight paths for him.'"

I Want to Be Ready!

Just as we should get ready for the coming of the Lord, we need to prepare for the arrival of our babies.

There are a million decisions to be made—cloth or disposable, breast-feeding or bottle, location of the crib, blue or pink, Winnie the Pooh or Sesame Street? There are things to buy—stroller, car seat, a layette, dresser, changing table, rocking chair, tiny little outfits that look like they were made for a doll.

What Others are Saying:

Ruth Bell Graham: Most everything is ready. So far I've made one white wool cap and sweater and booties set trimmed with Angora, three slips, one dress, three sheets, one pillowcase, five mattress covers and covered two pillows. My gowns and bed jackets are washed and pressed and hanging in the closet. . . . I love having a baby. Sure makes life richer. I feel so much more normal, too, and better balanced. Strange how a girl can look so absurd, feel so uncomfortable, and be so happy.[5]

KEY POINT

Preparation will ease many of your fears and make the whole experience more joyful.

A FRIGHTENING TIME

☞ **GO TO:**

1 Samuel 14:45; 2 Samuel 14:11; 1 Kings 1:52; Luke 21:18; Acts 27:34 (hairs)

Matthew 10:29–31 Are not two sparrows sold for a penny? Yet not one of them will fall to the ground apart from the will of your Father. And even the very hairs of your head are all numbered. So don't be afraid; you are worth more than many sparrows.

His Eye Is on the Sparrow, and I Know He Watches Me

Jesus is saying that we have no reason to worry. God is in control. He even knows when a sparrow falls, and we are so important to him that he knows the number of hairs on our head.

Think About It

Are you concerned about labor pain, and if you will be able to handle it? Does the possibility of a cesarean section frighten you? Are you worried that your insurance company is forcing you to go home from the hospital before you will be ready?

Take comfort from these words from the gospel of Matthew. Take your concerns to God in prayer and then talk to your doctor about every concern, even the silly ones.

What Others are Saying:

Chuck Swindoll: One of the most paralyzing problems in all of life is fear. . . . Sometimes it's worse than we anticipated! I've known times when I felt virtually paralyzed with feelings of panic. As fear gets a firm grip on us, we become its victim.[6]

Think About It

Read Psalm 27 and meditate on it as you prepare to give birth. Let God fill you with his peace as you rest in his **salvation**. Imagine him with warm loving arms just waiting to hold and comfort you.

What Others are Saying:

Gigi Graham Tchividjian: Lord, I am afraid. Anytime now this child that I am carrying will be born, and for some reason I am anxious. I fear delivery. . . the pain, the unknown. I question and I worry. Will this child be all right? If not, will I be able to accept and cope? Please, Lord, help me![7]

salvation: *deliverance from consequences of sin, death*

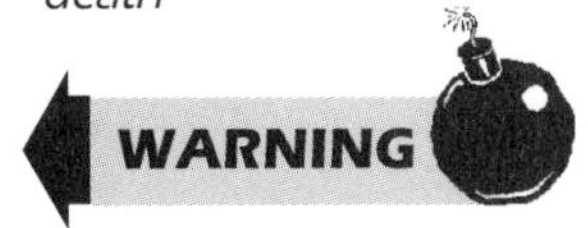

Don't let fear take away from the joy of giving birth.

> **Genesis 4:1–2** Adam lay with his wife Eve, and she became pregnant and gave birth to Cain. She said, "With the help of the LORD I have brought forth a man." Later she gave birth to his brother Abel.

An Understatement

The first birth was recorded with the simple words, "*she . . . gave birth.*" What an understatement. Those of us who have experienced birth know the truth. It is not simple, and for Eve it must've been terribly frightening. She must have witnessed multiple births amongst the animals and thus was prepared somewhat. But can anything really prepare us?

Three Stages of Labor

1. Labor

   Early—mild contractions about ten minutes apart. Try to relax.

   Active—harder contractions, three to five minutes apart. It is time to call the doctor.

   Transition—heavy contractions, close together. Shortest phase of labor. Baby is about to be born. Most help will be needed from husband. Try not to panic.

2. Pushing and Delivery

   This stage is hard work, but well worth the effort.

3. Delivery of Placenta

   A few contractions will deliver the placenta, but you will hardly notice as you hold your baby to your breast.

What Others are Saying:

Dr. William Sears and Martha Sears, R.N.: Childbirth is an intense experience, and substituting the word contraction for the word pain does not hide the fact that it can hurt. But it should be a good pain, one closely connected to pleasure. . . . Acknowledge the sensations of labor for what they are—the way being paved for your baby to emerge.[8]

For Single Moms—Find a "coach" who can walk through your delivery with you. This can be your mother, a favorite aunt, or a friend. They should take your birthing classes and help you prepare for the time that is nearing.

Jeremiah 4:31 I hear a cry as of a woman in labor, a groan as of one bearing her first child—the cry of the Daughter of Zion gasping for breath, stretching out her hands and saying, "Alas! I am fainting; my life is given over to murderers."

☞ **GO TO:**

Psalm 48:6; Isaiah 13:8; 21:3; Jeremiah 6:24; 30:6; 31:8 (labor)

Genesis 3:16; 1 Chronicles 4:9 (bearing)

Relax and Enjoy?

The pain that accompanies childbirth can be managed; it doesn't have to be endured. Hospitals and birthing centers teach relaxation techniques that will assist you through this phase of childbirth.

The most important thing to remember is to try to remain calm. When you resist and tense your muscles, they contract, and that only increases the pain.

Isn't it interesting that we call the pain of childbirth labor? Part of the curse placed on men at the Fall was that they would experience *"painful toil"* and we call that labor, too. Do you think it's a fair tradeoff?

Hints to Ease the Tension

- Change positions frequently, especially during early labor
- Recite Scriptures
- Pray
- Remember to drink plenty of fluids and relieve your bladder often
- Take a bath or a shower
- Lean on your husband or labor coach for help

> **1 John 4:18** There is no fear in love. But perfect love drives out fear, because fear has to do with punishment. The one who fears is not made perfect in love.

GO TO:

Romans 8:15 (fear)

How Long Is Long Enough?

Forty-five years ago, women who gave birth were in the hospital for a week. Twenty-five years ago, it was three days. Now the average hospital stay is down to one day. This can raise concern because there are so many unknowns especially if this is your first child.

Dr. William Sears and Martha Sears, R.N.: The controversy in the health insurance industry over how soon a new mother and baby should leave the hospital brings up an important issue. Mothers and babies have tended to do better once they get home to the familiar nest. That's not because they don't need the care, but because home is a friendlier place, the appropriate place for both newborn and mother. What needs to happen is for health care to provide continuing care at home so that breast-feeding can be monitored and the new mother taught basic newborn care. It is not right that new mothers are sent home to care for new-

KEY POINT

The more you know, the better prepared you will be for the unexpected.

borns before they are ready, just to save on the cost of additional days in the hospital. Home care, in the form of a *doula* (from the Greek word meaning "servant"), can provide all the lactation help and infant monitoring that mother and baby need at a fraction of the cost of extending the hospital stay. Ask your insurance company about how they will work with you to be sure you can get the care you need. Ask them to consider covering the cost of a *doula* in order for you to be able to have a shorter hospital stay.[9]

What about a Cesarean Section?

Natural childbirth is touted as the only way to go by friends, relatives, and health care professionals, but a quarter of all children born in the last decade were delivered by cesarean section. Critics say that almost half of those were unnecessary. But the rise in the numbers of C-sections can be directly related to a lowering of infant mortality rates from forty-seven deaths per one thousand births in 1940 to fewer than nine per one thousand today.

You are not a failure if you have a C-section. It may save your life or that of your baby.

If you've already had one cesarean section, it doesn't mean you have to have another. Again, talk to your doctor about your options.

What Others are Saying:

F. Sessions Cole, M.D.: C-sections are based on a baby's or mother's medical condition, not on the comfort of the mother.[10]

Bible Verses to Calm the Nerves

Psalm 4:8 .... peace and safety
Psalm 37:1–11 .... trust in the Lord
Psalm 127 .... the Lord watches
Proverbs 3:5–6 .... trust with all your heart
Isaiah 41:10 .... do not fear
John 14:27 .... do not be troubled
1 Peter 5:7 .... he cares for you
Psalm 22:9–11 .... you brought me out of the womb
Psalm 71:1–6 .... a refuge
Psalm 139 .... the Lord knows you
Proverbs 17:22 .... a cheerful heart
Matthew 11:28–30 .... rest for the weary
Philippians 4:4–9 .... rejoice in the Lord
1 John 4:13–18 .... God is love

Anxiety about the coming baby can increase tensions in your marriage. If you find that you're not communicating well, this might be a good time to seek out a Christian counselor. Perhaps your church has a support group for expectant parents. This is a good way to learn that what you are experiencing is normal.

Grow Your Marriage

Genesis 35:16–18 Then they moved on from Bethel. While they were still some distance from **Ephrath**, Rachel began to give birth and had great difficulty. And as she was having great difficulty in childbirth, the **midwife** said to her, "Don't be afraid, for you have another son." As she breathed her last—for she was dying—she named her son **Ben-Oni**. But his father named him **Benjamin**.

GO TO:

Ruth 1:2; Micah 5:2 (Ephrath)

Genesis 38:28 (midwife)

Ephrath: *older name for Bethlehem*

midwife: *woman who assists in childbirth*

Ben-Oni: *"son of my trouble"*

Benjamin: *"son of my right hand"*

Some Comforting Thoughts

Of the four million women who give birth each year, only about 250 die. Yet I know there are some of you who are afraid.

Try to find the source of your fear and ask God to take it away from you. Talk to your husband, your doctor, or even a Christian counselor. Memorize Scripture and think about the positive aspects of childbirth.

It is meant to be a joyful time. Don't let Satan rob you of it.

Think About It

Rachel cried out to her husband to give her sons or let her die. Isn't it ironic that she died in childbirth? Sometimes we get exactly what we pray for. Next time you pray, remember that.

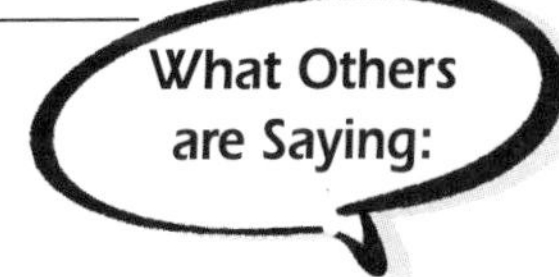

Reader's Digest Illustrated Dictionary of Bible Life & Times: The bible regards childbirth as an agonizing experience. . . . Women often gave birth under unsanitary conditions, and the mortality rate for both infants and mothers was high.[11]

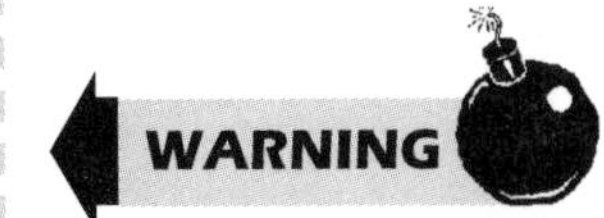

Don't let yourself dwell on the negatives. When you find yourself thinking about something negative, stop, and begin to praise the Lord for the life he has created.

Maternal Mortality Rate

(per ten thousand live births)

Year	Rate
1915	60.8
1920	79.9
1925	64.7
1930	67.3
1935	58.2
1940	37.6
1945	22.8
1950	8.3
1955	4.7
1960	3.7
1965	3.2
1970	2.2
1980	0.92
1990	0.82
1995	0.76

SOURCE: U.S. Bureau of the Census

Genesis 30:19–21 Leah conceived again and bore Jacob a sixth son. Then Leah said, "God has presented me with a precious gift. This time my husband will treat me with honor, because I have borne him six sons." So she named him **Zebulun**. Some time later she gave birth to a daughter and named her Dinah.

Zebulun: *"honor"*

GO TO:

Genesis 34 (Dinah)

Exodus 21:7 (daughter)

BOY OR GIRL, WHICH IS BETTER?

Numbers 36:8–9 Every daughter who inherits land in any Israelite tribe must marry someone in her father's tribal clan, so that every Israelite will possess the inheritance of his fathers. No inheritance may pass from tribe to tribe.

Boys Rule!

The words *son* and *sons* are used so often in the Old Testament that at first glance it can seem that the Bible pretty much ignores daughters. And partly that is true. Many more sons are mentioned than daughters.

But in fairness to the Scripture, the terms "son" and "sons" could be more accurately translated to mean "children." These were generic terms, just as we used to use the term "man" to mean "human beings."

Daughters had many of the same rights and privileges as sons did, and were valuable to the family. They were a source of labor, and, when a prospective husband paid a bride-price, it was also a means to greater wealth for the family. Daughters could inherit from their fathers, but then they had to marry within the clan. This was a way of protecting the family wealth.

In our society, there is no obvious desire for boys over girls like there is in other countries such as China and India.

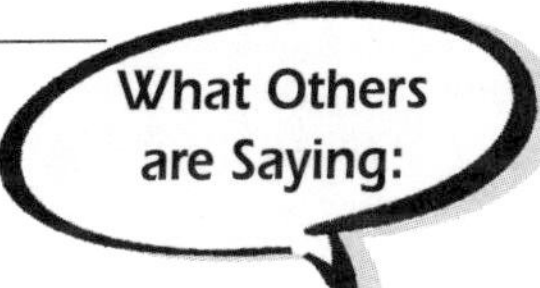

Laurie Lee: Ever since I was handed this living heap of expectations, I can feel nothing but awe. She is, of course, just an ordinary miracle, but she is also the particular late wonder of my life. This girl, my child, this parcel of will and warmth, was born last autumn. . . . This moment of meeting seemed to be a birth time for both of us, her first and my second life. Nothing, I knew, would be the same again, and I think I was reasonably shaken. They handed her to me, stiff and howling. I kissed her, and she went still and quiet, and I was instantly enslaved by her flattery of my powers. . . . I have got a daughter, whose life is already separate from mine. She will give me more than she gets, and may even later become my keeper.[12]

Sugar and spice and everything nice, that's what little girls are made of. Snips and snails and puppy dog tails, that's what little boys are made of.

Helen Good Brenneman: When we learn that a member is going to be added to our family, the sex has already been determined, along with all the other inherent possibilities of our child. . . . Let us thank God for the coming babe—boy or girl—and let him be his or her own God-inspired self.[13]

As your due date nears, physical intimacy can be difficult. Ask your doctor what is appropriate or read aloud to one another The Gift of Sex *by Clifford and Joyce Penner. This will open up the lines of communication on a topic that may be hard to discuss.*

THE BIRTH OF OUR SAVIOR

Luke 2:5–7 While they were there, the time came for the baby to be born, and she gave birth to her **firstborn**, a son. She wrapped him in **cloths** and placed him in a **manger**, because there was no room for them in the **inn**.

☞ **GO TO:**

Ezekiel 16:4 (cloths)

firstborn: *implies that Jesus had siblings*

cloths: *strips of material*

manger: *a feeding trough for animals*

inn: *a place travelers could stay for the night*

No Room at the Inn!

There is great disagreement about the "inn" that Mary and Joseph visited.

One tradition says that it was a home, probably of a relative. Because there were others who were also returning to Bethlehem to register, they just did not have room in the house and so they let Mary and Joseph stay in the stable, a cave in the hillside behind the house.

Others say that "inns" were structures that had been erected for caravans. Such a structure was probably like a fortress made of brick or stone, with a well in the center. Around the walls of this fortress were cells without windows or furnishings. Travelers were expected to provide their own food. Behind the cells were stables for bedding down the animals. This may have been the sort of place where Mary and Joseph were forced to rest for the night.

KEY POINT

God came to earth as a baby.

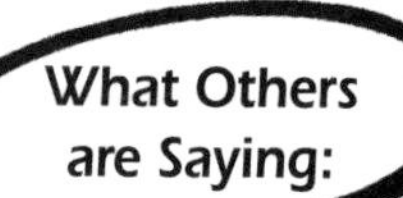

A. C. Bouquet: To place a newborn infant in a manger or trough was not an out-of-the-way proceeding, since the Hebrew word means both trough and cradle, and to this day troughs or mangers are used in the Near East for cradling infants.[14]

Exodus 1:15–21 The king of Egypt said to the Hebrew midwives, whose names were Shiphrah and Puah, "When you help the Hebrew women in childbirth and observe them on the **delivery stool** [see illustration, page 103], if it is a boy, kill him; but if it is a girl, let her live." The midwives, however, feared God and did not do what the king of Egypt had told them to do; they let the boys live. Then the king of Egypt summoned the midwives and asked them, "Why have you done this? Why have you let the boys live?" The midwives answered Pharaoh, "Hebrew women are not like Egyp-

☞ **GO TO:**

Jeremiah 18:3 (delivery stool)

delivery stool: *commonly used in biblical times by women in labor*

Delivery Stool

A woman in labor might sit on a delivery stool, such as this one, made of stone or brick. She would probably be attended by a midwife.

tian women; they are vigorous and give birth before the midwives arrive." So God was kind to the midwives and the people increased and became even more numerous. And because the midwives feared God, he gave them families of their own.

From Humble Beginnings

From this passage of scripture, we get a glimpse of what giving birth was like for a Hebrew woman. She was attended by two midwives, probably one to hold her upright on the delivery stool and the other to catch the baby.

Mary and Joseph were in a strange city when Mary gave birth to Jesus. Can you imagine her fear? There were no midwives, no mother, not even a mother-in-law to help her. There was only Joseph. He must've held her hand during her contractions and spoken words of encouragement as her labor grew more intense.

They probably talked about what they had been promised by the angel Gabriel and wondered about this child. Do you suppose they looked around at their circumstances and asked, "Why God? Why here? Why now? It seems like such an unlikely place for the Son of God to be born." (See illustration, page 104.)

After his birth, they wrapped him in cloths, which in other translations are commonly referred to as **swaddling clothes**. In the Hebrew culture after a baby was born, he or she was washed in water, rubbed in salt, and then wrapped in strips of cloth that bound the arms and legs tightly. (See GWWB, page 104.)

KEY POINT

There was nothing special about how Jesus was treated.

swaddling clothes: *strips of cloth*

Manger and Stable

Jesus' first bed might have been in a manger—a feed trough for animals—in a stable similar to the one pictured.

What Others are Saying:

penman: *author of the Scripture*

Adam Clarke's Commentary: Many have thought that this was a full proof of the . . . poverty of the holy family, that they were obliged to take up their lodging in a stable; but such people overlook the reason given by the inspired **penman,** because there was no room for them in the inn. As multitudes were going now to be enrolled, all the lodgings in the inn had been occupied before Joseph and Mary arrived. An honest man who had worked diligently at his business, under the peculiar blessing of God, as Joseph undoubtedly had, could not have been so destitute of money as not to be able to procure himself and wife a comfortable lodging for a night; and, had he been so ill fitted for the journey as some unwarrantably imagine, we may take it for granted he would not have brought his wife with him, who was in such a state as not to be exposed to any inconveniences of this kind without imminent danger.[15]

☞ GO TO:

John 6:35, 48 (Bread of Life)

Matthew 16:26 (Bread)

Think About It

The word *Bethlehem* means house of bread. Isn't it interesting that Jesus called himself the Bread of Life? Bread is also a symbol that we use during communion to remind us of his sacrifice for our sins on the cross.

What Others are Saying:

Philip Yancey: "The Little Lord Jesus, no crying he makes," seems to be a sanitized version of what took place in Bethlehem. I imagine Jesus cried like any other baby the night he entered the world, a world that would give him much reason to cry as an adult.[16]

FROM JUDY'S HEART

When I was pregnant, everyone had a story to tell about her pregnancy. Some were funny, most exciting, and one or two tragic. I tried not to think too much about what lay ahead of me. I concentrated on the day at hand and nothing more.

Each of my two deliveries was different and nothing like what I expected. Looking back, I can hardly remember the pain, but I do remember things like what I was doing when I went into labor. Later, I remember lying in a room attached to monitors. My husband was there holding my hand. When things got really bad, I grew angry and pushed him away, not caring if I ever saw him again. Nurses came and went. Finally, there was a mad rush to get me to the delivery room. They put my feet into stirrups and screamed, "Don't push, don't push." Then, "Push, push."

Excitement grew and there were "ohs" and "ahs" and then a tiny little cry. Suddenly my doctor held a little red body in the air and announced, "It's a boy." A nurse wrapped him in a cloth and laid him on my breast. He had a squished face, a furrowed brow, and dimples on his knuckles. He looked around, as if wondering what in the world was going on here. And I fell in love.

Study Questions

1. Contrast the waiting for the birth of a baby to the waiting for the Second Coming of Christ.
2. Why do they call it labor, and what does that have to do with the curse given Eve in Genesis?
3. What were the names of Adam and Eve's first two children?
4. Name two of the three Hebrew customs during childbirth that are mentioned here.
5. What is a manger and why do you think God chose this as Christ's birthplace?
6. What does Bethlehem mean and why is that significant?

CHAPTER WRAP-UP

- The last months of pregnancy are an exciting time, with much preparation taking place in the home and the heart. It's just as important to prepare ourselves for the coming of Christ.

- Childbirth can be prepared for by taking classes. The more you know the better. Also, leaning on the Lord during this time can help ease any fears.
- Maternal deaths during childbirth are almost nonexistent, but fear still can interfere with the joy of the experience. Prayer is as much a part of the preparation as breathing exercises.
- Midwives helped Hebrew women give birth. There were probably two of them and they used a birthing or delivery stool.
- Mary gave birth to Jesus in a stable. A humble beginning for the Son of God.
- Jesus was treated just like every other newborn of his time.
- No matter what the circumstances, every child born is a miracle and a cause for celebration.

JUDY'S BOOKSHELF

- *I Am a Woman by God's Design*, Beverly LaHaye, Fleming H. Revell. A classic look at the role of a godly woman.
- *The Complete Book of Christian Parenting & Child Care*, William Sears, M.D. and Martha Sears, R.N., Broadman & Holman. The basics are discussed by a doctor and his wife from prenatal to age six.
- *Mothers Together*, Ruth Bell Graham and Gigi Graham Tchividjian, Baker Books. A collection of journal entries, poems, and essays by the wife and daughter of Billy Graham.

6 A CAUSE FOR CELEBRATION

WHAT'S IN THIS CHAPTER

- Jesus' Birth
- Circumcision
- Names in Scripture
- The Importance of a Name

Here We Go

The birth of a baby is cause for celebration.

When it's an important birth, it makes the headlines and is carried on the national news. If it's a friend or relative, we give gifts for the new arrival and send flowers and cards to the new parents. Some new parents announce the birth by hanging signs from their garage doors saying, "It's a boy" or "It's a girl." They send birth announcements with pictures, and phone calls and e-mails go out across America. Newspapers even have a special section where they list the births at the local hospitals.

JESUS' BIRTH

Luke 2:8–12 And there were shepherds living out in the fields nearby, **keeping watch** over their flocks at night. An angel of the Lord appeared to them, and the glory of the Lord shone around them, and they were terrified. But the angel said to them, "Do not be afraid. I bring you good news of great joy that will be for all the people. Today in the **town of David** a **Savior** has been born to you; he is Christ the **Lord**. This will be a sign to you: You will find a baby wrapped in cloths and lying in a manger."

☞ **GO TO:**

Luke 1:11; Matthew 1:20, 24; 2:13, 19 (angel of the Lord)

Matthew 1:21; John 4:42 (Savior)

Acts 2:36; Philippians 2:11 (Lord)

keeping watch: *against thieves and predatory animals*

town of David: *Bethlehem*

Savior: *deliverer from sin*

Lord: *a designation reserved for God*

So, Sheepishly, They Made Their Way to the Manger . . .

KEY POINT

The birth, which changed the world forever, went almost unnoticed at the time.

The first to hear of Christ's birth were not the local officials or the leader of the Jewish religion, but a bunch of shepherds tending sheep (see illustration below) in the fields around Bethlehem. This sounds strange to us, but for God these were the right men.

Sheep were an important part of the economy. They were prized for their meat, fat, milk, wool, and skins, and were used for religious sacrifices (Exodus 29:22). The residents of Bethlehem had probably hired these shepherds to watch the sheep for everyone in the village. That means the shepherds were entrusted with the wealth of each family.

And God entrusted them with the wondrous knowledge that the Savior was born.

What Others are Saying:

Janette Oke: Shepherds were simple people, often ridiculed and sometimes even looked on with suspicion because they were unlearned, uncouth men of the land. It was not unusual for them to be in the fields by night, for shepherds often slept under the stars with their flocks. It was at night that the flock often faced the gravest danger, and the shepherds needed to be alert.[1]

Shepherds Tending Flocks

Although shepherds were considered lowly by people of their time, the angels appeared to them, heralding Jesus' birth.

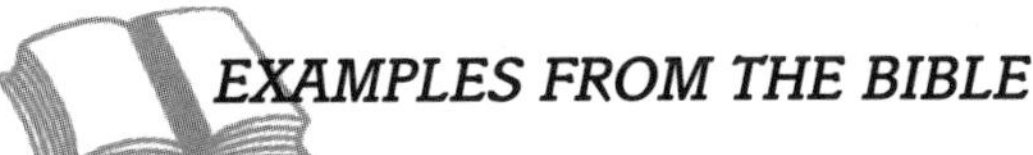

References to God as a shepherd and Israel as his flock abound in the Old Testament, and in the **gospel** of John, Jesus describes himself as a shepherd.

GO TO:

Genesis 48:15; 49:24; Ezekiel 34:15; John 10:11 (shepherd)

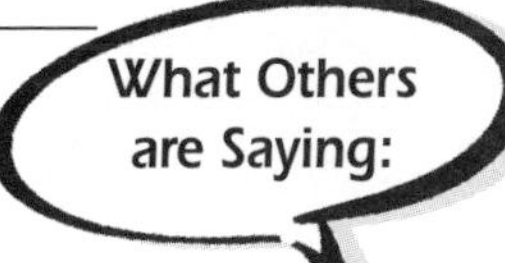

Philip Yancey: God's visit to earth took place in an animal shelter with no attendants present and nowhere to lay the newborn king but a feed trough. Indeed, the event that divided history, and even our calendars, into two parts may have had more animal than human witnesses. A mule could have stepped on him. "How silently, how silently, the wondrous gift is given."[2]

gospel: *first four books of the New Testament*

Parent's Dictionary

Amnesia: condition that enables a woman who has gone through labor to have sex again.

Impregnable: a woman whose memory of labor is still vivid.

Prenatal: when your life was still somewhat your own.

> **Luke 2:13–15** Suddenly a **great company** of the heavenly host appeared with the angel, praising God and saying, "Glory to God **in the highest**, and on earth **peace** to men on whom his favor rests." When the angels had left them and gone into heaven, the shepherds said to one another, "Let's go to Bethlehem and see this thing that has happened, which the Lord has told us about."

great company: *army*

in the highest: *in heaven*

peace: *a deep peace within the heart and soul of man*

GO TO:

John 14:27; Romans 5:1 (peace)

Pinch Me, This HAS to Be a Dream!

It's hard to believe what the shepherds had just seen and heard. An army of beings descending from heaven with strange lights glowing all around them. It must've been terrifying.

But it also must have been convincing, because the shepherds didn't run away; instead they looked at each other and said, "Let's go and see for ourselves."

Obedience is not a popular word. We want to do things our way and in our own time. We think obedience will mean being bored, or being made uncomfortable, or denying ourselves pleasures. But obedience can mean peace, joy, and fulfillment.

What Others are Saying:

Chuck Swindoll: Let's face it, we are a pretty wayward flock of sheep![3]

Lighten Up

A Letter to God

God,

Are there really angels? Do you have to be a girl? Can they really fly high?

But can angels still do normal things like eat pasta and play soccer?

You and the Pope are great,

Georgio (age 9)[4]

Think About It

What would you have done if you had been confronted by an army of celestial beings? Would you have run away? Would you have told anyone? Do you think they would have believed you?

What Others are Saying:

Janette Oke: Why did God send an angel to tell the good news to the shepherds? We do not know, but we do know that they listened, responded, and rejoiced. They understood the message. They didn't even doubt.[5]

GO TO:

Luke 2:7 (manger)

amazed: *in wonder and admiration*

> **Luke 2:16–17** So they hurried off and found Mary and Joseph, and the baby, who was lying in the manger. When they had seen him, they spread the word concerning what had been told them about this child, and all who heard it were **amazed** at what the shepherds said to them.

You Know, Mary, Nothing Surprises Me Anymore

KEY POINT

God uses the most unlikely people to carry his message.

Mary and Joseph must have been surprised when a bunch of shepherds showed up with a strange tale of heavenly hosts and angels. Or maybe they weren't. Maybe by this time, they were used to angels appearing at odd times.

The shepherds, after seeing with their own eyes, went and told others. And because of who they were, they were believed.

Reader's Digest Illustrated Dictionary of Bible Life & Times: Since sheep and goats can forage in nearly barren wasteland, they were the most **ubiquitous domestic** animals in the arid Holy Land. The shepherd's job required that he continually move his flock to new pastures, especially in summer months. . . . Shepherds were sometimes looked down upon by settled populations [Genesis 46:32–34]. Because both groups competed for the same land and water, there was often hostility between them, as the story of Cain and Abel [Genesis 4:1–16] suggests.[6]

What Others are Saying:

ubiquitous: *found everywhere*

domestic: *tame*

Luke 2:19–20 But Mary treasured up all these things and pondered them in her heart. The shepherds returned, glorifying and praising God for all the things they had heard and seen, which were just as they had been told.

GO TO:

Luke 2: 51 (treasured)

Matthew 9:8 (glorifying)

A Humble Heart

Mary must've looked into her baby's eyes as she breast-fed him and wondered about all she had heard. As she traced her finger across his cheek, there must've been some awe and maybe even a little worry. What would the future hold for her precious little one?

Patricia H. Rushford: If I could tell new mothers something for which they'd be eternally grateful, it would be to approach motherhood as a child. Mothers who enter motherhood as if they know all there is to know will miss some of life's most important lessons. Come into motherhood with the awe, the excitement, and the willingness to learn a whole new way of life. Come with the anticipation of a child on his or her first day of school. . . . Let your children lead and teach you, 'cause Mama—we've got a lot to learn.[7]

What Others are Saying:

How long has it been since you looked at your children and "treasured" them? Sometimes we get caught up in the daily grind of life. We're busy going to work, doing laundry, housework, running our children to and from all sorts of activities.

Think About It

Janette Oke: What thoughts and feelings occupied the young mother? Was there a mixture of joy and shame? Of promise and doubt? Of hope and fear? What thoughts did Mary wrestle with

What Others are Saying:

in the days following Jesus' birth? What secret prayers did she whisper in the days that followed as she ground wheat for the daily bread or carried water from the public well, her eyes always returning to study her infant son? Was it really true? Had she, Mary, a lowly maiden, really given birth to the Son of the living God?[8]

Don't approach motherhood thinking you know it all. We all can learn from experts, from our friends, our mothers, and even from our babies.

glorifies: *gives glory to (as in worship)*

> **Luke 1:46–55** And Mary said: "My soul **glorifies** the Lord and my spirit rejoices in God my Savior, for he has been mindful of the humble state of his servant. From now on all generations will call me blessed, for the Mighty One has done great things for me—holy is his name. His mercy extends to those who fear him, from generation to generation. He has performed mighty deeds with his arm; he has scattered those who are proud in their inmost thoughts. He has brought down rulers from their thrones but has lifted up the humble. He has filled the hungry with good things but has sent the rich away empty. He has helped his servant Israel, remembering to be merciful to Abraham and his descendants forever, even as he said to our fathers."

☞ GO TO:

John 4:24 (arm)

Matthew 5:6; John 6:35 (hungry)

Genesis 22:16–18 (merciful)

Mary's Song

Read this song carefully, as a mother. All that Mary had seen and heard, all that she knew about the child, humbled her. She knew she was unworthy, just as any of us would be. But yet God had chosen her and she gave him the glory.

She gives thanks to God for scattering the proud and for bringing down the unkind rulers and for keeping his promise to Abraham.

Did she believe that the baby she carried was going to be a political savior who would free the Israelites from the Roman Empire?

It must've puzzled her when her child was born in a stable. She must've wondered at the first visitors, shepherds instead of kings. Did Mary really understand what was coming?

Do you sometimes wonder, "God, what are you doing?"

You go to church regularly, you have daily quiet times, you pray for and with your children and give generously to the church, and yet your life is disappointing. The expected raise didn't come through, the landlord just raised your rent, your son has a reading disability, you struggle with depression, and your marriage is in trouble.

Are you feeling discouraged because life isn't turning out the way you think God promised? Look at Mary and ask yourself if her life turned out the way she expected it to?

If your marriage seems to be stuck in a rut, put new life into it by spending alone time together. New babies can take much time away from the oneness that you once had. Don't be afraid to find a reliable babysitter and concentrate on your husband for a few hours.

For Single Moms—You too need time away from your children. Find another single mom and trade babysitting. Attend church functions that offer babysitting. Don't bury yourself in your home. We all need adult contact to keep us sane.

CIRCUMCISION

> **Luke 2:21** On the eighth day, when it was time to **circumcise** him, he was named Jesus, the name the angel had given him before he had been conceived.

☞ **GO TO:**

Genesis 17:10–12, 14; Exodus 13:2, 12 (circumcise)

circumcise: *the cutting away of the covering of skin that encloses the head of the penis*

An Unkind Cut?

No Hebrew mother would have thought twice about having her baby circumcised. It was part of the Mosaic Law. "*This is my covenant with you and your descendants after you, . . . Every male among you shall be circumcised*" (Genesis 17:10). Circumcision was commanded by God as a symbol, to every generation and every nation, that he had a special relationship with the Hebrew people.

Today there is much discussion about the health risks associated with circumcision. According to a recent study, uncircumcised boys are four times as likely to develop urinary tract infections in their first year of life. But urinary tract infections only occur in less than 1 percent of infants. Uncircumcised men are also more at risk of developing penile cancer, but again the number of men who get this type of cancer is low (nine out of one million).

☞ GO TO:

1 Corinthians 7:19–20; Romans 2:29; Galatians 6:15 (circumcision)

Circumcised men are one-third to one-half more likely to contract a sexually transmitted disease, but these can easily be avoided by remaining faithful to one wife. In summary, medical risks do not have to be considered when making this choice.[9]

If you have any questions about this procedure, be sure to talk to your pediatrician.

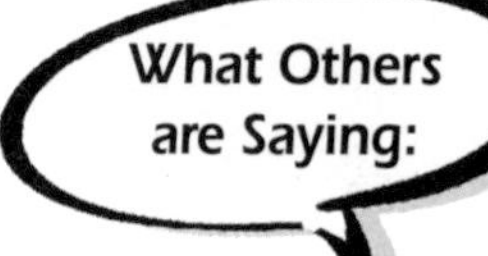

Dr. William Sears and Martha Sears, R.N.: Whether or not your newborn son should be circumcised is your decision to make. It is an issue you need to consider carefully, with thought, prayer, and discussion between both parents.[10]

☞ GO TO:

Acts 15:1, 5 (commitment)

Ephesians 2:14–18 (covenant)

> **Galatians 5:6** For in Christ Jesus neither <u>circumcision</u> nor uncircumcision has any value. The only thing that counts is faith expressing itself through love.

Some Folks Say One Thing, Some Folks Say Another . . .

In the early church there was much argument over the issue of circumcision. As **Gentiles** converted, some felt that, like the Jewish men, the new Christians should be circumcised as an outer sign of their <u>commitment</u> to Christ. But Paul and Peter both agreed that it wasn't necessary. To them what was more important was a heartfelt transformation.

Gentiles: *people who are not Jewish*

covenant: *agreement between one or more persons*

What Others are Saying:

Nelson's Illustrated Bible Dictionary: Paul declared that the new **<u>covenant</u>** of Christ's shed blood has provided forgiveness to both Jew and Gentile and has made circumcision totally unnecessary. All that ultimately matters for both Jew and Gentile, Paul says, is a changed **nature**—a new creation that makes them one in Jesus Christ.[11]

nature: *the core qualities of a person*

NAMES IN SCRIPTURE

> **Luke 1:31** You will be with child and give birth to a son, and you are to give him the name **Jesus**.

☞ **GO TO:**

Matthew 1:21 (Jesus)

***Jesus:** the Greek form of Joshua, which means "the Lord saves"*

Jesus Is the Sweetest Name I Know

Choosing the name of a child in the Jewish tradition was an important decision, for it was believed that a name represented the very nature of the person.

Personal names were formed from words that had their own meanings. Isaac was named "laughter" because his mother, Sarah, had done that when told she would bear him. Esau was named "hairy" because of his appearance, Jacob, "supplanter," because he grabbed his brother's heel, and Moses meant "drawn out of the water."

☞ **GO TO:**

Genesis 17:5 (Abram)

Genesis 17:15–16 (Sarai)

Genesis 32:28 (Jacob)

Matthew 16:18 (Simon)

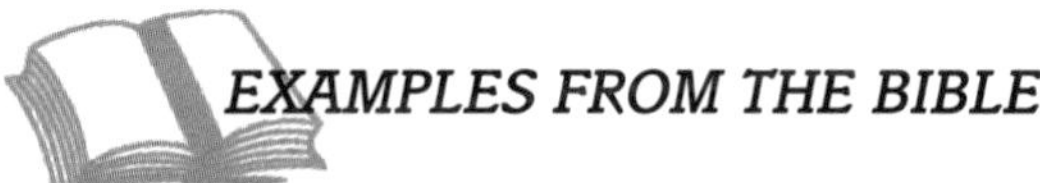

EXAMPLES FROM THE BIBLE

Names were changed to reflect a crucial turning point in a person's life. Abram (exalted father) was renamed Abraham (father of a multitude), Sarai (contentious) became Sarah (princess). Jacob (supplanter) became Israel (God strives), because he struggled with God. Simon was renamed Peter (rock) because he was the first apostle to confess his faith in Jesus.

What Others are Saying:

E. W. Heaton: All Israelite names were personal [that is, what we call first or "Christian"] names; no **surnames** were used, not because the connexion [sic] was unimportant, but because it was so important as not to need mentioning.[12]

***surnames:** last names*

☞ **GO TO:**

Matthew 1:13 (John)

***John:** "the Lord is gracious"*

***writing tablet:** a small wooden board covered with wax*

> **Luke 1:59–66** On the eighth day they came to circumcise the child, and they were going to name him after his father Zechariah, but his mother spoke up and said, "No! He is to be called **John**." They said to her, "There is no one among your relatives who has that name." Then they made signs to his father, to find out what he would like to name the child. He asked for a **writing tablet**, and to everyone's astonishment he wrote, "His name is John." Immediately his mouth was opened and his tongue was loosed, and he began to speak, praising God. The neigh-

bors were all filled with awe, and throughout the hill country of Judea people were talking about all these things. Everyone who heard this wondered about it, asking, "What then is this child going to be?" For the Lord's hand was with him.

The First of Many, Many, Many Boys Named John

From this scripture we can tell that sons were traditionally named after their fathers.

You can almost hear the gasp when Elizabeth says, "No, his name is to be John." In total dismay, the friends and relatives turn to Zechariah for the truth.

And when he affirms the choice, they are amazed, because Zechariah, who has been mute since the child was conceived, can now speak again.

Word goes out that this child is going to be someone very special.

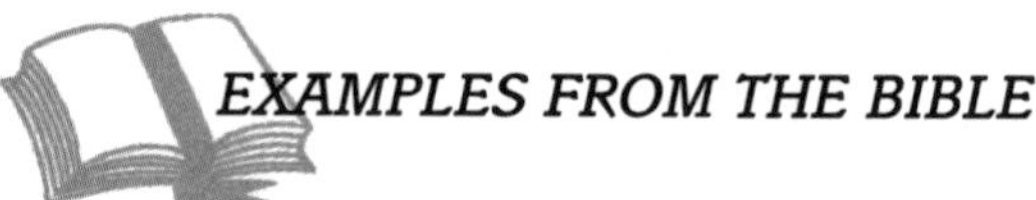

EXAMPLES FROM THE BIBLE

Both John and Jesus were announced, set apart, and named by the angel Gabriel even before their birth.

Exodus 3:13–14 Moses said to God, "Suppose I go to the Israelites and say to them, 'The God of your fathers has sent me to you,' and they ask me, 'What is his name?' Then what shall I tell them?" God said to Moses, "**I AM WHO I AM**. This is what you are to say to the Israelites: '<u>I AM</u> has sent me to you.' "

I AM WHO I AM: also, translated as I WILL BE WITH YOU

☞ GO TO:

John 8:58–59 (I AM)

Acts 10:42; John 14:6; 1 Timothy 2:5 (no other name)

Even God Has a Name

We really don't know someone until we learn his or her name, and so it was with Moses.

He wanted to know God's name.

The answer he got is significant, because it reveals God's character: He will be with us. He will never let us go. We can take much comfort in knowing the meaning of God's name. Acts 4:12 says, "*Salvation is found in no one else, for there is <u>no other name</u> under heaven given to men by which we must be saved.*"

Do you know God's name? Is he as personal to you, as his name implies? If not, begin today to develop a relationship with him. Spend time in his Word and on your knees in prayer.

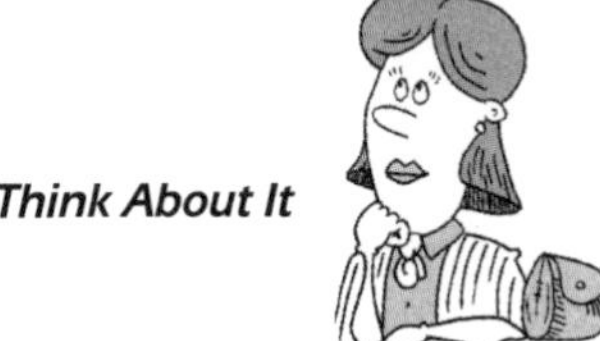

In the ancient world, knowing another's name was a special privilege that offered access to that person's thoughts and life. God favored his people by revealing himself by several names that offered special insight into his love and righteousness.

What Others are Saying:

Nelson's Illustrated Bible Dictionary: One of the most important names for God in the Old Testament is Yahweh, or Jehovah, from the verb "to be," meaning simply but profoundly, "I am who I am," and "I will be who I will be." The four-letter Hebrew word YHWH was the name by which God revealed Himself to Moses in the burning bush [Exodus 3:14]. This bush was a vivid symbol of the inexhaustible dynamism of God who burns like a fire with love and righteousness, yet remains the same and never diminishes. Some English translations of the Bible translate the word as Jehovah, while others use Yahweh.[13]

Names of God

Genesis 22:14	Jehovah-jireh	The-LORD-Will-Provide
Exodus 17:15	Jehovah-nissi	The-LORD-Is-My-Banner
Judges 6:24	Jehovah-shalom	The-LORD-Is-Peace
Ezekiel 48:35	Jehovah-shammah	The-LORD-Is-There
1 Samuel 1:3	Jehovah-tsebaoth	The-LORD-of-Hosts
1 Samuel 15:29	Jehovah Elohe Israel	LORD-God-of-Israel
Deuteronomy 5:9	Elohim	God
Genesis 21:33	El Olam	Everlasting God
Exodus 6:3	El Shaddai	God Almighty

Don't take the Lord's name lightly. The Jewish people thought it was so precious that they refused to pronounce it. Ask yourself if you've grown too blasé about the privilege of saying Jesus' name.

> **Acts 10:43** All the prophets testify about him that everyone who believes in him receives forgiveness of sins through his name.

In the Name of Jesus Christ

"Jesus, name above all names . . . " is a favorite praise hymn of many. There *is* something special about his name. When we want to bring authority to our prayer requests we say, "In the name of Jesus Christ . . . " and we can do this knowing that as a child of God, we have the authority to speak in his name. When we are hurting and at the end of our rope, we can cry, "Jesus, sweet Jesus" and he hears our cries and comforts us.

By his name people are saved, by his name people are healed, and by his name we are forgiven. Isn't it the most wonderful name you ever heard?

Names of Jesus

Adam
Advocate
Almighty
Alpha and Omega
Angel
Angel of his presence
Anointed
Apostle
Arm of the Lord
Author and Finisher of our faith
Beginning and end of the creation of God
Beloved
Blessed and only Potentate
Branch
Bread of life
Bridegroom
Bright and Morning Star
Brightness of the Father's glory
Captain of the Lord's host (army)
Captain of Salvation
Carpenter
Carpenter's son
Chief Shepherd
Chief Cornerstone
Chosen of God
Christ
The Christ (Messiah)
Christ, a King
Christ Jesus
Christ Jesus our Lord
Christ of God
Christ, the chosen of God
Christ the Lord
Christ, the power of God
Christ, the wisdom of God
Christ, the Son of God
Christ, Son of the Blessed
Commander
Consolation of Israel
Cornerstone
Counselor
Covenant of the people
David
Dayspring
Day Star
Deliverer
Desire of all nations
Door, the
Elect
Emmanuel
Ensign
Eternal Life
Everlasting Father
Faithful and True
Faithful Witness, the
Faithful and true witness, the
Finisher of faith
First and last
First begotten
First begotten of the dead

Names of Jesus (continued)

Firstborn
Foundation
Fountain
Forerunner
Friend of sinners
Gift of God
Glory of Israel
God (deity)
God blessed forever
God manifest in the flesh
God of Israel, the Savior
God of the whole earth
God our Savior
God's dear Son
God with us
Good Master
Governor
Great Shepherd of the sheep
Head of the ekklesia (body)
Heir of all things
High priest
Head of every man
Head of the corner
Holy child Jesus
Holy one
Holy one of God
Holy one of Israel
Holy thing
Hope (our)
Horn of salvation
I AM
Image of God
Israel
Jehovah
Jehovah's fellow
Jesus
Jesus Christ
Jesus Christ our Lord
Jesus Christ our Savior
Jesus of Nazareth
Jesus (of Nazareth), King of the Jews
Jesus, the Son of God
Jesus, the Son of Joseph
Judge
Just man, Just person, Just One
King
King of Israel
King of the Jews
King of Saints
King of Kings
King of Glory
King of Zion
King over all the earth
Lamb
Lamb of God
Lawgiver
Leader
Life
Light
Light of the world
Light to the Gentiles
Living Bread, the
Living Stone
Lion of the tribe of Judah
Lord
Lord of Lords
Lord of all
Lord our righteousness
Lord God Almighty
Lord from heaven
Lord Jesus Christ
Lord of glory
Lord of Hosts (armies)
Lord, mighty in battle
Lord of the dead and living
Lord of the Sabbath
Lord over all
Lord's Christ
Lord, strong and mighty
Man of sorrows
Master
Mediator, the only
Messenger of the covenant
Messiah
Messiah the Prince
Mighty God
Mighty one of Israel
Mighty one of Jacob
Mighty to save

KEY POINT

Each name of Jesus emphasizes a different part of who he is.

Names of Jesus (continued)

Minister of the sanctuary
Morning Star
Most holy
Most mighty
Nazarene
Offspring of David
Only begotten
Overseer
Passover, our
Plant of renown
Potentate
Power of God
Physician
Precious Cornerstone
Priest
Prince
Prince of Life
Prince of Peace
Prince of the kings of the earth
Prophet
Propitiation (expiation, our Sin-offering)
Rabbi, Rabboni
Ransom
Redeemer
Resurrection and the Life, the
Redemption
Righteous Branch
Righteous Judge
Righteous Servant
Righteousness
Rock
Rock of Offence
Root of David
Root of Jesse
Rose of Sharon
Ruler in Israel
Salvation
Sanctification
Sanctuary
Savior
Scepter
Second Man, the
Seed of David
Seed of the woman
Servant
Servant of rulers
Shepherd
Shepherd of Israel
Shiloh
Son of the Father
Son of God
Son of man
Son of the Blessed One
Son of the Highest One
Son of David
Star
Sun of Righteousness
Surety (Guarantee)
Stone
Stone of Stumbling
Sure Foundation
Teacher
True God
True Vine
Truth
Unspeakable Gift
Vine, the
Way, the
Which is, which was, which is to come
Eternal One, I AM THAT I AM
Wisdom
Wisdom of God, the
Witness
Wonderful
Word
Word of God
Word of Life

What Others are Saying:

Philip Yancey: Jesus' own name comes from the word Joshua—"he shall save"—a common name in those days. [As major-league baseball rosters reveal, the name Jesus remains popular among Latin Americans.] Its very ordinariness, not unlike "Bob" or "Joe" today, must have grated on Jewish ears in the first century as they listened to Jesus' words. Jews did not pronounce the Honorable Name of GOD, save for the high priests one day a year, and even today Orthodox Jews carefully spell out G_D. For people raised in such a tradition, the idea that an ordinary person with a name like Jesus could be the Son of God and Savior of the world seemed utterly scandalous. Jesus was a man, for goodness' sake, Mary's boy.[14]

THE IMPORTANCE OF A NAME

> **Numbers 1:2** "Take a **census** of the whole Israelite community by their clans and families, listing every man by **name**, one by one."

census: *a list*

name: *a mark of individuality*

Kjellen? Could You Spell That, Please?

Naming your child is a huge responsibility. It can be something he will wear proudly for the rest of his life, or be the source of frustration and even anger. Some of the things you need to consider are:

- Is it too cute? Jimmy may fit nicely when he's one or even two, but what about when he's forty and running for president?
- Is it too trendy? In the sixties, hardly anyone was named Jennifer, but by the seventies, it was the top name given to girl babies. Every classroom in America probably had two or three.
- Is it hard to pronounce? Sylvester Stallone named one of his children Seargeoh. Now for the rest of his life, the boy will have to correct people who mispronounce it.
- Is it hard to spell? Emylee may seem clever when you're filling out the birth certificate, but will Emylee thank you after she has to spell her name a million times to receptionists?
- Will it be made fun of? Children love to take a name and twist it into something funny. Sometimes this is hard to predict, but with other names it's obvious.
- How does it sound with your last name? Harry Carey probably had a hard time growing up.

- What do the initials spell? Nathan Edward Riley-Dodd will probably be teased by his peers if they ever figure this one out.
- Is it too pretentious? Everest may sound nice to your ears, but will your son really like being named after a mountain peak?

Names of the Nineties

Amanda	Chelsea	Dylan	Miles
Ashley	Chloe	Emily	Morgan
Brandon	Cody	Jake	Owen
Caitlin	Courtney	Kyle	Zachary

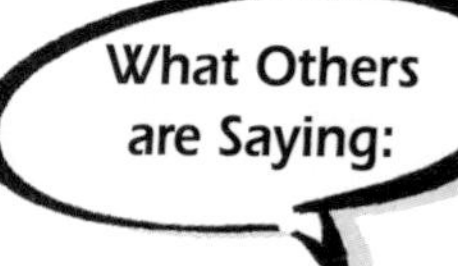

Helen Good Brenneman: It doesn't matter so much what you name your baby—Ruth, or Shirley, or Tom, or Kirk. What does matter is how you feel toward that child. Do you see in him a son of God, a beloved person, an individual capable of making a unique contribution to his world? Jesus saw Simon Peter's many blunderings, when He said, "So you are Simon the son of John? You shall be called Cephas [which means Peter]" [John 1:42]. We know that Peter means "rock" and that Peter became a pillar in the early church, a strong and solid character, fulfilling Jesus' expectations of him.[15]

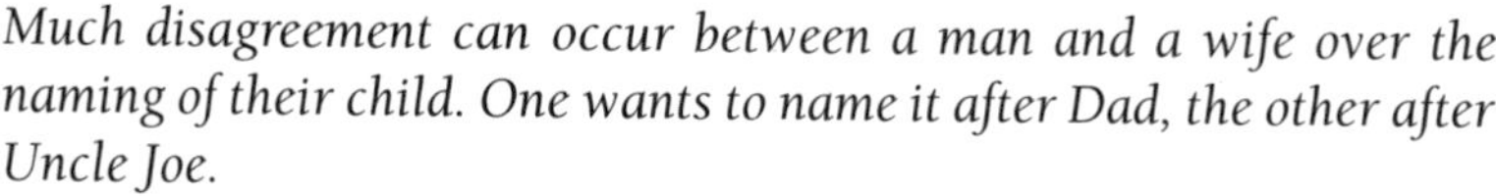

Much disagreement can occur between a man and a wife over the naming of their child. One wants to name it after Dad, the other after Uncle Joe.

A good solution is to find a third possibility that will please you both. Your marriage is too important for you to allow an issue like this to come between you.

For Single Moms—Naming your child will be entirely up to you. Make your decision carefully. Ask the advice of a trusted family member or friend.

I write fiction. An important part of the process is developing characters. Each one must be as real to me as my children or husband are. The characters must have distinct personalities, with their own desires and goals and pain. The sound of their voices and the way they put their words together must be unique, so that the reader can identify them just by the words written on the page.

It's a difficult process and one I labor over long and hard before I begin to write the story. I will think about the plot elements and the story line, plan the setting, and maybe even write the beginning, but until I know my characters it is a waste of time to even begin.

Often my characters come to me while thumbing through a baby name book. Each name listed resonates with personality—Edith immediately brings to mind someone who is efficient, possibly an accountant or math teacher. Yvonne is tall with blonde hair and walks regally in her perfectly tailored suits. Ramon is romantic, with dark hair and large brown eyes. Brandon is immature, while Harley is old for his age.

Once I have given my characters their names, they come alive for me. They "become" their names.

Do we? Do we develop certain personalities because of our names? It's something each of us should consider before we label our child Fifi or Pixie or Speck (actual names given to children of popular movie personalities).

After careful consideration, we chose to name our sons Matthew and David. Matthew is intellectual, more serious, and persistent. David is competitive, bright, and social. They are as distinct as they can be. Did they become their names? Or, did their names become them? I don't know that it matters. I can't imagine them being named anything else.

Study Questions

1. Who were the first to hear of Jesus' birth? Why do you think they were chosen?
2. Name three things Mary gave thanks for in her "song."
3. What did circumcision symbolize in the Old Testament?
4. Is circumcision necessary for a Christian? Why or why not?
5. What was God's name?
6. What does the name Jesus mean and who picked it?
7. Name three people in the Bible whose names were changed, and explain why.

CHAPTER WRAP-UP

- The birth of every baby is cause for celebration. Jesus' birth was announced, not to the public or religious officials, but to the shepherds by an army of angels.

- On the eighth day Jesus was circumcised just like every Hebrew child. Circumcision was a symbol of God's commitment to the Israelites that he would never leave them, that he is with them always.
- Circumcision is still practiced today, but it's not a requirement for a Christian. God is more concerned with our inner commitment to him than with an outward symbol that may mean nothing.
- The angel Gabriel told Mary and Joseph to name their baby Jesus. It means "the Lord saves."
- John's name was given to his parents by an angel. It was so unusual, word spread rapidly that there was something special about him.
- In the Bible names had specific meanings. Moses received his name because he was drawn out of water, Esau because he was hairy, Isaac because his mother laughed when she was told she would give birth to him.
- God's name is I AM WHO I AM. It means that he is with us always.
- Jesus had many names that reflected who he was and what he did while he was here on earth.
- Today our children are given names for a whole host of reasons, but much thought should go into each one, because we tend to "become" our names.

JUDY'S BOOKSHELF

Some light reading to cheer you up:

- *Chicken Soup for the Mother's Soul,* edited by Jack Canfield, Health Communications, Inc. A collection of 101 stories that will warm your heart.
- *God's Little Instruction Book,* Honor Books. A collection of sayings that will make you smile.
- *At Home in Mitford,* Jan Karon. Fiction that will be like taking a vacation.
- *Rubes Bible Cartoons,* Leigh Rubin, Hendrickson Publishers. A fun look at the Bible.

7 PROMISED TO THE LORD

WHAT'S IN THIS CHAPTER

- The Firstborn Male
- Promising Children to God
- Modern Traditions

Here We Go

There's something special about our firstborn child.

Is it because the whole birth experience is so new and frightening and wonderful? Is it because there's only one to look after?

Or, is there something within us that understands a biblical principle that we are not even aware of?

THE FIRSTBORN MALE

Exodus 13:1–2 The LORD said to Moses, "**Consecrate** to me every firstborn male. The first offspring of every womb among the Israelites belongs to me, whether man or animal."

GO TO:

Exodus 13:11–13; 34:19; Leviticus 27:26 (consecrate)

consecrate: *treat with special care as a possession of God*

tenth plague: *the killing of every firstborn male in Egypt*

Number One Son

After the Israelites escaped from Egypt, God placed a special claim on the firstborn male offspring of both man and beast. This meant that the firstborn male was to be treated as someone special. He was given extra privileges and responsibilities.

REMEMBER  THIS

During that period, several nations living around the Israelites practiced human sacrifice of firstborn males.

What Others are Saying:

NIV Study Bible: God had adopted Israel as his firstborn [Exodus 4:22] and had delivered every firstborn among the Israelites, whether man or animal, from the **tenth plague** [Exodus 12:12–13]. All the firstborn in Israel were therefore his.[1]

redeem: *ransom*

shekels: *coins weighing two ounces*

> **Numbers 18:16** When they are a month old, you must **redeem** them at the redemption price set at five **shekels** of silver, according to the sanctuary shekel, which weighs twenty gerahs.

☞ **GO TO:**

Psalm 130:7–8; John 8:34; Romans 6:18 (sin)

Redemption

The Jewish tradition was that every firstborn male, because he belonged to God, was presented to the priest. To get the boy back the parents were required to pay a ransom that could not exceed five shekels.

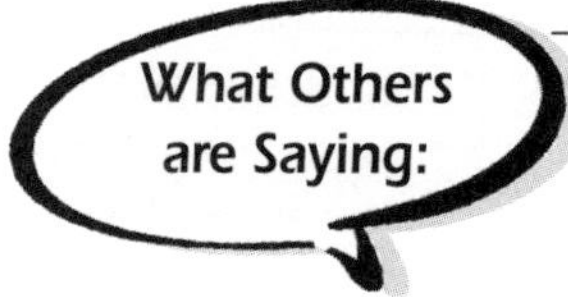

Nelson's Illustrated Bible Dictionary: In the Old Testament redemption was applied to property, animals, persons, and the nation of Israel as a whole. In nearly every instance, freedom from obligation, bondage, or danger was secured by the payment of a price, a ransom, bribe, satisfaction, or sum of money paid to obtain freedom, favor, or reconciliation. Men may redeem property, animals, and individuals [slaves, prisoners, indentured relatives] who are legally obligated to God or in bondage for other reasons.[2]

Deuteronomy 15:15 (enemy oppressors)

Job 19:25–26; Psalm 49:8–9 (death)

God alone is able to redeem us from the slavery of sin, enemy **oppressors**, and the power of death.

Think About It

Isn't it interesting that Jesus, God's firstborn son, is called our redeemer (see 1 Peter 1:19; Ephesians 1:7)? What was the price he paid (see 1 Corinthians 6:19–20; 1 Peter 1:13–19)? What was the result? If you don't understand what he did for you on the cross, then talk to your pastor.

☞ **GO TO:**

Galatians 4:3–5; 5:1 (law)

Hebrews 2:14–15 (fear of death)

EXAMPLES FROM THE BIBLE

We have been freed from the oppressive bondage of slavery to sin, the law, and the fear of death. *"Therefore if the Son makes you free, you shall be free indeed"* (John 8:36).

C. S. Lewis: Some will not be redeemed. . . . I would pay any price to be able to say truthfully "All will be saved." But my reason retorts, "Without their will, or with it?" If I say "Without their will" I at once perceive a contradiction; how can the supreme voluntary act of self-surrender be involuntary? If I say "With their will," my reason replies "How if they *will not* give in?"[3]

oppressors: *burden with unjust authority*

Grow Your Marriage

Are you worried because your husband isn't the spiritual head of your home? Try asking him questions about what he believes and then, in a respectful way, listen to him. Seek his advice on spiritual matters. You may witness an incredible change.

> **Deuteronomy 21:17** He must acknowledge the firstborn by giving him a double share of all he has. . . . That son is the first sign of his father's **strength**. The right of the firstborn belongs to him.

☞ **GO TO:**

Genesis 49:3; 2 Chronicles 21:3 (strength)

strength: *a man's ability to reproduce*

Come on, Dad, He Gets the Lion's Share of Everything!

In Israel the firstborn son was loved in a special way by his parents, and inherited a double portion of the estate and leadership of the family. The rest of the shares were divided equally among the rest of the children, including daughters.

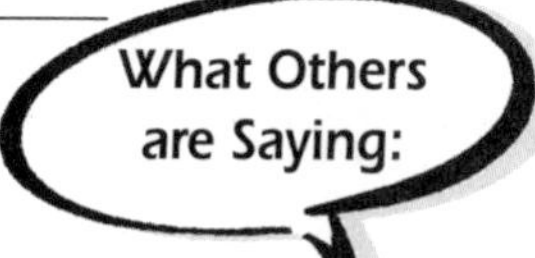

Alan Beck: Between the innocence of babyhood and the dignity of manhood we find a delightful creature called a boy. Boys come in assorted sizes, weight, and colors, but all boys have the same creed: to enjoy every second of every minute of every hour of every day and to protest with noise (their only weapon) when their last minute is finished and the adult males pack them off to bed at night.[4]

transfiguration: *the supernatural change of Jesus on the mount*

Jesus was God's firstborn Son. At his baptism (Matthew 3:16–17) and again at the **transfiguration** (Matthew 17:5) God spoke and said, *"This is my Son, whom I love; with him I am well pleased."*

Think About It

As head of the home after his father's death, the eldest son customarily took care of his mother until her death, and of his sisters until they married. He was also the family's spiritual head.

What Others are Saying:

Nelson's Illustrated Bible Dictionary: In the New Testament, the inheritance that Jesus gives is salvation. Hebrews 9:15 states that "those who are called may receive the promised eternal inheritance."[5]

1 Chronicles 5:1–3 Reuben was Jacob's firstborn, but when he defiled his father's marriage bed, his rights as firstborn were given to the sons of Joseph, son of Israel (Jacob); so Reuben could not be listed in the genealogical record in accordance with his birthright, and though Judah was the strongest of his brothers and a ruler came from him, the rights of the firstborn belonged to Joseph.

☞ **GO TO:**

1 Chronicles 11:2; 17:7; 2 Samuel 5:2; 6:21; 7:8 (ruler)

. . . But the Birthright Could Be Taken Away

As you can see from this text, the birthright of an eldest son could be lost. In this case, Reuben lost his for sleeping with his father's **concubine** (Genesis 35:22). A high standard of behavior was expected from an eldest son.

concubine: *a woman who lives with a man without marriage*

Think About It

The oldest son did something disgraceful, but look how God used it for good. Joseph went on to be one of the major characters in God's plan for the Israelites. Joseph saved Egypt from the plague and it became a refuge for David's family. The Israelites lived there for four hundred years before being set free by Moses.

Don't take your inheritance of salvation too lightly. It cost the life of Jesus Christ.

Genesis 25:29–34 Once when Jacob was cooking some stew, Esau came in from the open country, famished. He said to Jacob, "Quick, let me have some of that red stew! I'm famished!" (That is why he was also called **Edom**.) Jacob replied, "First sell me your birthright."

"Look, I am about to die," Esau said. "What good is the birthright to me?"

But Jacob said, "**Swear to me** first." So he swore an oath to him, selling his birthright to Jacob.

Then Jacob gave Esau some bread and some **lentil** stew (see GWHN, page 39). He ate and drank, and then got up and left.

So Esau despised his birthright.

Edom: *"red"*

Swear to me: *a verbal, binding agreement*

lentil: *a small pea-like plant which turns red when cooked.*

It Could Also Be Given Away

Here you can see that Esau placed little value on his birthright and traded it away for a mere bowl of stew (see GWBI, page 20).

This is an instance of God using evil for his own purposes. Jacob was a schemer, and he cheated his brother out of his birthright. God allowed this for his own larger purpose.

Don't allow your birthright to be stolen away by sin or frittered away by things of this world.

Think About It

Isn't it interesting that Esau despised his birthright and the younger was allowed to take his place? This can be likened to the Jewish people who also rejected their birthright (Jesus) and the Gentiles received it.

What Others are Saying:

J. Alec Motyer: What Esau saw as "taking a relaxed view" the Bible calls "sexually immoral" and "godless" [Hebrews 12:16]—the attitude that lives this life as if there were no eternal life, no absolute values. For Esau, there was no place of repentance [Hebrews 12:17].[6]

PROMISING CHILDREN TO GOD

> **Luke 2:22–24** When the time of their <u>purification</u> according to the Law of Moses had been completed, Joseph and Mary took him to Jerusalem to present him to the Lord [as it is written in the Law of the Lord, "Every firstborn male is to be consecrated to the Lord"], and to offer a <u>sacrifice</u> in keeping with what is said in the Law of the Lord: "a pair of doves or two young pigeons."

☞ **GO TO:**

Leviticus 12:8 (purification)

Leviticus 12:8 (sacrifice)

Jesus Was Consecrated

When the time came, Mary and Joseph traveled about five miles to Jerusalem to present their firstborn male child at the temple. Following the birth of a child, a woman was considered unclean for forty days. At that time she had to offer a sacrifice in order to be made clean. There is no mention, however, of redeeming Jesus for the price of five shekels.

In the Old Testament, God clearly set up the tradition of consecrating the firstborn child. Jesus was God's firstborn and here he is being consecrated for special service to him. Only God knew exactly what that meant.

Paul D. Gardner: In accordance with tradition, Jesus was presented in the Temple as a child. Again it is important to see that this incident is recounted, not just as a pleasant childhood story, but because of its significance for Jesus' identification as the one who was Saviour and redeemer and because of what it said about his calling and mission.[7]

☞ **GO TO:**

Genesis 28:20–22; Numbers 21:2; Psalm 50:14 (vow)

> **1 Samuel 1:10–11** In bitterness of soul Hannah wept much and prayed to the LORD. And she made a vow, saying, "O LORD Almighty, if you will only look upon your servant's misery and remember me, and not forget your servant but give her a son, then I will give him to the LORD for all the days of his life, and no razor will ever be used on his head."

A Promise Made

How many of us have gone to the Lord with a heavy heart and begged him for something we wanted so badly, we promised God anything, anything if he'd just answer our prayer? Here, Hannah is so desperate for a son that she promises her firstborn to God's service.

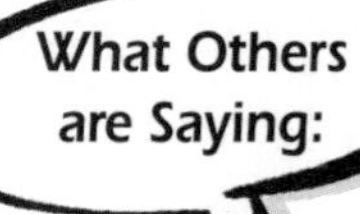

Kay Arthur: Are you going through a difficult situation, a trial? Does it feel like more than you can bear? It is not. The situation, whatever its shape or form, is designed to make you, not to destroy you. It has been permitted by God to mold you into the image of His Son rather than disfigure you for life. God doesn't test us to see if we'll fail but to show us how strong we are. He does it for the sake of proving us, and He wants us to score a hundred on the exam![8]

Margaret Wold: Hannah had no training in prayer, and her theological understandings of the nature of prayer can be questioned by theologians. She was bitter. She bargained with God. But Hannah prayed! Publicly. And even though her voice was soft and perhaps hoarse with the intensity of emotion, she prayed. God does not regard professionalism in prayer as important. It's the heart that matters and the fact that one prays at all.[9]

> **1 Samuel 1:20–22, 24–28** So in the course of time Hannah conceived and gave birth to a son. She named him Samuel, saying, "Because I asked the LORD for him." When the man Elkanah went up with all his family to offer the annual sacrifice to the LORD and to fulfill his vow, Hannah did not go. She said to her husband, "After the boy is **weaned**, I will take him and present him before the LORD, and he will live there always." . . .
>
> After he was weaned, she took the boy with her, young as he was, along with a three-year-old bull, an ephah of flour and a skin of wine, and brought him to the house of the LORD at Shiloh. . . . they brought the boy to Eli, and she said to him, "As surely as you live, my lord, I am the woman who stood here beside you praying to the LORD. I prayed for this child, and the LORD has granted me what I asked of him. So now I give him to the LORD. For his whole life he will be given over to the LORD." And he worshiped the LORD there.

☞ GO TO:

1 Samuel 1:3–4; Leviticus 7:16; Psalm 50:14 (annual sacrifice)

1 Samuel 1–4 (Eli)

weaned: *it was customary to nurse children three years or more*

A Promise Kept

Hannah was an extraordinary woman.

She must've spent the first years of Samuel's life treasuring every moment, watching him crawl, then walk, and run. Impressing his first words into her memory, and his smile when he held a newborn lamb or as he played games with his half brothers and sisters.

The pain must've been almost unbearable as she made the trip to Jerusalem to leave her son, her precious child whom she had waited for so long, with strangers.

How many times she must've wavered, and yet she kept her word. She gave Samuel into the care of the Lord.

KEY POINT

Motherhood is a partnership with God.

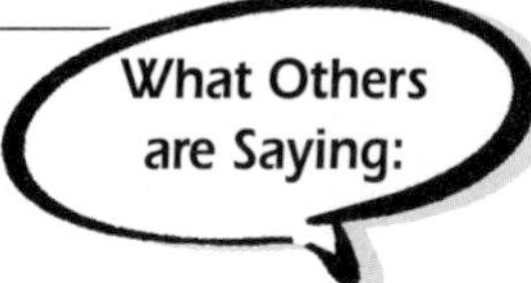

Cheri Fuller: Then the time came for [Hannah] to fulfill her vow and take [Samuel] to the temple to live and serve God. He was probably no more than three years old. How difficult it must have been for her to let go of her beloved firstborn son, the one she'd prayed and wept for! But as she had trusted God to answer her prayers, so she trusted Samuel into Eli's hands and God's safekeeping, dedicating him to the Lord's service in the temple.[10]

Begin today to keep your word. If you tell someone that you'll do something, do it. Whether you are at work or at home, the people around you need to see that a Christian does what she says. If you can't do something, then be up front and let that person know.

Grow Your Marriage

Think about how hard it must've been for Hannah's husband to allow her to keep the vow she'd made. He was an extraordinary man. Are you married to someone like him? Let him know today how much you appreciate his willingness to let you be all God wants you to be.

For Single Moms—Did you make the decision to give your baby up for adoption? You probably had many fears and doubts as you wrangled back and forth with that decision. Perhaps you, more than any of us, can empathize with Hannah.

GO TO:

Judges 1:34 (Danites)

Genesis 11:30; 16:1; Genesis 25:21; 1 Samuel 1:2; Luke 1:7 (sterile)

Genesis 16:7 (angel of the Lord)

Numbers 6:1–21 (Nazirite)

***Nazirite:** one separated or set apart for the service of God*

Judges 13:2–5 A certain man of Zorah, named Manoah, from the clan of the Danites, had a wife who was sterile and remained childless. The angel of the Lord appeared to her and said, "You are sterile and childless, but you are going to conceive and have a son. Now see to it that you drink no wine or other fermented drink and that you do not eat anything unclean, because you will conceive and give birth to a son. No razor may be used on his head, because the boy is to be a **Nazirite**, set apart to God from birth, and he will begin the deliverance of Israel from the hands of the Philistines."

Another Promise Made

This was how Samson's mother received the announcement of his birth. She, like so many other women of the Bible, was sterile and longing for a child. When the angel appeared to her, she was ready to make a commitment to carry out the requirements for his birth. Like Hannah, she dedicated her son, before she even conceived him, to the work of the Lord.

The Nazirite (Nazarite) vow was a strict way of living. It involved abstaining from wine, vinegar, grapes, raisins, and grape juice. These were staples in the Hebrew diet and would be like giving up bread or sugar for us today.

A Nazirite had to let his hair grow long, and must not go near a dead body, even if his own mother or father or brother or sister died. Nazirites must keep themselves holy. These restrictions were the outward signs of total devotion to God.

Most Nazirite vows were for a period of time and could be ended with a series of offerings, but Samson's was to be a lifetime commitment. (See GWWB, page 128.)

Manoah, the father of Samson, must have prayed many times for the wisdom to raise this boy so that Samson would fulfill his destiny. At times, Manoah probably felt unworthy and scared.

☞ **GO TO:**

Judges 13:8, 12 (work of the Lord)

What Others are Saying:

Herbert Lockyer: This faithful, self-sacrificing holy woman then, must have had a life corresponding to the separated character of the son she was to bear, and grace was hers to dedicate him to the Lord before his birth.[11]

A Letter to God

Dear God,

Was Samson and the haircut thing a big disappointment to you?

Love,

Charlie (age 11)[12]

FROM JUDY'S HEART

Did you consecrate your firstborn to the Lord?

I remember lying in my hospital bed with that little miracle feeding at my breast. He stared at me with those dark blue eyes as if he had something important he needed to tell me. Was it a message from God whose presence he had just left? I like to think that if he could have talked he would've said, "Hi Mom. I'm really glad to meet you. God told me that he had picked someone special to be my mother. He said you like to laugh and that you know lots of fun games to play. He said you would love me more than life itself. I was a little nervous, but I can see by the look in your eyes that God was right.

"He made me special just for you and Dad. I'm not perfect, but then God warned me that you aren't either. He said we'll all help each other grow up. All I need from you is love and encouragement.

"He also wanted me to tell you that he loves you very much and that he will be right alongside of you helping you to raise me. Even when you fail, he'll be there. So you're not to worry so much. My life is in his hands."

And this is what I would have said back to him, "Okay kid, I want you to grow up to be everything God intended because I know he has some purpose for your life. In order to accomplish this I will teach you about God and his ways. I will discipline you when you need it and I will kiss your hurts away and I will love you as much as is humanly possible. God, who loves you even more than I, will direct your paths. This won't always be easy, but he has something greater in mind than I do. He knew you before he gave you to me and he wants you to spend eternity with him. You might experience suffering, but it is always with a purpose—your salvation. Nothing is more important to God or to me."

I didn't call it consecration, but that's pretty much what I promised God that day in that hospital room.

Things You Learn from Your Children

- Superglue is forever.
- Legos will pass through the digestive tract of a four-year-old.
- 911 has at least a three-minute response time.

MODERN TRADITIONS

> **1 Corinthians 7:14** For the unbelieving husband has been **sanctified** through his wife, and the unbelieving wife has been sanctified through her believing husband. Otherwise your children would be **unclean**, but as it is, they are holy.

GO TO:

Malachi 2:15 (sanctified)

Acts 10:14, 28; 11:8 (unclean)

sanctified: *to make holy*

unclean: *ceremonially impure*

Baby Dedications

The Christian church no longer practices circumcision or the consecrating of babies on the thirtieth day. However, other rituals have replaced these Jewish traditions.

In some churches, babies are brought before the congregation sometime in their first year. They are presented by the parents, prayed over by the congregation, and blessed by the pastor. This is a pact between the participants that they will all work together to raise this child up to be a believer.

They believe, as is implied by this scripture, that children are covered by the grace of God until they are of an age to make their own decision about whether or not to be a follower of Jesus Christ.

What Others are Saying:

Reverend Michael Lindvall: Tina, eighteen and unwed, brought her baby, Jimmy, one Sunday to be baptized. She looked so young and vulnerable standing there all alone. I read the opening part of the service and then I asked, "Who stands with this child?" Expecting only her mother to respond, my eyes went back to the service book. I was just about to ask Tina the parent's question when I became aware of movement in the pews. One by one, people stood until the whole congregation was on its feet standing with little Jimmy.[13]

For Single Moms—If you are a single mom, the church should be there for you.

Don't hesitate to reach out to various ministries, mom's groups, and Sunday school. If you withdraw into your home because you are ashamed, no one will know of your needs.

It may be uncomfortable at first, but once the other men and women get to know you, they will be there for you.

> **Acts 16:33** At that hour of the night the jailer took them and washed their wounds; then immediately he and all his family were <u>baptized</u>.

☞ GO TO:

Acts 16:15 (baptized)

Should Babies Be Baptized?

An argument for baptizing babies is found in this verse. This household surely had infants in it. Were they baptized right along with the adults?

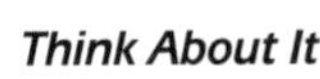

There are basically two camps on this issue. One holds that baptism is reserved for those who have made a confession of faith, and since babies are incapable of doing this, baptizing them is unnecessary. The other holds that it is necessary, because unbaptized infants who die cannot enter heaven, but are instead consigned to a state of limbo, and if such a fate is to be avoided babies must be baptized to remove the guilt of their "original sin" and receive new life.[14]

Support for the latter view includes:

- The above scripture where a whole household was described as being baptized, with the belief that these households must've contained children (see also Acts 16:15).
- Jesus' treatment of children. Jesus commanded the disciples to bring the children to him. When they did so, he blessed them (Mark 10:13–16). Because of this example from Jesus, it would seem inconsistent to deny baptism to children today.
- Baby baptism can be likened to circumcision of the Old Testament, which was a sign of God's covenant relation with his people and a reminder that this child was to live a holy life.
- Infant baptism has been practiced in the church from early times, certainly as early as the second century.[15]

An issue that divides those groups that practice infant baptism is the question of which infants should be baptized.

In general, the covenant theologians (Presbyterians, Lutherans, and the various Reformed groups) insist that only the children of believing parents should be included.

Roman Catholics, however, baptize even infants and children whose parents have not made such a commitment, believing that the rite itself has the power to bring about salvation. There is some faith necessary here, too. The person administering such a baptism must believe that the sacrament has saving power; also, whoever brings and presents the child is showing at least a certain degree of faith by doing so.

Those who do not practice infant baptism argue that the Bible teaches the implicit faith of infants (Matthew 18:6; Luke 1:15; 1 John 2:13). They argue that, if Jesus could speak of *"these little ones who believe in Me"* (Matthew 18:6), and if John the Baptist was filled with the Holy Spirit even from his mother's womb, then little children can have implicit faith and do not need baptism until they are old enough to know what it means.

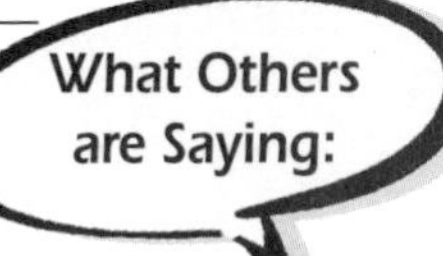

Nelson's Illustrated Bible Dictionary: The problem of the faith of children is not a difficult issue. It is a potential faith. So also is the salvation. God promises to give the benefits signified in baptism to all adults who receive it by faith. This same promise is extended to all infants who, when they grow to maturity, remain faithful to the vows that were made on their behalf at the time of their baptism. In this view, baptism's saving work depends on the faith that will be, rather than upon the faith that is.[16]

Jewish Customs Today

The custom of redeeming the firstborn son is still practiced among the Jews today. When the baby is thirty days old, the father invites a **Kohen** to the house. The father shows the Kohen the child and tells him that the mother is Jewish. The Kohen asks the father which he prefers, his child or five shekels. The father pays the Kohen five shekels and the Kohen then pronounces the Aaronite blessing.[17]

Kohen: *a descendant of Aaron*

☞ **GO TO:**

Numbers 6:22–27 (Aaronite blessing)

Study Questions

1. What is the significance of the firstborn male?
2. Name the privileges and responsibilities of the firstborn male.
3. What were the similarities between Samuel and Samson's mothers?
4. What were the differences?
5. What is the purpose of modern baby dedications and baptisms?
6. Name three reasons churches practice baby baptism.

CHAPTER WRAP-UP

- In the Jewish tradition, all firstborn males were to be consecrated to the Lord. Thirty days after their birth, they were taken to the Temple and redeemed with five shekels of silver.
- The firstborn male was well-loved by his parents and inherited a double portion of the family wealth, but he also bore the burden of caring for the family after the death of his father.
- The firstborn male could lose this privilege if he misbehaved or treated his position with disrespect, such as Reuben and Esau did.
- Jesus was the firstborn of God. He had to be redeemed.
- The mothers of Samuel and Samson dedicated their firstborns to the service of God before the boys were even born. This

meant great sacrifice for both mothers, but each of their children grew into great men of God.

- Many churches practice baby dedication and baptisms. There are many reasons for these rituals, one of which is for the whole community to make a pact with the parents to help raise their children to believe in Jesus Christ as their Lord and Savior.

JUDY'S BOOKSHELF

- *Parenting: Questions Women Ask*, Gail MacDonald, Karen Mains, and Kathy Peel, Multnomah. Common questions mothers ask and practical answers from godly women.
- *Building Your Child's Faith,* Alice Chapin, Thomas Nelson. Practical things you can do to build your child's faith.
- *Normal Is Just a Setting on Your Dryer,* Patsy Clairmont, Focus on the Family. Humorous look at what "normal" really means.

Part Three

RAISING UP

REVEREND FUN

"Your father has agreed to stay awake in church today since it is Mother's Day . . . it would be nice if you would do the opposite for once."

8 MAINTAIN A POSITIVE ATTITUDE

WHAT'S IN THIS CHAPTER

- Learn to Laugh
- Build Your Faith
- Get Some Help

Here We Go

Motherhood is a tough job. Those who think they will leave the hospital with a cute little bundle who will give them the love they've been seeking are quickly disappointed. Children are takers. Their daily needs and demands drain us of our energy, our patience, and our sense of humor.

Oh yes, there are moments of pure joy when they say, "I love you" and our hearts melt, or when they fall asleep and look like little angels. But there are other moments when we can't get them to stop crying no matter what we try, when they fight with their brother or sister endlessly, when they break our favorite lamp, or get into trouble at school.

If we aren't careful, the negative can overwhelm us and turn motherhood into an ordeal to be endured rather than a blessing from God. The key is our attitude. Let's look at what the Bible has to say.

LEARN TO LAUGH

> **Genesis 21:6** Sarah said, "God has brought me **laughter**. . . ."

☞ **GO TO:**

Genesis 17:17 (laughter)

laughter: *temporary disbelief*

Are We Having Fun Yet?

Sarah burst out laughing from total disbelief when she was told that she was going to have a baby. She, an old woman, was going to have a baby! She probably chuckled throughout her pregnancy and made jokes to her maidservants and laughed with Abraham at night. So tickled was she that she named her son Isaac, which means "laughter." (See GWWB, page 40.)

After putting her children to bed, a mother changed into old slacks and a droopy blouse and proceeded to wash her hair. As she heard the children getting more and more rambunctious, her patience grew thin. At last she threw a towel around her head and stormed into their room, putting them back to bed with stern warnings. As she left the room, she heard her three-year-old say with a trembling voice, "Who was that?"

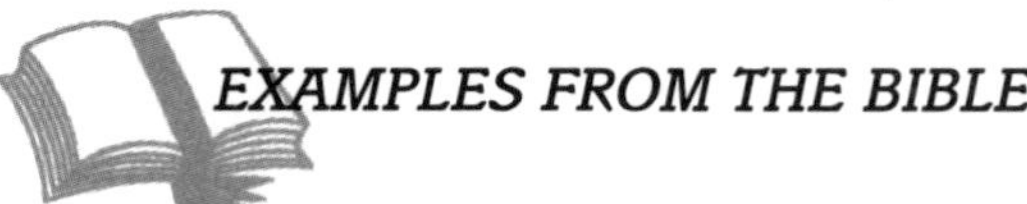

In Genesis it says we are made in God's image. This includes our emotions. We get angry, we love, we weep, and we laugh.

Think About It

Laughter releases morphine-like substances, called endorphins, in the brain. They cause pleasure and relieve pain. When was the last time you laughed right out loud? If you can't remember, then make a plan to put some fun back into your life.

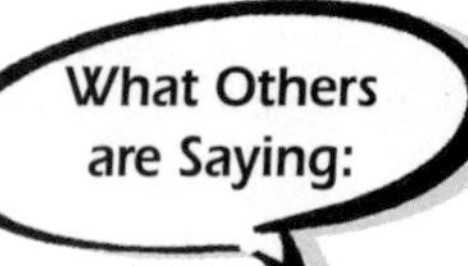

Patricia H. Rushford: Laughter is a natural spring that bubbles up inside us. Having been created in the image of God, we are born with the ability to laugh. . . . Can you remember the last time you laughed so hard you cried, fell to the floor, and rolled from side to side, holding your aching tummy? If you can't, it's been too long.[1]

> **Genesis 21:6b** ". . . , and everyone who hears about this will **laugh** with me."

☞ **GO TO:**

Genesis 17:17; 18:12; Exodus 32:6 (laugh)

laugh: *merriment*

KEY POINT

Enjoying your child is a key element to good parenting.

Laugh, and the World Laughs with You

Laughter is contagious.

If you don't believe me, next time you go to the grocery store, smile at everyone you meet. They will automatically smile back.

The same is true of your children. If you are laughing and smiling, they can't help but catch it from you.

It's a big responsibility, but Mom sets the tone for the whole household.

How does your child perceive you? (Check one.)

- ❑ The director?
- ❑ The organizer?
- ❑ The cleaner?
- ❑ The cook?
- ❑ The disciplinarian?
- ❑ The tutor?
- ❑ The grammarian?
- ❑ The shopper?
- ❑ The postponer?

KEY POINT

Schedule fun times with your children.

What Others are Saying:

Barbara Johnson: Laughter CAN be contagious, not to mention unpredictable. As somebody said, perhaps laughter is the cheapest luxury we have. It stirs up the blood, expands the chest, electrifies the nerves, clears away the cobwebs from the brain, and gives the whole system a cleansing rehabilitation. A good laugh is the best medicine, whether you are sick or not. In fact laughter is to life what salt is to an egg.[2]

> **Proverbs 31:25** She is clothed with strength and dignity; she can **laugh** at the days to come.

☞ **GO TO:**

Psalm 32:11; Isaiah 55:12; Nehemiah 8:12 (laugh)

laugh: *to rejoice, be joyful*

A Merry Heart Doeth Good Like a Medicine

In this verse, we encounter a different kind of laughter. It's a spontaneous feeling of joy.

This woman looks into the future and laughs.

She knows that she can't control tomorrow or next week or next year, but only the moment.

She can choose to fuss and fume and make everyone miserable or she can choose to live in the moment and trust the future to God.

What Others are Saying:

Liz Curtis Higgs: Any woman who can, as the Hebrew declares, "smile, laugh, make merry, celebrate, rejoice, and have no fear" about the future is my kind of role model. She didn't just smile, she snorted. She didn't just giggle, she guffawed. She didn't just snicker, she roared. What a woman![3]

Randy Rolfe: Your day as a parent can be filled with humor, little jokes, insights, little tricks, and realizations of profundity, if only you know how to detect and appreciate them. With these you can be constantly replenishing your parental energy and faith, even in the midst of everyday challenges both big and small.[4]

Don't laugh at your children, only with them. And if they bring home inappropriate humor from school, resist being outraged. Instead, explain calmly why it's harmful.

☞ **GO TO:**

2 Corinthians 6:6; Ephesians 4:2; 5:9; Colossians 3:12–15 (fruit of the Spirit)

1 Timothy 1:9 (law)

joy: *calm delight*

> **Galatians 5:22–23** But the fruit of the Spirit is love, **joy**, peace, patience, kindness, goodness, faithfulness, gentleness and self-control. Against such things there is no law.

Picking the Fruit of the Spirit

Joy is a byproduct of the Holy Spirit dwelling in our lives. We don't earn it and we don't deserve it. We just need to partake by allowing the Holy Spirit to work in us.

Notice the singular "fruit."

If you are a believer, then joy is in you.

It's not something you earn by doing good deeds and it's not something you need to create in yourself.

It's like oil under the ground that only needs to be tapped into.

Think About It

If you're not feeling joy, could it be that you've allowed something to block it out? Are you too busy? Do you worry too much? Do you spend regular time developing a relationship with the Lord? Do you spend time just enjoying your children?

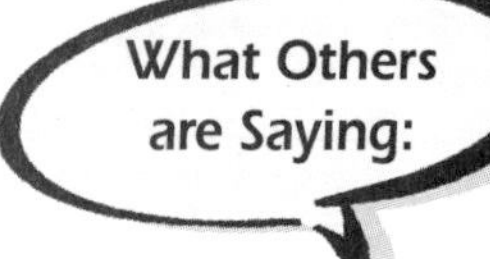

Chuck Swindoll: Worry is serious business. It can drain our lives of joy day after day. And there is not one of us who doesn't wrestle with the daily grind of it.[5]

☞ **GO TO:**

John 20:29 (seen)

> **1 Peter 1:8** Though you have not seen him, you love him; and even though you do not see him now, you believe in him and are filled with an inexpressible and glorious joy.

The Ultimate Source of Joy

We look for joy in our children, in our relationships with our husbands, in the things we do. However, true joy, the kind that wells up deep within us, has only one source—Jesus Christ. Seek a relationship with him and joy will be a part of your everyday life.

Sources of Joy

Suffering ....John 16:20; Romans 5:3–4
Persecution ..... Matthew 5:11–12; Acts 5:41
Faith................ Romans 15:13
Hope .... Romans 5:2
Joy of others .... Romans 12:15
God .... Psalm 35:9; 43:4; Isaiah 61:10; Luke 1:47; Romans 5:11; Philippians 3:1; 4:4

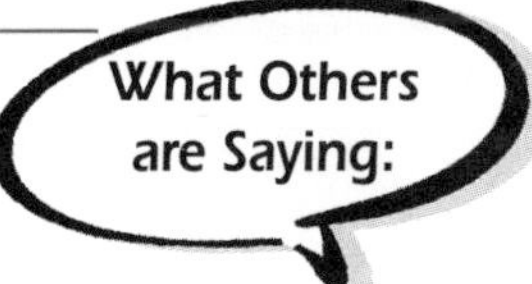

Dr. John Townsend: Your child needs to see that you are a better parent to him by virtue of being connected to God. As you go to the Source in prayer, worship, and study, you receive what you need to love your child better.[6]

Learn to laugh with your husband.

Share with him funny things that happen during your day. Read a humorous book and share the highlights. Go see a comedy at your local movie theater.

There are lots of ways to lighten up your marriage, if you'll just look for the sunny side of things. Make it a rule not to bring up negative issues while you are having fun. Keep the issues for another time. Learn to enjoy your times together.

Your children will reap the benefits.

BUILD YOUR FAITH

THE BIG PICTURE

1 Samuel 1:9–28 Hannah is barren. She pleads with God to give her a son and vows to give him over to the service of the Lord. God hears her and when a son is born, she faithfully keeps her promise. When he is about three years old, she takes him to the temple and gives him over to the care of Eli.

Cultivating Faith

One of the best things we can do for our children is to cultivate our own faith.

Here Hannah made a vow to God and then kept it. She was faithful even though it must've caused her unbearable pain. She set an example to everyone around her. The result was that her son Samuel went on to be one of the greatest prophets in the Old Testament, and she was also rewarded with more children.

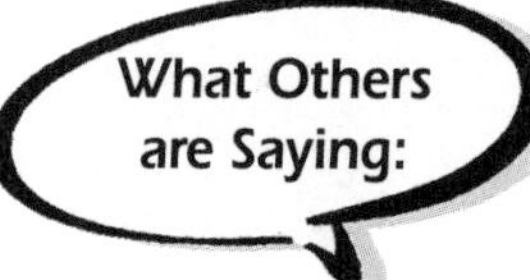

Cheri Fuller: What were the results of Hannah's bringing her need to God in prayer and trusting her child to him? Her sorrow turned to joy. Freedom and blessing abounded. As she dedicated Samuel to God, her heart sang a song of praise which begins with "*My heart exults in the Lord.*" Later God blessed her with three more sons and two daughters. Samuel grew before the Lord, becoming God's chosen spokesperson in a time in history when words and vision from God were rare.[7]

Karen Mains: Imagine your children having the same kind of relationship with Christ that you have. Is that what you desire for them? If you want more for them, begin seeking more for yourself so your children can follow your example.[8]

Charles Meigs: What is home without a Bible? 'Tis a home where daily bread for the body is provided, but the soul is never fed.[9]

John MacArthur: [Mothers,] take inventory in your own hearts. Do you thirst for God as the deer pants after the water? Or is your own life sending your children a message of hypocrisy and spiritual indifference? Is your own commitment to Christ what you hope to see in your children's lives? Is your obedience to His Word the same kind of submission you long to see from your own kids? These are crucial questions each parent must face if we really want to be successful parents and good role models for our children. Parents who are lax in these areas virtually guarantee that their sons and daughters will fail spiritually. For parents to be derelict in their own spiritual lives is tantamount to cutting down all the shade trees for the next generation in their family.[10]

If your husband is not a believer, you can still set a role model for your children.

Develop a relationship with God and let the fruit of the Spirit show through everything you do and say. Encourage your husband, but don't nag or place Scriptures in his lunch or give him tracts in the guise of Christmas cards. Let your behavior win him over (1 Peter 3:1–6).

Matthew 8:26 He replied, "You of <u>little faith</u>, why are you so afraid?" Then he got up and rebuked the <u>winds</u> and the waves, and it was completely calm.

GO T

Matthew 4
(little fait

Psalm 65:7; 89:9; 107:29 (winds)

Faith Drives Out Fear

In this passage Jesus correlates fear with a lack of faith. If we have faith we can accomplish anything, and peace will reign in our hearts even when there is a storm raging all around. (See GWBI, page 296.) Children need a mother who can stay calm no matter what the crisis.

What Others are Saying:

Gigi Graham Tchividjian: God gives us the strength as mothers to do what is "unnatural." It is against our nature to get up three or four times a night, yet we do it. It is against our nature to wipe dirty bottoms, clean up vomit, wipe runny noses, wash piles of dirty laundry, yet we do it. It is against the natural to be unselfish, yet as mothers, we have to be. . . . El Shaddai means the all-sufficient one. Because of His all-sufficiency we can be sufficient for the task.[11]

Fear is often the source of anger.

Think about the last time your child put himself in danger. What was your reaction? Was it anger? Do you worry about stretching your money from paycheck to paycheck and find yourself angry whenever anyone wastes food, or paper towels, or toothpaste?

You won't be able to bring calm back into your life until you discover the source of your anger. Next time you find yourself angry with your children, look for the underlying fear.

Don't be too perfect. Our children need to know that sometimes we feel afraid, too. One way to communicate this is by sharing our own childhood fears with them. This assures them that fear is a normal part of growing up and that, even when you can't be with them, God is.

. nite: *a Gentile; not .ne Jewish faith*

demon-possession: *under the control of a demon*

☞ **GO TO:**

Matthew 4:24; Luke 8:28; John 10:21 (demon-possession)

Matthew 9:22 (faith)

Matthew 15:22–28 A **Canaanite** woman from that vicinity came to him, crying out, "Lord, Son of David, have mercy on me! My daughter is suffering terribly from **demon-possession**."

Jesus did not answer a word. So his disciples came to him and urged him, "Send her away, for she keeps crying out after us."

He answered, "I was sent only to the lost sheep of Israel."

The woman came and knelt before him. "Lord, help me!" she said.

He replied, "It is not right to take the children's bread and toss it to their dogs."

"Yes, Lord," she said, "but even the dogs eat the crumbs that fall from their masters' table."

Then Jesus answered, "Woman, you have great faith! Your request is granted." And her daughter was healed from that very hour.

Pray for Your Child's Needs

In this passage a woman who is not of the Jewish faith comes and begs Jesus to heal her daughter. She must have been persistent, because the disciples tell Jesus to ignore her. At first Jesus says no to her request, implying that his works are only for the Jewish nation. Her reply that even the dogs are allowed to eat the crumbs under the table impresses him. Because of her faith, he heals her child.

We can take our children's needs to the Lord and he will listen. And because of our faith he will answer our prayers on their behalf.

What Others are Saying:

Dr. William Sears and Martha Sears, R.N.: If you have a Christian physician, you can ask him or her to pray with you for your child when your child is sick. This practice gives your child total Christian medical care. We are given clear instructions on how to pray for the sick in James 5:14–15. If there is a particularly disturbing medical problem, we recommend you call the elders of the church and ask them to come and pray over your child, perhaps even anointing with oil, for healing.[12]

Alice Chapin: Many of us wait until a problem arises, or until tragedy occurs, before we disrupt our routines for a moment of prayer. And then, when we finally do take time to pray, too often we hurriedly stumble before the throne of grace, mumbling a "forgive me for my sins" preface, hoping we have thereby won the favor and blessing of God. Shame on us if we pass along to our children such a haphazard unscriptural approach to prayer![13]

> **James 2:14–17** What good is it, my brothers, if a man claims to have faith but has no deeds? Can such faith save him? Suppose a brother or sister is without clothes and daily food. If one of you says to him, "Go, I wish you well; keep warm and well fed," but does nothing about his physical needs, what good is it? In the same way, faith by itself, if it is not accompanied by action, is dead.

☞ **GO TO:**

Matthew 25:35–36; Luke 3:11; 1 John 3:17–18 (physical needs)

Galatians 5:6 (faith by itself)

Set the Example

In this letter, James comes across as almost shouting. What good is faith without deeds?!

And he has a very good point. Faith, if it's genuine, will automatically produce good deeds.

Otherwise, it would be like a dog not wagging its tail! A dog, if he is truly a dog, will wag his tail. He can't help it.

On the other hand, just because an animal wags its tail doesn't mean it's a dog.

When we try to do good deeds out of our own strength, we will burn out. Nowhere is this more true than in motherhood.

If we are trying to do too much out of a sense of obligation, then our actions become burdens, not delights. But when we act out of a spirit that is full of God's love, then our deeds become joys.

Perfectionism can come from a false belief that we can earn the approval and love of our family. This never works because we are loved for who we are, not for what we do.

Randy Rolfe: Let your child see you and be around you and share with you in every area of your life that is important to you. You may not think something is important. In fact, if you spend any time doing it regularly it must be important. So share all of your life.[14]

GET SOME HELP

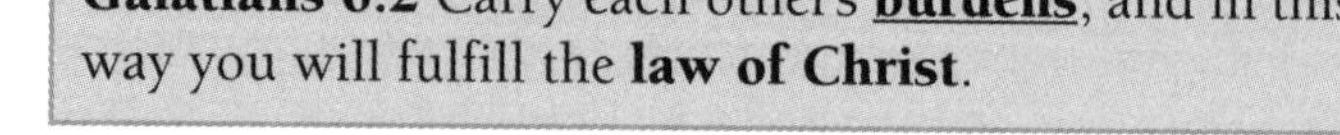

Galatians 6:2 Carry each other's **burdens**, and in this way you will fulfill the **law of Christ**.

☞ **GO TO:**

Psalm 68:19; 81:6; Romans 15:1–3 (burdens)

burdens: *problems in life or moral weaknesses*

law of Christ: *the teachings of Christ*

Just Ask

Another attitude you need to take on is one of dependence. Here it is clear that God wants to help bear our burdens, but how many of us wait until they are so heavy that we are almost broken before we allow God to help us. The same is true of accepting help from our friends, our relatives, our husbands, and even our children.

We think we should be able to do it all, but that's a big mistake.

Too often we get into trouble because we don't ask God or others for assistance. Parenting can be tough at times. Asking for help is not a sign of weakness; it's a sign of strength.

Being too dependent can be just as harmful as being too independent. If you "use" your friends, relatives, and family, and don't take your share of responsibility, you are at risk of losing their support, because the ones who love you will get tired of holding you up.

For Single Moms—Search out a church that has a ministry that can support the needs of a single mom. Volunteers can often do simple car maintenance like changing your oil. They also can help you move, provide needed bags of groceries, or even do yard maintenance.

What Others are Saying:

Dr. Henry Cloud and Dr. John Townsend: One of the most common problems we . . . hear from parents . . . is isolation. You cannot assume that being a parent means you are automatically in community. Take steps to find what resources are in your area for both parenting and personal spiritual growth help.[15]

Barbara Johnson: There is no magic place to go when we face unsurmountable problems. There is no never-never land, there is no place where "troubles melt like lemon drops, 'way above the chimney tops." We may have to live with mountains that will not move, but we can face the inevitable and realize that we have greater reserves and resources than we thought possible. We can never get our lives together until we stop looking back; we must "launch out into the deep" with God's promises. . . . Don't hesitate to open every floodgate, cross every bridge that comes. Accept the sovereign hand of God to sort out the possibilities. Remember that regardless of the turn of the tides, God alone is the source of your adequacy.[16]

> **1 Timothy 5:7** If anyone does not provide for his relatives, and especially for his immediate family, he has denied the faith and is worse than an unbeliever.

GO TO:

Luke 10:38–42; John 11:1–3 (relatives)

After All, What Are Families For?

Pride often keeps us from asking for help, but if it's hurting your family, then you are going against God's will.

Take on an attitude of seeking help, whether it be for financial counseling, marriage counseling, tutoring for your children, or medical needs. Maybe you just need a break from your kids one afternoon a week. Find a babysitting co-op or form one with a couple of neighbors.

Don't think you are in this alone. There is much wisdom out there that only need be tapped into.

Don't forget prayer. We need to spend time on our knees asking that God will meet the needs of our families.

When you reach out and ask someone for help, it gives her permission to ask you in return. And in the giving and taking, true friendships can blossom.

> **Ecclesiastes 4:9–12** Two are better than one, because they have a good return for their work: If one falls down, his friend can help him up. But pity the man who falls and has no one to help him up! Also, if two lie down together, they will keep warm. But how can one keep warm alone? Though one may be overpowered, two can defend themselves. A cord of three strands is not quickly broken.

I Get By with a Little Help from My Friends

How could any of us survive without friends? They celebrate our victories, wipe our tears, hug us, and hold our hands after our failures. They love us in spite of ourselves. Without friends life would be unbearable.

What Others are Saying:

Margaret Wold: Mary stayed with Elizabeth for three months. . . . What a marvelous time of renewal it must have been for them both! Mary had strength to go back to Nazareth and face the townspeople, her family, and Joseph.[17]

C. W. Neal: Picture a long-distance runner who has support personnel driving alongside in a car. The runner goes through the paces on her own, but she has arranged to have a support team available whenever she shows signs of need. In this journey you will have moments when an encouraging voice, a proud smile, a nod of approval, or someone to talk things over with will prove extremely valuable.[18]

Mamie McCullough: The more friends you have and the more people you know, the more support personnel you will have on your team.[19]

For Single Moms—The best thing you can do for yourself and your children is to become a friendly neighbor. Get to know the people who live around you. Insist on meeting the parents of your children's friends. The more people you know, the wider your circle of friends will grow.

FROM JUDY'S HEART

There was a period in my life when I thought I had no friends. I would look out my window at my neighbors as they talked with one another at the mailbox and feel left out. At church, there were a few women I worked with in ministry and a couple more who were in my home fellowship group, but there was no one that I thought I could call when I was hurting. No one who would understand the struggles I had.

Then one day, I read, *"Love your neighbor as yourself."* Now I had read this line a million times wondering how I could possibly love my neighbor when I didn't love myself. But this particular time, I had a new insight. It was as if God was speaking to me. "I never called you to *be* loved; I called you *to* love." He brought to mind the times I'd wished someone would call me and he pointed out that maybe, just maybe, the woman who wanted to call me was sitting at home wishing someone would call her.

And so I began a new way of living. Whenever I found myself feeling sorry for myself, I reached out to someone with a phone call, a written note, or an invitation to lunch. I made it a practice to be more interested in the women around me than they were in me. And in a world full of discouragement, I began to encourage.

The result? I now have friends. Close friends I can share many things with, who are there when I'm hurting and help me celebrate my triumphs. They are at work, at church, and in my neighborhood. Today when I see my neighbors talking at the mailbox I join them, and we have a great time enjoying one another's company.

> **Acts 4:34–35** There were no needy persons among them. For from time to time those who owned lands or houses sold them, brought the money from the sales and put it at the apostles' feet, and it was distributed to anyone as he had need.

☞ **GO TO:**

Acts 2:44, 45 (need)

That Radical Church

Today we would call this church radical. Sell our land and houses and give to the church to be distributed to those in need? My goodness, that is radical.

But remember there was no welfare system, no government handouts, and no social workers. Many of these new converts may have lost their jobs, been thrown out of their families, divorced by their spouses. There were legitimate needs and the church was the only source of help for these people.

The church is still a good resource for families. There is Sunday school, Bible studies, food programs, co-ops, women's groups, parenting classes, children's programs, marriage seminars, and counseling.

Take advantage of these programs and even volunteer back your time.

The church is like a family. Jesus described it as a body, with him being the head. The best thing we can do for ourselves, no matter what ages our children, is to get involved at our local church.

Think About It

A MOPS (Mothers of Preschoolers) member said, "MOPS means I am able to share the joys, frustrations and insecurities of being a mom. Our meetings provide the opportunity to hear someone else say, 'I was up all night,' or 'they're driving me crazy!' or 'He doesn't understand.' While listening to others, I may discover a fresh idea or a new perspective that helps me tackle the job of parenting, home management, or being a good wife. It's important to feel normal and not alone. Burdens are lifted when the woman next to me says, 'I know exactly how you feel.' "[20]

Parent's Dictionary

Feedback: the inevitable result when the baby doesn't appreciate the strained carrots.

Ow: the first word spoken by children with older siblings.

Whodunit: none of the kids that live in your house.

> **1 Corinthians 11:11** In the Lord, however, woman is not independent of man, nor is man independent of woman.

Hey, We're a Team!

In this verse, the terms *woman* and *man* could be interpreted as wife and husband. Together they make a family work more smoothly.

Ask your husband for help. Be specific about what you need, and then don't criticize him for the job he did. He may not dress the kids the way you would, but if you criticize him, he'll probably never do it again. "My way, or no way" is the slogan of a woman who gets no help around the house voluntarily.

KEY POINT

When I come to the end of my rope, God is there to take over.

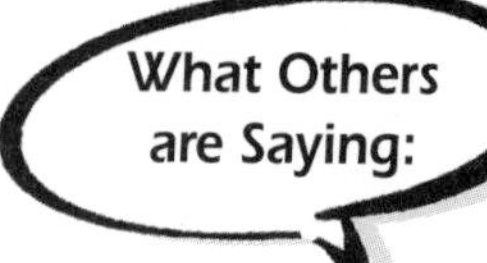

John MacArthur: The husband who thinks God ordered the family so that his wife would be at his beck and call has it backward. He is to love and serve her. The father who thinks of his wife and children as personal possessions to be under his command has a skewed concept of the responsibility that is his as head of the family. His headship means first of all that he is to serve them, protect them, and provide for their needs. In short, his duty is love—and all that is encompassed in that word.[21]

Adam Clarke's Commentary: Men and women equally make a Christian society, and in it have equal rights and privileges.[22]

Think About It

If you work full-time, consider hiring someone to come in and clean once a week. It might not be as expensive as you imagine. This will free up your weekends so that you can enjoy your family.

Trust Me, This Is for Your Own Good!

Allow your children to help around the house. Give them age-appropriate chores and then praise them richly for their work. They need to know that they are an important part of a team. This is true especially if you're a single mom.

Your children might gripe and complain and it may at times seem easier to do the chores yourself, but you need to stand firm in your requests. You are training them for more than just "house-work." You are training them for life.

What Others are Saying:

Patricia H. Rushford: If you are doing too many things that go unnoticed or unappreciated, perhaps your children aren't doing enough. I firmly believe children should be given an equal share in household chores. We wouldn't want to keep them from receiving their reward in heaven, would we?[23]

Dr. William Mitchell and Dr. Charles Paul Conn: Making children a part of a family team is of critical importance to the kinds of adults that they will become.[24]

Study Questions

1. Why is it important to laugh?
2. List the fruit of the Spirit. Identify which one is the weakest in your spirit and ask God to show you how to strengthen it.
3. Define "joy."
4. On a scale of one to ten, with ten being the highest, rate your faith. List three things you can do today that will build your faith.
5. What is the practical importance of a strong faith for a mom?

6. Name four sources of help for you and your family. What does God say about pride and independence?
7. Name three people whom you can call today, just to see how they're doing. What is the second greatest commandment?

CHAPTER WRAP-UP

- Many aspects of being a mom are tough. Attitude can make a big difference between enjoying the process and just surviving it.
- Laughter can brighten even the darkest day. Learning to laugh won't solve all your problems, but will make them seem easier. Laughter is also contagious.
- Faith in God will bring peace even in the darkest storms. Faith can be built through time in the Word, prayer, giving, attending church regularly, and sharing your faith with your children.
- Asking for help is not a sign of weakness, but a sign of strength.
- Sources of help are our church, family, neighbors, friends, husband, and children.

JUDY'S BOOKSHELF

- *What Kids Need Most in a Mom*, Patricia H. Rushford, Fleming H. Revell. Practical stuff with a touch of humor.
- *Raising Great Kids*, Dr. Henry Cloud and Dr. John Townsend, Zondervan. Focus is on building the character of your child.
- *The Christian Working Woman*, Mary Whelchel, Fleming H. Revell. Practical advice on parenting, working with difficult people, shuffling schedules, and being a Christian in the workplace.

9 FACE YOUR RESPONSIBILITY

WHAT'S IN THIS CHAPTER

- Training Your Children in the Way They Should Go
- Teaching Your Children about the Bible
- Parent as Teacher
- Biblical View of Discipline

Here We Go

As Christian mothers, our deepest desire for our children should be that they grow up knowing the Lord.

Nothing in life, not a career, or a nice home, or success, or a loving family, can steer them through the rocky waters of life like a personal relationship with the Lord can. Only a strong faith can give them the foundation they need to survive the rejection, failure, and heartbreak that they, like all people, will most likely face.

Faith will give them the hope they need to go forward even when things seem hopeless. It will provide them the confidence of knowing God specially chose them. It will give them peace knowing God is always there to protect. It will give them the joy they need to face each day knowing the Creator of the universe loves them. It also will give them the self-control they'll need to say no to the temptations that will come their way.

No one can teach them better than you. No one will influence them quite the way you do. It's a big responsibility. Are you willing to take it on?

TRAINING YOUR CHILDREN IN THE WAY THEY SHOULD GO

Proverbs 22:6 <u>**Train**</u> a child up in the <u>way he should go</u> and when he is **old** he will not depart from it.

 **GO TO:**

1 Kings 8:63; Proverbs 1:8 (train)

Genesis 18:19 (way he should go)

train: *start*

old: *grown*

KEY POINT

Your goal as a Christian mother is to raise your children to have a faith of their own.

Training Begins at Home

The word "train" in this scripture can also be translated, "initiate" or "dedicate." *"In the way he should go"* is the right way, the way of wisdom (Proverbs 4:11).

Our job is to not just give our children worldly wisdom and training towards a career, but, even more importantly, to introduce them to God and his teachings and, ultimately, a personal relationship with Jesus Christ—a faith independent of our own.

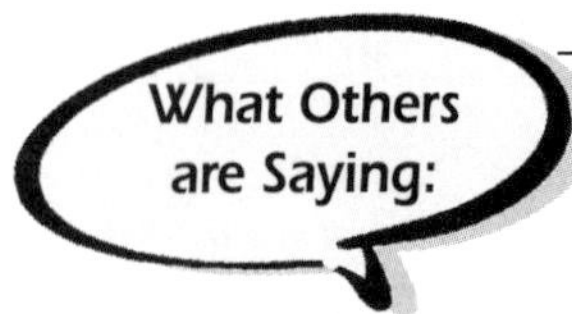

Dr. William Sears and Martha Sears, R.N.: To train a child in the way she should go, you must know which way she should go. Almost all parents truly love their children; however, parents vary in the degree to which they *know* their children.[1]

If left to their own devices, your children might choose a path of sin. It's up to you to direct them onto the right path.

GO TO:

Matthew 15:14 (blind man)

Luke 6:39 He also told them this parable: "Can a blind man lead a blind man? Will they not both fall into a pit?"

Show Them the Way

Jesus is using a story to teach his disciples a simple truth. That only those who can "see" are able to lead the spiritually "blind."

Think About It

The religious training of your children begins with you. You cannot teach them something that you don't know yourself.

If your faith is weak or if you are unsure of what you believe, now is the time to get into the Word. Take Bible study classes. Ask questions. Apply what you learn to your life.

You can't teach your children about a faith you don't have.

Luke 6:40 A student is not above his teacher, but everyone who is fully trained will be like his teacher.

Just Like Jesus

Again, Jesus uses something that every one of the disciples has experienced to teach them a point—that not one of them is higher than his teacher (Jesus), but that when they do become fully trained, they will be like him. Isn't that what we all want? To be like Jesus?

From the moment our children are born, their training begins.

Some of it is obvious. We teach them "This little piggy went to market." We teach them their ABC's, names of colors, how to count to ten, and the words to "Jesus Loves Me." We teach them how to feed themselves, tie their shoes, and go to the bathroom.

But most of what they learn is subtle, and taught by our example: love, forgiveness, anger, ridicule, acceptance, hope, worry, and faith.

We may want to teach our child the love of God, but if they never see it modeled in our behavior, they will have trouble grasping what "love" means. If they never experience acceptance, they will never understand what it means to accept others. If they hear others ridiculed for their human frailties, they will grow up ashamed of their own.

KEY POINT

Children are natural mimics—they act like their parents in spite of every attempt to teach them good manners.

What Others are Saying:

Liz Curtis Higgs: One of the reasons that the job of mother is valued by so many of us is because of the important place our own mothers had in our lives. Of the hundreds who answered the question, "Who serves as a role model for you in your family life?" more than two hundred of us listed our mothers.[2]

> **Matthew 5:6** **Blessed** are those who hunger and thirst for **righteousness**, for they will be filled.

☞ **GO TO:**

Psalm 1:1; Revelation 1:3 (blessed)

Isaiah 55:1–2 (thirst)

Genesis 18:25; Deuteronomy 32:4; Romans 9:14 (righteousness)

blessed: *a deep, spiritual joy not dependent on circumstances*

righteousness: *holy and upright living*

A Thirst for God

During his famous Sermon on the Mount, Jesus promises his listeners that those who long to be holy and pure, and live lives that are pleasing to God, will be satisfied.

If you want your children to seek God, then you must begin by developing your own craving for the things of God.

If you find it hard to take time to pray, or to attend church, or to read your Bible, then ask God to give you the desire to make the time for these things. Seek it with your whole heart. If following God is a burden, then you don't fully understand what a relationship with him is all about.

Seek the answers you're looking for. You *will* find them.

Think About It

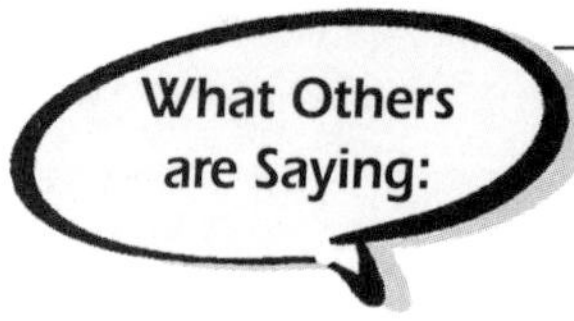

Dr. Deborah Newman: God promises that He will be found. Jeremiah 29:11–14 and 2 Chronicles 7:14 are promises that if we seek Him, He will reveal Himself to us.[3]

light: small clay lamp that burned olive oil

> **Matthew 5:16** In the same way, let your **light** shine before men, that they may see your good deeds and praise your Father in heaven.

Let Your Light Shine

GO TO:

Titus 2:14 (good deeds)

Matthew 9:8 (praise)

Jesus instructs the people to let their faith show every day in every way so that those who watch will know that God is responsible.

Think About It

Your children need to see the difference that being a believer has made in your life. In Jesus' day, small clay lamps were used as a source of light (see illustration below). These lamps burned olive oil drawn by a wick. In the above scripture, Jesus is comparing our good deeds to a lamp, a light. When things are dark, a lamp lights the way. It also draws people to it.

This is the way Jesus is asking us to be—a light that will draw our children to him.

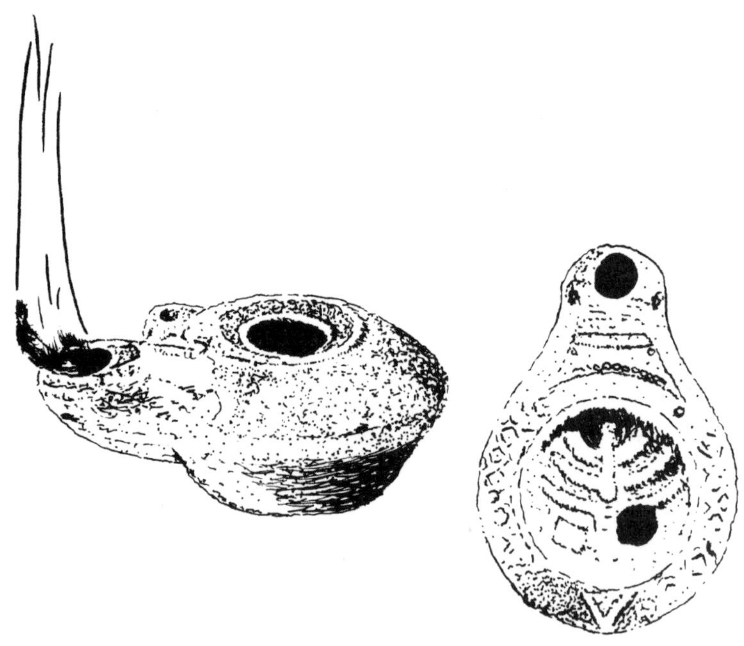

Clay Lamp

Pictured here is a clay lamp like one Jesus might have used. Note the lamp had two holes, one for oil and one for a wick. Lamps of that time burned day and night, and also had great symbolic importance, as illustrated in Scripture ("Let your light shine before men").

What Others are Saying:

Chris Fabry: Some of the most ineffective Christians today learn more about the Bible than anyone else. . . . they only listen to the Word and don't do it in their lives.[4]

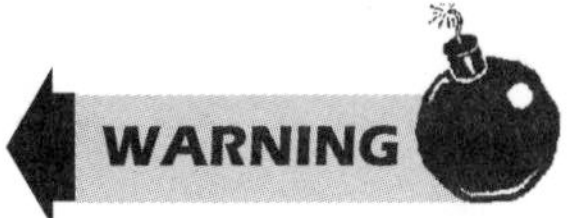

It's easy to take the credit ourselves for the good things Jesus accomplishes through us. Be sure to point your child to the source of all good things so that Jesus gets the praise, not you.

What Others are Saying:

Alvin Vander Griend: You can do everything else right as a parent, but if you don't begin with loving God, you're going to fail.[5]

> **Ephesians 5:21–24** **Submit** to one another out of reverence for Christ. Wives, submit to your husbands **as to the Lord**. For the husband is the head of the wife as Christ is the head of the church, his body, of which he is the Savior. Now as the church submits to Christ, so also wives should submit to their husbands in everything.

GO TO:

1 Corinthians 14:34; Colossians 3:18; 1 Timothy 2:12; Titus 2:5; 1 Peter 3:1, 56 (submit)

1 Corinthians 11:3 (head)

Ephesians 2:16; 4:4, 12, 16 (body)

submit: *yield one's own rights*

as to the Lord: *a woman should submit to her husband as an act of submission to the Lord.*

You're the Man!

The word "submit" can immediately make some of us defensive, but that is because we don't understand what is being said here.

First of all, we are to submit to one another, husbands to wives, wives to husbands. We are to take on an attitude that considers our mate's needs as more important than our own. It's mutual. It's seeking the best of one another. We are to do this *"as to the Lord."* Everything we do should be as if we are doing it for the Lord.

When this kind of attitude permeates our homes, our children will grow up understanding what love really means and are more likely to treat their mates with the same kind of respect.

The word "submit" does not mean "obey." The only time the word "obey" is used is when the Scripture talks about children and slaves (Ephesians 6:1, 5).

For Single Moms—Single moms only need submit themselves to the Lord. Deuteronomy 10:17–18 says, *"For the LORD your God is God of gods and Lord of lords, the great*

God, mighty and awesome, who shows no partiality and accepts no bribes. He defends the cause of the fatherless and the widow."

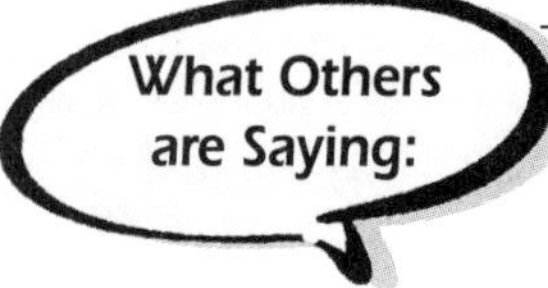

Beverly LaHaye: Women need to recognize and accept the truth that God did not create them inferior.[6]

Think About It

Is your marriage a model for your children? Or do you and your husband quarrel and belittle one another in front of the children? Do you undermine your husband's authority by letting your children disobey his orders? Do you call him names in front of them?

Your attitude will make a big difference in how they view their father and how they will view being parents.

Joseph Joubert: Children have more need of models than of critics.[7]

Grow Your Marriage

Speak highly of your husband in front of your children. This will not only strengthen your marriage, but it will be an encouragement to your children. When they know that their parents love and respect one another, they feel more secure and loved themselves.

> **Ephesians 5:33** However, each one of you also must love his wife as he loves himself, and the wife must **respect** her husband.

respect: *to consider worthy of high regard*

He's All That

Nowhere in Scripture are wives commanded to love their husbands, but here it is quite clear that they should respect them.

Why? Because love is something that comes naturally to women, but respect for our mates is hard. We have to work at it.

One of the worst things we can do to undermine our family is to usurp the authority of our husbands. Nowhere is this more important than when we are disciplining our children.

You and your husband need to show a united front, or you will lose the respect of your children. Once that respect is gone, you've lost all authority to discipline them.

If you disagree about anything, talk about it while alone together, not in front of the children.

Also check your tone of voice. It can say far more than your words.

Dr. James Dobson: Real love, in contrast to popular notions, is an expression of the deepest appreciation for another human being; it is an intense awareness of his or her needs and longings for the past, present and future. It is unselfish and giving and caring.[8]

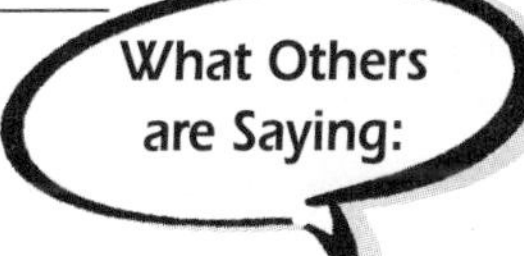

For Single Moms—If you are divorced, you can still respect the father of your children. Don't run him down in front of your children. Point out his good qualities to them. Be civil to him when you are together with the children or when you are talking with him on the phone.

> **1 Corinthians 13:1–8** If I speak in the tongues of men and of angels, but have not **love**, I am only a resounding gong or a clanging cymbal. If I have the **gift** of prophecy and can fathom all mysteries and all knowledge, and if I have a faith that can move mountains, but have not love, I am nothing. If I give all I possess to the poor and surrender my body to the flames, but have not love, I gain nothing. Love is patient, love is kind. It does not envy, it does not boast, it is not proud. It is not rude, it is not self-seeking, it is not easily angered, it keeps no record of wrongs. Love does not delight in evil but rejoices with the truth. It always protects, always trusts, always hopes, always **perseveres**. Love never fails.

☞ GO TO:

Mark 16:17 (tongues)

Ephesians 4:11 (prophecy)

1 Corinthians 12:9 (faith)

Luke 19:8 (poor)

Daniel 3:27 (flames)

1 Corinthians 8:1 (proud)

1 Corinthians 11:18–22 (rude)

The Greatest Thing in the World

Nothing is more important than teaching our children to love. In this world we are taught that love is a feeling, but in God's kingdom, love is an action and we do it even when we don't feel like it. No spiritual gift is greater. No calling is higher.

love: *a selfless concern for the welfare of others*

gift: *spiritual gift, such as that of tongues, prophecy, faith, or charity*

perseveres: *lasts*

Think About It

Do you model this kind of love for your children?

Do they see you being kind to the next-door neighbor who is rude? Do they see you becoming angry with a store clerk who has made a mistake, or a waitress who is slow bringing your meal?

Those little eyes are watching you, and learning what love truly means. What are you teaching them?

Teach your children to forgive by giving them forgiveness. Show them the right way to express anger (James 1:19) by modeling it yourself. Don't speak ill of others or gossip, thus giving your children an attitude that they are better than others (James 3:8).

Model the right way to love. It'll be the best lesson that you can give them, and your greatest legacy.

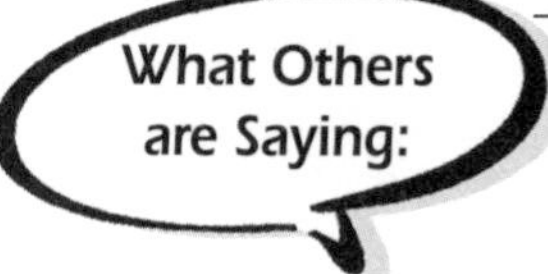

Max Lucado: There are times when we . . . are called to love, expecting nothing in return. Times when we are called to give money to people who will never say thanks, to forgive those who won't forgive us, to come early and stay late when no one else will notice.[9]

TEACHING YOUR CHILDREN ABOUT THE BIBLE

> **1 Corinthians 13:12** When I was a child, I talked like a child, I thought like a child, I reasoned like a child. When I became a man, I put childish ways behind me.

The Bible Tells Me So

Our goal of *"training a child up in the way he should go"* clearly involves some formal Bible training.

From the earliest families in Genesis to today, teaching has been the key to raising our children to adulthood. Parents the world over teach their children how to survive and even thrive in their respective societies. These lessons may include basic hygiene, good manners, proper speech, food preparation, reading, writing, arithmetic, and a trade.

Our most important task of all, however, as Christian mothers, is to teach our children about Jesus Christ.

Adam Clarke's Commentary: We understand only as children understand: speak only a few broken articulate words, and reason only as children reason; having few ideas, little knowledge but what may be called mere instinct, and that much less perfect than the instinct of the brute creation; and having no experience. But when we became men-adults, having gained much knowledge of men and things, we spoke and reasoned more correctly, having left off all the manners and habits of our childhood.[10]

What Others are Saying:

EXAMPLES FROM THE BIBLE

Jesus used examples from life to teach the apostles. For instance, in Matthew 22, the Pharisees are trying to trap him with a trick question. *"Is it right to pay taxes to Caesar or not?" He answered them by asking for a coin. "Whose portrait is this?" he asked. "Caesar's," they replied. Then he said, "Give to Caesar what is Caesar's, and to God what is God's."*

> **Deuteronomy 6:6** These **commandments** that I give to you today are to be upon your hearts.

commandments: *rules*

☞ GO TO:

Deuteronomy 11:18; 30:14; 32:46; Psalm 26:2; 37:31; 40:8; Proverbs 3:3 (hearts)

The Right Stuff

Teaching the principles in the Bible is different than teaching someone his or her ABC's. The latter is head knowledge, but the former is something that needs to be imprinted upon the heart.

Oh yes, we need Bible memorization, and children are naturally interested in the Bible stories of Daniel in the lions' den, Moses' narrow escape in a reed basket, and Jonah being swallowed by a whale.

But if these things are taught without application to the child's life, then the main message will be missed. These stories are intended to teach a way of living, a way of thinking, and a way of behavior that will develop our children's character.

Dr. John Townsend: We view character as the structures and abilities within ourselves that make up how we operate in life. In other words, character is *the sum of our abilities to deal with life as God designed us to*. . . . You can make great strides in helping your child be a person of character, or you can also miss its importance and see its effects in painful ways later in life.[11]

What Others are Saying:

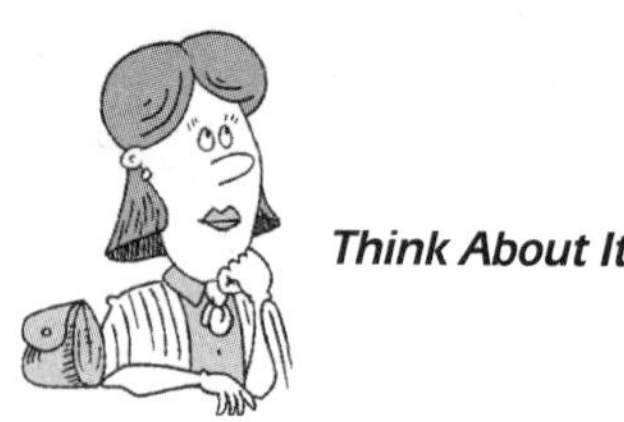

Think About It

When you begin to be more concerned with the "heart" of your children, then your discipline style will change. Instead of looking at your child's outward behavior alone, you will also look at attitude. It's no good if your child "behaves" out of fear of a spanking, of losing a privilege, or of the withdrawal of your love. How much better that they learn to behave because it's what they want to do.

Then when they have flown the nest, they will maintain the values you've taught them.

What Others are Saying:

Jean Hodges: You are never so high as when you are on your knees.[12]

Deuteronomy 6:7–9 Impress [God's commandments] on your children. Talk about them when you sit at home and when you walk along the road, when you lie down and when you get up. Tie them as symbols on your hands and bind them on your foreheads. Write them on the doorframes of your houses and on your gates.

☞ **GO TO:**

Matthew 23:5 (phylacteries)

phylacteries: *boxes containing scripture verses worn on the forehead and arm*

Object Lessons

The Israelites took this scripture literally. They tied boxes called **phylacteries** on their foreheads and arms and placed wooden or metal containers on the doorframes of their homes.

You need to take every opportunity to teach your children.

When you see a dead bird, talk about what it means to go to heaven. When you see a person with a disability, explain why God allows some people to suffer. When your children misbehave, turn it into a lesson for life. When something objectionable comes on TV, explain why this isn't pleasing to God.

When your little boy comes home from school after being called a name, take the time to let him know that God loves him, that God made him special, and that there is no one else just like him.

We can't leave our children's spiritual education to Sunday school.

Jim Raburn: It's a sin to bore children with the gospel.[13]

Here are some things to think about if your children are complaining about attending church. Are you overcommitted at church? Maybe they are resenting the time you spend there. Do you complain about church or the other members in front of your children? Maybe your attitude is rubbing off on them.

Are your children bored? It doesn't have to be that way. You could do some thinking about what might be the cause of their boredom, and what could be done about it. Maybe, for instance, your children are more advanced in their knowledge than many others their age and would get more out of an adult situation.

> **Exodus 16:32** Moses said, "This is what the LORD has commanded: 'Take an **omer** of **manna** and keep it for the generations to come, so they can see the bread I gave you to eat in the desert when I brought you out of Egypt.'"

omer: *an ancient Hebrew unit of measurement*

manna: *the food that God provided miraculously for the Israelites in the wilderness during their Exodus from Egypt*

Memory Makers

Moses was required by God to save some of the manna to remind future generations of what the Lord had done for the Israelites in the desert.

GO TO:

Exodus 16:15, 31, 33; Numbers 11:6–9 (manna)

Another way to teach is by keeping things that have spiritual meaning.

We take pictures of our children and store them in albums. We save all of their precious drawings, awards, trophies, and report cards. But what about events that mark their spiritual growth? Frame the certificates they earn at Sunday school. Celebrate their baptisms. Make confirmation as big an event as graduating from high school.

Turn religious holidays into times for them to remember what Christ has done for them. Don't just put up a Santa Claus; use a **nativity scene** and tell the story of his birth over and over. At Easter, remind them not just of the Easter bunny, but of Jesus' great sacrifice, and, most of all, tell them of his **resurrection**.

nativity scene: *portrayal of the birth of Christ*

resurrection: *rising from the dead*

GO TO:

John 20 (resurrection)

Alice Chapin: It is the inescapable calling of parents to lead their sons and daughters into the Book of books early in life. Today's children must somehow be taught that while the world changes, God does not. They must be led to seek the guidance, instruction and unchanging truth that transcends time and transforms lives. They must see Scripture as a precious heritage preserved just for them.[14]

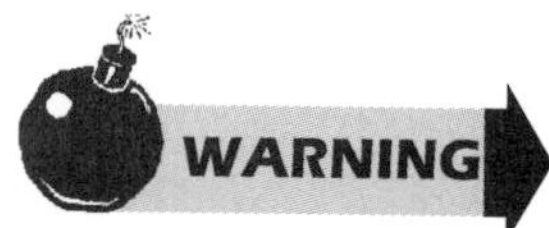

Don't get so caught up in tradition that religious events and holidays become meaningless. Seek out new and interesting ways to communicate the stories behind them. As your children grow older, bring in more details, and challenge them to think about the events and what they mean to your children personally.

Gilgal: *the first campsite of the people of Israel after they crossed the Jordan River and entered the Promised Land*

> **Joshua 4:20–22, 24** And Joshua set up at **Gilgal** the twelve stones they had taken out of the Jordan. He said to the Israelites, "In the future when your descendants ask their fathers, 'What do these stones mean?' tell them, 'Israel crossed the Jordan on dry ground.' He did this so that all the peoples of the earth might know that the hand of the LORD is powerful and so that you might always fear the LORD your God."

He's Got the Power

Joshua built a memorial to help the Israelites and their descendants remember what God had done for them there in the Promised Land, to show the rest of the world what a powerful God they served.

Think About It

Teach your children how God is working in your life. Pray for your needs with your children, and then celebrate when God answers your prayers. Share the small and big miracles in your life and in theirs. Pray for their health when your children are sick, and then give God the praise when they get better. Let them know that God is powerful and will answer their prayers.

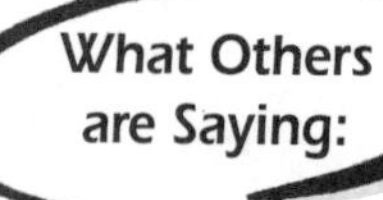

Cheri Fuller: [Charles Stanley] attributes much of his own hunger to know and trust God to the godly influence of his mother. As he was growing up, each night he and his mom knelt together beside his bed and prayed. They thanked God for His provision and protection and took their everyday concerns to Him.[15]

Don't set your children up to believe that God will answer every prayer exactly the way they want. Teach them to be realistic in their beliefs.

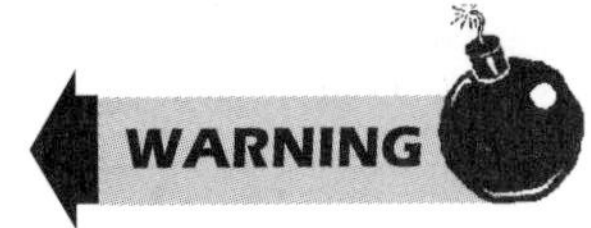

Judges 2:10–12, 14 After that whole generation had been gathered to their fathers, another generation grew up, who knew neither the LORD nor what he had done for Israel. Then the Israelites did evil in the eyes of the LORD and served the **Baals**. They forsook the LORD, the God of their fathers, who had brought them out of Egypt. . . . In his anger against Israel the LORD handed them over to raiders who plundered them. He sold them to their enemies all around, whom they were no longer able to resist.

☞ **GO TO:**

Genesis 15:15 (fathers)

Exodus 1:8 (knew)

Judges 3:7, 12; 4:1; 6:1; 10:6 (evil)

Judges 6:1; 13:1 (handed)

Judges 3:8; 4:2; 10:7 (sold)

Baals: *false gods worshiped by the Canaanites*

Their Just Desserts

This is an account of what happened to a whole generation of Israelites because they were not taught the things that God had done for them. The Israelites had been brought out of Egypt, wandered in the desert for forty years, and had finally taken hold of the Promised Land. When that generation died off, the next generation quickly forgot what God had done for them and turned to the worship of other gods. They no longer had a real leader, and lived in anarchy (Judges 21:25). Out of anger, God let them be taken over by their enemies.

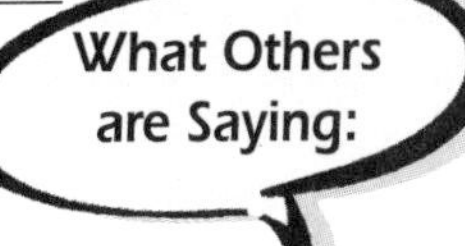

Dr. Ross Campbell: A popular misconception goes like this: "[My child] shouldn't feel he has to believe what I believe. I want him to learn about different religions and philosophies; then when he has grown up he can make his own decision." This parent is copping out or else is grossly ignorant of the world we live in. A child brought up in this manner is indeed one to be pitied. . . . One of the finest gifts parents can give to a child is a clear, basic understanding of the world and its confusing problems.[16]

If we don't teach our children what God has done for us, they are in danger of quickly forgetting God and of following, instead, the tempting gods of this world—materialism, beauty, success, and hedonism. They are all too likely to reject our values, turning to their peers for guidance.

Baal was the god worshiped by the Canaanites and Phoenicians. They believed he gave fertility to the womb and life-giving rain to the soil. The worship of Baal involved prostitution and sometimes even child sacrifice.

PARENT AS TEACHER

Both the mother and father are responsible for teaching the children. Both parents have unique gifts to bring to a marriage. One may have a love for great literature, the other for outdoor activities. Together they can provide a well-rounded education for the children.

What Others are Saying:

Nelson's Illustrated Bible Dictionary: To be a parent meant to teach. Both parents were involved in the child's education; however, the father was responsible to see that his children were properly educated [Proverbs 1:8–9]. A young son stayed with his mother when the father went to the fields to work. Therefore, a boy's first significant instruction came from his mother. As the boy grew, the father's involvement in his son's education increased, especially as they began to work together in the fields or in the father's trade. A daughter stayed on with her mother and continued under her instruction. In the close-knit family structure of that day, as parents became grandparents they also became involved in teaching their grandchildren [Deuteronomy 4:9; 2 Timothy 1:5; 3:14–15]. A parent's responsibility for instructing children continued until death.[17]

John 13:13 "You call me 'Teacher' and 'Lord,' and rightly so, for that is what I am.

The Ultimate Teacher

Jesus was called "teacher" throughout his ministry. Here, he affirms that title. We can learn much from his style of teaching when working with our children.

What Others are Saying:

Nelson's Illustrated Bible Dictionary: During the period between the Old and New Testaments, Synagogue schools were established. Generally, each rabbi taught in a village school supported by the parents of the children who attended. The teacher or rabbi of the school helped the parents by instilling religious truths in the boys' minds; however, the parents still were responsible for their children's education. In choosing a rabbi as a village teacher, the parents were more concerned with his personal character than with his ability to teach. His example was more important than his teaching skills. The ideal rabbi was a married man who also was industrious and serious. He would never joke with the boys, nor would he tolerate any wrongdoing. However, it was considered important that he be a patient man. Both rabbi and parents took God as their model for proper teaching. God was the Master Teacher (Isaiah 30:20–21), who taught by word and example (Psalm 78:1; Deuteronomy 8:2–3).[18]

> **Proverbs 1:8–9** Listen, my son, to your father's instruction and do not forsake your mother's teaching. They will be a garland to grace your head and a chain to adorn your neck.

☞ **GO TO:**

Proverbs 6:20 (mother's teaching)

Homeschooling

Many parents are now opting to homeschool their children for a variety of reasons. Whether or not you choose this option is up to you. You know your limitations and your strengths. You might take time to pray about it, read some material from your local library, and talk to other parents who are doing it or have tried it.

Some parents homeschool until junior high or high school. Others do it until their children enter college. You don't have to have a teaching certificate to make this choice, and there are a lot of support groups that weren't available even a few years ago. Here in Washington State, you can send your children to the public schools for music or sports or academic subjects you feel weak in.

A great homeschooling resource can be found online at www.homeschoolplus.com.

The education of your children is in your hands. Only you know what is right for them.

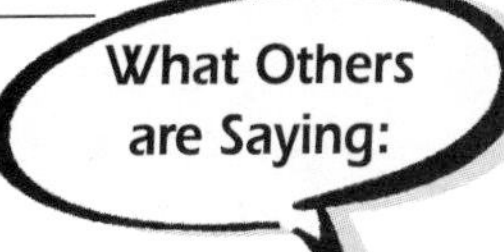

Randy Rolfe: The only reason we need teachers for school-age children is to engage in that special activity of teaching—that is, instructing some twenty kids, all the same age, all doing more or less the same things when that's not what they want to be doing. A parent who just continues teaching the way she did before school age never has to change hats. Many caring parents today get deeply involved in the child's school activities. They can think of home education simply as "eliminating the middleman."[19]

☞ **GO TO:**

Matthew 18:3; Matthew 19:13–14 (kingdom of God)

Mark 9:36–37 (such as these)

Matthew 19:13–14; Mark 5:23 (hands)

kingdom of God: *a future hope where God rules*

Mark 10:13–16 People were bringing little children to Jesus to have him touch them, but the disciples rebuked them. When Jesus saw this, he was indignant. He said to them, "Let the little children come to me, and do not hinder them, for the **kingdom of God** belongs to such as these. I tell you the truth, anyone who will not receive the kingdom of God like a little child will never enter it." And he took the children in his arms, put his hands on them and blessed them.

Some of My Best Friends Are Children

Jesus liked the openness and receptivity of children. Sin and cynicism had not blinded their eyes, false doctrines had not yet filled their minds, and self-pride had not hardened their hearts. He treated children with respect and counted them as important as the adults. When the disciples tried to keep the children away, he chastised them.

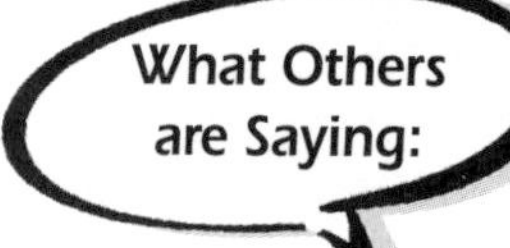

Barbara Johnson: Kids love the way light shines through crystal, ricochets off diamonds, emanates from rainbows. Crystals, diamonds, and rainbows are all designed by God. He put them in the world to remind us to take things *lightly*. He means for us to wonder and imagine what could be hidden in the darkest piece of coal or the rainiest day on earth. As Christians, part of our assignment is to be curious. Kids never think they have all the answers, and we shouldn't either. Thinking we know it all closes our hearts to what is beautiful and new.[20]

KEY POINT

Treat your children with respect, just as Christ did.

EXAMPLES FROM THE BIBLE

The kingdom of heaven (kingdom of God) was a future period foretold by the prophets in the Old Testament. The kingdom of heaven is the experience of blessedness, like that of the Garden of Eden, where evil is fully overcome and where those who live in the kingdom know only happiness, peace, and joy.

parables: *fictitious stories illustrating moral attitude or religious principle*

Matthew 13:10, 13 The disciples came to him and asked, "Why do you speak to the people in **parables**?" . . . This is why I speak to them in parables: "Through seeing, they do not see; though hearing, they do not hear or understand."

Try Parables

Jesus used short simple stories to pass along spiritual and moral truths to the people of his day. These stories were easy to remember, and related to everyday things in the peoples' lives with which they could quickly identify.

Try using a similar method with your own children. Take experiences and activities from their everyday lives and turn them into object lessons. (See GWBI, pages 191–192.)

Parables Used by Jesus

Sower .... (Matthew 13:1–23; Luke 8:4–8; Mark 4:1–20)
Mustard Seed .... (Matthew 13:31–32; Luke 13:19; Mark 4:30–32)
Vineyard...................................... (Matthew 21:33–46; Luke 20:9–19; Mark 12:1–12)
The lost son .... (Luke 15:11–32)
The Good Samaritan .... (Luke 10:25–37)
Wheat and the tares .... (Matthew 13:24–30)
The leaven .... (Matthew 13:33)
The hidden treasure .... (Matthew 13:44)
Pearl of great price .... (Matthew 13:45–46)
The dragnet................................. (Matthew 13:47–52)
Four lost things .... (Luke 15:3–32)
Pharisee and the tax collector...... (Luke 18:9–14)
Prodigal son .... (Luke 15:11–24)
Great supper .... (Luke 14:15–24)
Unfinished tower .... (Luke 14:28–32)

> **Matthew 5:13** "You are the salt of the earth. But if the salt loses its saltiness, how can it be made salty again? It is no longer good for anything, except to be thrown out and trampled by men."

Try Analogies

Another technique used by Jesus was the analogy. An analogy, like a parable, also uses an everyday item and turns it into a spiritual or moral lesson.

In the previous example, Jesus uses the analogy of salt. Another time, he used a light hidden under a bowl.

Common everyday things can take on new meaning for your child when used like this for teaching. This way of teaching is especially helpful to children whose learning style is predominantly tactile; that is, if touching helps them retain material.

A seashell can turn into an example of God's creation. As you look at the intricate details, the unique colors, the perfection of a house for this particular animal, you can liken it to how God has created each and every one of us unique and different.

GO TO:

Job 5:7; Psalm 58:3; John 9:34 (sinful at birth)

Matthew 22:37–40 (God's law)

John 13:34 (be love)

Romans 15:3; 1 Corinthians 13:5; 2 Timothy 3:2, 4; 2 Thessalonians 2:3–4 (selfishness)

BIBLICAL VIEW OF DISCIPLINE

Psalm 51:5 Surely I was sinful at birth, sinful from the time my mother conceived me.

Sinful from Birth?

When we think of sin, we think of the evils of this world like lying, cheating, murder, stealing, and cruelty. But the true definition of sin is the breaking of God's law, and all of God's laws can be summed up in one word: love. God is love, and his desire for us is to be love. The antithesis of love is selfishness and egotism. Selfishness is at the bottom of all disobedience.

Think About It

When you hold a tiny infant, it's hard to believe that he or she is capable of sin. That's because you probably don't understand the meaning of the term. When we understand that sin is selfishness then it becomes easy to see that our children are sinners. Our job as parents is to help our children become selfless, and sometimes that involves discipline.

What Others are Saying:

John MacArthur: Many parents live in terror that something they do wrong might mar their child's otherwise virtuous character in some irreparable way. They think if something goes wrong in childhood, the child might begin to drift spiritually or wander morally. But the truth is that our children are already marred by sin from the moment they are conceived. The drive to sin is embedded in their very natures. All that is required for the tragic harvest is that children be allowed to give unrestrained expression to those evil desires. . . . [Children] are born sinful, and that sinfulness manifests itself because of what their parents do *not* do.[21]

EXAMPLES FROM THE BIBLE

In Matthew, Jesus summed up the law with two commandments, that we love God with all our heart, and that we love our neighbor as ourself. The world teaches a very different way of living. Self-love is exalted as the only true source of happiness. Self-fulfillment is touted as a goal we all should strive for. We are number one, and if we don't look out for our own interests no one else will.

GO TO:

Matthew 22:37–40 (two commandments)

> One father, Jonathan Katz, says, "My daughter has me totally wrapped around her little finger. I don't even try to win anymore. I just try and save face. I say things to her like, "Go to your room at your earliest convenience. O.K. Daddy's going to count to fifteen hundred."

What Others are Saying:

Dr. Henry Cloud: When Jesus commanded us to love others as ourselves, he was not teaching "self-love." He was teaching about the deep connection of empathy. As a result of our actions, we identify with how the other person feels. We care about their pain as if it were our own. Teach your children that their behavior affects others.[22]

> **Proverbs 29:17** Correct your son, and he will give you rest; yes he will give delight to your soul.

Love Is Hard Work Sometimes

Letting our children have their way can feel like love, but is it really?

Sometimes we don't discipline because we don't want to deal with the tantrum. Most of us work outside the home, and, let's face it, we're tired. Letting our children stay up a half hour longer is easier than the argument that we know we'll face if we say "no." Sometimes we don't discipline because we are looking to our children for love and acceptance. We don't want them to "hate" us. And sometimes we don't discipline because we're afraid. We're unsure of our skill and we worry about damaging our children's psyches.

KEY POINT

If children learn to say "no" from their parents, who teaches them to say "mine"?

Proverbs 29:17 makes it clear, though, that if we are willing to invest time and energy now, in the long term we will be rewarded.

What Others are Saying:

C. H. Spurgeon: Train your children in the way in which you know you should have gone yourself.[23]

FROM JUDY'S HEART

I'll never forget the first time my precious baby challenged my authority. He was about fifteen months old and, like most children at that age, he liked to pick things up, examine them, put them in his mouth, and discard them on the floor.

I had to decide whether to put my "good" stuff away or leave it out. I took a middle-of-the-road approach. Things that I absolutely could not bear if they were broken, I put up. But, I left a few items out because I knew I had to teach my son that some things were off limits for his safety and for the safety of every home we would visit. The one thing I could not put away was my bookcase.

Books to me are precious. They contain magical stories, wisdom, and time-honored facts. To destroy a book would be like destroying a valuable work of art. Therefore, every book I ever read (including my college textbooks) I kept and proudly displayed on my bookcase. There were cookbooks, mysteries, great works of literature, romance novels, how-tos, why-nots, what-ifs, and, of course, a few different Bibles.

My son was drawn to these colorful objects and often toddled over to take a closer look. A simple "no" and a distraction with a toy was the usual end to his exploration, until this one particular day.

This time he toddled over and pulled one of my books off the shelf and then looked at me as if to say, "What are you going to do about that?" (He was so cute.) I said "no" and took him into the living room and gave him a toy. He played with it a few minutes and then went back to the bookcase. He again looked at me and then pulled another book off the shelf. This time I said "no" with a little more firmness in my voice and pulled him away. He cried, but then with an obstinacy that I had never seen, went back to his forbidden fun. This time he swept several off onto the floor.

At that moment, I knew this was a clear challenge to my authority. He was saying to me, "I'm going to do what I'm going to do, and you can't make me stop."

This time I said "no" and slapped his pudgy little hand. He

plunked down on the floor and cried big salty tears. I felt like the meanest mother in the world. But to my disbelief, he pulled himself up and went back toward those books.

I repeated my discipline, he cried, and then tried it one more time. This was the same little guy who gave me big sloppy kisses and hugged my neck and cuddled so sweetly in my arms and made me laugh over his cute little antics. But this was starting not to be cute anymore, and I recognized that.

That day set the tone for the rest of his childhood and even into his teen years. I earned his respect and my authority was established. There came a time when he was bigger and stronger than me, but he never challenged me ever again in that way.

We flew through his teen years with few problems and today he is a successful adult who is responsible, caring, and hard-working. I often wonder how things would have turned out if he'd won the battle that day.

Sit down with your husband and discuss your opinions on discipline. In most marriages there is one parent who is lenient and one who is strict. Recognize this before your children do, and decide to work together. Don't let your children pit one of you against the other. Work together as a team. Your marriage will be stronger and your children not as likely to rebel.

> **Ephesians 6:4** Fathers, do not **exasperate** your children.

GO TO:

Romans 10:19 (exasperate)

exasperate: *provoke to anger*

That's Harsh!

One of the dangers of discipline is spelled out clearly in this scripture. No matter what form of discipline you use, it must not provoke your child to anger. Immediately you might think of **corporal** punishment, but that isn't necessarily the only example of this danger. Unclear rules, rules applied unfairly, and even no rules at all can have this same affect.

corporal: *physical*

Good discipline begins with clear rules. Then when they are broken, there must be consequences that are age-appropriate, consistent, practiced without anger, and followed up with reconciliation.

KEY POINT

There is only one thing worse than being too strict and that is being too lenient.

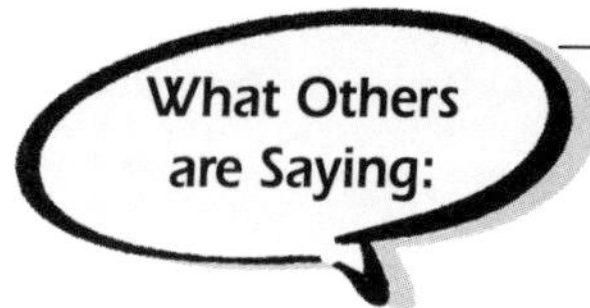

Dr. James Dobson: Methods and philosophies regarding control of children have been the subject of heated debate and disagreement for centuries. The pendulum has swept back and forth regularly between harsh, oppressive discipline and the unstructured permissiveness of the 1950s. It is time that we realize that *both* extremes leave their characteristic scars on the lives of young victims, and I would be hard pressed to say which is more damaging.[24]

Dr. Ross Campbell: [Corporal] punishment is occasionally necessary but because of its negative effects from overuse, punishment should be used *only as a last resort*. It is far, far better to handle misbehavior positively, especially with genuine love and affection, than to punish a child, especially with corporal punishment.[25]

GO TO:

Judges 13–16 (Samson)

Exodus 34:11 (forbidden by law)

EXAMPLES FROM THE BIBLE

Samson's parents gave in to his request to marry a Philistine woman even though it was forbidden by law. This led to much heartache for Samson (see GWBI, page 54). How different things might have been if they had not given in to their son's desires.

Think About It

If you do not give your children consequences for their bad behavior, God will. A child who is allowed to run wild when young just might grow up to be an adult with little regard for God's laws. Personal tragedy is sure to follow.

Ephesians 6:4 Bring them up in the **training** and **instruction** of the Lord.

training: *disciplinary instruction*

instruction: *mild rebuke*

A Better Way

The two words used here, "training" and "instruction," are translated from other versions which use "nurture" and "admonition." These words speak to a type of discipline that, if practiced properly, will develop godly children.

The discipline that we should practice should include instruction, not just consequences. Sending your child to his or her room for telling a lie needs to be followed up with a time of explaining why lying is a bad thing. And admonition means mild, not harsh, rebuke.

GO TO:

Genesis 18:19; Deuteronomy 6:7; Proverbs 13:24; 22:6 (bring them up)

2 Timothy 3:16 (nurture)

1 Corinthians 10:11; Titus 3:10 (admonition)

Children tend to be sensitive, and often a word spoken at the right moment and in a soft tone of voice can be enough to correct unwanted behavior.

Think About It

The words *"Bring them up"* make it clear that we need to do the work. Children cannot raise themselves. They need our loving guidance and discipline. They need our time and attention. If we don't give it to them, they might look for it somewhere else.

Patricia H. Rushford: Discipline says, "I love you and I care about how you grow."[26]

We are not called to be our children's best friends. We are called to be their parents.

> **Proverbs 29:15** The **<u>rod</u> of correction** imparts wisdom, but a child left to himself disgraces his mother.

☞ **GO TO:**

Proverbs 13:24 (rod)

rod of correction: *any form of discipline*

A Big Stick?

The "rod of correction" refers to any form of punishment, not literally a "rod." The verse itself, however, leaves little doubt that discipline is necessary, and that without it children will disgrace their mothers.

Think About It

Spanking has become a controversial word. You can even be turned in to child welfare agencies for practicing it. But the Bible says there is a time and a place for it. The experts may disagree, but if corporal punishment is practiced within the godly guidelines of love, then there are times when it is appropriate.

A Letter to God

Dear God,

I want to confess that I stole bubble gum from the 7 and 11 store last year. That was a long time ago but that was still bad. I want to tell you that I did not like the gum (it made me sick) and the baseball cards in it had no all stars. Mostly just guys from the Cleveland Indians and the seattle team. So was punished like I deserved.

Please forgive me,
XXX (age 9)[27]

What Others are Saying:

Dr. James Dobson: Corporal punishment is reserved specifically for moments of willful, deliberate, on-purpose defiance by a child who is old enough to understand what he is doing. These challenges to authority will begin at approximately fifteen months of age and should be met with loving firmness. A thump on the fingers or a single stinging slap on the upper legs will be sufficient to say, "You must listen when I tell you no." By your persistence you will establish yourself as the leader to whom the child owes obedience. At the same time, however, you must seek numerous and continual ways of telling this youngster how much you adore him. That formula of love and discipline has been tested and validated over many centuries of time, and it will work for you.[28]

Study Questions

1. Who are your children's greatest role models? Why?
2. Examine your spiritual life and list three ways you can make it stronger.
3. What is the biblical definition of love?
4. Who is responsible for the spiritual training of your children? Why?
5. Why is discipline important to your children?
6. What does the Bible say about spanking? Contrast that with what the world teaches and explain why there is such a difference of opinion.

CHAPTER WRAP-UP

- Whether we want to believe it or not, we are the most important role models our children have. Everything we do and are affects them deeply.
- We cannot teach our children a faith we do not have ourselves. The deeper our walk with the Lord, the more likely they are to "catch" our faith.
- Love is the basis for our parenting. It is more than a feeling, it's an action and a way of life. Without love we are nothing but clanging bells and our children will know it.

- Teaching our children about God is more than sending them to Sunday school. We need to talk to them about our own faith and make object lessons out of everyday life situations. If we don't teach them, no one else will.
- If we love our children, we will discipline them. It will teach them self-control, consideration for others, and the right way to live.

JUDY'S  BOOKSHELF

- *Successful Christian Parenting*, John MacArthur, Word Publishing. A biblical look at parenting responsibilities and challenges.
- *Parenting Isn't for Cowards*, Dr. James Dobson, Word Publishing. A popular book on parenting from my favorite radio personality. His advice is practical and down-to-earth.
- *The Mom Factor*, Dr. Henry Cloud and Dr. John Townsend, Zondervan. A look at how our mothers affect our parenting.
- *Your Thirty Day Journey to Being a World-Class Mother*, C. W. Neal, Oliver Nelson. A daily devotional that will help you be a better mother. Short exercises are included.

10 MEETING THE NEEDS OF YOUR CHILDREN

WHAT'S IN THIS CHAPTER

- Meeting Our Children's Physical Needs
- Meeting Our Children's Emotional Needs
- Meeting Our Children's Spiritual Needs
- When Your Husband's Not a Believer

Here We Go

From birth, children need us. There are the obvious physical needs—food, clothing, and shelter—but there are also emotional and spiritual needs that may not be quite so obvious.

But if these important needs aren't filled, it can stunt the growth of our children just as surely as if we deprived them of food.

Before we can meet these needs we must understand what they are and what they are not. Let's take a look at what the Bible has to say about the needs of our children.

MEETING OUR CHILDREN'S PHYSICAL NEEDS

> **1 Timothy 5:8** If anyone does not **provide** for his relatives, and especially for his immediate family, he has denied the faith and is worse than an unbeliever.

GO TO:

Romans 12:17; 2 Corinthians 12:17 (provide)

Luke 12:45; 1 Corinthians 14:23; 2 Corinthians 6:14 (unbeliever)

provide: *look out for*

Worse Than an Unbeliever

Paul was writing to Timothy about a problem in the church—widows and orphans. There were no pension plans, government welfare programs, Medicare, or Medicaid. Someone needed to care for them, and it looks as if they were turning to the church for help when they should have been helped by their families.

Meeting the needs of our family is so basic to human nature that to not do it is almost unthinkable. Paul called these people worse than the unbelievers who, even though they were not following Christ, still took care of their immediate families.

John MacArthur: Children are born weak and unable to fend for themselves. Of all the higher mammals in God's creation, man alone is born with no ability whatsoever to sustain himself. Newborns are utterly unable to walk, crawl, or even roll over. Parents assume the responsibility of feeding them, changing them, making sure they get proper rest, and protecting them from all harm. If someone does *not* do all that for them, they will die.[1]

For Single Moms—These widows probably had children that needed care. I wonder what Paul would think of Christian parents who skip out on their child care payments after a divorce?

portions: *delegates responsibilities*

> **Proverbs 31:15** She gets up while it is still dark; she provides food for her family and **portions** for her servant girls.

KEY POINT

When you've forgotten to take something out of the freezer, "What's for dinner?" can be the most irritating question!

Martha Stewart Doesn't Live Here

The Proverbs 31 woman sounds almost too good to be true, but remember that all of the food eaten by her family had to be made from scratch, and, since there was no way to store it for more than a few hours, it had to be prepared daily. The latter part of this scripture means that she delegated responsibilities to her servant girls, which means she had help. She didn't do it all herself!

Think About It

Microwave ovens, precooked foods, frozen entrees, take-out, fast-food restaurants, and home delivery have made meal preparation much easier, but it still hasn't gone away. Day in and day out, the responsibility for feeding the family most often falls on us. There's menu planning, grocery lists, trips to the grocery store, storage, and preparation. All this and still staying within a budget, satisfying everyone's tastes, and meeting the family's nutritional needs (see GWHN, page 29). It's a big responsibility that often goes unnoticed and unappreciated.

☞ GO TO:

Judges 7:13; Ruth 2:17 (barley)

leavening: *yeast*

In biblical times women made bread every day from wheat or barley flour, salt, water, and **leavening**—usually a bit of old dough to make the new dough rise. The loaves were round and flat and were baked on hot stones or in an oven (see illustration, page 185).

Bread Baking

Professional bread makers placed flat cakes of bread (like pancakes) into large ovens like the one shown here. Homemakers cooked bread on the smooth, outside surface of their ovens, which were smaller and more beehive shaped than this one.

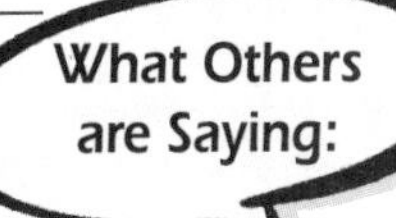

Kathy Collard Miller: Before we think this wonderful woman is fixing food for both her family and her servant girls, we need to know that the word "portions" actually means she apportioned or delegated the work of her household. Mothers without hired help can apply this instruction by including their children in the work of the home. Although children will complain, they will actually feel included, necessary, and important, plus they will learn valuable skills for later in life.[2]

> **Deuteronomy 32:15 Jeshurun** grew fat and kicked; filled with food, he became heavy and sleek. He abandoned the God who made him and rejected the Rock his Savior.

☞ GO TO:

Isaiah 44:2 (Jeshurun)

Deuteronomy 31:20 (filled)

Genesis 49:24 (Rock)

Jeshurun: *"the upright one," that is, Israel*

apostasy: *renunciation of religious faith*

Too Much on Our Plates?

The metaphor used here is that of a pampered animal, which, instead of being tame and gentle, becomes mischievous and vicious as a consequence of good living and kind treatment. The Israelites acted this way too through various acts of rebellion, murmuring against God, and idolatrous **apostasy**.

Think About It

Did you know that in this country one-third of our children ages three through seventeen are heavy for their age?[3] Getting enough to eat is no longer the big problem; it's getting too much to eat compounded with inactivity. It's our job as moms to help. Here are some things you can do:

- Limit the amount of television, Nintendo, and computer use. These are sedentary activities. If these "path-of-least-resistance" choices are taken away, your child will choose physical activities. If your neighborhood is unsafe, enroll your children in girls' and boys' clubs, or organized sports in your community or church.
- Set an example. Be more active yourself, and eat healthy foods.
- Create physical activities you can do together, like hiking, skiing, rollerblading, or ice-skating. This will strengthen the family too.
- Limit the amount of fast food your family eats. It's high in fat and calories.
- Impress upon your children the importance of fruits and vegetables. Don't insist that they clean up their plates. Don't worry about finicky eaters. When a child gets hungry, he or she will eat.
- Don't purchase or even serve high-calorie items like cake, pie, and ice cream, except on special occasions.

Don't put your child on a diet without consulting your pediatrician.

Think About It

Isn't it interesting that being too full led to the backsliding of Jeshurun? Why do you think that is? Is it because he had no self-discipline, or was it because when his belly was too full he grew lazy?

What Others are Saying:

Gwen Shamblin: Studies show that we are fatter than ever. And it seems that the more weight-obsessed we are, the less we lose and the more we revile the pudgy, the plump, the rotund, the fat, and the morbidly obese. . . . Years of focusing on food and giving all our boredom, distress, and troubles to a pan of brownies have only increased our stress. Dieting has drained us emotionally, if not financially, and has exacerbated rather than solved our problems.[4]

Luke 18:18–25 A certain ruler asked him, "Good teacher, what must I do to inherit eternal life?"

"Why do you call me good?" Jesus answered. "No one is good except God alone. You know the commandments: 'Do not commit adultery, do not murder, do not steal, do not give false testimony, honor your father and mother.'"

"All these I have kept since I was a boy," he said.

When Jesus heard this, he said to him, "You still lack one thing. Sell everything you have and give to the poor, and you will have treasure in heaven. Then come, follow me."

When he heard this, he became very sad, because he was a man of great wealth. Jesus looked at him and said, "How hard it is for the rich to enter the kingdom of God! Indeed, it is easier for a camel to go through the eye of a needle than for a rich man to enter the kingdom of God."

☞ GO TO:

Mark 10:15; Luke 10:25; Romans 6:23 (must I do)

Exodus 20:12–16; Deuteronomy 5:16–20 (honor)

Matthew 6:19–21; Mark 10:21 (treasure in heaven)

Ecclesiastes 5:10 (wealth)

You Can't Take It with You

This is an interesting exchange between a rich young man and Jesus. The young man wanted to know what he could do to earn his way into heaven.

Jesus gave him an unexpected answer when he replied, "Sell all you have." Jesus knew that this man's true treasure, what he valued in this life, was wealth. Money itself was not keeping this man from entering heaven, but he had made it his god. It was the most important thing to him, and he was unwilling to give it up.

Think About It

Are you teaching your children to value money over a relationship with Jesus Christ? Do you spend time earning money that you don't really need to provide things you really don't want? When we do, we pass along the message that wealth is far more valuable than a relationship with God, or even relationships with other people.

Lighten Up

A wealthy man was close to death. He begged and begged God to allow him to take his wealth into heaven. Finally God relented and said, "Okay, you can bring one suitcase." After he died, the rich man stood at the gates of heaven with his suitcase in hand. Peter approached him and asked, "What's that?" The rich man proudly opened his suitcase that he had filled with gold. Peter laughed and said, "Why would you want to bring paving stones into heaven?"

> **Isaiah 5:8** Woe to you who add house to house and join field to field till no space is left and you live alone in the land.

Too Much House?

☞ **GO TO:**

Micah 2:2; Nehemiah 5:1–8 (houses)

Leviticus 25 (jubilee)

Isaiah warns against possessing many houses or even having a large, beautiful home, because this is contrary to the Law of Moses—which stated that when the children of Israel entered the land of Canaan, the land should be equitably divided.

To help each family retain its own God-given land and identity, he ordained the "jubilee," occurring once every fifty years, by which every man and every family should have their former possessions restored to them, and Hebrew slaves would be freed.

Yet, in defiance of this requirement and the spirit of the law, the people in the time of Isaiah had become generally covetous.

Think About It

Ask yourself if you have too much house. Do you have to work outside the home to make the house payments? Could you live in a smaller home and be more available to your children?

Is the appearance of your home more important to you than the people who live in it? Do your children feel free to bring their friends over, or are you so fussy about tracking on the carpet or messing up the playroom that they don't feel comfortable or wanted?

What Others are Saying:

Mamie McCullough: I knew a young bride who would not develop any relationships . . . because she was too busy: she had to clean her house every day. . . . When she had children, her clean house came first with her. She didn't allow her family to enjoy their home because it was a shrine to her housekeeping skills. She did not take the kids on picnics or go to their ball games; she did not take them fishing or to church. The children are gone now. . . . She realizes at last that family—not furniture—should have filled her days.[5]

Earline Steelberg: I have held many things in my hands and lost them all; but the things I have placed in God's hands, those I always possess.[6]

Are you looking for fulfillment in the wrong places? You won't find it in a bigger home that's beautifully decorated and landscaped. You'll only find it in a relationship with Jesus Christ. Turn to him right now and ask forgiveness for your attitude, and ask him to change you so that you can get your eyes off what is temporary and onto what is eternal, your kids.

contentment: *satisfaction*

clothing: *Greek term used here; can include housing*

trap: *a hole dug in the earth, filled full of sharp stakes, and slightly covered over with turf. Whatever steps on it falls in, and is pierced through and through with these sharp stakes.*

griefs: *sorrows*

> **1 Timothy 6:6–10** But godliness with **contentment** is great gain. For we brought nothing into the world, and we can take nothing out of it. But if we have food and **clothing**, we will be <u>content</u> with that. People who want to get rich fall into temptation and a **trap** and into many foolish and harmful desires that plunge men into ruin and destruction. For the <u>love of money</u> is a root of all kinds of evil. Some people, eager for money, have wandered from the faith and pierced themselves with many **griefs**.

☞ GO TO:

Philippians 4:11–13 (content)

Colossians 3:5; Ephesians 5:5; 1 John 2:15 (love of money)

It's a Trap

Paul warns us that seeking riches here on earth is a dangerous trap. With wealth comes all kinds of temptations that ultimately do not bring the happiness that we are expecting.

True happiness comes with being content with what we have. If we can pass that attitude along to our children, then no matter what their circumstances they will be happy, and isn't that what we really want for them?

Do you tell your children that you are content with what you have? Or do you say in front of them that you desire more—a bigger house, a newer car, a bigger TV, etc.? Is what you wear more important than who you are on the inside? How often do you tell them that you desire a closer relationship with the Lord?

What we do and say has a powerful impact on what our children value.

Are you overusing your credit card to get the things you want? If so, work out a plan right now with your husband. Cut up your cards and begin to live on a budget. It will bring peace to your heart and your home.

EXAMPLES FROM THE BIBLE

The Israelites were known for making wool into cloth. It was spun from fleece and woven into lengths of fabric (see illustration below) that were hand-sewn together to make garments. The rich wore garments colored with dye made from plants and insects. Women's clothes were often more colorful than men's. Everyone who could afford it wore sandals made of leather.

> **Matthew 8:20** Jesus replied, "Foxes have holes and birds of the air have nests, but the Son of Man has no place to lay his head."

GO TO:

Mark 8:31 (Son of Man)

Where Did Jesus Live, Anyway?

God has poured his riches out on this country. The poorest in our land live better than most of the population in India, China, Mexico, and Pakistan. Yet, we are turning farther and farther away from Jesus' teachings.

Weaving

Pictured here is a woman weaving on a loom. In biblical times, many homes had looms like this one.

God, who created everything, came to earth as a man. He could have lived in the biggest castles and been served by multiple servants. He could have been ushered around in the fanciest chariots and worn the finest linen.

Instead, he often walked long distances to get where he was going, and he depended on the hospitality of others to provide his nourishment and a place to lay his head.

What Others are Saying:

Philip Yancey: Were they living in modern times, with the crackdown on homelessness, Jesus and his disciples would likely be harassed by police and forced to move on.[7]

Think About It

Make it a daily habit to thank God for his many blessings. Name them specifically, and as you do you will begin to find satisfaction in what you have and your desire for more will begin to fade.

MEETING OUR CHILDREN'S EMOTIONAL NEEDS

> **1 Chronicles 28:20** David also said to Solomon his son, "Be strong and courageous, and do the work. Do not be afraid or discouraged, for the LORD God, my God, is with you. He will not fail you or **forsake** you until all the work for the service of the temple of the LORD is finished.

GO TO:

Deuteronomy 31:6; 1 Chronicles 22:13; 2 Chronicles 19:11 (courageous)

Deuteronomy 4:31 (forsake)

forsake: *give up on*

I Believe in You

In this scripture David is telling his son, Solomon, that he has faith in him and, more importantly, that God will not forsake him and will help him accomplish the task of rebuilding the Temple.

When our children are young, they need to be undergirded by that same kind of faith until they can learn it for themselves.

It's like teaching our children to ride a bicycle. At first we hang onto the handlebars and seat. As they progress, we let go of the handlebars. Slowly we loosen our grip on the seat until we've let go, but we still run alongside, ready to catch them when they fall. Once they're proficient, we don't even need to be there.

Until the day they have faith in their own abilities, they need our encouragement.

Randy Rolfe: Your expression of faith in [your child's] own positive destiny, his many options, and his maturing inner guidance system will allow him to seek his potential with confidence. Even when your wills conflict, your faith will keep the conflict in perspective, so that you both will hang in there with love and respect until a resolution can be found.[8]

What do you think about your child? Do you always think the worst, or do you think the best? Your attitude can make a big difference not only in your relationship, but how he views himself.

Words of Faith: Repeat Often

- I love being your parent.
- You're easy to love.
- You make me so proud.
- I love having you around.
- God gave me a special blessing when he gave me you.
- I'm proud of who you are.
- I like spending time with you.

FROM JUDY'S HEART

I used to dread parent-teacher conferences. On the one hand, my oldest son was an overachiever, and his teachers thought he was the brightest and best and most talented she or he'd ever had. He excelled in everything he did. The fifteen minutes I spent with each of his teachers were the proudest of my life.

Then there was my other son. His conferences were another story. Every year I heard almost the same thing, and I began to dread them. Being one grade behind his big brother, he had big shoes to fill. Intellectually those shoes fit fine, but emotionally he seemed to be behind. He had fits of temper, especially when he lost in a game or failed to live up to his own expectations. The teachers were concerned. Was there some way that we could get this kid to relax and accept himself? They never came out and said it, but I kept getting the feeling that they blamed me for what they saw as an inferiority complex. I knew they thought we said to him every morning with his cereal, "Why can't you be more like your big brother?"

I'd come away feeling depressed about this kid whom I knew was bright and in many areas even brighter and more creative than his brother, but there was something in him, something almost inborn that asked a lot of himself. He was never satisfied with "good enough," he was never happy coming in second, he liked to compete, and he took on projects that were way beyond his capacity, like the time he chose to read a book in second grade that was more appropriate for fifth or sixth. But he wouldn't listen. He insisted he could read it although of course he didn't, and ended up unhappy.

How do you get a kid like that to relax? How do you help him be satisfied with the status quo? The answer is, you don't. You can't change your son or daughter into anything other than what he or she is. You can bend them a little, you can redirect them, but you can't change them. You can only accept them. You can also look at those negative personality traits and ask yourself, "Is there a positive side to this trait?"

The answer is "yes." This emotional son who was never happy with himself went on to be president of his senior class, and at the end of that year he won a full-ride scholarship to a highly rated private university. Now, I don't know anyone who is more comfortable with himself and more sure of what he wants out of life. You know, I'm kind of glad he was never happy with the status quo.

> **Romans 12:10** Be devoted to one another in **brotherly love**. Honor one another above yourselves.

☞ **GO TO:**

1 Thessalonians 4:9; Hebrews 13:1; 1 Peter 1:22 (brotherly love)

brotherly love: *translated from the Greek word philadelphia which means love among brothers*

There's No Present Like Time

More than they need food, water, and shelter, our children need our attention. This means we have to put them ahead of the many tasks that rob us of time with them. They need specific times when we are all theirs.

Some parents "date" their children. (Friday night is Jennifer's night out with Mom. Tuesday evening is Sam's night out with Dad.) Other parents play board games, take their children bowling, spend ten minutes saying goodnight to each one individually.

You need to decide what will work best for you and your children, and then do it. In that way they will know they are loved, and you will get to know who your children are.

What Others are Saying:

Dr. William Sears and Martha Sears, R.N.: As the size of your family increases, . . . Take some time out every day or every few days to do something special with each child individually. This special time helps satisfy each child's bid for equal time and gives each the feeling of individual worth.[9]

Dr. Henry Cloud: You cannot grow children on just "quality time." Growing children, first of all, takes quantities of time. . . . You're children will grow. . . . You must be there throughout the process. . . . Children internalize things from the outside world as they grow, you have to be ever-present, monitoring the things they internalize. . . . Children need to grow in relationship with another person in order to develop character.[10]

For Single Moms—This is going to be particularly hard for single moms because there is no one to share the responsibility of household chores. Examine your life and sort the tasks that have to be done immediately from those that can wait a week.

For example, if the lawn doesn't get mowed today, it will still be there tomorrow or the next day, and the world won't come to an end. The dishes can be left in the sink one more hour or even one more day. They will wait, but your son and daughter won't. You will turn around one day and your children will be gone. They might even leave early, looking for love somewhere else.

What Others are Saying:

Ruth Bell Graham and Gigi Graham Tchividjian: A young child died suddenly. After the funeral, . . . the mother returned home. She found little fingerprints on a windowpane. Only a few days before she would have taken Windex and cleaned the glass. Now, she carefully covered them to seal and preserve them. Death changes things. Don't wait till then to learn perspective.[11]

Matthew 18:10 "See that you do not look down on one of these little ones. For I tell you that their **angels** in heaven always see the face of my Father in heaven."

GO TO:

Psalm 34:7; 91:11; Hebrews 1:14 (angels)

angels: *guardian angels not exclusively for children*

Just a Little Respect

Jesus is saying that those who are like little children (new Christians) should not be looked down upon, for even they have angels in heaven who watch out for them.

When our children disappoint us, it's easy to slip into a disrespectful attitude. We say things like "How could you do this?" "You're so stupid." "I've told you a hundred times to be careful." Words like this cut into your child's heart and assaults his or her character. Would you speak that way to a coworker or your best friend?

Jesus here is calling us to not look down on our children. They are only acting out of their immaturity. What else can we expect of children?

Lady Bird Johnson: Children are likely to live up to what you believe about them.[12]

A Job Description for Mothers

Wanted: Athlete in top condition to safeguard tireless toddler. Needs quick reflexes, boundless energy, infinite patience. ESP helpful. Knowledge of first aid essential. Must be able to drive, cook, and work despite constant distraction. Workday: fifteen hours. Will consider pediatric nurse with Olympic background. Training in psychology desirable. Should be able to referee and must be unflappable. Tolerance is chief requirement.[13]

> **James 1:19** My dear brothers, take note of this: Everyone should be quick to listen, slow to speak and slow to become angry.

☞ **GO TO:**

James 1:26 (speak)

Please Listen to Me

Listening is a skill that must be learned in order to be a good parent. It can be hard to take the time when we're tired, or when our child is rambling on about something we think is unimportant. But if we don't listen to the unimportant, there will come a time when our children will not share the important, either.

KEY POINT

The more a child becomes aware of a mother's willingness to listen, the more a mother will begin to hear.

Think About It

Things That Block Our Hearing

- We think we've heard it before.
- We "leave our motor running" so we can answer the minute our child stops talking.
- We are distracted by the television or radio or phone.
- We're more interested in getting our point across than hearing what they have to say.
- We take on a self-righteous attitude of "I'm right and they're wrong."

Examine your listening habits. Make a concerted effort to improve, and see what a difference it can make in your communication with your child. Sometimes children who babble do so out of a need to be heard.

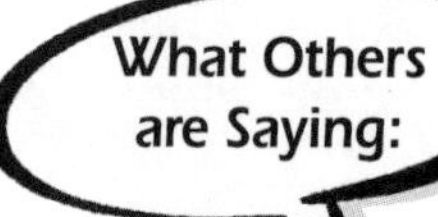

Patricia H. Rushford: A part of really loving someone is to give your attention by listening intently to what is said. While children learn to read and write, few of them have been taught to speak and fewer to listen.[14]

love: *not an emotion but an active love*

sincere: *true and honest*

> **Romans 12:9 Love** must be **sincere**. Hate what is evil; cling to what is good.

They Need Our Love

This may seem rather obvious, but it needs to be addressed, because loving our children can be difficult at times. Oh, yes, it's easy when they are behaving and cute and responsible and getting along with one another, but it's hard when they have just gotten into trouble at school, or have ruined a brand new pair of shoes, or are fighting with their brother again, or failed to take out the garbage even after being reminded three times. But that's when we need to love them the most. That's when we need to pull out the big guns, our trust and faith in the Lord, and love them anyway.

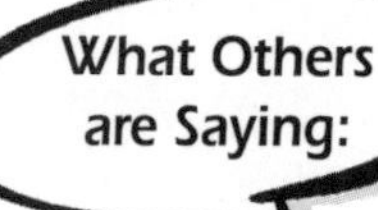

Sandra Stanley: Lord, remind me each day that these precious children are so different from each other and from me! You created them so uniquely. Show me, as their mother, how to love each one of them just the way they need to be loved individually. Help me love them according to their own personality and needs and not just the way that comes easiest to me. Give me discernment as I learn their needs, and creativity as I learn to love them accordingly.[15]

Remember that even when we were sinners God loved us. Don't withdraw love as a form of punishment or reward. Don't give your child the message that he or she is only loved conditionally.

> **Romans 15:7** Accept one another, then, just as Christ accepted you, in order to bring praise to God.

☞ **GO TO:**

Romans 14:1; Philemon 12 (accept)

Please Accept Me as I Am

Every child comes to us already packaged by the Father.

From the womb we can see that one is compliant, another defiant. One is optimistic, the other pessimistic. One is quiet, the other noisy.

It's up to us to help them develop into their unique selves, and the first step in that process is acceptance. Trying to make our children into something they aren't is the saddest thing that can happen to them.

What Others are Saying:

Pablo Picasso: My mother said to me, "If you become a soldier you'll be a general; if you become a monk you'll end up as the pope." Instead, I became a painter and wound up as Picasso.[16]

> **Luke 6:41–42** "Why do you look at the speck of sawdust in your brother's eye and pay no attention to the plank in your own eye? How can you say to your brother, 'Brother, let me take the speck out of your eye,' when you yourself fail to see the plank in your own eye? You **hypocrite**, first take the plank out of your eye, and then you will see clearly to remove the speck from your brother's eye.

☞ **GO TO:**

Matthew 6:2; 7:5 (hypocrite)

hypocrite: *a person who puts on a false appearance of virtue or religion*

Judge Not!

Jesus uses an exaggeration here to point out how foolish it is to be judgmental of others when we are blind to our own faults. This is usually thought of in terms of our relationships with adults, but also can be easily applied to our relationships with our children.

Sometimes the things we like least about our children are the things we don't like about ourselves. For example, if you procrastinate, you may be most critical of your children when they put off their homework until the last minute.

GO TO:

Proverbs 29:3 (companion)

gluttons: *loose morally*

> **Proverbs 28:7** He who keeps the law is a discerning son, but a companion of **gluttons** disgraces his father.

Good Friends

Even in biblical times, parents were concerned about their children's companions. There are Scriptures that warn against the company we keep.

Our child's choice of friends is extremely important, especially if he or she is a follower. There is probably no other area where parents feel so helpless. But are you really?

There are a number of things you can do to have some input here. Make sure that your son or daughter brings their friends home so you can meet them. Make it a point to also introduce yourself to their parents. If you are uncomfortable with a relationship, then steer your child away, not by discouraging the friendship, but by giving him or her opportunities for making new friends. Get your children involved in a local youth group, sign them up for sports they'd like to try, give them art lessons, swimming lessons, or Karate lessons.

Spend time on your knees praying about your children's friendships.

Michelle Howe: Youngsters don't have the same finely tuned ability to distinguish between acceptable imperfections and unacceptable ones. Thus, moms need to be keenly aware of their children's acquaintances before close friendships develop.[17]

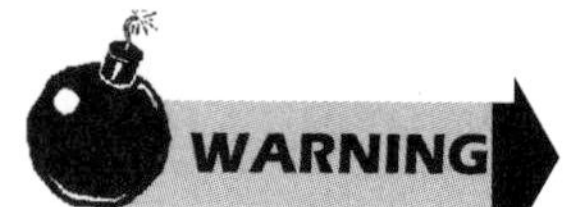

Make sure that your concerns about a certain friend are based on moral behavior and not on socioeconomics or race.

Zechariah 8:5 The city streets will be filled with boys and girls playing there.

Fun Is Serious Business

This scripture implies that during this time the Jewish nation would be so secure that the children could play in the streets.

Think About It

Children need time to play. This seems obvious, but sometimes we keep them so busy going to ballet lessons, soccer practice, and church activities that we ignore the importance of time for them to simply just be kids.

What Others are Saying:

Patricia H. Rushford: For the sake of having fun, be frivolous for a change. It won't mar your image. Go for a wild run on the beach with your hair flying in every direction. Create a sand castle. Write "I love you" in the sand. Fly a kite and let the wind take your soul along for the ride. Make a mud pie. Let a puppy lick your face. Climb a mountain. . . . Make a snow angel or a snowman.[18]

Toys used by children in New Testament times are similar to ones used by children today. There were dolls (see illustration below) and games, and balls. There is even a record of spinning tops and hoops and a form of hopscotch.[19]

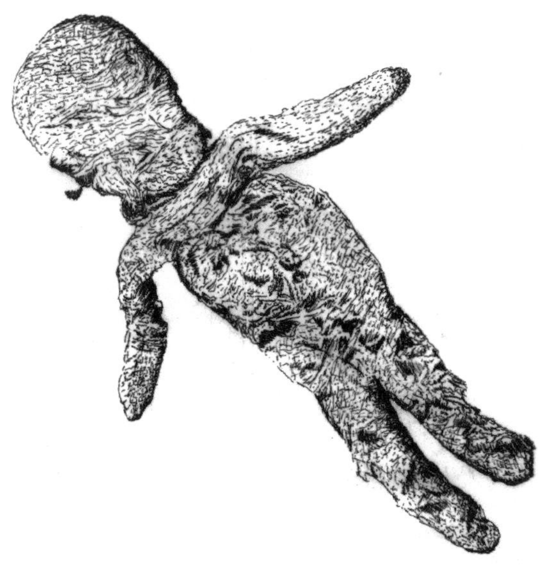

Rag Doll

This is the sort of rag doll that may have been played with by a child during New Testament times.

MEETING OUR CHILDREN'S SPIRITUAL NEEDS

3 John 4 I have no greater joy than to hear that my children are walking in the truth.

Your Child's Greatest Need Is a Relationship with Jesus Christ

Not money, not an education, not high moral values, not a myriad of friends, not even a solid family can give our children what they need most in life—a relationship with Jesus Christ. This alone will give them the foundation they need to survive everything that life will throw at them.

What Others are Saying:

John MacArthur: Your top priority as a parent, then, is to be an evangelist in your home. You need to teach your children the law of God; teach them the gospel of divine grace; show them their need for a Savior; and point them to Jesus Christ as the only One who can save them. If they grow up without a keen awareness of their need for salvation, you as a parent will have failed in your primary task as their spiritual leader.[20]

What Your Child Needs Most

Following is a list of the Gospel highlights. Learn them so that you can teach them to your children. Use terms they can understand. Don't pressure them into a decision they are not ready for. Let them know there is a price for following Jesus and that it shouldn't be done lightly. When you know your children are ready, present them with the Gospel and then step back and let them decide.

- God is holy, and his law therefore demands perfect holiness. (1 Samuel 6:20; 1 Peter 1:16)
- Because he is holy, God hates sin. (Psalm 5:4; 7:11)
- Sinners cannot stand before him. (Psalm 1:5; 5:5)
- Sin is violation of God's law. (Romans 7:7)
- Sin is what makes true peace impossible for unbelievers. (Micah 2:1)
- All have sinned. (Romans 3:23)
- Sin makes the sinner worthy of death. (Ezekiel 18:4)

- Sinners can do nothing to earn salvation. (Isaiah 64:6; Romans 3:20)
- Sinners cannot change their own sin nature. (Jeremiah 2:22)
- Jesus is eternally God. (John 1:1–3)
- Jesus is Lord of all. (Revelation 17:14)
- Jesus became man. (Philippians 2:6–7)
- Jesus is utterly pure and sinless. (Hebrews 4:15)
- He became a sacrifice for our sin. (2 Corinthians 5:21)
- He shed his own blood as payment for sin. (Ephesians 1:7)
- He died on the cross to prove a way of salvation for sinners. (1 Peter 2:24)
- He rose triumphantly from the dead. (Romans 1:4)
- His righteousness is given to those who trust him. (1 Corinthians 1:30)
- He freely justifies all who trust in him. (Galatians 2:16)
- Repent. (Acts 3:19)
- Turn your heart from all that dishonors God. (1 Thessalonians 1:9)
- Follow Jesus. (Luke 9:23)
- Trust him as Lord and Savior. (Acts 16:31)

What Others are Saying:

Alice Chapin: Some parents say that they do not want to influence a child's religious beliefs. They will allow him to decide for himself when he grows up, they reason. But this is an irresponsible attitude. After all, these same parents DO choose to be an influence in their youngster's activities, choice of friends, education, clothing, manners, etc., so why should they shirk the responsibility to influence their child's spiritual beliefs?[21]

WHEN YOUR HUSBAND'S NOT A BELIEVER

> **1 Corinthians 7:14** For the unbelieving husband has been **sanctified** through his wife, and the unbelieving wife has been sanctified through her believing husband. Otherwise your children would be unclean, but as it is, they are holy.

sanctified: *purified or made holy*

Unequally Yoked?

There was a problem in the Corinthian church. As one spouse turned to Christ, but the other did not, the question arose about whether or not the believer should stay married to the unbeliever. Paul argued that divorce wasn't necessary because the believer influenced the unbeliever and her children. That faith, when acted out in the home, had a great influence over the entire household, making it likely that everyone would eventually make his or her own personal commitment to Christ.

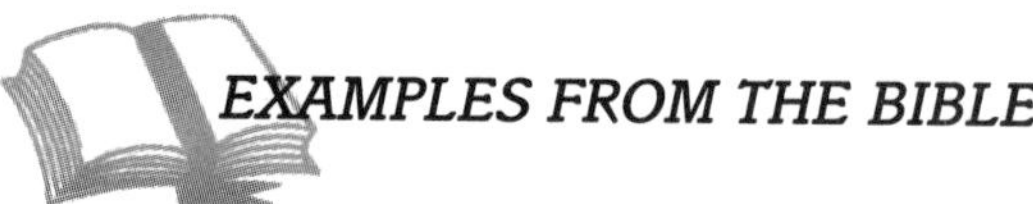

EXAMPLES FROM THE BIBLE

Timothy's father was not a Christian and yet Timothy went on to become one of the most beloved of Paul's companions (see chapter 16).

☞ **GO TO:**

1 Peter 2:13–17 (submissive)

submissive: *recognize authority, respect another's opionion*

the word: *the Gospel message*

purity: *innocence*

reverence: *awe*

1 Peter 3:1–6 Wives, in the same way be **submissive** to your husbands so that, if any of them do not believe **the word**, they may be won over without words by the behavior of their wives, when they see the **purity** and **reverence** of your lives. Your beauty should not come from outward adornment, such as braided hair and the wearing of gold jewelry and fine clothes. Instead, it should be that of your inner self, the unfading beauty of a gentle and quiet spirit, which is of great worth in God's sight. For this is the way the holy women of the past who put their hope in God used to make themselves beautiful. They were submissive to their own husbands, like Sarah, who obeyed Abraham and called him her master. You are her daughters if you do what is right and do not give way to fear.

Six Steps to Winning Your Husband to Christ

Some women cringe at this passage of Scripture, but that's because they don't fully understand what is being said. If you want to change your husband, live the kind of life that will not only bring him to the Lord, but also will make you happy. Here are six ways to do it.

1. Act out your faith. Let your husband see the difference your faith makes in your life. He won't be very impressed

if you continue to blow up at everyone over small things or spend your time gossiping about the neighbors.

2. Let God work on your heart. Ask God to help you become all that you can be. Let him work in you to bring out the fruit of the Spirit: love, joy, peace, patience, kindness, goodness, faithfulness, gentleness, and self-control. It won't happen overnight, but as you grow and change, your husband will notice.
3. Be submissive. This doesn't mean that you are to be considered inferior to your husband or that you must bow down to his every whim, but it means to make him the head of your home. Consider his opinions, make what he cares about important to you, and treat him with respect.
4. Keep silent. As women we often try to talk our way into and out of situations. But if you want to win your husband to the Lord, keep silent.
5. Compliment and encourage your husband honestly. Begin to encourage your husband in positive ways. Point out to him what he does right and how important he is to the family. Tell him how he's a great father and how much you appreciate his help. You will see him grow and change in ways you never believed possible.
6. Do not be afraid. Fear keeps us from doing and being what God has called us to. Fear is at the core of anger. Fear of not being lovable makes us push people away, instead of welcoming them toward us. Fear of losing ourselves keeps us from following Jesus completely. Fear of losing control keeps us from discovering the true freedom we have when we believe in Christ Jesus.

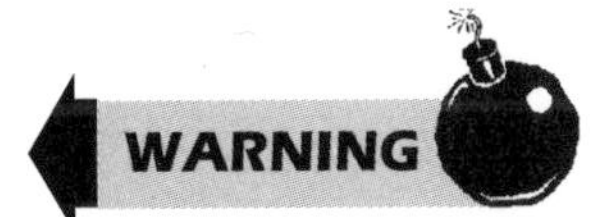

If you don't let your husband lead your household, he will abdicate his role and let you be in charge. Ask yourself if this is what you really want before you make that mistake.

Study Questions

1. Explain what Jesus meant when he told the rich young ruler to go sell all he had?
2. List some "treasure" that you can take to heaven.
3. Name at least four emotional needs that your children have.

4. Make a mental list of each of your children's strengths and weaknesses. Notice how different they are from each other.
5. Identify your child's greatest need and make a plan to meet it.
6. Write out the Gospel presentation in your own words.

CHAPTER WRAP-UP

- It is our responsibility to provide for the physical needs of our children. These include food, shelter, and clothing.
- It is also our responsibility to teach our children to be content with whatever they have and to learn that true happiness is not found in the things of this world, but in the things of Christ.
- Our children have many emotional needs. They include things like time, attention, respect, listening, love, and acceptance.
- Our children's greatest need is for salvation. All else pales in comparison. With salvation comes personal satisfaction with who they are, a peace that passes all understanding, joy no matter what the circumstances, and faith that will get them through anything life hands them, and a life everlasting.
- A believing wife can win an unbelieving husband to the Lord.

JUDY'S  BOOKSHELF

- *The Weigh Down Diet*, Gwen Shamblin, Doubleday. A different kind of diet book that concentrates on your relationship with the Lord. I highly recommend it for anyone who is struggling with his or her weight.
- *Building Your Child's Faith*, Alice Chapin. This little book is full of great ideas and activities for family devotions. Recommended by Focus on the Family.
- *Going It Alone*, Michelle Howe, Hendrickson Publishing. Chock full of practical ideas for single moms.

11 FACING THE TOUGH ISSUES

WHAT'S IN THIS CHAPTER

- Working outside of the Home
- Day Care
- Divorce
- Rebellious Children
- Out-of-Control Children
- How to Help the Children

Here We Go

Even though we are Christians, we still struggle. We're torn about whether or not we should work outside the home, and if we do, we worry about the kind of day care our children are in.

Some of us are divorced, or thinking about it. We are scared about the affect it will have on our children and wonder how we can best help them through it.

Still others of us have children who have drug and alcohol problems, eating disorders, are sexually promiscuous, have broken the law, have been kicked out of school, or are totally out of control.

There are no guarantees that just because we are Christians that our children will turn out okay. Let's look at what the Bible has to say to those of us struggling with these tough issues.

WORKING OUTSIDE OF THE HOME

Proverbs 31:10, 13–28 A wife of noble character who can find? She is worth far more than rubies. . . . She selects wool and **flax** and works with eager hands. She is **like the merchant ships**, bringing her food from afar. She gets up while it is still dark; she provides food for her family and portions for her servant girls. She considers a field and buys it; out of her earnings she plants a vineyard. She sets about her work vigorously; her arms are strong for her tasks. She sees that her trading is profitable, and her lamp does not go out at night. In her hand she holds the **distaff** and grasps the **spindle**

☞ **GO TO:**

Ruth 3:11 (noble character)

flax: *a plant whose fibers are made into linen*

like the merchant ships: *enterprising*

distaff: *a staff that holds unspun flax or wool for spinning into thread*

spindle: *a weighted spool that holds the spun wool*

☞ **GO TO:**

Genesis 41:42; Judges 8:26; Luke 16:19; Revelations 18:16 (fine linen and purple)

2 Samuel 15:2–6 (city gate)

Judges 14:12–13; Isaiah 3:23 (linen garments)

city: *a walled settlement of no more than ten acres*

gate: *heavily fortified entrance, with stout wooden doors that could be shut and braced by bars*

> with her fingers [see illustration below]. She opens her arms to the poor and extends her hands to the needy. When it snows, she has no fear for her household; for all of them are clothed in scarlet. She makes coverings for her bed; she is clothed in fine linen and purple [see GWRV, page 272]. Her husband is respected at the **city gate**, where he takes his seat among the elders of the land. She makes linen garments and sells them, and supplies the merchants with sashes. She watches over the affairs of her household and does not eat the bread of idleness.

Too Good to Be True?

We can look at this "perfect" woman and cringe. But notice, she "worked" not only inside the home—cooking, cleaning, making wool, weaving, sewing, and making sure the household lamps were always lit—but outside the home, too. She bought land, she planted a vineyard, she bartered her valuables, she sold linen garments, and she supplied merchants with sashes. Finally, in her spare moments, she helped the poor!

Spinning

Pictured is a woman using a spindle and distaff to make yarn. She is likely to be working with wool taken from her family's flocks.

This actually describes many mothers today. Ask yourself how many "tasks" you do.

Your list will differ depending on whether you work full-time or part-time, in or out of the home.

The truth is, all mothers work. We all have twenty-four hours in a day, and how we fill it depends on our talents, our priorities, and our circumstances.

The key here is that the Proverbs 31 woman had help (servants), she made the most of her days, she had a husband who highly esteemed her, and she made the Lord her first priority.

If you are feeling overwhelmed by all the responsibilities you have, consider getting some help. Here are some ideas:

- Delegate to your husband and children.
- Have a housecleaner come in one day a week.
- Take your husband's shirts to the laundry.
- Cut back at work or go part-time.
- Share a job with another mother.
- Work a ten-forty week. That will give you three days off to get your "household work" done.
- Prioritize your to-do lists.
- Take time for yourself.

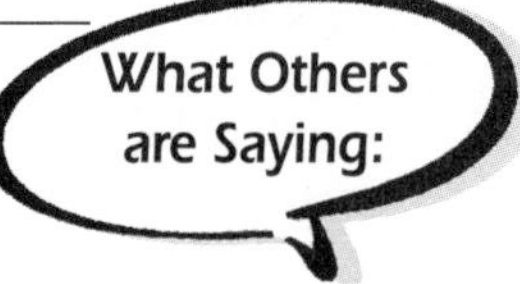

Gail MacDonald: There is probably no greater stress on a mother than feeling torn between husband and children. Add a job to the mix, and your stress level may go off the charts. The first step toward reducing the pressure that comes from trying to fill several roles is to assess your expectations. Ask yourself: What is my definition of a good wife and mother? And, given the busy circumstances of my life, is it possible for me to meet these expectations? . . . It is just not realistic to expect to do everything, every day that perhaps a stay-at-home mom might be able to do.[1]

John MacArthur: God's design for the woman is to be in the home—to be submissive to her own husband, to be caring for her own children, and to be tending the needs of her own home. Mothers who want to be successful parents cannot forsake those tasks and expect the Lord's blessing in their parenting.[2]

A spindle was a round stick with tapered ends used to form and twist the yarn in hand spinning. The spindle and the distaff are the most ancient of all instruments used in the craft of spinning. About eight to twelve inches long, spindles were used to guide the thread as it was fashioned into cloth. The weaver sometimes turned the spindle by rolling it across her thigh.

GO TO:

Acts 16:40; Philippians 1:1–10; 4:3 (Lydia)

Revelation 1:11 (Thyatira)

Acts 11:14 (household)

dealer in purple cloth: *a businesswoman*

household: *not only family but slaves and hired workers*

> **Acts 16:14–15** One of those listening was a woman named Lydia, a **dealer in purple cloth** from the city of Thyatira. When she and the members of her **household** were baptized, she invited us to her home.

A Modern Woman in Biblical Times

Lydia was a successful businesswoman. She not only owned a house, but the term "household" meant she had slaves and employed servants.

When she became a Christian, she did not give up her business; instead, she used it to benefit the apostles and the other Christians in her area. She made her home the center for Christian activity.

EXAMPLES FROM THE BIBLE

Scholars agree that Paul is including Lydia (see GWWB, page 281) in his opening remarks to the church at Philippi and when he refers to the women who have contended for the faith.

What Others are Saying:

Herbert Lockyer: Lydia not only sold her dyes—she served her Saviour. She stayed in business that she might have the money to help God's servants in their ministry. How her generous care of Paul and Silas, and of many others, must have cheered their hearts. Lydia was, first of all, a consecrated Christian, then a conscientious businesswoman who continued to sell her purple dyes for the glory of God.[3]

REMEMBER THIS

Thyatira was famous for its dyeing works (see illustration, page 209), especially royal purple. It was the most expensive and most coveted dye in the ancient world. The dye was found in the glands of the murex snail, which was harvested in the spring and fall when the seas were calmest. The recipe was kept secret for generations, making purple cloth even more valuable.

> **Titus 2:4–5** Then they can train the younger women to love their husbands and children, to be self-controlled and pure, to be **busy at home**, to be kind, and to be subject to their husbands, so that no one will malign the word of God.

busy at home: *good housekeepers*

Every Mother Is a Working Woman

The above scripture is often used to show that women should not work outside of the home, but the word used here for "busy at home" means housekeeping. The passage can be translated "the older women should train the younger women how to keep their homes."

Think About It

If we are following Jesus Christ and seeking his will in our lives, then we will know where he wants us, working full-time outside of the home or working full-time inside of the home. He will make it clear to us through our emotions, through feedback from our husbands, children, and friends.

The Making of Purple Dye

After murex snails are harvested, the liquid from their hypobranchial gland is simmered for nine days, strained, and then used for dyeing wool purple. These men are using tools to break open the shells and take out the glands.

Do not judge other women for the choices they are making for themselves and their families. That judgmental attitude may do more to discredit the name of Jesus than anything they are doing.

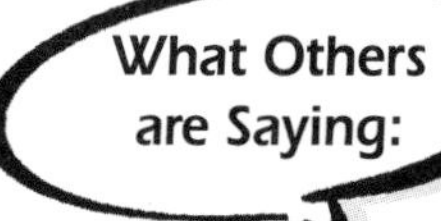

John MacArthur: Mothers in particular pay a high price when they leave the home to pursue a career. Not only do they step out of the role God has designed for wives, but they often must also abandon their most crucial role as the primary caregiver to their own children. I believe one of the worst errors a mother can make is to sacrifice time with her own children for the sake of pursuing a career.[4]

DAY CARE

Naomi: *mother-in-law to Ruth, the mother of the infant*

> **Ruth 4:16** Then **Naomi** took the child, laid him in her lap and cared for him.

Day Care in the Bible

☞ GO TO:

Genesis 35:8 (nurses)

nurses: *women who breast-fed other people's infants and helped raise the children*

Hiring help to take care of children is not something new. The Bible records that the Israelites had **nurses**. *"So they sent their sister Rebekah on her way, along with her nurse and Abraham's servant and his men"* (Genesis 24:59). Nurses were surrogate mothers and breast-fed the babies until they were weaned and then helped raise them. Some nurses were respected members of households, even after the child became an adult.

What Others are Saying:

Mary Whelchel: With all the publicity these days about child abuse in day-care centers, I think working mothers and fathers have a heavy responsibility to insure their children's environment is not only safe but conducive to their growth and maturity. I have to say that a center would have to be exceptional for me to leave my young child there day in and day out.[5]

Mildred B. Vermont: Being a full-time mother is one of the highest salaried jobs in my field since the payment is pure love.[6]

FROM JUDY'S HEART

When my sons were one and three, I went back to work full-time to pursue my career. I was offered a once-in-a-lifetime opportunity to work as a dietitian in a facility managed by the woman who had written my college textbooks. Not only that, Nancy a wonderful Christian friend, called and offered to take care of my children.

My workday started at 6:00 AM, but my husband would get our sons up, dress them, and take them to Nancy's at 9:00 AM. I would pick them up at 3:00 PM. It seemed perfect for everyone.

My sons liked going to Nancy's and even would cry when I picked them up. They always wanted to stay and play longer. Nancy didn't just "baby-sit." She developed age-appropriate activities, purchased educational toys, planned menus, and provided cubbyholes for their belongings.

Things moved along smoothly for a couple of years and then my oldest started insisting that I wake him up in the morning to say good-bye. His simple request touched my heart. However, that meant I would have to wake him up at 5:30 every morning. I worried about his rest, but he insisted and so I agreed. Religiously I shook him awake so we could hug and kiss and say good-bye. One morning I was late and forgot. My husband reported to me later that our son had cried and carried on something terrible.

Thinking that he must have just had a bad dream, I brushed it off. Besides, I didn't have time to worry about it. I had responsibilities, and my son would just have to understand. He'd get over it.

I continued waking him up and giving him an extra-hard squeeze, reassuring him of my love. He seemed to be happy once again and I thought we were back to our normal routine.

Then one morning I walked into his bedroom. Shook him once and then twice. He sleepily raised his arms. I hugged him, brushed his blond head, and whispered, "I love you." He snuggled back into his covers. I backed the car out of the garage and for some reason I looked up. He was standing in the window, his arms spread, screaming hysterically.

I stopped the car and ran inside. I grabbed him in my arms. He sobbed, "You didn't say good-bye, you didn't say good-bye." I held him realizing that he must not have wakened enough to know that I had. It took quite a while to calm him down enough so I could leave.

My well-ordered world was suddenly shattered. I prayed all the way to work, seeking God's will. It was clear. I needed to be home with my kids. I wanted to be home with my babies.

It took me a year, but finally I was able to quit. It cut our income in half and we struggled financially for years, but I have never regretted that decision.

DIVORCE

> **Malachi 2:16** "I hate divorce," says the LORD God of Israel, "and I hate a man's covering himself with violence as well as with his garment," says the LORD Almighty. So guard yourself in your spirit, and do not break faith.

God's View of Divorce

To write a book on mothering and not mention divorce would be a great oversight. Divorce is at an all-time high and the saddest thing is that, according to pollster George Barna, it is now occurring at a higher percentage rate among Christians than non-Christians. The results are devastating our children. The American Academy of Pediatrics says it is "like a death." Children never get over it.

Think About It

If your marriage is struggling, then work to keep it together, but if you're already divorced, learn what you can do to help your children recover. You can't undo all the damage, but you can keep it from becoming more severe.

What Others are Saying:

Ann Landers: In 1993 I asked my readers this question: "Looking back, do you regret having moved so rapidly to be divorced, and do you now feel that had you waited, the marriage might have been salvaged?" . . . To my surprise, out of nearly 30,000 responses, almost 23,000 came from women. Nearly three times as many readers said they were glad they divorced, and most said they wished they'd done it sooner.[7]

If you are in the process of divorcing, here are some things you can do to help your children:

1. Prepare your children as best you can. You and your husband both tell them together, and explain to them where they will live, go to school, and if they can take their dog.

2. Don't assume your children are okay, even if they're acting fine. They may be hiding their feelings to protect you from more pain.
3. Reassure them that it's not their fault and that you love them.
4. If at all possible, do not uproot your children.
5. Find a support group that can help them go through the grieving.
6. Maintain important relationships with grandparents, aunts, uncles, and cousins.
7. Get counseling for yourself.
8. Don't belittle your ex-spouse. Don't force your children to choose sides. Assure them that it is okay to spend time with the other parent.

Matthew 19:4–9 "Haven't you read," he replied, "that at the beginning the Creator 'made them male and female,' and said, 'For this reason a man will leave his father and mother and be united to his wife, and the two will become one flesh'? So they are no longer two, but one. Therefore what God has joined together, let man not separate."

"Why then," they asked, "did Moses command that a man give his wife a certificate of divorce and send her away?"

Jesus replied, "Moses permitted you to divorce your wives because your hearts were hard. But it was not this way from the beginning. I tell you that anyone who divorces his wife, except for marital unfaithfulness, and marries another woman commits adultery."

☞ **GO TO:**

Matthew 19:8; Mark 10:5; 16:14; Deuteronomy 10:16; Jeremiah 4:4 (hearts were hard)

Why Divorce Was Permitted

Divorce was permitted by Moses, not because it was God's will, but because of the cruelty of men. When men (or women) are caught in a marriage and they think there is no way out, they can be pretty cruel to one another. Divorce, however, was never part of God's original plan.

In this passage Jesus is talking about men because under Jewish law, women were not permitted to divorce. Today, with more and more women entering the workforce and able to support themselves, things have changed. Women now file 70 to 80 percent of divorces.

GO TO:

Exodus 34:14; Deuteronomy 4:24; 32:16, 21; Joshua 24:19; Psalm 78:58; 1 Corinthians 10:22; James 4:5 (jealous)

Numbers 16:31–34; Joshua 7:24 (households)

jealous: *desires exclusive devotion*

> **Exodus 20:5–6** "I, the Lord your God, am a **jealous** God, punishing the children for the sin of the fathers to the third and fourth generation of those who hate me, but showing love to a thousand [generations] of those who love me and keep my commandments."

Consequences of Divorce

Those Israelites who blatantly violated God's covenant and thus showed that they rejected the Lord as their King brought judgment on themselves and their households for generations. Divorce can affect a family like that. Children whose parents are divorced are two-thirds more likely to divorce themselves, which makes it more likely that their children will divorce, and on and on.

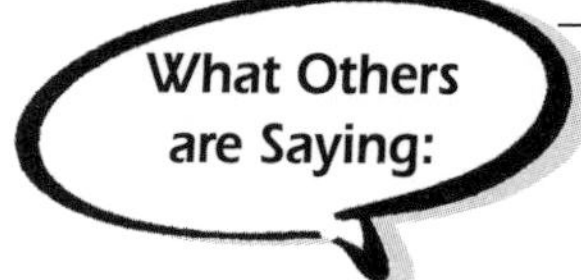

Jay Kessler: As Christian parents, we long for the pain a failed relationship or death inflicts on our children to disappear without a trace. But it doesn't.[8]

Researcher and author Judith Wallerstein followed a group of 131 children of divorce for twenty-five years. Eighteen months after the breakup she didn't find a single child who was well-adjusted. Five years later, she found a third of the children experienced moderate or severe depression, and at ten years a significant number were just drifting and underachieving. Even after twenty-five years, over half of the now-grown children had psychological problems they attributed to the divorce.[9]

Does This Sound like the Brady Bunch to You?

Putting blended families together is like rolling dice. You really won't know what you have until you are settled into a home trying to live together as a family. Suddenly the oldest child may become a younger child with older siblings bossing him around. The children may have to share a room or move out of their home. Discipline by the new parents is often resented, and their love rebuffed. It can take years to work out the kinks in these new families.

What Others are Saying:

Gail MacDonald: It's important to remember that for children living in a blended family, the rules have suddenly changed in the middle of the game. Having a stepmother was not the children's choice. And the loss of a mother, whether through divorce or death, has triggered a very necessary time of grief. You need to give children plenty of time and emotional breathing space to adjust to a new family.[10]

Think About It

Now would be a good time to find one or two other mothers who are trying to stepparent. Sharing your frustrations with someone else who is in your situation can ease some of the frustration and give you hope that things will get better.

REMEMBER THIS

Abraham Lincoln was raised by his stepmother, and he gave her all the credit for making him into the man he was.

REBELLIOUS CHILDREN

> **Genesis 19:30–38** Lot and his two daughters . . . lived in a cave. One day the older daughter said to the younger, "Our father is old, and there is no man around here to lie with us, as is the custom all over the earth. Let's get our father to drink wine and then lie with him and preserve our family line through our father." That night they got their father to drink wine, and the older daughter went in and lay with him. He was not aware of it when she lay down or when she got up. The next day the older daughter said to the younger, "Last night I lay with my father. Let's get him to drink wine again tonight, and you go in and lie with him so we can preserve our family line through our father." So they got their father to drink wine that night also, and the younger daughter went and lay with him. Again he was not aware of it when she lay down or when she got up.
>
> So both of Lot's daughters became pregnant by their father. The older daughter had a son, and she named him Moab; he is the father of the **Moabites** of today [see illustration, page 217]. The younger daughter also had a son, and she named him Ben-Ammi; he is the father of the **Ammonites** of today.

***Moabites** and **Ammonites:** two bitter enemies of Israel*

Wicked Daughters

There is nothing tougher than when our children do something wicked, especially when we believe we've done all the right things. We've taken them to church, given them all the advantages, taught them from infancy what was right and what was wrong. And yet, some children will choose to do evil.

Here is one reason—peer pressure.

The older daughter convinced the younger daughter to lay with her father. The consequences reverberated through the history of the Israelites because the descendants of these daughters became bitter enemies of Israel.

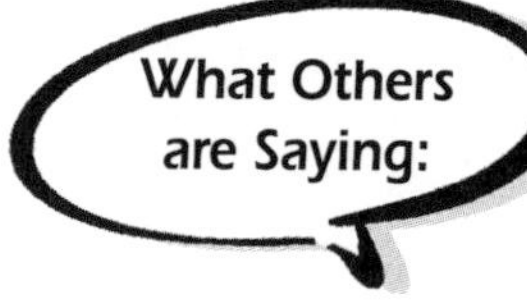

Herbert Lockyer: The lack of any true morality whatever in Lot's daughters is evident by what happened in that cave once all three were clear of the smoking Sodom. . . . How revolting was the conduct of the daughters when they made their father drunk in order to make him the unwilling father of their children. . . . They remain for all time a solemn reminder of the truth that "God is not mocked" for whatsoever a man soweth, that shall he also reap" (Galatians 6:7).[11]

☞ **GO TO:**

Genesis 10:19; 19 (Sodom)

John MacArthur: Most parents . . . have turned their kids over to their peers. . . . They have permitted all their children's spiritual, moral, and ethical instruction to come from television, movies, music, and other children. Even in the best cases, parents rely too much on school teachers, Sunday school teachers, and youth leaders—all outside the purview of the family. Parents must realize that character is neither inbred by genetics nor picked up by osmosis. Children are *taught* to be what they become. If they have become something other than what the parents hoped for, it is usually because they have simply learned from those who were there to teach them in their parents' absence.[12]

Lance R. Odden: [I have come] to peace with the notion that our children act one way around us and another with their peers, that they have an intense need to respond to that peer audience, and that there is only so much we can do about this beyond setting good examples and being involved in their lives through meaningful, honest conversations as often as is possible.[13]

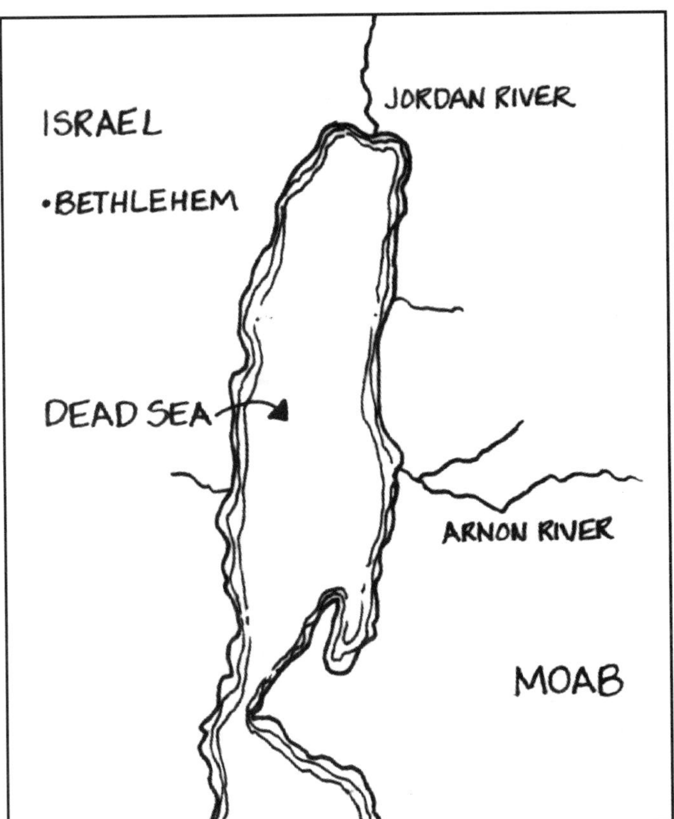

Location of Moab

The territory of the Moab nation was located east of the Dead Sea, as shown.

When a child is rebellious it can lead to disunity in a marriage, especially if you have different views on discipline. This is a time when your child needs you to keep a united front to help her combat the evil that she is acting out. If you can't agree with your husband on how to deal with this, then seek the help of a professional.

1 Samuel 2:22–25 Now **Eli**, who was very old, heard about everything his sons were doing to all Israel and how they slept with the women who served at the entrance to the Tent of Meeting. So he said to them, "Why do you do such things? I hear from all the people about these wicked deeds of yours. No, my sons; it is not a good report that I hear spreading among the LORD's people. If a man sins against another man, God may mediate for him; but if a man sins against the LORD, who will intercede for him?" His sons, however, did not listen to their father's rebuke, for it was the LORD's will to put them to death.

Eli: *prophet of the Lord*

☞ GO TO:

Exodus 27:21; 28:43; 29:4 (Tent of Meeting)

1 Samuel 2:12 (wicked)

Even the Prophet's Sons

No one is exempt from the tragedy of rebellious children. Eli was a high priest and a judge, and yet his sons did not know the Lord and even did evil things in their leadership roles at the Temple. Don't assume that, because you make a lot of money, or have a husband who is in a powerful job or a pastor or elder, that your children will turn out to be good.

Think About It

Is it our fault when our children make wrong choices? It might be, or it might not be. Our children have free will, and we have to honestly admit we have limited control over them, especially as they grow older. The lesson we must learn is that we cannot abdicate our role as parents.

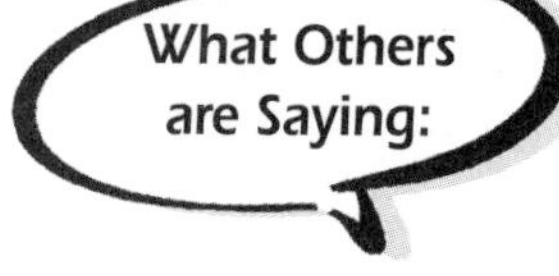

Barbara Johnson: As parents we must remember we are not responsible for our children's choices. But we must examine ourselves in times of crisis and admit to failures—then put them aside. God does go after the prodigals. As parents, it is our job to love our children; it is God's job to bring to pass His work of salvation in their lives.[14]

It we do not discipline our children, God will. Some consequences are unavoidable.

What Others are Saying:

Virginia Page Rohrer: Lord, I cry for wisdom to guide our troubled son. The enemy challenges his trust in You. Give me a heart to understand his deep distress, a mouth to express Your grace, and arms to show my precious child divine strength and protection. Oh, Love, You will not let him go. I rest my weary soul in You.[15]

Think About It

It's difficult to admit to our church family that we have a rebellious child, because we fear we will be judged. Don't suffer in silence.

When you share your struggle, you may be surprised to find other parents who have encountered similar behavior in their children. They can be a great support to you and may know of some helpful resources.

Don't suffer in silence. In the New Testament we are urged to "*carry each other's burdens, and in this way you will fulfill the law of Christ*" (Galatians 6:2).

Things You Learn from Your Children

- A ceiling fan is not strong enough to hold a forty-two-pound boy wearing a Superman outfit.
- A six-year-old can start a fire with a flint rock even though a thirty-six-year-old man says they can only do it in the movies.
- No matter how much Jell-O you put in a swimming pool, you still can't walk on water.

> **1 Samuel 8:3** But [Samuel's] sons did not walk in his ways. They turned aside after dishonest gain and accepted bribes and perverted justice.

Some of Us Never Learn

It's hard to imagine that Samuel, who replaced Eli as high priest and judge, did not learn from the mistakes of his mentor. And yet his sons also did wicked things, accepted bribes, and perverted justice. History often repeats itself, if we don't stop it.

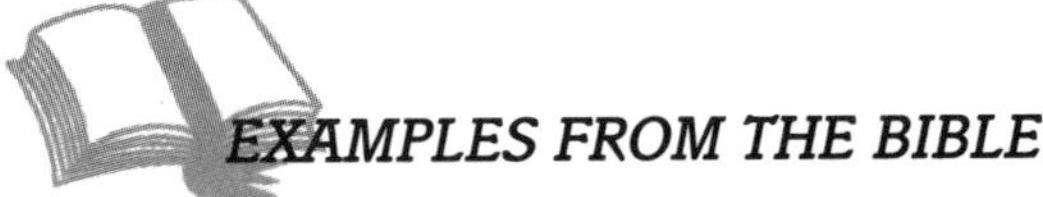

The failure of Eli and Samuel's sons led the people of Israel to demand a new form of government. They wanted a king, like their neighbors had. Thus, the door was opened for Saul to be the first king of Israel, preceding David (see GWBI, page 58). God often uses human weakness to bring about his greater plan.

When our children are experiencing trouble, it's easy to feel guilty. This can only make matters worse, because it opens us up to being manipulated by children who really need us to be strong. You might have made mistakes, but that does not excuse the behavior of your children.

Ruth Bell Graham: Lord, there are so many subtle temptations today. Please help the children learn early in life the fine line between right and wrong and make a habit to choose the right.[16]

OUT-OF-CONTROL CHILDREN

Ephesians 5:18 Do not get drunk on wine, which leads to **debauchery**.

debauchery: *excessive indulgence in sensual pleasures*

Drugs and Alcohol

Drug and alcohol abuse among teenagers concerns every parent. Here Paul explicitly warns against getting drunk because it can lead to worse problems, a life that is lived indulging oneself in sensual pleasures.

Think About It

Drinking lowers our children's inhibitions, which then makes them more vulnerable to do what they normally wouldn't. As parents we need to warn our children of the dangers of drinking and drug abuse, and the earlier the better. Don't assume, because your child is attending Sunday school and has Christian friends, that he won't be tempted at some time in his life.

The use of alcohol typically begins around the age of thirteen. Nine and a half million children between the ages of twelve and twenty had at least one drink in the last month. Half of those (4.4 million) were binge drinkers. They consumed five or more drinks in a row on at least five different days.[17]

The number one problem on college campuses today is drinking. Ivy League universities report that every weekend three to five students end up in health care centers for alcohol abuse. In the last year for which statistics were collected, 384 students between the ages of fifteen and twenty-four died from alcohol poisoning.[18]

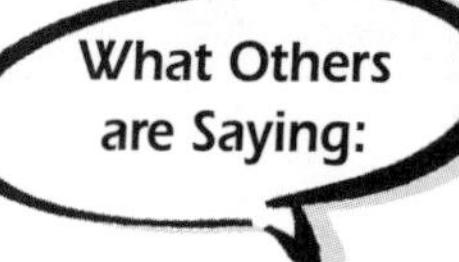

Melinda Sacks: Experts estimate that 60 to 75 percent of the teens and young adults who abuse drugs and alcohol have parents who are abusers. . . . The most powerful thing a parent can do to moderate, if not eliminate, the chances their children drink may also be the most difficult: It is to set a good example.[19]

Bill Pollack, author of *Real Boys*, says, "Boys may exhibit **bravado** and **braggadocio**, but they find it more difficult to express their genuine selves." He believes that young boys have learned about their emotional lives primarily from their mothers, and the modern family does not allow enough time or energy for the kind of emotional nurturing that boys need in order to accept their emotional side. As a consequence, boys are more likely to imitate their fathers, who don't know how to handle their emotions, either.[20]

Think About It

bravado: *swaggering display of courage*

braggadocio: *bragging*

Reader's Digest Illustrated Dictionary of Bible Life & Times: Wine was typically enjoyed at most meals, but the Israelites disapproved of drinking too much.[21]

> **1 Thessalonians 4:3–7** It is God's will that you should be **sanctified**: that you should avoid **sexual immorality**; that each of you should learn to control his own body in a way that is holy and honorable, not in passionate lust like the heathen, who do not know God; and that in this matter no one should wrong his brother or take advantage of him. The Lord will punish men for all such sins, as we have already told you and warned you. For God did not call us to be impure, but to live a holy life.

sanctified: *set apart*

sexual immorality: *sexual relations outside marriage*

☞ **GO TO:**

1 Corinthians 5:1 (sexual immorality)

Sexual Sins

We may think we live in a sexually charged society, but at the time Paul wrote this the moral standards were equally low. In fact, many Christians considered his command unreasonable.

But God has called us to be set apart, to be different from the society we live in. That is one reason we need to teach our children high moral values.

And there is another reason—sexual immorality has consequences: venereal diseases, unwanted pregnancy, AIDS, emotional scars, pain, and humiliation. God wants to protect our children, not just deny them worldly pleasure.

Two common misconceptions held by Christian parents are that their own children don't have this problem and that sex education is a deterrent. The first belief is like sticking your head in the sand, and the latter is totally false. Research has shown that sex education results in earlier sexual experiences.

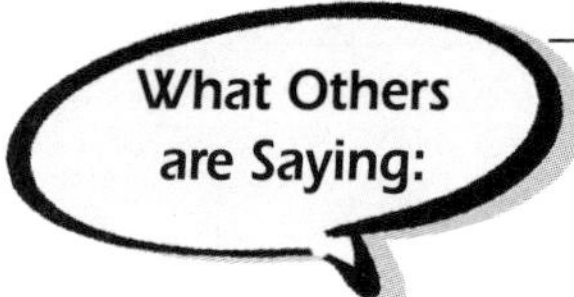

Gary Thomas: Although the rate of teen pregnancy has been decreasing in the 1990s, about one million teens become pregnant each year in the United States, according to the Medical Institute for Sexual Health; one-third of these pregnancies result in an abortion. Of the children carried to term, about 72 percent are born out of wedlock. This social devastation is exacerbated by an alarming health crisis among young people. In 1996, five of the top ten reportable infectious diseases—including the top four—were sexually transmitted. Adolescents (10–19) and young adults (20–24) are the age groups most at risk for acquiring a sexually transmitted disease.[22]

Richard Nadler: When adults teach kids how to have sex, how to use contraceptives, and where to get them, the kids simply have more sex. And this approach is the heart and soul of sex-ed ideology.[23]

Anorexia and Bulimia

One of the problems now facing our young is the obsession with weight. Thin is in, fat is unacceptable. Children as young as ten are worrying about their weight and talking about dieting. Twenty to 30 percent of fourth and fifth grade girls want to get thinner, and 40 to 60 percent of all high school girls are on diets.[24] This is only exacerbated by "perfect" women they see in the movies, on television, and in advertising. (Models weigh on average 110 pounds and are six feet tall.)

anorexia nervosa: *extreme food restriction and excessive weight loss*

bulimia nervosa: *a cycle of binge eating followed by purging using vomiting, laxatives, or excessive exercise*

This preoccupation with weight can lead to two eating disorders called **anorexia nervosa** and **bulimia nervosa**. The resulting weight loss is sometimes so severe that it can lead to serious illness and even death. Anorexia and bulimia have leveled off in the past few years, yet one and a half percent of young women still have serious cases of bulimia, and another less than one percent (still a significant number) have anorexia nervosa.[25]

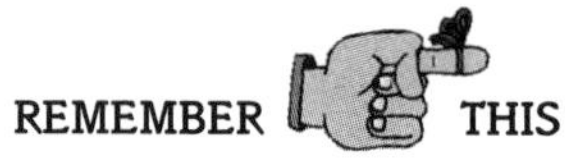

If your child seems obsessed with eating and is below normal weight, talk to a doctor or counselor about your concerns. The sooner you get your child some help, the easier recovery will be.

Full Armor of God

Equipment	Quality	Interpretation
Belt	Truth	Openness and honesty bind Christians together (Ephesians 4:15, 25)
Breastplate	Righteousness	Morality and purity are to mark every life (Ephesians 5:3)
Sandals (shod feet)	Gospel of peace	Unity and harmonious relationships must be maintained (Ephesians 4:3)
Shield	Faith	Confidence and hope should be placed in God (Ephesians 3:20)
Helmet	Salvation	Awareness of our identity as members of Christ's Body brings assurance (Ephesians 3:6)
Sword of the Spirit	Word of God	Only this equipment has not been discussed previously in Ephesians, so it is defined now (6:17)

SOURCE: *The Revell Bible Dictionary*, Lawrence O. Richards, ed. (Grand Rapids, MI: Fleming H. Revell, 1990), p. 94.

HOW TO HELP THE CHILDREN

Ephesians 6:12–13 For our struggle is not against **flesh and blood**, but against the rulers, against the authorities, against the powers of this dark world and against the spiritual forces of evil in the **heavenly realms**. Therefore put on the full armor of God, so that when the day of evil comes, you may be able to stand your ground, and after you have done everything, to stand.

Put on the Armor of God

When our children are in the middle of a crisis, we are too. We're angry and hurt and we yell and scream at them, thinking our battle is with them. But it's not. It's with the power of darkness, and what better way to destroy our faith than through our children.

Paul admonishes us to put on the full armor of God, not just for our sake, but for our children's sakes, too.

☞ **GO TO:**

1 Corinthians 15:50; Hebrews 2:14 (flesh and blood)

Romans 8:38 (powers)

Ephesians 1:3 (heavenly realms)

flesh and blood: *human beings*

heavenly realms: *the place where Christ now resides*

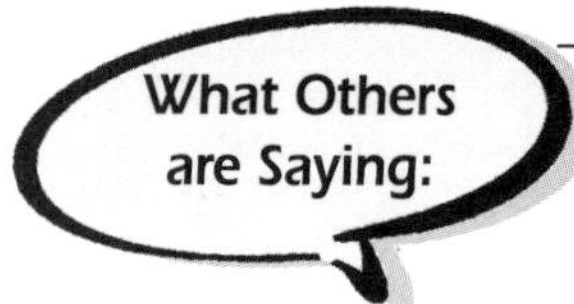

Jim Cymbala: Our oldest daughter, Chrissy, had been a model child growing up. But around age sixteen she started to stray. . . . There were many nights when we had no idea where she was. Her boyfriend was everything we did not want for our child. . . . The more I pressed, the worse Chrissy got. . . . I knew I had to let go of the situation. Back home in New York, I began to pray with an intensity and growing faith as never before. Today she is a pastor's wife in the Midwest with three wonderful children. Through all this, Carol and I learned as never before that persistent calling upon the Lord breaks through every stronghold of the devil, for nothing is impossible with God.[26]

GO TO:

Isaiah 11:5 (belt)

Isaiah 59:17 (breastplate)

Ephesians 6:14–16 Stand firm then, with the belt of truth buckled around your waist, with the breastplate of righteousness in place, and with your feet fitted with the readiness that comes from the gospel of peace. In addition to all this, take up the **shield** of faith, with which you can extinguish all the flaming arrows of the evil one.

shield: *large Roman shield covered with leather and soaked in water so it will put out flaming arrows*

Be Proactive, Not Reactive

Here we are being told to put on the belt of truth and the breastplate of righteousness and then to take up the shield of faith. All of these are protective devices that will thwart the arrows, doubt and fear, that Satan likes to shoot at us.

Think About It

When we have a troubled child, anxiety takes over and we overreact to everything. One solution is to be proactive.

Instead of waiting for the next incident, sit down with your children and clearly spell out what you expect from them, and the consequences if they fail to keep those rules. Do not threaten or get angry.

If they break a rule, then follow through with the consequences. Don't allow them to wiggle out. Your children need you to be strong for them.

What Others are Saying:

Barbara Johnson: Some people live with a low-grade anxiety tugging at their spirit all day long. They go to sleep with it, wake up with it, carry it around at home, in town, to church, and with friends. Here's a remedy: Take the present moment and find something to laugh at. People who laugh, last.[27]

A little girl was diligently pounding away on her mother's word processor. When Mom asked what she was doing, she said she was writing a story. "What's it about?" Mom asked. "I don't know," she replied, "I can't read."

Grow Your Marriage

Quarrels are often the result of looking to our mate to fulfill our needs or provide our sense of security and take away our fear. Begin to look to your relationship with the Lord for these things. Present a united front to problems you face and see if you don't notice a change in your attitude toward your husband.

> **Ephesians 6:17** Take the **helmet** of salvation and the sword of the Spirit, which is the word of God.

GO TO:

Isaiah 59:17 (helmet of salvation)

helmet: *provided protection and was used as a symbol of military victory*

Let Go, Let God

The helmet protected one of the most vital parts of the body, just as salvation protects us spiritually. The sword was also used to protect self and loved ones. The word of God said over our children has the same kind of power.

We want to fix our troubled children, but often we can't. They are too old to be sent to their rooms, or they just laugh at us when we lay down the rules.

This is when we need to turn to God and let go and let him. Take up the Bible and begin to read it. Pray the Word over your children, bathe your home in prayer. Get yourself right with God and begin to claim his promises.

Your child might be out of your reach, but he or she is never out of the reach of God.

Think About It

What Others are Saying:

Cheri Fuller: Trust when you pray for your kids, it's never in vain. It's time well spent for eternity. When mothers and fathers pray, no matter where they are or what their life circumstances are, God hears, and their children's lives are influenced forever.[28]

For Single Moms—If you are a single mom and you have a child who is out of control, you can really feel all alone. Look for help. Talk to your pastor and see if there are other men or women in the church who would reach out to your troubled teen. Maybe one of them would even be willing to mentor your child. It's sometimes amazing what another adult who isn't the child's parent can accomplish! Continue to seek and knock until you find someone to help you.

> **Ephesians 6:18** And pray in the Spirit on all occasions with all kinds of prayers and requests. With this in mind, be alert and always keep on praying for all the saints.

Pray without Stopping

The battle for our children's souls, hearts, and minds is a spiritual battle. Prayer is the most powerful weapon we have. Never underestimate it.

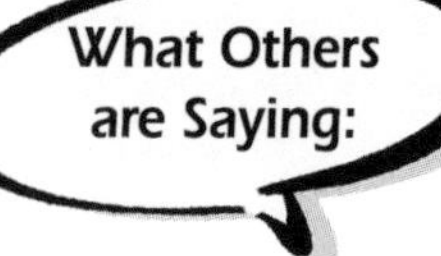

Susanna Wesley, mother of John and Charles, was married to a difficult man who got them deeply into debt. She gave birth to nineteen children, but only nine survived. Their home burned to the ground twice, destroying everything they owned. In spite of all these hardships she was determined to raise her children to glorify Christ. Every day she spent two hours in prayer for them.

John became a powerful preacher, both in England and America, and founded the Methodist movement. Charles wrote many of the hymns we sing in our churches today.

What Others are Saying:

Ruth Bell Graham: Be tender, Lord, we plead for those with runaways for whom moms bleed. But be tenderest of all with each whose child no longer cares . . . is out of reach.[29]

Study Questions

1. Name examples from the Bible of women who worked outside of the home.

2. Describe a biblical "nurse" and contrast that with a modern day care center.
3. Why was divorce permitted by Moses?
4. The prophet Eli's sons rebelled against the Lord. His successor, Samuel, also had sons who rebelled. Why do you think Samuel failed to learn from Eli's mistakes?
5. Why is drinking too much forbidden in Jewish Law?
6. What are some of the physical and emotional consequences of sexual immorality?
7. Name the parts of the armor of God.
8. Make a plan to pray for each of your children daily.

CHAPTER WRAP-UP

- Whether or not to work outside of the home is an individual decision neither specifically forbidden nor condoned in the Bible. Two examples of women who worked outside of the home as businesswomen were Lydia and the Proverbs 31 woman.
- Nurses were used to help raise children. They were often loyal members of the household.
- Divorce is never God's best. The consequences on children can be devastating. Even after twenty-five years they can be emotionally damaged by the divorce.
- Even the best of parents can have children who rebel. There are several examples in the Bible—Eli's sons, Samuel's sons, and Abraham's son Ishmael.
- It is up to parents to warn their children of the dangers of too much drinking/drugs, sexual immorality, eating disorders, etc.
- Being proactive in getting them help is one of the best solutions.
- Our real struggle is not against flesh and blood (our children), but against the rulers, the powers, the authorities of this dark world. To overcome the evil, we need to turn on the light by putting on the full armor of God to protect ourselves and our children.
- Prayer is one of the best things we can do for our children. We should begin from the time of conception until the Lord takes us home.

JUDY'S BOOKSHELF

- *When Mothers Pray,* Cheri Fuller, Multnomah. Will show you how, where, when, and why prayer is so necessary for a mother.
- *Prayers from a Mother's Heart,* Ruth Bell Graham, Thomas Nelson. A nice gift book full of inspirational prayers that will warm your heart.
- *Fresh Wind, Fresh Fire,* Jim Cymbala, Zondervan. A book that changed my view of the power of prayer.

12 MISTAKES MOTHERS MAKE

WHAT'S IN THIS CHAPTER

- Faultfinding
- Misplaced Values
- Favoritism
- Too Busy to Parent
- Misguided Love
- Disrespect for Her Husband
- Setting a Bad Example

Here We Go

As mothers we have an incredible influence on our children for good and bad. Like it or not, we can make mistakes that will affect them the rest of their lives.

Sometimes poor parenting skills are learned from our parents or from well-meaning child psychologists or popular media. Sometimes our mistakes are made out of our own needs.

Whatever the reason, we must do all we can to be the best we can be.

Let's take a look at some of the mistakes parents made in the Bible and see what we can learn from them.

FAULTFINDING

> **Colossians 3:21** Fathers, do not **embitter** your children, or they will become **discouraged**.

embitter: *provoke to anger*

discouraged: *disheartened*

Teaching or Tearing Down?

This is directed at fathers, but easily can be applied to mothers as well. Paul is cautioning against parents who continually find fault with their children. Nothing they do is ever good enough, whether it be school, sports, cleaning their room, the way they eat, or the way they look.

This can do great harm to children who want to please their parents, and instead of getting encouragement, they are discouraged. After banging their heads against the wall for a few years, they eventually stop caring. When children become sullen and indifferent there is no motive strong enough to get them to do anything, because they know it will never be good enough.

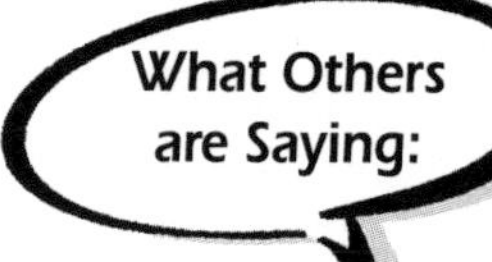

Patricia H. Rushford: Ella May, mother of three, felt it was her duty to consistently point out her children's mistakes. "For crying out loud, Andy," she yelled after him as he slipped out the door to play with his friends. "Why can't you be more like your sister? I always have to clean up after you and I'm getting tired of it. Do you hear me?" . . . Andy is a grown man now. . . . His mother still nags. She is still disappointed in him. And he, after all these years, still wants to please her, but he can't. He never could.[1]

Dr. Ross Campbell: If parents normally use pleasant requests, the occasional use of direct commands will be quite effective. The more parents use authoritative ways of telling a child what to do, the less response they will have. This is especially true if they are also angry, hostile, or hysterical when they do it.[2]

MISPLACED VALUES

THE BIG PICTURE 

Genesis 19:1–26 Two angels went to Sodom. At the **city gate** they meet Lot who invites them into his home for the evening. While they were eating, men from the city knock at the door demanding the visitors come out so that they can have sex with them. Lot refuses to send the men out, but offers them his two virgin daughters instead. They refuse to listen and pressure Lot to give in. The two angels go to the door and strike everyone blind and tell Lot to get everyone out who belonged to him for the city is going to be destroyed. Everyone refuses to go and even Lot hesitates. The angels grasp the hands of Lot, his wife, and daughters and lead them outside of the city. The angels tell Lot and his family to flee and to not look back. But Lot's wife looks back, and she becomes a pillar of salt.

☞ GO TO:

Genesis 16:7; 18:2 (two angels)

Luke 17:32 (Lot's wife)

city gate: *administrative and judicial center where legal matters were discussed and prosecuted*

From a Pillar in the Community to a Pillar of Salt

Lot's wife liked where she was living. She liked the luxuries, the fancy parties, and the high position her husband held. She didn't realize how wicked her world had become and so as she fled the city, she couldn't help but look back at all she was leaving behind. Her community meant more to her than her family. Instead of seeing this as a chance to get her daughters away from a sinful society, she looked back, and God turned her into a pillar of salt. Unfortunately she had already passed her values along to her daughters.

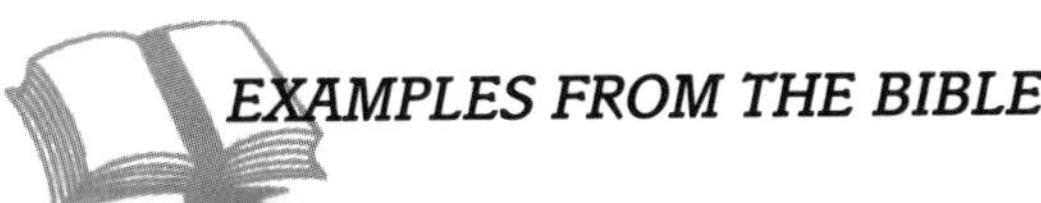

Later Lot's daughters commit incest with their father. The mother was partially to blame by bringing these girls up to value the things of this world over the things of God. If they had a believing faith, they would have waited on God to supply them with proper husbands. Instead they took circumstances into their own hands and lay with their father.

GO TO:

Genesis 19:30–38 (incest)

FAVORITISM

> **James 2:1** My brothers, as believers in our glorious Lord Jesus Christ, don't show favoritism.

GO TO:

James 2:9; Deuteronomy 1:17; Leviticus 19:15; Proverbs 24:23; Acts 10:34 (favoritism)

Mom Likes Me Best!

God loves each of us the same. In his eyes there is no one better than another; we are all equal. We should treat each other and especially our children the same way. When we don't, it brings disharmony into the home. Jealousy grows as one child sees the other being treated differently.

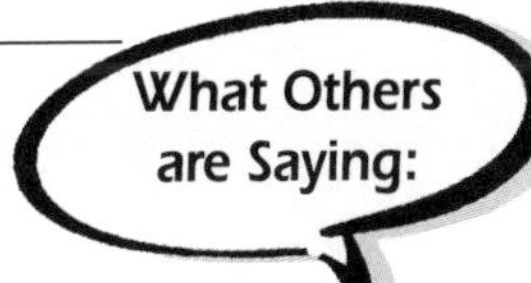

C. W. Neal: To be a world-class mother, you must consider the individuality of each child.[3]

> **Genesis 25:28** Isaac, who had a taste for wild game, loved Esau, but Rebekah loved Jacob.

GO TO:

Genesis 37:3 (loved)

Playing Favorites

Esau and Jacob were the twin sons of Rebekah and Isaac. The two boys were as different as night and day.

Esau was hairy and ruddy in complexion. Very much an outdoorsman, he liked to hunt and fish and was uncomfortable around the more civilized camp. He was used to providing for his own needs and had little use for the niceties of civilization. Isaac loved Esau more than Jacob because he saw himself reflected in this man among men.

Jacob, Isaac's younger son, was a puzzle to his father. Isaac couldn't understand Jacob's contentment in just hanging around the tent and doing "woman's work."

Jacob, unlike Esau, was fair-complexioned. He was comfortable around the things of camp. He looked after the sheep and cattle and probably took care of the needs of the household. He liked to cook, and probably sat for hours talking with the women who were busy sewing, weaving, and baking. Rebekah liked him best because he reflected the things she valued—civilization, a caring attitude, and refined conversation. Maybe to his mother Esau seemed like a wild man, without manners, and she probably feared the day he would be in charge of the household.

Think About It

What kind of arguments did Esau and Jacob hear between their parents? Did Isaac and Rebekah compare children within earshot of the boys? Did they unfairly defend one against the other? Did the boys grow up to be so different because of the open favoritism shown by their parents?

Grow Your Marriage

Maybe we can't help but be drawn to the child who is more like us in temperament. But we need to be careful that we don't allow this to tear apart a marriage. We must present a united front, not only in regard to discipline, but also in regard to love for our children. It will help them feel loved and accepted by both parents, and it also will strengthen your marriage.

☞ GO TO:

Genesis 49:1–28 (blessing)

Genesis 27:6–17 Rebekah said to her son Jacob, "Look, I overheard your father say to your brother Esau, 'Bring me some game and prepare me some tasty food to eat, so that I may give you my blessing in the presence of the LORD before I die.' Now, my son, listen carefully and do what I tell you: Go out to the flock and bring me two choice young goats, so I can prepare some tasty food for your father, just the way he likes it. Then take it to your father to eat, so that he may give you his blessing before he dies."

> Jacob said to Rebekah his mother, "But my brother Esau is a hairy man, and I'm a man with smooth skin. What if my father touches me? I would appear to be tricking him and would bring down a curse on myself rather than a blessing."
>
> His mother said to him, "My son, let the curse fall on me. Just do what I say; go and get them for me."
>
> So he went and got them and brought them to his mother, and she prepared some tasty food, just the way his father liked it. Then Rebekah took the best clothes of Esau her older son, which she had in the house, and put them on her younger son Jacob. She also covered his hands and the smooth part of his neck with the goatskins. Then she handed to her son Jacob the tasty food and the bread she had made.

A Recipe for Heartache

Rebekah is deceptive. She wants her favorite son to inherit her husband's blessing so that Jacob will get the bulk of the inheritance and be in charge of the household after his father's death. She gets Jacob to help her, and together they deceive Isaac into giving his blessing, not to his favorite son, Esau, but to Jacob.

When Esau finds out, he is furious, so Jacob is forced to flee to his uncle, Laban. There he stays for fourteen years laboring to earn his wife Rachel. While he is gone his mother dies. The price she paid for her deception was to never see her son again.

☞ **GO TO:**

Genesis 29–33 (Laban)

What Others are Saying:

Margaret Wold: [God spoke to Rebekah and said,] "I want you to remember what I am about to tell you because you will have to be the one who sees that my word is carried out. . . . I have chosen to reverse the usual order of things. . . . I have chosen the second-born child to take the place normally reserved for the firstborn." . . . Rebekah has often been characterized by biographers as a devious, scheming wife, but was she not carrying out her God-given responsibility as preserver of the covenant?[4]

Think About It

We can come down pretty harshly on Rebekah for her behavior, but how often do we do the same thing? We cover over the mistakes of our children and tell them "we won't tell Daddy this time." Or their father disciplines them, but we let them off the hook early or even do their penance for them. We say little things when their father is gone that show our own willingness to deceive.

REMEMBER THIS

A blessing is the act of declaring, or wishing, God's favor and goodness upon others. The blessing is not only the good effect of words; it also has the power to bring them to pass. Once given it cannot be revoked.

What Others are Saying:

Dr. James Dobson: Are we without spiritual resources with which to support our sons and daughters? Absolutely not! We are given the powerful weapon of intercessory prayer which must never be underestimated.[5]

☞ **GO TO:**

Genesis 27:28–29 (blessing)

Amnon: *David's oldest son*

Tamar: *David's daughter by Maacah of Geshur and full sister to Absalom*

TOO BUSY TO PARENT

THE BIG PICTURE

2 Samuel 13:1–29 Amnon, the son of David, desires his half sister **Tamar**. Feigning illness he lures her into his bedroom where he rapes her. Afterwards, he despises her and throws her out of his room. She runs to her brother Absalom and tells him the whole tale. When David hears of this he is furious, but does nothing. Anger burns in Absalom's heart and he looks for an opportunity to get even. Two years later, he gets his brother drunk and orders his men to kill his brother. After the deed is done Absalom and his men ride away.

Who's Watching the Kids?

David was a successful king, yet when it came to his family he was a failure. Was it because he was too busy? Running a kingdom had to be time consuming, with wars to wage, peace agreements to be worked out, budgets to balance, and speeches to be given.

But if he was too busy, where were the mothers of these children? Something needed to be done, but nothing was done. Amnon suffered no consequences for his actions even though he had destroyed his sister and broken the Law of God (Leviticus 18: 9, 11).

Are you too busy to discipline your children? It takes time to maintain order in the home and carry out discipline in a fair manner. If you send a child to his room, then you have to make sure he stays there. If you send him out to rake leaves, then you have to follow up and see that he did what you asked. And when you don't, your children will come away either thinking you don't care or that they got away with breaking a rule.

Tamar's rape meant she was no longer a virgin and could not be offered by her father to any other potential husband.

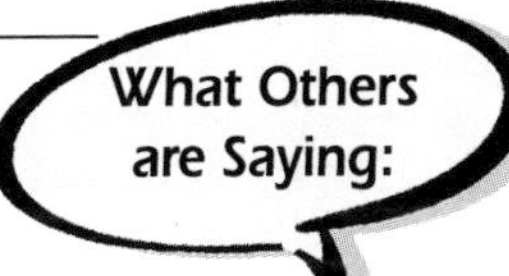

John MacArthur: The most dominant thing you notice about a child when he comes into the world is that he is totally selfish. He wants what he wants immediately, and he thinks everything in reach belongs to him. It is difficult to teach a child how to share, what to say at appropriate times, and how to be humble. None of those things come naturally to any child.[6]

MISGUIDED LOVE

> **Judges 14:1–4** Samson went down to Timnah and saw there a young **Philistine** woman. When he returned, he said to his father and mother, "I have seen a Philistine woman in Timnah [see illustration, page 236]; now get her for me as my wife."
>
> His father and mother replied, "Isn't there an acceptable woman among your relatives or among all our people? Must you go to the uncircumcised Philistines to get a wife?"
>
> But Samson said to his father, "Get her for me. She's the right one for me."

Philistine: *an aggressive tribal group that occupied part of southwest Palestine from about 1200 to 600* B.C.

Manoah, You're Spoiling That Kid!

Late in life, Samson's parents were given a special son. From conception he was set apart from everyone else. During pregnancy his mother refrained from eating anything that came from a grapevine, drinking anything that was fermented, or eating any unclean food.

☞ **GO TO:**

Judges 13
(Samson's parents)

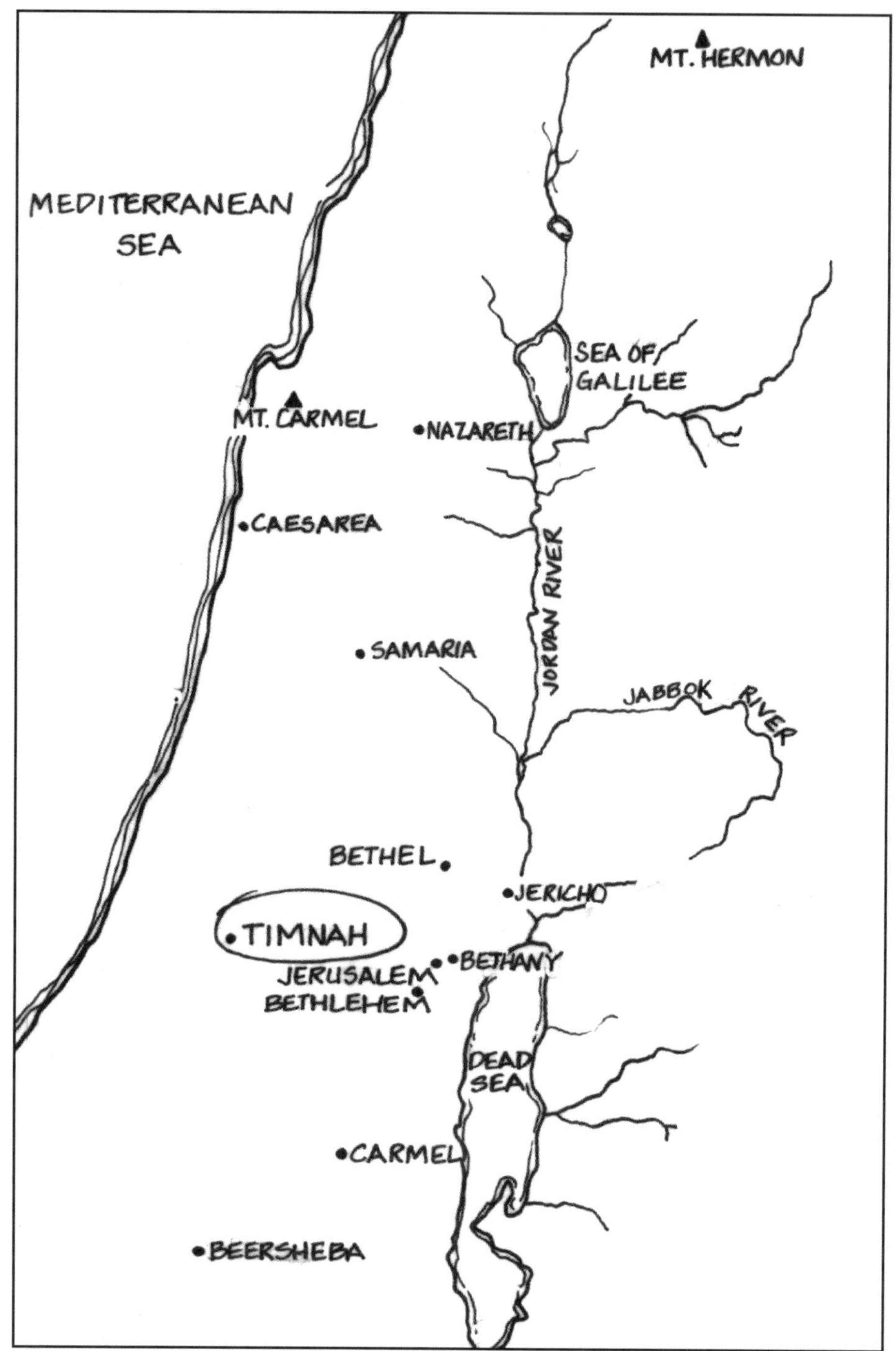

A Map of Palestine Showing Timnah

Timnah, in the hill country, was the home of Samson's wife and inhabited by Philistines.

They knew that Samson was especially chosen by God to free the Israelites from the Philistines. (See GWBI, page 54.) Because of that, they overindulged him. When he came begging to marry a Philistine, they gave in even though they knew it was wrong.

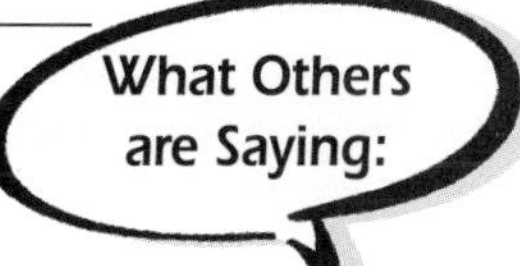

Patricia H. Rushford: Lack of discipline is a fearful thing. We all, even as adults, need boundaries and rules to keep us from running wild. . . . Children who control their homes because parents are afraid to or refuse to discipline, are miserable tyrants.[7]

> **1 Samuel 3:13–14** For I [God] told him [Eli] that I would judge his family forever because of the sin he knew about; his sons made themselves contemptible, and he failed to restrain them. Therefore, I swore to the house of Eli, 'The guilt of Eli's house will never be atoned for by sacrifice or offering.' "

GO TO:

Leviticus 24:14 (contemptible)

1 Samuel 2:27–36 (swore)

Exodus 33:7 (Tent of Meeting)

Tent of Meeting: *where the people met before the Tabernacle was built*

Who's Accountable?

Eli's sons were wicked. They had no regard for the Lord, they treated the Lord's offering with contempt, and slept with the women who served at the entrance to the **Tent of Meeting** (see illustration, page 238). When Eli found out, he rebuked his sons but did not remove them from office, thus showing his weakness of character. He was unable to control his own family.

What Others are Saying:

Dr. James Dobson: Parents today are much too willing to blame themselves for everything their children do. Only in this century have they been so inclined. If a kid went bad 100 years ago, he was a bad kid. Now it's the fault of his parents. . . . When their kids entangle themselves in sin and heartache, guess who feels responsible for it? Behavior is caused, isn't it? The blame inevitably makes a sweeping U-turn and lodges itself in the hearts of the parents.[8]

GO TO:

Exodus 37:1–9 (Ark of the Covenant)

1 Samuel 4:12–18 (died)

Ark of the Covenant: *the most sacred item of the ancient Israelites. It contained a sample of manna, the stone tablet on which were written the Ten Commandments, and Aaron's rod.*

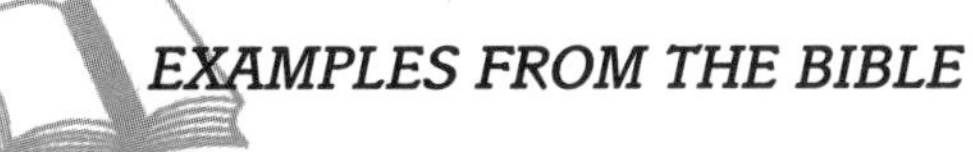

Because of the sin of Eli's sons, God allowed the Philistines to attack and capture the **Ark of the Covenant** (see illustration, page 239). The Philistines defeated the Israelites in battle and both of Eli's sons were killed. When he heard the terrible news, Eli fell backward off his stool and died. A high price to pay for allowing his children to run wild.

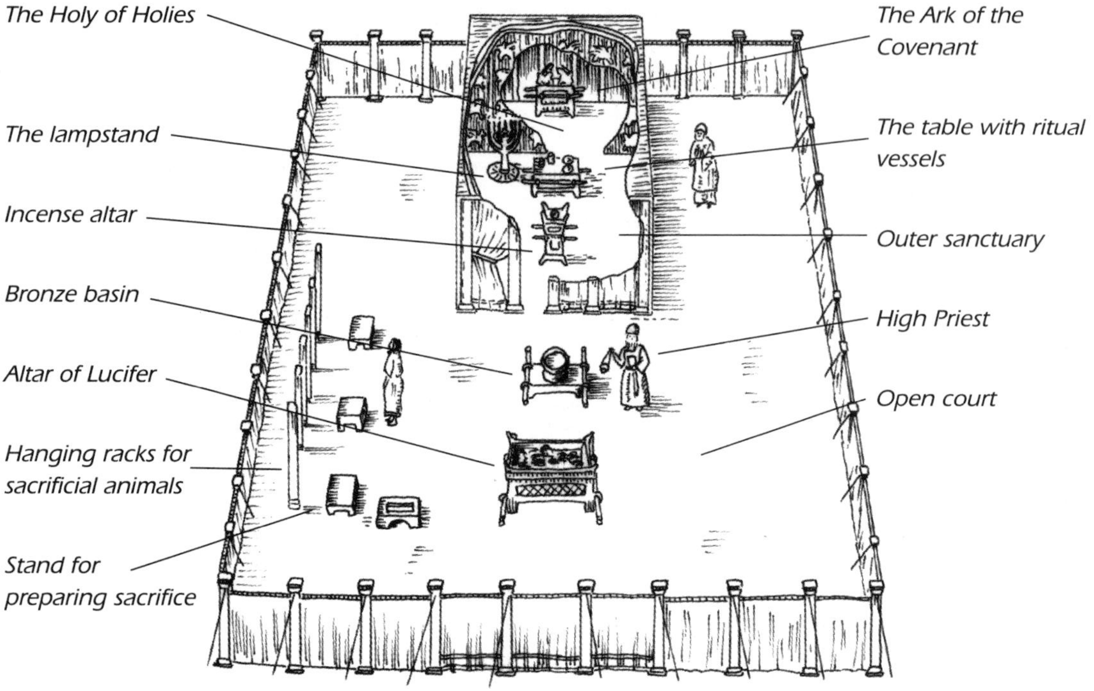

The Holy of Holies

The Ark of the Covenant

The lampstand

The table with ritual vessels

Incense altar

Outer sanctuary

Bronze basin

High Priest

Altar of Lucifer

Open court

Hanging racks for sacrificial animals

Stand for preparing sacrifice

Tent of Meeting

Pictured here is the Tent of Meeting, where Eli and his sons served.

FROM JUDY'S HEART

I know a couple, good solid Christians, who have a son who has been caught stealing and doing drugs, and has been kicked out of school. They've gone to the church, school, and police. They've tried praying, counseling, and intervention. He promises to pull himself together, and then they discover he's sneaking out at night and lying to them. Sometimes they feel like giving up, but they can't. This is their son and they want to help him. But how do you help someone who doesn't want it?

There are no easy answers for kids like this. There are no quick formulas or simple solutions. There's not a Bible verse you can give his parents or a book they can read that will solve their problem.

They blame themselves and wonder what they did wrong. Guilt is their constant companion.

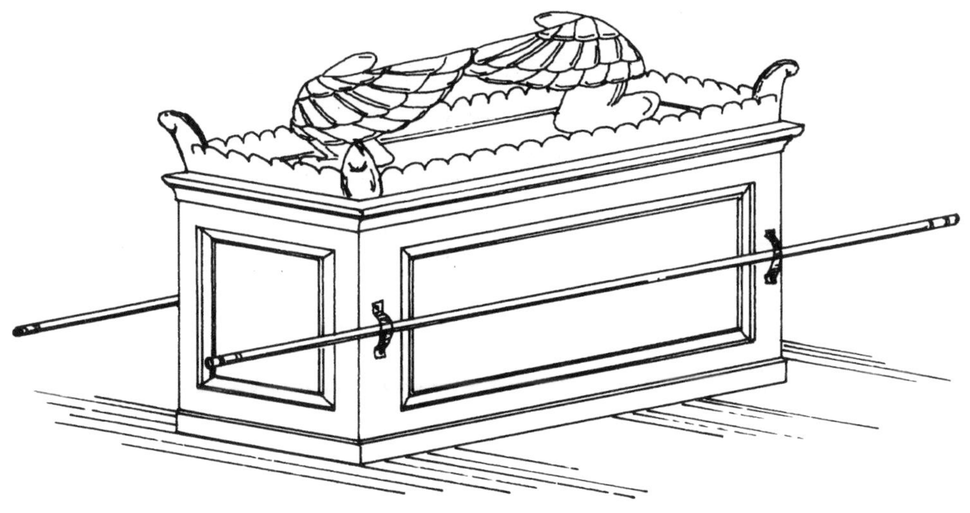

The Ark of the Covenant

The Israelites believed that this was where God lived.

It's at times like this that we need to come alongside one another, to *"carry each other's burdens, and in this way you will fulfill the law of Christ"* (Galatians 6:2).

If you know parents like this, make it a point to become their friend. They need all the support they can get. Pray with them, meet with them for lunch, have them in your home. You might not help their son, but you sure will help this couple survive.

Genesis 21:9 But Sarah saw that the son whom Hagar the Egyptian had borne to Abraham was **mocking**.

☞ **GO TO:**

Genesis 16 (Hagar)

Genesis 19:14; 26:8; 39:14, 17 (mocking)

mocking: *laughing at*

Mothers Who Love Too Much?

Hagar, an Egyptian slave, is asked by her mistress, Sarah, to sleep with Sarah's husband, Abraham, and provide them a son. She is obedient and gives birth to Ishmael whom she loves more than life. This makes her proud, for she loves her child too much. She thinks that the child has given her a place in this household that is not rightfully hers. She chides the childless Sarah and this attitude is passed along to her son, Ishmael. He grows up with an attitude of being better than his half brother Isaac.

EXAMPLES FROM THE BIBLE

Hagar bore Abraham his first son, Ishmael, and thus became the founder of the Ishmaelites, the Arab peoples from whom came Mohammed, the founder of Islam.

What Others are Saying:

Dr. Ross Campbell: Inappropriate love . . . hinders a child's emotional growth by failing to meet a child's emotional needs, which fosters an increasingly dependent relationship upon a parent and hampers self-reliance. [Two common ones are possessiveness, which] is a tendency of parents to encourage a child to be too dependent on his parents, and [vicariousness, which] is living one's life or dreams through the life of a child.[9]

> **1 Kings 1:5** Now **Adonijah**, whose mother was Haggith, **put himself forward** and said, "I will be king." So he got chariots and horses ready, with fifty men to run ahead of him.

Adonijah: *David's fourth son, after Absalom*

put himself forward: *an attempt to usurp the throne*

☞ **GO TO:**

2 Samuel 15:1 (fifty men)

Pride Goes before a Fall

Haggith was David's fifth wife. Can you imagine how proud she must have felt at giving birth to a handsome son? She must have told Adonijah time and time again that he deserved to be on the throne, especially now that his older brothers were all dead.

His father had never interfered with this very handsome fourth son (born after Absalom) by asking, "Why do you behave as you do?"

Believing that he was above the law, which stated David had the right to choose his own successor, Adonijah set out to make himself king. Haggith did little to curb her son's prideful attitude and probably even encouraged it in light of the fact that David seemed to care so little about what his children did.

EXAMPLES FROM THE BIBLE

Adonijah's coup attempt failed and, later, he was executed by his half brother Solomon for asking to marry David's nurse. Solomon saw this as another bid to take over the kingdom (1 Kings 2:19–25).

DISRESPECT FOR HER HUSBAND

> **2 Samuel 6:16** As the ark of the LORD was entering the City of David, Michal daughter of Saul watched from a window. And when she saw King David leaping and dancing before the LORD, she despised him in her heart.

Honey, You're Embarrassing Me!

Here is a woman in the Bible who shows disrespect for her husband. Michal ridicules David as he dances before the Ark of the Covenant.

Another such biblical example is of Zipporah, the wife of Moses, who, afraid for her husband's life, steps in, takes charge, and circumcises their sons. The tone of her voice is full of sarcasm as she says (referring to circumcision), "*Surely you are a bridegroom of blood to me*" (Exodus 4:24–26).

GO TO:

Exodus 4:24–26 (disrespect)

EXAMPLES FROM THE BIBLE

Michal never again was alone with David and so died without children (see GWWB, pages 224–225). Zipporah did not make the journey to the Promised Land with her husband. Her name and the names of her children, instead of being etched on history, disappeared never to be heard from again (see GWWB, pages 222–233).

What Others are Saying:

Karen Mains: Kids pick up on our attitudes about the opposite sex from the way they see us treating our mates.[10]

John MacArthur: Women try to take charge and overturn the divine order in the home and men respond with a domineering, tyrannical authority God never granted them. . . . Conflicts between husbands and wives are a fruit of humanity's fallenness.[11]

SETTING A BAD EXAMPLE

> **1 Kings 22:51–52** Ahaziah son of Ahab became king of Israel in Samaria in the seventeenth year of Jehoshaphat king of Judah, and he reigned over Israel two years. He did evil in the eyes of the LORD, because he walked in the

GO TO:

1 Kings 16:30–33 (Ahab)

> ways of his father and mother and in the ways of Jeroboam son of Nebat, who caused Israel to sin.

Bad Apples

Evil became progressively worse with each generation in the nation of Israel. Ahaziah's mother was Jezebel, daughter of Ethbaal, king of the Sidonians. She worshiped Baal. Her influence was felt throughout the kingdom as Ahab, her husband, built an altar to Baal and an Asherah pole.

These forms of worship were strictly forbidden by Jewish law, but that didn't matter to Ahab or his wife. They passed their pagan worship and disdain for the things of God along to their son, who did even more evil in the eyes of the Lord.

What Others are Saying:

Randy Rolfe: Punishing a child for what you do yourself is going to feel pretty bad to most parents and utterly unfair to most kids. Instead, do your best to clean up your own act. Get a life you can be proud of.[12]

Dr. Henry Cloud and Dr. John Townsend: Every parent is a bit of a perfectionist. You want to parent the right way, and you don't want your failures to hurt your children. The sad reality is that you have failed in the past and that you will fail in the future. You can't love, provide structure for, and teach your children perfectly every time. And your failures do affect your children. . . . The good news is that children are resilient, and they can recover and flourish under imperfect parents. . . . Be a parent who is not afraid of failure, but sees it as a way to grow.[13]

Study Questions

1. Why is constantly finding fault with your children so damaging?
2. What is the significance of Lot's wife being turned into a pillar of salt?
3. Rebekah loved Jacob more than Esau. What was the consequence?
4. What happened because of David's unwillingness to punish Amnon?
5. What was Eli's greatest weakness?
6. Why is showing disrespect to your husband (or ex-spouse) so damaging to your children?
7. Name two inappropriate forms of love.

CHAPTER WRAP-UP

- Finding fault with children can lead to discouragement. They begin to believe that nothing they do is ever good enough and so they quit trying.
- Valuing the things of this world over the things of God can lead to disaster.
- Showing favoritism for one child over another and openly disagreeing with your husband can tear a home apart, lead to deception, and end up causing heartache.
- Overindulgence and overprotection can lead a child into trouble and can have consequences for generations to come.
- Disrespecting your husband or ex-spouse can give children a confused idea of God's original plan for marriage.
- Allowing our children to be prideful instead of teaching them humility can lead to their downfall.
- Nothing we can say will teach our children more than what we do.

JUDY'S  BOOKSHELF

- *How to Really Love Your Child,* Dr. Ross Campbell, Victor Books. A Christian psychologist writes about appropriate and inappropriate love and how to discipline with love.
- *Being a Believer in an Unbelieving World,* Wayne Brouwer, Hendrickson Publishing. A look at the Sermon on the Mount and how we can apply it to our day-to-day lives. Maturing as a Christian will help you be a better parent.
- *God Uses Cracked Pots,* Patsy Clairmont, Focus on the Family. A humorous look at our imperfections.
- *Where Does a Mother Go to Resign?,* Barbara Johnson, Bethany House. The poignant and sometimes funny story of how Barbara coped with the crippling of her husband, the death of two sons, and the homosexuality of a third.

Part Four

LETTING GO

REVEREND FUN

13 LETTING GO IS AN ATTITUDE

WHAT'S IN THIS CHAPTER

- Unique from Birth
- Weaning—the First Important Step
- The School Years
- The Adolescent Years

Here We Go

From the moment our children are born, we begin the process of training them up so we can let them go. If we don't do it right, they will be handicapped. Just like a bird with a clipped wing, they won't be able to fly away.

Letting go is an attitude that begins early as we wean them from the breast and send them off to school. The teen years are difficult only because they are breaking bonds that would keep them from finding their own place in the world.

Let's look at what the Bible says that can help us help them to take this necessary step in their maturation.

UNIQUE FROM BIRTH

> **Jeremiah 1:5** "Before I formed you in the womb I knew you, before you were born I set you apart."

Molders Not Makers

Before birth, God planted into each of our children the raw materials they need to become wholly who he intended. Our job is to come alongside God and help him shape and mold them through nurture, love, instruction, and discipline, and then to let go. This doesn't begin when they leave home as young adults, it begins at birth.

GO TO:

Job 10:8 (shape)

Job 10:9 (mold)

What Others are Saying:

Randy Rolfe: Your child is a fully formed person from birth. Her life is as full spiritually, physically, emotionally, and intellectually as your own. She has a life path beyond your direction or control. We no longer subscribe to the idea of a clean slate that we must write on.[1]

What Others are Saying:

Dr. William Sears and Martha Sears, R.N.: There are several major weanings throughout a child's life—from the womb, from the breast, from home to school—and many minor ones. The pace at which children make these transitions and attain these milestones needs to be respected.[2]

WEANING—THE FIRST IMPORTANT STEP

> **Genesis 21:8** On the day that Isaac was weaned Abraham held a great feast.

Let's Celebrate!

In biblical times weaning took place at about the age of three and was cause for a celebration. Today most children, if they are breast-fed, are weaned in the first year and often with a great deal of difficulty. When weaning is done properly it should have the affect as stated by the writer in Psalm 131:2, *"But I have stilled and quieted my **soul**; like a **weaned child** with its mother, like a weaned child is my soul within me."* What a beautiful picture of peace and tranquility.

☞ **GO TO:**

Psalm 6:3 (soul)

1 Samuel 1:22–23 (weaned)

Matthew 18:3 (child)

soul: *one's very self as a living, conscious, personal being*

weaned child: *a child of about three*

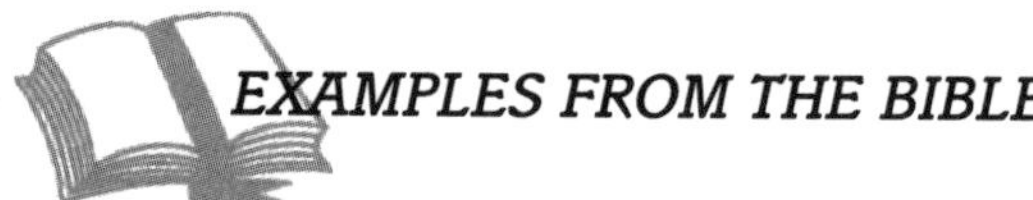

Bible commentators believe that Samuel was weaned when he was about three years of age. From the account in 1 Samuel, it seems as if there was no preset time and that it was left up to the intuition of the mother. Moses was nursed by his mother probably just as long.

What Others are Saying:

Dr. William Sears and Martha Sears, R.N.: A child who is weaned before his time from any childhood need and hurried into independence may rebel both inwardly and outwardly and show what we call "disease of premature weaning." Many of the usual behaviors of infancy and childhood, such as aggression, excessive clinginess, frequent mood swings, and aloofness may, in fact, be diseases of premature weaning.[3]

Exodus 1:22–2:4 Then **Pharaoh** gave this order to all his people: "Every boy that is born you must throw into the Nile, but let every girl live." Now a man of the house of Levi married a **Levite woman**, and she became pregnant and gave birth to a son. When she saw that he was a fine child, she hid him for three months. But when she could hide him no longer, she got a papyrus basket [see illustration below] for him and coated it with tar and pitch. Then she placed the child in it and put it among the reeds along the bank of the Nile. His sister stood at a distance to see what would happen to him.

Pharaoh: *a royal title rather than a personal name*

Levite woman: *Jochebed, Moses' mother*

☞ **GO TO:**

Exodus 6:20 (Levite woman)

Exodus 15:20 (his sister)

A Desperate Choice

Moses' mother, Jochebed (see GWWB, pages 123–124), must have been frantic with fear as she released her baby into the water of the Nile River. She had no other alternative. She could hide him no longer, and if he were discovered he would be killed.

As she watched the basket float out of sight she must have wondered many things. Would he survive the water? Would he be found by someone who would then carry out the Pharaoh's order? Would he float forever until he died of dehydration?

There were so many unknowns, just like there are many unknowns when we send our children out into the world.

Think About It

Most mothers are not forced to take such drastic measures in order to save their children. But sometimes it can feel like it as we watch our precious ones go off to school or as we leave them in the hands of a day care center full of strangers whom we must trust so that we can work and put food on the table.

Reed Basket

Pictured is a reed basket like the one that may have been used to hide Moses.

Notice that Jochebed had a spy. Her daughter, Miriam, kept watch over the basket, and we can do the same thing. We can check up on the schools, get to know the teachers, principals, and support staff. We can drop in unannounced at the day care center just to see how things are going.

REMEMBER THIS

The account of Moses' remarkable deliverance in infancy foreshadows the deliverance of the Jews from Egypt. (See GWBI, page 23.)

What Others are Saying:

Herbert Lockyer: It was Jochebed's love, faith and courage that saved her child from a cruel death and preserved him to bless the world. A mother who loves the Saviour, and who has a more severe anguish when she knows that, not the life of her child is at stake, but its soul, can rest in the assurance that Jochebed's God still lives, and is able to save her dear one from eternal death.[4]

EXAMPLES FROM THE BIBLE

We can hardly imagine the suffering that Jochebed went through under the Egyptian rulers. Yet, we can tell that she must have been a woman of great faith. And God rewarded her mightily with three children that will continue to be remembered throughout the history of time—Miriam, Aaron, and Moses.

☞ **GO TO:**

Exodus 15:20–21; Numbers 12:1–15; 20:1; 26:59; Deuteronomy 24:9; Micah 6:4 (Miriam)

Exodus; Numbers 20:22–29 (Aaron)

1 Samuel 1:28 "So now I [Hannah] give him [Samuel] to the LORD. For his whole life he will be given over to the LORD." And he worshiped the Lord there.

A Heart-Wrenching Release

Hannah has promised God that if he gives her a son, she will return him to the service of the Lord for all the days of his life. God gives her Samuel and when he is three years old, she returns to the temple and gives him to Eli, a prophet and judge, to be raised by others. We can hear the tears in her voice and the anguish in her heart as she hands him over to this gruff old man.

How do you suppose Hannah prepared herself and Samuel for this day? Did she cling to him every moment, treasuring his every word, coddling him? Or do you think she pushed him emotionally away from her so that she could bear the pain?

Think About It

I like to think she prepared him by teaching him to be independent, respectful of his elders, polite at the dinner table, self-controlled; that she made sure he was sleeping in his own bed and was potty trained.

She probably told him over and over what an honor it would be for him to serve the Lord, and shared as much of her faith with him as possible. She didn't want her son to be a burden. She wanted him to be able to make the transition.

Hannah must have had a great deal of faith in order to make this sacrifice.

☞ GO TO:

1 Chronicles 6:49 (tribe of Aaron)

Samuel went on to be a great man of faith. He replaced Eli as the chief judge of the nation of Israel even though he wasn't from the tribe of Aaron.

What Others are Saying:

Dr. James Dobson: It is better, I believe, to begin releasing your children during the preschool years, granting independence that is consistent with their age and maturity. When a child can tie his shoes, let him—yes, require him—to do it. When he can choose his own clothes within reason, let him make his own selection. When he can walk safely to school, allow him the privilege. Each year, more *responsibility* and *freedom* [they are companions] are given to the child so that the final release in early adulthood is merely the final relaxation of authority. This is theory, at least. Pulling it off is sometimes quite difficult.[5]

> **1 Peter 2:1–3** Therefore, rid yourselves of all malice and all deceit, hypocrisy, envy, and slander of every kind. Like newborn babies, crave pure spiritual milk, so that by it you may grow up in your salvation, now that you have tasted that the Lord is good.

Spiritual Milk

Just as a baby craves milk, we are commanded to crave spiritual milk so that we may grow and mature as Christians. At conversion we are like babies, dependent on others to guide and direct us, to teach us what's in the Bible, and to correct us when we make mistakes.

But we are called to go beyond a surface knowledge of who Christ is and discover what it means to rely on him for every need.

If you do not crave the things of God, then pray and ask God to give you a new hunger and thirst. *"As the deer pants for streams of water, so my soul pants for you, O God"* (Psalm 42:1). He will answer your honest plea.

You cannot pass along a faith to your children that you do not possess. They need to see it acted out in your everyday life, not just taught to them at Sunday school or read to them out of books. Hannah most likely set the kind of example that Samuel needed.

What Others are Saying:

Barbara Johnson: Jesus told us to receive forgiveness for past sins and refuse to worry about tomorrow. In this way, living fully in the present moment, we become more like children with hearts open for laughter and joy.[6]

THE SCHOOL YEARS

1 Samuel 2:18–21 But Samuel was ministering before the LORD—a boy wearing a **linen ephod**. Each year his mother made him a **little robe** and took it to him when she went up with her husband to offer the annual sacrifice. Eli would bless Elkanah and his wife, saying, "May the LORD give you children by this woman to take the place of the one she prayed for and gave to the LORD." Then they would go home. And the LORD was gracious to Hannah; she conceived and gave birth to three sons and two daughters. Meanwhile, the boy Samuel grew up in the presence of the LORD.

☞ GO TO:

1 Samuel 22:18; 2 Samuel 6:14 (linen ephod)

1 Samuel 15:27; 18:4 (robe)

linen ephod: *a priestly garment worn by those who served in the sanctuary, close fitting, sleeveless, and hip length*

little robe: *a sleeveless garment reaching to the knees, worn over the undergarment and under the ephod*

A Faithful Visitor

Even though Hannah sent her son to be raised in the Temple by Eli, she faithfully visited him, bringing him robes that she made with her own hands. Her visits must have been looked forward to by her small son, and they may have lasted for several days. During those visits they must have had much to share. Her godly influence continued in Samuel's life for as long as she lived.

Letting go of our children doesn't mean abandoning them. We must continuously be involved in their lives, letting our influence wash over them at every opportunity. When our children come home from school, it's a good time to sit down with them and review the events of the day. We sometimes think we've heard it all, but remember Hannah, who only got to have one visit a year. Make the most of every opportunity.

EXAMPLES FROM THE BIBLE

Eli's sons were wicked men and they had no regard for the Lord. Yet Samuel, whom he also raised, grew up to serve the Lord. The difference had to be the influence of Samuel's mother.

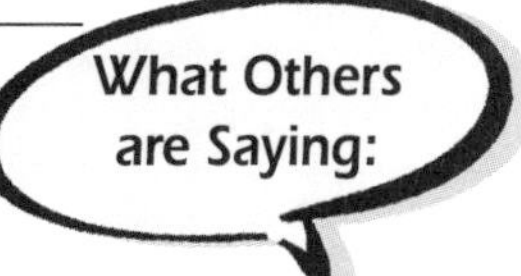

Margaret Wold: Although [Hannah] left [Samuel] in the temple, she never ceased caring for him. Every year she made a little robe for him and brought it to the temple in Shiloh. We can be quite sure that every stitch was a prayer and every visit a joyful reunion. Samuel was not abandoned. He knew he was loved by his parents, his brothers and sisters, and by God.[7]

> **1 Thessalonians 4:11–12** Make it your ambition to lead a quiet life, to mind your own business and to work with your <u>hands</u>, just as we told you, so that your daily life may win the respect of <u>outsiders</u> and so that you will not be dependent on anybody.

☞ GO TO:

Ephesians 4:28; 2 Thessalonians 3:10–12 (hands)

Mark 4:11 (outsiders)

Encouraging Independence

This scripture was written to the Greeks, who thought that manual labor was beneath them and were often idle and getting into other people's business.

We must teach our children to do manual labor and to do it as if they were doing it for the Lord. Hard work brings rewards in better grades, better jobs, respect from outsiders, and independence, and it also keeps them out of trouble.

Your children may gripe and complain about doing chores around the house, but chores are a valuable training tool. Kids need to mow the lawn, clean the gutters, rake leaves, wash the dishes, and do the laundry so that when they leave home they will be independent. There is nothing more pitiful than a college student who destroys all of his or her clothes by washing the colors with the whites or shrinking the woolens in the dryer.

Once they've left home, they will be glad they know how to iron a shirt or sew on a button. They may not thank you at the moment they are learning, but someday they will appreciate that you loved them enough to show them how to change the oil in the car or fix a flat.

For Single Moms—Teaching your children to help around the house not only helps them prepare to leave home, but can give you much-needed help when you're struggling to do everything yourself.

What Others are Saying:

John MacArthur: Your children will work if you stand there with a whip. But will they work if you don't? They're going to have to learn to work on their own initiative if they are going to be successful in life.[8]

Bill Cosby asked a young girl of seven, "Do you help your mother clean up the house?"

"No," she sweetly replied, "I help make the mess."

Hebrews 5:13–14 Anyone who lives on milk, being still an infant, is not acquainted with the teaching about righteousness. But solid food is for the **mature**, who by constant use have trained themselves to distinguish good from evil.

mature: *Christians of sound judgment and discernment*

Right and Wrong

Children will not develop if they are fed only milk. There is a time when they must be weaned to solid food in order to grow and mature physically.

This is also true of moral training.

Children must learn to distinguish right from wrong.

At first they will have to be told over and over, but there will come a time when they will have to learn on their own. The same is true of spiritual growth. There is a time to move beyond the elementary and learn some of the more difficult aspects of being a Christian.

In an age when many of our schools teach that there is no right or wrong or absolutes, training up your children will take much diligence on your part. Take the opportunity whenever you see an example of the **philosophy of relativism** to contrast that with what the Bible teaches.

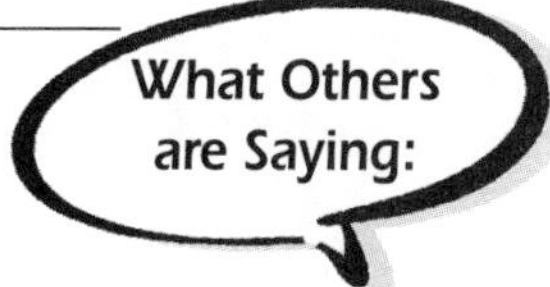

Dr. William Sears and Martha Sears, R.N.: Between five and six years of age most children begin to depart from home—in their waking hours away from home—in school, even on overnights, or on group trips, such as scouting or church activities. They are exposed to outside values. How firmly they are grounded in the values at home influences whether or not they will "depart."[9]

philosophy of relativism: *everything is permitted under the right circumstances*

> **Isaiah 28:9–10** "Who is it he is trying to teach? To whom is he explaining his message? To children weaned from their milk, to those just taken from the breast? For it is: Do and do, do and do, **rule on rule**, rule on rule; a little here, a little there."

☞ GO TO:

Hebrews 5:12–13 (milk)

rule on rule: *meaningless sounds, possibly a mimicking of the prophet's words*

Too Many Rules!

The people are complaining that the prophets give too many rules, treating the people like they are infants. What they want is to be treated like adults. They want explanations, illustrations, and discussion.

Think About It

Too many rules, especially if they don't give freedom of choice to children, can lead to rebellion.

We must give age-appropriate choices.

Instead of insisting that your children drink milk, ask if they want a full glass or half a glass. Instead of insisting that they wear certain clothes to school, ask if they want, for instance, the blue dress or the pink outfit.

Children love choices, and to choose gives them a sense of freedom. As they grow older, these choices will change, but the principles will remain the same.

What Others are Saying:

Randy Rolfe: Don't expect to be able to let go in all areas at the same time to the same extent. As a child is exploring one area courageously, she might in fact be surprisingly dependent in another area, if only to keep a kind of balance, as it were. A child who is winning squash tournaments at the state level, for example, may still be afraid to be left alone at night.[10]

KEY POINT

Your home should be Christ-centered, not child-centered.

Is your home child-centered? This means that everything you do revolves around the children.

You give up your social life to be with your children. You skip church to go to soccer games. You drop out of church activities to chauffeur your children to their activities. You're too busy with coaching Little League or being a den mother to spend time alone with your husband.

Do you find yourself cooking three different things for dinner to satisfy everyone's wishes? Do you constantly serve your husband "kids' food," and ignore his requests for meat loaf or liver and onions?

When homes get out of balance, then children begin to feel as if they are the most important people in the home. They begin to lose their desire to grow up because they don't see that being an adult has any benefits.

Make your husband the most important person in the home and see what a difference it makes in everyone's attitude.

> **Luke 8:14** The seed that fell among thorns stands for those who hear, but as they go on their way they are choked by life's worries, riches and pleasures, and they do not mature.

☞ GO TO:

Matthew 19:23; 1 Timothy 6:9–10, 17 (worries)

Oh, Grow Up!

This is a verse taken from the Parable of the Sower and refers to the Word of God being like a seed, which sometimes falls among thorns. Our children can also be likened to seeds. To bring them to maturity we must weed out the thorns and teach them to trust in God and not in the things of this world.

When our children worry about a test they are facing or whether or not a certain friend likes them or whether or not they have the coolest shoes, this is an opportunity for instructing them that the things of this world may seem important, but they are only temporary.

It's a hard lesson when our children have to face the reality that their parents can't afford the pair of shoes that cost eighty dollars, or that their parents can't afford to buy them a brand new car when they turn sixteen, or send them to Hawaii on vacations "like all their friends."

But giving our children everything they desire would stunt their growth.

They wouldn't appreciate what they have, and wouldn't learn the wonderful experience of working for what they get.

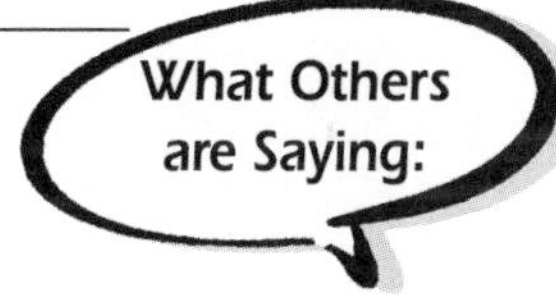

Todd Howard, president of the childrenswear division of Tommy Hilfiger: By the time they are 6 or 7, they are talking about brands in school; and by the time they are 9 to 10, they are making all the decisions. And Mom and Dad's involvement is just paying.[11]

One of the worries that children face today is whether or not their mom and dad are going to stay together. Don't forget to grow your marriage right along with growing your children. Plan date nights with your husband. Go out together, have fun, and just talk.

> **James 1:2–4** Consider it pure joy, my brothers, whenever you face trials of many kinds, because you know that the testing of your faith develops **perseverance**. Perseverance must finish its work so that you may be mature and complete, not lacking anything.

GO TO:

Matthew 5:11–12; Romans 5:3; 1 Peter 1:6 (joy)

perseverance: *hopeful endurance*

Hardship Develops Character

James is writing to Jewish Christians scattered throughout the world who were facing many trials. They were losing their homes, their families, and even their lives, but he says to them to consider it "joy" because trials would help them mature as Christians. In the same way, trials help mature our children.

It's awfully tempting to jump in when our children are facing trials and "fix it." When they are having problems with a bully at school, or they are behind in their schoolwork because they put it off until the last minute, or they have a friend who moves away, it's tempting to take care of the problem or tell them to "just get over it."

But trials can build perseverance. Let them work through their own problems, and only step in when appropriate.

KEY POINT

Sometimes children need to fix their own problems.

If our child is caught shoplifting and we go to the police to get them out of the consequences, then what will they have learned? Isn't it better that they receive the punishment that they need so that they will learn that stealing is wrong even if all their friends are doing it and even if it was their first time?

An eight-year-old boy in Illinois learned one lesson the hard way. He was entranced by Mary Poppins and her magical umbrella, so one day while Mom was at work and Dad was playing golf, and his fifteen-year-old sister was in charge, he took an umbrella up to the roof of the house and jumped off to see if he could fly. The umbrella reversed and he came crashing to the ground. It scared his sister to death! But a few sutures, and he was good as new. He never tried it again.[12]

GO TO:

Exodus 23:14–17; Deuteronomy 16:16 (Feast of the Passover)

twelve years old: *age when boys began preparing to take their place in the religious community*

Luke 2:41–52 Every year his parents went to Jerusalem for the Feast of the Passover. When he was **twelve years old**, they went up to the Feast, according to the custom. After the Feast was over, while his parents were returning home, the boy Jesus stayed behind in Jerusalem, but they were unaware of it. Thinking he was in their company, they traveled on for a day. Then they began looking for him among their relatives and friends. When they did not find him, they went back to Jerusalem to look for him. After three days they found him in the temple courts, sitting among the teachers, listening to them and asking them questions. Everyone who heard him was amazed at his understanding and his answers. When his parents saw him, they were astonished. His mother said to him, "Son, why have you treated us like this? Your father and I have been anxiously searching for you."

"Why were you searching for me?" he asked. "Didn't you know I had to be in my Father's house?" But they did not understand what he was saying to them.

We Looked Everywhere for You!

Mary and Joseph must have been frantic as they searched for their son. Three days is a long time for a child to be missing. Thoughts of him going hungry with no place to sleep and worse must have tortured them just as they would parents today. To find him in the Temple, sitting among the teachers must have been one of the last places they looked. When they saw him, they surely were angry as they said, "Why have you treated us like this?" Jesus' answer announces to them that he is now fully aware of who he is and that he must soon begin his ministry.

Notice that Mary and Joseph did not understand what Jesus was saying to them. Do you think they were in denial about this rather ordinary child being the Messiah, or do you think that they were like most parents who can't see the special qualities that have been planted in their children?

Sometimes we just need to get out of the way and let our children be what God has called them to be.

THE ADOLESCENT YEARS

Romans 12:12 Be joyful in hope, patient in affliction, <u>faithful in prayer</u>.

GO TO:

Luke 18:1; 1 Thessalonians 5:17 (faithful in prayer)

Attitude

Paul was speaking to the Christians in Rome when he wrote this scripture. He urged them to be joyful, because their suffering was only temporary, and if they were patient, kept their eternal rewards in mind and remained faithful in prayer, they would be able to endure their trials.

The same can be said to mothers who are struggling through their children's challenging teen years!

Think About It

No other scripture quite captures the attitude that mothers need during the teen years.

First, go into them with a joyful attitude. These years can be the best. Your teen has a developing intellect and you can now have deep discussions on a variety of topics. Teens are excited about life, and will introduce you to a variety of experiences that you might have never tried. Their sense of humor may seem wild and wacky, but don't put them down for it. Learn to laugh with them.

Second, be patient. Don't take everything to heart. One moment they may be angry with you, but the very next they will want you to hold them. For a few short years, toughen your hide and don't let their prickly words get under your skin. Remember they are under a lot of pressure from school and peers and you. They have not yet developed the skills to cope with all that life and what their hormones are throwing at them.

Last, spend time in prayer every day for the choices they will make.

EXAMPLES FROM THE BIBLE

How often should a Christian pray? The Scripture doesn't give us a specific number of times. David prayed seven times a day (Psalm 119:164); Daniel, three times a day (Daniel 6:10). Jesus spent many hours in prayer.

Every one of us should set aside a time each day for communication with the one who loves us the most.

What Others are Saying:

Cheri Fuller: One frustration many moms have expressed is not knowing what to pray for their teenagers. . . . As hard as it is, I believe one prayer we must pray for our children is that they will be caught when they're guilty. . . . A second, and almost instinctive, prayer we can pray for our teens is for protection.[13]

Everything that has gone before is now being tested. Your child is struggling for freedom and discovering his or her identity. What your son or daughter believed so easily at age eight, because you "said so," is now questioned.

If you are pro-life, they may look at the other side to see if they truly agree with your stand. If you are conservative in your dress, they may seek to be flamboyant. If you are politically conservative, they may be liberal. If you have brought them up as Christians, they will examine that faith with a fine-tooth comb, turning it over, to see if it's really true. And for a time they may even reject it.

Don't take everything that your teen says personally. Keep in mind that the closer they are to you emotionally the more difficult the separation process can be.

For Single Moms—This can be an especially tough time for a single mom because there is no one to help her go through this. If she has a son, he will be seeking a father figure. If she has a daughter, she may be looking for the love of a father through early relationships with boys.

What Others are Saying:

Dr. Henry Cloud: Adolescence is a time when all of the past developmental issues are reworked in a different context. Instead of developing these qualities while he is still "under" the parent, your teenager is working out those issues in the context of independence in preparation for adulthood. Therefore two things are happening. First, he is going through the issues in a different, more independent way. Second, the issues are open to reworking and repair if he missed them the first time around.[14]

FROM JUDY'S HEART

My dread grew as my sons traveled through grades four, five, and six. I worried: would they go off the deep end like so many of my friends' children had?

One of my friend's children had tried to commit suicide; another's was running away; a third's was stealing from the parents and getting into trouble with the law. These were all good kids with loving, caring parents.

Would this happen to my sons?

My husband, on the other hand, chose to take on the attitude that these would be the best years. He even looked forward to them as a time when we could finally reap the benefits of all our work. He was excited to see what paths their lives would take, and was eager to do all he could to help them achieve whatever they wanted out of life.

I wouldn't say we sailed through those difficult years, but I have to admit that my husband's attitude played a big role in how certain events were perceived. He didn't panic the first time one of them stayed out all night without calling us. He took it in stride when our first son bought a car and then had an accident. He bore the brunt of many rude comments that, if he had allowed them to get under his skin, would have been cause for an angry explosion.

The result was that those years were fun. We enjoyed the adult conversations around the dinner table, many of which challenged our deeply held beliefs. There was much laughter as we allowed them to tell us about the funny things that they'd done at school or the outlandish movie they'd just seen. We tried to be interested in everything they were doing.

We did ask that their music be kept low, that they not bring any R-rated movies into the house, that they tell us where they were going and what time we could expect them to be home. If they were going to be late they needed to call, no matter how late it was.

In their eyes, the worst thing we did was refuse to carry cable TV. It meant that we had fewer choices for ourselves, but it also kept MTV and other questionable channels out of our home.

They weren't perfect years, but they were peaceful. And it must not have been too bad around here because all their friends hung around a lot and called us Mom and Dad. I think the credit belongs to my husband.

THE BIG PICTURE

Luke 15:11–32 Jesus tells the story of a man with two sons. The younger asks for his inheritance and so the father divides his property between his two sons. The younger sets off for a distant country where he squanders his wealth in wild living. When all his money is gone he takes a job tending pigs, but even they eat better than he does.

Eventually he realizes that even his father's hired men have food to spare, and so he decides to return home.

While he is still a long way off, his father sees him and is filled with compassion. He runs to his son, throws his arms around him and kisses him. The son asks for forgiveness, for he feels he is no longer worthy to be called "son."

But the father throws a big feast to celebrate his younger son's return. When the older son hears about

> this he is angry, because he has stayed and labored and no one has ever thrown a feast for him.
>
> "My son," the father says, "you are always with me, and everything I have is yours. But we have to celebrate and be glad, because this brother of yours was dead and is alive again; he was lost and is found."

Luke 19:10; Matthew 10:6; 18:10–14 (was lost and is found)

Let Them Fail?

The story of the **prodigal** son is familiar to many of us and there are many lessons to learn from it. Note that the father allowed the son to go off and make his own mistakes. He let him learn his lesson the hard way. There are natural consequences to squandering money, getting into debt, driving recklessly, and sometimes we have to let our children learn those lessons.

prodigal: *reckless and extravagant*

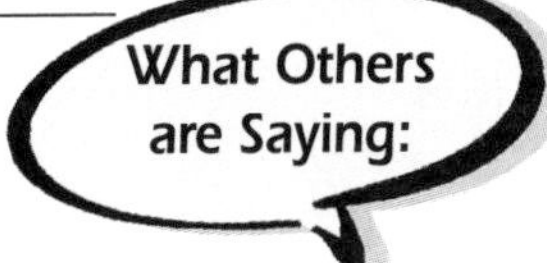

The father fully forgave his son, but did not give him any more money. Notice he says to the older brother, "All I have is yours." Earlier, he had divided up the estate; there was nothing left to give.

What Others are Saying:

Harry Emerson Fosdick: When a mother prays for her wayward son, no words can make clear the vivid reality of her supplications. . . . She does not really think that she is persuading God to be good to her son, for the courage of her prayer is due to her certain faith that God also must wish that boy to be recovered from his sin. She rather is taking on her heart the same burden that God has on his, is joining her demand with the divine desire. In this system of personal life which makes up the moral universe, she is taking her place alongside God in an urgent, creative outpouring of sacrificial love. Her intercession is the utterance of her life; it is love on its knees.[15]

Dr. James Dobson: What are your reasons for restricting the freedom of your grown or nearly grown children? In some cases, if we're honest, we need them too much to let them go. They have become an extension of ourselves, and our egos are inextricably linked to theirs. Therefore, we not only seek to hold them to us, but we manipulate them to maintain our control. . . . We use guilt, bribery, threats, intimidation, fear and anger to restrict their freedom. And sadly, when we win at this game, we and our offspring are destined to lose.[16]

Daniel 1 Nebuchadnezzar, king of Babylon, seized Jerusalem. He ordered the chief of his court's officials to bring in some of the Israelites from the royal family, young men without any physical defect, handsome, showing aptitude for every kind of learning, well-informed, quick to understand, and qualified to serve in the king's palace. He was to teach these young men the language and literature of the Babylonians.

Among those chosen were **Daniel**, Shadrach, Meshach, and Abednego. They refused to eat the rich food and drink the wine of the king. Instead they ate only vegetables and drank water. At the end of their training they were presented to the king, who found them **ten** times better in every matter of wisdom and understanding than all the magicians and enchanters in his whole kingdom.

***Daniel:** "God is my judge"*

***ten:** symbolic number for completeness*

Your Mother Raised You Right!

Daniel and his three friends were taken from their homes and brought into the palace for training by the chief official (see GWDN, page 18).

These young men were of superior character, and therefore we can conclude they came from godly homes, where God's laws were taught and taken to heart.

This is clear when they refused to eat the royal food. They considered it contaminated because the first portion of it was offered to idols. Likewise a portion of the wine was poured out on a pagan altar.

Their refusal could have meant sure death if Daniel had not offered that they be tested, showing again a keen mind and a proper respect for authority.

Daniel's mother would have been very proud of him.

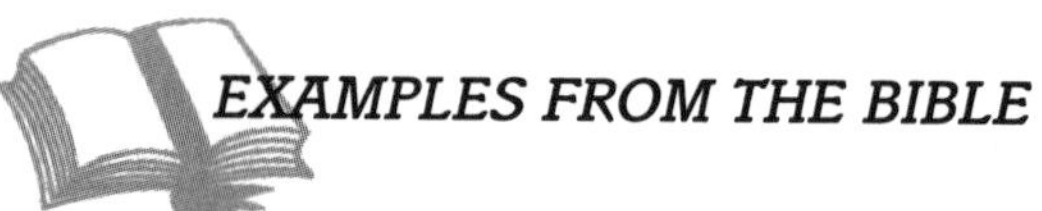

EXAMPLES FROM THE BIBLE

Other examples of fine young men are: Joseph, who was sold into slavery and rose to prominence in Egypt; Joshua, who replaced Moses as leader of the Jewish nation; and young David, who became King of Israel.

Colossians 4:12 Epaphras, who is one of you and a servant of Christ Jesus, sends greetings. He is always **wrestling** in prayer for you, that you may stand firm in all the will of God, mature and fully assured.

Epaphras: *a convert of Paul who carried the Gospel to Colosse*

wrestling: *laboring fervently*

Mature and Fully Confident

This scripture is directed to the church of Colosse, but could well apply to how we feel about our children.

Paul's goal was that they grow up to stand firm in their faith and develop into mature Christians. Our goal is that our children grow up to be well-adjusted, confident adults who will also stand firm in their faith.

Study Questions

1. Why did Abraham throw a feast for Isaac when Isaac was three years old?
2. Name two mothers who gave up their children early, and contrast their situations.
3. Name three lessons your children will learn from manual labor.
4. What was Jesus' response to his parents after they discovered him in the Temple?
5. Two fathers are mentioned in the passage in Luke. Who was Jesus referring to?
6. What three attitudes will help you survive your children's teen years?
7. Why did Daniel refuse to eat the royal food and drink the royal wine?

CHAPTER WRAP-UP

- Letting go of our children begins at birth. It is our job to take the raw material of our children's personalities and help mold them into adults who are confident, mature, and fully committed to Christ.
- Weaning is the important first step. In biblical times a baby wasn't weaned until he or she was about three years old, and a great feast was held to honor the event. Today we wean most children before the age of one, and it can turn into a painful event for the child and the mother.
- The first big step out of the house is school. We must encourage our children to become independent and yet at the same time protect them from harm.

- We should not fight our children's battles for them. They must learn to solve their own problems if they can.
- The best teacher is natural consequences. When our children step over the line, there should always be a price to pay.
- Manual labor keeps our children out of trouble, and also teaches them valuable lessons about life and humility.
- Our homes should be Christ-centered, not child-centered. The latter gives our children the wrong impression of their value and can retard their desire to grow up.
- Attitude is everything with teenagers. Go into these years expecting them to be the best so far. Find joy in every day, be patient with their sometimes sharp tongues, and pray diligently.

JUDY'S BOOKSHELF

- *Family: The Ties That Bind and Gag*, Erma Bombeck, McGraw-Hill. Humor as only Erma can dish it up.
- *Joy Breaks*, Patsy Clairmont, Barbara Johnson, Marilyn Meberg, and Luci Swindoll, Zondervan. Short inspirational stories for women.
- *Mama, Get the Hammer! There's a Fly on Papa's Head*, Barbara Johnson, Word. Barbara's humor helps those who are hurting.

14 THE EMPTY NEST

WHAT'S IN THIS CHAPTER

- The Stages of Mourning
- Rediscovering an Old Love
- Developing a Revitalized Relationship with God
- Developing Your Gifts
- The True Value of a Friend
- Living without Regrets

Here We Go

All too quickly, it's time for them to leave. We have bathed and fed them, changed their diapers and wiped their runny noses, bandaged their skinned knees and held them as they cried over a broken toy.

We taught them to ride their bikes and then drive a car, not fully realizing we were giving them the tools they needed to drive out of our lives.

Now all we can do is watch, for it is likely that they never again will be under our roof. Our job is done. They are free, and we are left with a quiet house, a full refrigerator, and empty hearts.

When they first arrived, they filled our lives with themselves. Now that they have left, it's time to discover what can be.

Yes, it's an ending, but it's also a beginning.

THE STAGES OF MOURNING

Ecclesiastes 3:1–8 There is a time for everything, and a season for every activity under heaven: a time to be born and a time to die, a time to plant and a time to uproot, a time to kill and a time to heal, a time to tear down and a time to build, a time to weep and a time to laugh, a time to mourn and a time to dance, a time to scatter stones and a time to gather them, a time to embrace and a time to refrain, a time to search and a time to give up, a time to keep and a time to throw away, a time to tear and a time to mend, a time to be silent and a time to speak, a time to love and a time to hate, a time for war and a time for peace.

☞ **GO TO:**

Ecclesiastes 8:6 (time for everything)

Isaiah 28:24 (plant)

Esther 4:14 (time to be silent)

To Everything There Is a Season

This scripture is often used at funerals to soothe the hearts of those who are mourning. It says that God is in control and that he knows the hour of every event in our lives. Just as there is a time for planting, there has now come a time for your child to leave home.

FROM JUDY'S HEART

I thought I was prepared. I had a part-time job that I loved. I was active in an organization that hosted a large conference for writers in the Pacific Northwest. My relationship with my husband had never been better and I had never felt closer to God. On top of all that, my writing career was beginning to take off. I had a lot to look forward to and with all my activities, having my last child out of the house would be a relief, not the tragedy that I read about.

When we dropped him off at college, I cried, but that seemed a normal reaction and I was sure that I soon would get over it. But I didn't. I missed him terribly. I hadn't realized how much of my life revolved around him. There was no one to watch the football games with or share the highlights in the paper the next day. His wacky sense of humor that filled my days with laughter was now hundreds of miles away. Our long political and religious discussions that had sharpened my thinking and honed my own beliefs were gone. His friends, who were in and out and often at our table and who called me Mom, no longer came by. Our cocker spaniel drooped around the house and spent long hours asleep by his bedroom door waiting for him to get up.

Oh sure, there was always milk in the refrigerator and pop in the pantry, and the grocery bill dropped by a third. Laundry was a breeze and the bathroom stayed clean. I could come and go as I pleased and if I didn't feel like cooking we could have popcorn for dinner or even waffles. I now had a car to myself and we could have adult food like liver and onions, tuna casserole, and meat loaf more often. And I would tell my friends how wonderful it was, but I cried over the silliest things and could hardly force myself to get excited about turning out another article or going to another meeting. I moped around the house and watched way too much TV.

He came home often that year, Thanksgiving, Christmas, spring break, but with each good-bye my heart would break. I thought I had filled my life so full that I wouldn't miss him, but I don't think there is any way you can fill the hole that they leave in your heart.

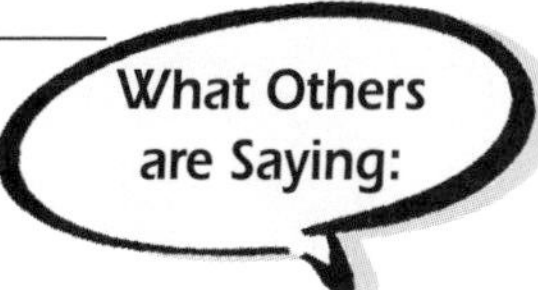

***Patricia H. Rushford*:** My babies have been whisked away on the winds of life. Will they survive? Will they be carried on the wind into dangerous ground? Will they settle among the thorns and be choked out? Will they fall on fertile ground? Autumn was a time for wondering where I had gone right—or wrong. It was a time of anticipation and guilt. I think perhaps the harvest was the hardest time of all. When they all have flown away. . . .[1]

Cheri Fuller: Your grocery bills are less, your loads of laundry are fewer, and occasionally a phone call is actually for you. Your children aren't the only ones who experience culture shock when they move away from home for the first time—whether they're heading for college, a trade school, or a full-time job. For the first time, your kids aren't under your roof, aren't underfoot, and aren't under your "wing." . . . It's tempting—and candidly, maybe a bit of a relief—to think, "they're on their own now," and let both our communication and prayer support dwindle.[2]

Laurie Beth Jones: It is no coincidence that the eyes through which we view life depend on tears to keep them open.[3]

We are subject to times and changes over which we have little or no control. God predetermines all of life's activities (see Psalm 31:15; Proverbs 16:1–9).

REDISCOVERING AN OLD LOVE

> **Proverbs 31:10, 12** A wife of noble character who can find? She is worth far more than rubies. She brings [her husband] good, not harm, all the days of her life.

☞ GO TO:

Ruth 3:11; Proverbs 12:4 (noble character)

Proverbs 18:22; 19:14 (good)

That Second Honeymoon?

The Proverbs 31 woman was rare, and when a man found such a wife she was to be treasured far more than rubies. She was used as an example when a man was looking for a wife and as a role model for Jewish women.

For so many years, your attention has been split between your husband and children. Now is the time to put all of your energy into your marriage and rediscover a richer, deeper love that may have gotten lost in the busyness of raising children.

Turn off the TV and spend your evening talking. Discover activities that you can do together like hiking, camping, or fishing. Take day trips to historic sites in your state, learn to golf, go out for breakfast. Become more curious about what interests your husband.

Make getting to know him a priority in every conversation and you will see him blossom before your eyes. Share with each other the memories of your youth and of your children. In the process you will discover a new and richer love that has grown through the years while you weren't even looking.

WARNING

Don't expect your husband to fill the hole your children have left. If you lean on him too much, you may find him moving away from you instead of toward you.

What Others are Saying:

Jean Lush: A woman of **mystique** is constantly changing and growing. She is a mystery to men and women because she involves herself deeply in the things of God. Her days are spent in learning God's ways and carrying out His will for her life through Bible study and prayer. She is in love with life, celebrating each moment, each day, as if it were her last. She is vital, growing, alive, and filled with the Spirit of God. She is a mystery because God is mystery and His Spirit lives in her.[4]

mystique: *an air or attitude of mystery and reverence*

Liz Curtis Higgs: It seems the Hebrew word *chayil* that describes this wonder woman is sometimes interpreted as "virtuous" or "excellent" but more commonly means "wealthy, prosperous, valiant, boldly courageous, powerful, mighty warrior." Now, that's a *lot* more than "good"! And the word for *wife*, in Hebrew, *ishshah*, simply means a "mature female." In other words, if you're a single woman, there's something of value for you here too.[5]

DEVELOPING A REVITALIZED RELATIONSHIP WITH GOD

Matthew 22:37–38 Jesus replied: "'**Love** the Lord your God with all your heart and with all your soul and with all your mind.' This is the first and greatest commandment."

love: *the word used here is* agapao, *the commitment of devotion that is directed by the will and can be commanded as a duty*

More Time to Focus on God

Here Jesus is commanding us to love God with all our *heart, mind*, and *soul*, which means we are to love God with our whole being. Now that our children are grown there is more time for prayer and contemplation, reading of Scripture, expanding our understanding through Bible studies and reading.

KEY POINT

Loving God and your neighbor summarizes the whole Old Testament teachings.

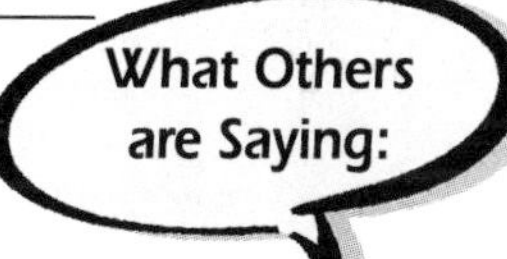

Dr. Deborah Newman: Glorifying God saves me from myself. I realized that if I am not glorifying God, I am glorifying myself. When I glorify myself, I often hurt others in the process. I don't accomplish the desires in my soul to love and be loved. This world is created to be in balance. It is only when God is in His rightful place as the center of our lives that we can live in balance. God rescues me from existing to glorify myself, because this position damages me. It is only as we seek to glorify God that unity is established within ourselves, with others, and with God.[6]

Thelma Wells: It doesn't matter what time of day or night it is; what day of the week it is; who else is talking to him, or what the problem is. He is always available to listen and to help us without static or interference. His omnipotence has blocked out anything and everything that would keep him from hearing and answering us.[7]

☞ GO TO:

1 Corinthians 12:12–31 (gifts)

Ephesians 4:11 (teaching)

DEVELOPING YOUR GIFTS

Romans 12:3–8 Just as each of us has one body with many members, and these members do not all have the same function, so in Christ we who are many form one body, and each member belongs to all the others. We have different gifts, according to the **grace** given us. If a man's gift is **prophesying**, let him use it in proportion to his faith. If it is serving, let him serve; if it is teaching, let

grace: *a gift given by God, not something that is earned*

prophesying: *a communication from the mind of God imparted to a believer by the Holy Spirit* *encouraging:* exhorting others with an uplifting cheerful call to worthwhile accomplishments

showing mercy: caring for the sick, the poor, and the aged

> him teach; if it is **encouraging**, let him encourage; if it is contributing to the needs of others, let him give generously; if it is leadership, let him govern diligently; if it is **showing mercy**, let him do it cheerfully.

You Want Me to Do What?

KEY POINT

God's grace is dispensed to others when we exercise our gifts.

Each of us has one or two spiritual gifts given to us by the grace of God. Often, we are not aware of these gifts because we have not exercised them, or we just haven't had them pointed out to us.

Now is a good time to get involved in church activities that maybe you never had time for before, and to put to use the gifts that God has given to you.

Think About It

If you've had a bad experience volunteering, perhaps it was because you weren't using your spiritual gifts. Teaching three-year-olds in Sunday school may have been a disaster, but that may have been because your real gift is leadership, which includes things like organization.

Maybe you're better equipped to be a biblical counselor or a greeter at the front door or the person who washes the communion cups. Perhaps you're being called to work with the homeless or in a hospice.

Listen to your heart and let God guide you to the "perfect" job.

A good way to find out what your spiritual gifts are is by taking a spiritual gifts test. There are many available. Ask your pastor which one he recommends. You may be surprised by what it reveals or it may confirm what you already know.

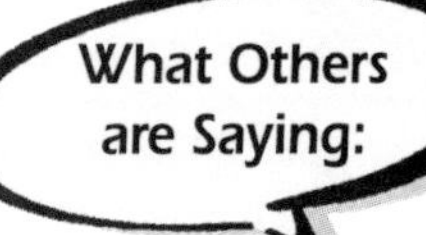

Marilyn Meberg: God has created within all human beings a tremendous drive to survive and a capability to succeed to the level of our God-given gifts. Isn't it fantastic to realize that most of us have barely tapped into our potential? We could be creating and contributing so much more.[8]

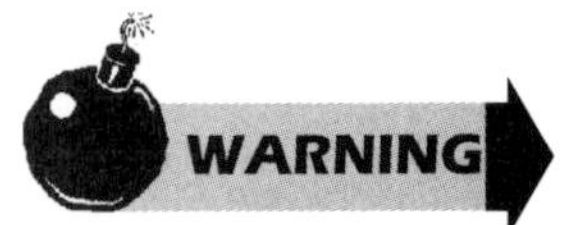

It's easy to desire a gift that may not be yours. Remember that each gift has been given to us by God and that there is not one that is better than the other. For example, the gift of teaching may look desirable, but there is much responsibility that goes along with that position.

Philippians 3:13–14 Brothers, I do not consider myself yet to have taken hold of it (total understanding and knowledge of Christ and the power of resurrection). But one thing I do: Forgetting what is behind and straining toward what is ahead, I press on toward the goal to win the **prize** for which God has called me **heavenward** in Christ Jesus.

prize: *the winner of Greek races received a wreath of leaves and sometimes a cash reward; the Christian receives an award of everlasting glory*

heavenward: *the place where Christ resides*

Reach for the Prize

The Christian life is like a race. A runner trains with one goal in mind, to win the race. He makes many sacrifices in order to get himself in top shape. The day of the race, he thinks of nothing else. His focus is on the finish line and he knows he cannot look back or be distracted by anything if he is going to win.

We too must prepare ourselves and not be distracted by the things of this world. Anything that gets in the way like money or career or position, we must be willing to give up. Our goal should be to finish the race.

Our prize? A crown that is incorruptible in heaven.

☞ **GO TO:**

Colossians 3:1–2 (heavenward)

Think About It

If you don't find eternity with Christ a goal worthy of attaining, then check out your spiritual health. You probably don't understand who Christ was and what he has done for you in the past and is doing in your life today.

We can never totally forget what is in our past, but we can choose to leave it behind and think about what is in the future.

Oswald Chambers: My goal is God himself. . . . At any cost, dear Lord, by any road.[9]

Luci Swindoll: Do your work as unto the Lord. And do it with gusto! What are you going to be when you grow up? Whatever it is, people like me will be deeply indebted to you for your service. When you go to work today, thank the Lord for the meaningful work you have and for your opportunity to help others. Give 'em a smile.[10]

THE TRUE VALUE OF A FRIEND

Ephesians 4:23 Be made new in the attitude of your minds.

☞ **GO TO:**

Romans 12:2; Colossians 3:10 (minds)

Time to Change Hats!

Paul is talking about the Christian life, but it applies to the transition you are making from being a mom to being a friend.

If you have not prepared your children and yourself for the transition they are making, they will continue to be dependent on you the rest of their lives. They will treat you like they always have. You will be the giver, and they the receivers.

But, if you have allowed them to become adults in their own right, now is the time to develop a new relationship—friendship. Friends give and receive. Healthy friendships are not one-sided. If they are, they won't last very long.

Put on a new attitude. Begin to think of your children as friends, and treat them as such.

Think About It

What are the traits you value in your friends? Make a list and then begin to change your relationship with your children.

This may mean saying "no" to them or asking them to call before they just drop in for dinner. It may mean asking them to take responsibility for certain bills like car insurance. It may mean sharing with them, adult-to-adult, some of the problems that you have "protected" them from in the past.

It may also mean that you go a whole week before you call to check up on them.

Changing relationships sometimes can be painful, but in the end it will be healthier for everyone.

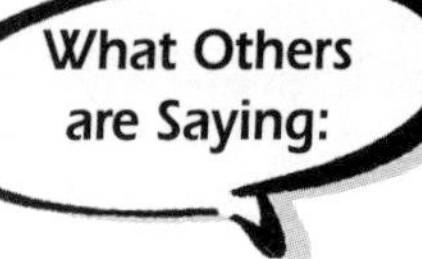

Dr. James Dobson: "Our parents never seemed able to grasp the reality of the fact that we had grown from dependent children, to capable, responsible adults. They did not recognize or appreciate our abilities, responsibilities or contributions to the outside world."[11]

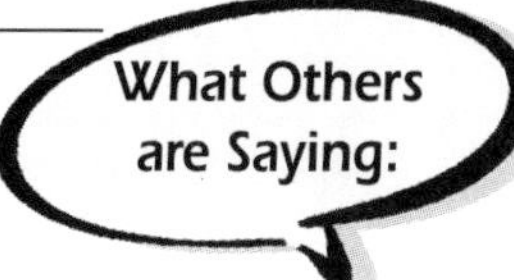

Karen Mains: My relationships with my adult children have evolved into a mixture of mother and friend. I'll admit it's been a learning process, working out this dynamic of becoming mother/friend rather than just parent/child. I'm still freeing them, affirming them, and giving them permission to grow. And they're still trying to get my ear. I'm a friend, but I truly am Mother, and always will be. What I'm beginning to realize is that this shift in our relationship is a process—one that needs regular evaluation both on my part and theirs.[12]

> **1 John 4:11–12** Dear friends, since God so loved us, we also ought to love one another. No one has ever seen God; but if we love one another, God lives in us and his love is made complete in us.

☞ GO TO:

John 3:16 (God so loved us)

John 15:12 (love one another)

John 1:18 (seen God)

1 John 2:5 (complete)

You've Got a Friend

Since the source of love is God, his love reaches full expression when we love others. The God whom "no one has ever seen" is seen in those who love, because God lives in them.

It's our job, our mission, to spread that love extravagantly throughout the world, and what better way to do that than by developing friendships, close personal friendships which, before, we may not have had time for?

Making friends may mean that you have to go first.

Call someone and ask her to go to lunch with you. Write someone else a note of encouragement. At church, smile and introduce yourself to people you don't know.

Don't assume that other women have lots of friends and don't need you.

What Others are Saying:

Patsy Clairmont: Friendship is the ship the Lord often launches to keep my boat afloat. I seem to require people in my life. Scads of them. I am not the type who wants to be an island unto myself. . . . Interacting with others encourages, nurtures, challenges, hones, and helps refine me.[13]

LIVING WITHOUT REGRETS

2 Corinthians 7:10 Godly sorrow brings **repentance** that leads to **salvation** and leaves no regret, but **worldly sorrow** brings death.

☞ **GO TO:**

Matthew 9:13; Luke 5:32 (repentance)

repentance: *a turning away from sin, disobedience, or rebellion and a turning back to God*

salvation: *deliverance from the power of sin; this leads to eternal life*

worldy sorrow: *self-centered sorrow over the painful consequences of sin*

No Regrets

Not one of us is a perfect mother. We have all made mistakes that we regret.

Perhaps we allowed a career to be more important than our children. Maybe we yelled at them too much, gave them too much, were too strict, too lenient, or too critical. Maybe we divorced their father or even abandoned them for a while.

Now that they are gone, we may for the first time really appreciate them and wish that we could do some of those things over, but we can't.

Recognizing our sin is godly sorrow. It's a deep regret and full understanding of the pain we've caused another. The good news is that godly sorrow leads us to repent.

What we *can* do is ask forgiveness from God. If it warrants, you may even need to ask forgiveness from your children.

Then grasp God's forgiveness and feel the freedom that comes from it. You'll find the regrets floating away as you begin to live in the present, a new person through God's unfailing grace.

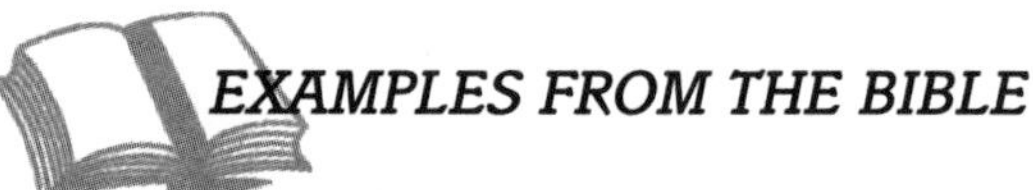

After David sinned with Bathsheba and then had her husband killed, he was confronted with his sin. Read Psalm 51 to see how deeply he regretted his sin, how he asked for forgiveness, and then put it behind him by accepting God's wonderful grace (see GWBI, page 65).

The salvation that comes through Christ may be described in three tenses: past, present, and future.

When a person believes in Christ, he is saved from the consequences of his past sins (Acts 16:31). In the present, we are being saved from the power of sin in our daily lives (Romans 8:13; Philippians 2:12). At the times of our salvation, God releases the power of Christ's resurrection in us

(Romans 6:4) and allows us a taste of our future life as his children (2 Corinthians 1:22; Ephesians 1:14).

Our experience of salvation will be complete when Christ returns (Hebrews 9:28) and the kingdom of God is fully revealed (Matthew 13:41–43).

Do you need to ask your children for forgiveness? Now would be a good time to do that.

Don't put it off for a better time. That time may never come.

You don't need to bring up every little thing, just say, "Will you forgive me for hurting you?" Don't just say, "I'm sorry." It doesn't require an answer and has become almost a cliché in our society. Wait for their answer.

Be prepared just in case they're not ready to forgive. You may have to ask more than once.

Don't allow yourself to wallow in the past. You might get stuck there.

Erma Bombeck: I could hardly wait to leave the "crud detail" as I called it. I wanted to go to a place where you were important and people listened to what you had to say. Mothering hadn't done that . . . and yet . . . wouldn't it be ironic if my turf yielded the most important commodity being grown today? A family? A crop of children, seeded by two people, nourished by love, watered by tears, and in eighteen or twenty years harvested into worthwhile human beings to go through the process again. What if nothing else I would do would equal it in importance? Wouldn't you have thought someone would have told me?[14]

Study Questions

1. Define the term "mystique," and name two ways to make yourself more interesting.
2. What is the greatest commandment?
3. Name the spiritual gifts as listed in Romans 12:3–8. Which do you think you possess?
4. What is the difference between being a parent and being a friend?
5. Why is regret so harmful, and what can be done about it?

CHAPTER WRAP-UP

- When our children leave home, it can be a time of mourning. It should be expected as a natural process of parenting. It's the end of a cherished role that defined who we were. It is also the time for a new beginning.
- Our energy can now be refocused on our marriages. This can be a wonderful time of rediscovering an old love that has grown richer because of the memories you share.
- Now there will be more time to develop a relationship with the Lord. Our quiet times will not be interrupted. New volunteer activities can be explored. We can even take that evening or day Bible study that we've always wanted.
- Spiritual gifts can be put to work. We can volunteer in the nursery, teach a Sunday school class, take a leadership position, or wash communion cups. Outside of the church we can explore other opportunities to serve in places that need the touch of a godly woman.
- Friends are especially important at this time of life. They will support us as we make this transition and give us other people to think about than our children.
- No mother is perfect. We have all made mistakes. Examining our regrets and then asking God (and maybe our children, too) for forgiveness, will free us from the weight of these mistakes and allow us to live a full rich life as God intended.

JUDY'S BOOKSHELF

- *Grow Something Besides Old,* Laurie Beth Jones, Simon & Schuster. A beautifully illustrated gift book full of one-liners that will make you think and short shorts that will make you laugh.
- *Emotional Phases of a Woman's Life,* Jean Lush, Fleming H. Revell. A down-to-earth writer and popular speaker talks about the emotional phases of a woman's life. It helped me realize that what I'm experiencing is normal.
- *Then God Created Woman,* Dr. Deborah Newman, Focus on the Family. The author discusses our search for wholeness and then tells us how to find it.

15 FACING THE UNTHINKABLE

WHAT'S IN THIS CHAPTER

- Eve's Heartbreaking Loss
- Bathsheba and David Lose a Baby
- Mary Was There
- A Time to Mourn
- The Comforter Comes

Here We Go

For a mother, there is no greater fear than the death of her child, and yet sometimes it happens. It can occur in the womb, during birth, in infancy, childhood, the teen years, or even in adulthood. It doesn't matter when; it is still always devastating.

There are no easy answers in the Bible to questions like why. But there are examples there of mothers who lost their children, like Eve, Bathsheba, and, of course, Mary.

And there is great comfort to be found in the writings of those who suffered.

EVE'S HEARTBREAKING LOSS

> **Genesis 4:8** Now **Cain** said to his brother **Abel**, "Let's go out to the field." And while they were in the field, Cain attacked his brother Abel and killed him.

☞ **GO TO:**

1 John 3:12 (Cain)

Matthew 23:35; Hebrews 11:4 (Abel)

Cain: *"brought forth or acquired"*

Abel: *"breath," or "temporary"*

A Violent Death

In one terrible act Eve lost two sons. One was murdered and the other forced to leave home and wander the earth.

Eve's reaction isn't recorded in this passage, but it must have been one of disbelief, anger, and heartbreak. Her faith in a God who would allow such a thing would have been stretched to the limits.

God's statement *"I will greatly increase your pains in childbearing"* (Genesis 3:16) would now have a new meaning.

This murder was especially monstrous, for Cain not only murdered his own brother who was a good man, but he deliberately deceived Abel into going out into that field. It shows how quickly evil entered the world after the Fall.

Think About It

A violent death seems as if it would be the most awful way to die. But research has shown that the body releases opiate-like painkillers during times of extreme stress that actually ease the pain and give the victim a sense of peace and tranquility.

Scientists give nature the credit, but it seems, if you believe in God, that it is as if he himself steps in and eases the trauma.[1]

What Others are Saying:

Sherwin B. Nuland, *writing about the violent murder of Katie Mason and subsequent look of tranquility on her face:* I am convinced that nature stepped in, as it so often does, and provided exactly the right spoonful of medicine to give a measure of tranquility to a dying child. . . . Joan Mason [Katie's mother], too, seems to have been protected by her **endorphins**. She told me that had it not been for her own feeling of almost supernatural warmth and the sense of being surrounded by a thick insulating aura, she believes that she might have had a heart attack and died there on the street alongside her daughter.[2]

endorphins: *a painkiller released by the body during extreme stress*

☞ GO TO:

Exodus 8:2; Exodus 12:23; 1 Samuel 25:38; Isaiah 19:22 (struck)

Ezra 8:23; Esther 4:15 (fasted)

BATHSHEBA AND DAVID LOSE A BABY

> **2 Samuel 12:15–18** After Nathan had gone home, the LORD **struck** the child that Uriah's wife had borne to David, and he became ill. David pleaded with God for the child. He **fasted** and went into his house and spent the nights lying on the **ground**. The **elders of his household** stood beside him to get him up from the ground, but he refused, and he would not eat any food with them. On the seventh day the child died.

struck: *inflicted with disease*

fasted: *cover over the mouth*

ground: *floor of his room*

elders of his household: *chief servants*

A Harsh Consequence

This verse speaks only of David's misery, but Bathsheba must have been suffering at least as much and probably more, for David had many other children. This was Bathsheba's first.

While David fasted and prayed on the floor in his room, Bathsheba spent seven days memorizing the features on her baby's face, placing cold cloths on his forehead, changing his diapers, kissing his little face, and weeping—alone.

This is a controversial scripture that even Biblical scholars avoid, for it's hard to reconcile how a loving God, one who would die on a cross for our sins, would strike a child with a deadly disease. He was the innocent victim. It was his parents who had sinned. Why would God do such a terrible thing?

Remember this: David, as King of Israel, held a great responsibility to be an example for his people and for the surrounding nations. Not only did he do a terrible thing, sleep with another man's wife and then have the man murdered, but he also shamed the name of the Lord.

Herbert Lockyer: Both David and Bathsheba must have had much agony of soul as they became deeply conscious that the death of their son, conceived out of wedlock, was a divine judgment upon their dark sin.[3]

Guilt is one of the stages of the grieving process. Parents blame themselves and even each other. The "if onlys" haunt them day and night. If only they hadn't left the child alone. If only they'd taken the child to the doctor sooner. If only they'd been better parents.

This scripture could be used to heighten that guilt by adding the burden of guilt over sin. But is this true? Does God send punishment upon our children for our sins? Does this scripture imply that when a child becomes ill or is injured in an accident that it is a punishment from God?

No. In Matthew it says clearly, *"He causes his sun to rise on the evil and the good, and sends rain on the righteous and the unrighteous"* (Matthew 5:45).

Bad things happen to everyone. Guilt and blame are not from God.

What Others are Saying:

Marjorie Holmes: My God is a god of mercy, of fair play and compassion as well as a god of power. . . . My God would never deliberately bring harm to anyone. But if it happens—if it simply happens due to wind and rain and weather and man's own mistakes, then God has promises to keep: Life continuing. An even richer, fuller, brighter ongoing life to compensate.[4]

☞ **GO TO:**

1 Chronicles 22; 23:1; 2 Chronicles (Solomon)

Leviticus 20:10; 24:17 (adultery and murder)

Solomon: *derived from the Hebrew word for peace*

> **2 Samuel 12:24** Then David comforted his wife Bathsheba, and he went to her and lay with her. She gave birth to a son, and they named him **Solomon**.

God's Forgiveness

David finally goes to Bathsheba and comforts her in her grief. How lonely she must have felt during those seven days as she watched her baby dying.

David had his loyal servants watching over him, but who was there for Bathsheba? Had her family and friends abandoned her because of her sin? Did David's other wives accept her?

The customary penalty for adultery and murder was death. The Lord showed great mercy in allowing David to live and continue to rule over Israel. David and Bathsheba experienced great mercy at the hands of God.

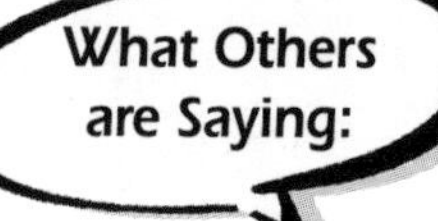

Herbert Lockyer: What about Bathsheba? With David, was she made conscious of her share in the iniquitous transaction of the past? Co-responsible in David's sin, did her tears of repentance mingle with those of her husband's? It would seem so, because God blessed them with another son whom they called Solomon. . . . Then, is not Bathsheba's inclusion in the genealogy of Jesus [Matthew 1] another token that God had put her sins behind His back?[5]

Larry G. Peppers, Ph.D. and Ronald J. Knapp, Ph.D.: Guilt usually comes in waves. At times, it penetrates the very core of the mother's existence.[6]

☞ **GO TO:**

Genesis 37:35 (go to him)

> **2 Samuel 12:20–23** Then David got up from the ground. After he had washed, put on lotions and changed his clothes, he went into the house of the LORD and worshiped. Then he went to his own house, and at his request they served him food, and he ate. His servants asked him, "Why are you acting this way? While the child was alive, you fasted and wept, but now that the child is dead, you get up and eat!" He answered, "While the child was still alive, I fasted and wept. I thought, 'Who knows? The LORD may be gracious to me and let the child live.' But now that he is dead, why should I fast? Can I bring him back again? I will go to him, but he will not return to me."

A Better Place

David's behavior seems irrational even to his servants. For seven days he has lain prostrate on the floor refusing to eat or be comforted, begging the Lord to spare the life of his son.

Now that the child is dead, he washes, puts on lotions, changes his clothes, and worships the Lord. When asked why, he clearly states that he was hoping the Lord would change his mind.

Now that the child is gone, there is nothing to be done but to accept God's judgment and wait until the time when they will be reunited in another world that the Hebrews called **Sheol**.

☞ **GO TO:**

Job 3:13–19; Psalm 9:17; Isaiah 38:10 (Sheol)

Sheol: *realm of the dead*

The Hebrew people regarded Sheol as a place where the righteous and unrighteous go at death, a place where punishment is received and rewards are enjoyed. They also believed that God was present there.[7]

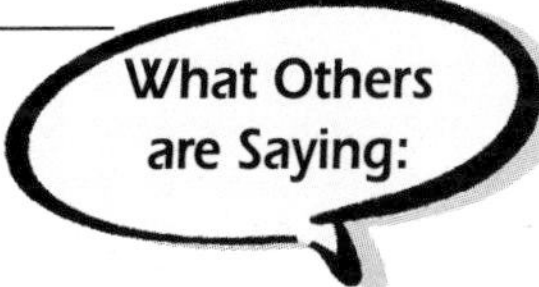

Marjorie Holmes: When one of us leaves the earth, it is for another destination. As surely as if he had climbed on a train that becomes just a plaintive wail in the distance, or a plane that dwindles to a speck in the sky. The rest of us can no longer see the plane or train or bus or car or its occupant. But we know it is taking him somewhere. Good-bys are always hard. . . . But it helps, how it helps to know that the one we miss so acutely has not ceased to exist, but simply lives in a place where we can't join him yet.[8]

KEY POINT

There is a better place waiting for all who believe.

Think About It

David believed in Sheol, but Jesus described an even better place. To his disciples he said, *"In my Father's house are many rooms; if it were not so, I would have told you. I am going there to prepare a place for you. And if I go and prepare a place for you, I will come back and take you to be with me that you also may be where I am"* (John 14:2–3).

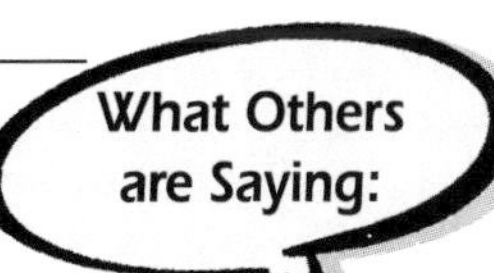

Barnes' Notes: We see that the death of a Christian is not to be dreaded, nor is it an event over which we should immoderately weep. It is but removing from one apartment of God's universal dwelling-place to another—one where we shall still be in his house, and still feel the same interest in all that pertains to his kingdom.[9]

Matthew 19:14 Jesus said, "Let the little children come to me, and do not hinder them, for the kingdom of heaven belongs to such as these."

☞ **GO TO:**

Matthew 18:3 (kingdom of heaven)

Heaven Belongs to Children

This scripture is often used to demonstrate that Jesus cared about little children and that because of their innocence, they belonged in the kingdom of heaven. He didn't require baptism or a baby dedication or even that the parents be baptized.

Jack Hayford: Here is the truth: the child of "early flight"—the stillborn, the newborn who dies, the miscarried, the aborted—is not a "nothing" that has gone nowhere. . . . Rather, each of those little ones are present with the Father. They have identity, individuality and deserve to be known for what they are—eternal beings.[10]

THE BIG PICTURE

Revelation 21:1–27 John was shown the Holy City where there will be no mourning or crying or pain. It had a great, high wall with twelve gates, and with twelve angels at the gates. The city was laid out like a square, as long as it was wide. The angel measured the city with a golden rod and found it to be **12,000 stadia** in length, and as wide and high as it was long. Its wall was **144 cubits** thick and made of jasper, and the city of pure gold, as pure as glass. The foundations of the city walls were decorated with every kind of precious stone. The twelve gates were each made of a single pearl.

12,000 stadia: *1,400 miles*

144 cubits: *200 feet*

Christ Builds a Home

This is the description of the Holy City where all those who believe in Christ as their Savior will one day live. It is beyond anything we can imagine here on earth.

Everything that is rare here, like gold and precious gems, will be common there, but everything that is common here, like crying and mourning, will not exist there.

If you have lost a child, you can be assured that he or she is waiting for you on the other side. You can be just as sure as David was. You may not be able to put off mourning for your lost little one as quickly as he did, but you can take hope in the fact that you will see each other again.

MARY WAS THERE

> **John 19:25–27** Near the cross of Jesus stood his mother, his mother's sister, Mary the wife of Clopas, and Mary Magdalene. When Jesus saw his mother there, and the **disciple whom he loved** standing nearby, he said to his mother, "Dear woman, here is your son," and to the disciple, "Here is your mother." From that time on, this disciple took her into his home.

☞ GO TO:

Matthew 27:55, 56 (mother)

Luke 8:2; John 20:1, 10–18 (Mary Magdalene)

disciple whom he loved: *John*

Mary's Death Watch

Mary watched and waited as her son hung on that cross and the life drained out of him. She had others to comfort her, a few women and one of the disciples, but still it must have been an unimaginable ordeal.

Jesus' last thoughts were of his mother. He placed her care in the hands of the beloved disciple John. (See GWWB, page 117.)

KEY POINT

Jesus had a mother who suffered.

What did Mary experience? Why didn't Jesus spare her this terrible agony? Note that Jesus' brothers were not present; some think it's because they did not believe. Maybe the only thing that carried Mary through was her faith.

We have popularized the cross. We wear it around our necks and dangle it from our ears. We display it proudly on our churches and in our art.

However, death on a cross was a cruelty beyond imagining. It wasn't until the fourth century that the cross became a symbol of the faith. C. S. Lewis points out that the cross did not become common in art until all who had seen a real one died off.[11]

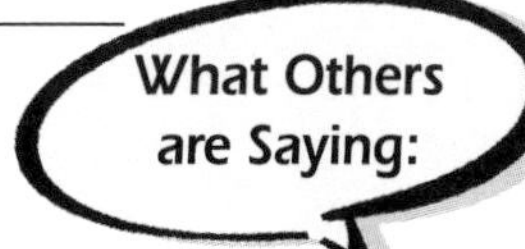

Herbert Lockyer: As [Jesus] dies, [Mary] stands in silence. Those around her had no conception of her inner grief as she stood where her Son could see her. . . . Before He died Jesus recognized His human relationship to Mary, which He had during His ministry put in the background, that His higher relationship must stand out more prominently. Commending Mary to John, Jesus did not address her by name, or as His mother, but as "Woman." . . . But even then she did not desert her Son. Some of His disciples forsook Him and fled, but her love never surrendered, even though her Son was dying as a criminal between two thieves.[12]

Most High: a title for God

☞ **GO TO:**

Genesis 14:19; 2 Samuel 22:14; Psalm 7:10 (Most High)

Psalm 45:6; Revelation 11:15 (forever)

Luke 2:51 (treasured)

Luke 1:32–33; 2:19 "He will be great and will be called the Son of the **Most High**. The Lord God will give him the throne of his father David, and he will reign over the house of Jacob forever; his kingdom will never end." But Mary treasured up all these things and pondered them in her heart.

High Expectations

Wow! Mary is being told by an angel of the Lord that her son is going to be the Messiah and that he is going to reign over the house of Jacob forever. He would be the new king.

She must have pondered over this message in the quietness of the night, while she was washing the laundry, cooking, and grinding flour for bread.

Think About It

Mary's imaginings would never have concluded that Jesus' life would end the way it did.

Did she think, like so many, that he would be a great political leader? Did she believe that he would be King of the Jews? What a great disappointment it must have been to see him die like a common criminal after the angel had promised her so much more.

Simeon: *"one who hears and obeys"*

☞ **GO TO:**

Luke 20:17, 18; 1 Corinthians 1:23; 1 Peter 2:6–8 (falling and rising)

Luke 2:34–35 Then **Simeon** blessed them and said to Mary, his mother: "This child is destined to cause the falling and rising of many in Israel, and to be a sign that will be spoken against, so that the thoughts of many hearts will be revealed. And a sword will pierce your own soul too."

A Terrible Prophecy

Simeon was a devout Hebrew in a time when religion was at a low ebb in Israel. He clung tenaciously to a belief that he would see the Messiah before he died and so, when he held Jesus, he experienced great joy.

But with his joy was mixed a sadder truth: A sword would pierce Mary's heart, just as it would pierce Jesus'. Mary must have wondered at this prophecy from this old man.

It had just been days before when the shepherds had visited at

Jesus' birth, and the words of the angel were still ringing in her ears, *"He will be great and called the son of the Most High."*

It was the first sign to Mary that things would not be all she dreamed of for her son and herself.

Larry Richards: Crucifixion was practiced as a method of torture and execution by the Persians before it was adopted by the Romans. Roman law allowed only slaves and criminals to be crucified. Roman citizens were not crucified. The victim's arms are stretched out above him, fastened to a cross bar fixed near the top of a stake slightly taller than a man. Suspended this way, blood is forced to the lower body. The pulse rate increases, and after days of agony the victim dies from lack of blood circulating to the brain and heart. . . . **Scourging** before crucifixion hastened death, as did breaking a victim's legs.[13]

Scourging: *to punish by whip or lash*

FROM JUDY'S HEART

When I was a child, Easter meant a whole lot more to me than it does today. I think it's because I have become immune to the story. Like a movie I've seen over and over, I know the details and I know how it turns out. Jesus' pain seems unreal.

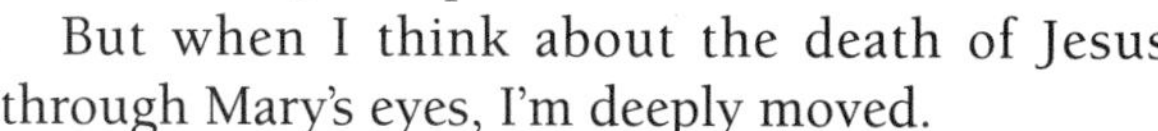

But when I think about the death of Jesus through Mary's eyes, I'm deeply moved.

Like Mary I am a mother of sons. The moment I held them I was filled with a love that only a mother can know. At that moment I would have given my own life to save theirs. I would have climbed Mount Everest or swam the ocean if it was what they needed.

Of course, their demands weren't that dramatic, but I did change my life to care for them. In one night, I went from caring about my own needs to caring about someone else's even more. I gave up a great job. I pulled my tired, sleepy body out of bed in the middle of the night. I wiped dirty bottoms and cleaned burps off the floor and me. When they couldn't sleep, I walked them until my arms felt like they would fall off.

Any illness panicked me. I worried that they wouldn't live, and often listened for their breathing or movement in the night. There was always this fear that something would happen to them.

As my children grow older (they're now 22 and 24) I have come to realize those feelings of care and responsibility never change. That must be how Mary felt about Jesus, too. She must have died a million deaths as she watched her baby hanging on that cross. She probably would have changed places with him if she could have.

A mother's grief. That I understand, and it breaks my heart and gives me a new understanding of the sacrifice that Jesus made for me. He died that I might have eternal life. If you don't know what that means, then please run, don't walk, to your nearest church and ask the pastor to help you understand.

A TIME TO MOURN

> **2 Samuel 14:2** So Joab sent someone to **Tekoa** and had a wise woman brought from there. He said to her, "Pretend you are in mourning. Dress in mourning clothes, and don't use any cosmetic lotions. Act like a woman who has spent many days grieving for the dead."

☞ **GO TO:**

Amos 1:1 (Tekoa)

***Tekoa:** a town a few miles south of Bethlehem*

Biblical Mourning Practices

From these scriptures we learn that there was special clothing worn during mourning and that women wore no makeup or lotion and that there was a certain "look" expected by those who mourned. In Zechariah 12:12 it says that men and women often mourned separately.

Jewish funerals were held either the same day or within twenty-four hours. The corpse was washed, anointed and bound with special grave clothes and placed on a simple **bier**. Then it was buried or placed in a cave. There was a time of great **lamentation** and wailing for the dead. Sometimes the family hired professional mourners.

***bier:** a frame or stand on which a corpse is laid*

***lamentation:** act of expressing grief*

There are no records that show any religious service was conducted at funerals for Jews. At the time of Christ, the **Pharisees** believed in a resurrection, while the **Sadducees** rejected the very notion of a personal immortality. The Jews never cremated their dead.[14]

***Pharisees:** a religious and political party known for insisting that the law of God be strictly observed*

***Sadducees:** the most powerful members of the priesthood*

> **2 Chronicles 35:25** Jeremiah composed laments for Josiah, and to this day all the men and women singers commemorate Josiah in the laments. These became a tradition in Israel and are written in the Laments.

☞ **GO TO:**

Jeremiah 22:15, 16 (Josiah)

Writing Out Their Grief

One of the ways that Jeremiah coped with the death of his friend Josiah was to write lamentations. He poured his heart out on paper for all to see and share. His grief was not private, but very public.

This is one way that many mothers also have used to cope with an unbearable loss.

Grief is a process. It is unique to everyone who goes through it. But there are some commonalities of experience.

It may take six months, a year, or two years to work through your grief and the stages may vary in length. You may think that you are finally through one stage only to revisit it later. Stages can even overlap.

Things that have helped others go through the process are journaling, joining a group, reading books of comfort like the Bible, and counseling.

If you have lost a child, let yourself experience the grief fully and give yourself time to recover.

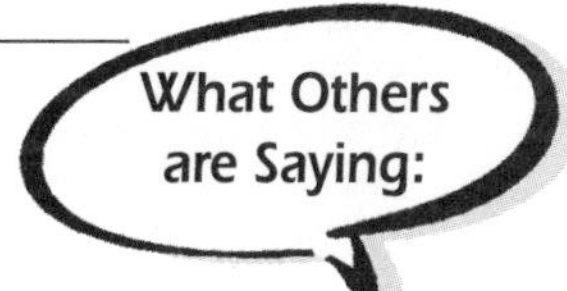

Larry G. Peppers, Ph.D. and Ronald J. Knapp, Ph.D.: We have discovered through our interviews that the grief that mothers experience may never be completely resolved. Portions of it will always remain tucked away, appearing from time to time when they least expect it.[16]

Stages of Grief

Stage of Grief	Symptom
Shock	Denial, refuse to believe, screaming, hysterical; some become emotionally paralyzed. Can last for minutes, hours, or months.
Disorganization	Confusion abounds. There are many questions and no answers. One feels disoriented. It's a time for talking, holding, hugging, and caressing. Not a time for making decisions.
Volatile emotions	Anger and rage. May be sudden and violent and directed at family members.
Guilt	Blame of self and others. The big question is, why? Sense of failure.
Loss and loneliness	The most difficult stage of grief. Feelings of emptiness. Deep depression. Loss becomes oppressive when alone. Arms ache to hold the baby. Difficult to be around babies and pregnant women.
Relief	Misery and despair begin to fade. Appetite returns, sleeping problems fade, anger subsides, depression goes away. Renewed interest in people.[15]

Psalm 69:20 I looked for sympathy, but there was none, for comforters, but I found none.

Comfort Hard to Find

The writer of this psalm pens the feelings of many who suffer. They feel alone and isolated. It seems as if there is no one who can truly understand what they are going through.

What Others are Saying:

Marjorie Holmes: This hurt, oh God, this hurt. It is a shock, it dazes and numbs me. So that for a little while I can move blindly, almost insensate, about my duties. Then it revives, it comes again in waves, rhythmic beatings that seem almost not to be borne. Yet I know that I must bear them, as a woman endures the pains of birth.[17]

THE COMFORTER COMES

Psalm 46:1 God is our refuge and strength, an ever-present help in trouble.

☞ **GO TO:**

Psalm 9:9; 37:39; 61:3 (refuge)

Psalm 18:1 (strength)

Psalm 34:18 (ever-present)

Psalm 18:6; Luke 1:54 (help)

Psalm 25:17 (trouble)

Isaiah 61:2–3 (mourn)

blessed: *an inner joy not dependent on outer circumstances*

There Is a Place to Go

This is but one example of a Psalm that will comfort, express your feelings for you, and help you through the grieving process. In Hebrews it clearly says "*Never will I leave you; never will I forsake you*" (Hebrews 13:5). You may not feel his presence, you may even feel angry at him, but he is there.

Matthew 5:4 Blessed are those who mourn, for they will be comforted.

A Promise Made

Jesus begins his most famous sermon with a promise to those who mourn—they will be comforted. This doesn't mean that the believer won't face trials and tribulations, but that through them the believer will experience God on a personal basis.

What Others are Saying:

Marjorie Holmes: "Help me," I kept crying to my God. . . . He came in the quiet of the night; he was there in the brilliance of the morning. He touched my senses with hope; he healed my despair. And with the awareness of his presence came the deliverance I sought.[18]

> **Galatians 6:2** Carry each other's burdens, and in this way you will fulfill the law of Christ.

Solace in Helping Others

This scripture describes a way to find healing: help others in their grief. In that way the one who hurts will find solace.

What Others are Saying:

Melissa Sexson Hanson: Looking back, I realize that God did not leave me comfortless throughout my times of grief. Friends were sent to support me through this terrible trial. Although many of them didn't know the best way to encourage me, others who had been through similar circumstances knew just what to say and do.[19]

> **Isaiah 61:2–3** To comfort all who mourn, and provide for those who grieve in Zion—to bestow on them a **crown of beauty** instead of ashes, the **oil of gladness** instead of mourning, and a garment of praise instead of a spirit of despair. They will be called oaks of righteousness, a planting of the LORD for the display of his splendor.

☞ **GO TO:**

Isaiah 49:13; 57:19; Jeremiah 31:13; Matthew 5:4 (comfort all who mourn)

Psalm 23:5; 45:7; 104:15 (oil of gladness)

crown of beauty: *turban or headdress*

oil of gladness: *olive oil used on joyous occasions*

Oil of Gladness

Grieving is for a little while in comparison to an eternity with our beloved ones.

Here God promises that those who mourn will wear beautiful headdresses, or tiaras, instead of the ashes commonly used to signify that one is in mourning. They also will trade in their clothes of mourning for ones of celebration, and they will be anointed with the oil of gladness.

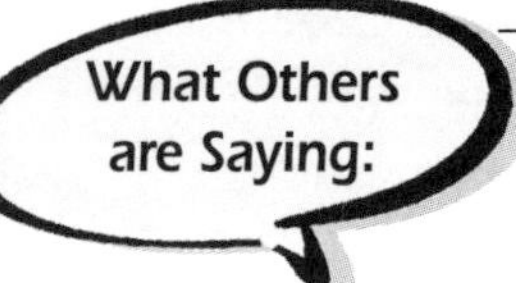

Hannah Whitall Smith: If we want to be comforted, we must make up our minds to believe every single solitary word of comfort God has ever spoken; and we must refuse utterly to listen to any words of discomfort spoken by our own hearts, or by our circumstances.[20]

Study Questions

1. Why was Abel's murder so evil?
2. Why did David mourn so openly while his baby lay dying and then stop so suddenly after the child died?
3. List three expectations that Mary, the mother of Jesus, might have had for her son.
4. List the stages of grief.
5. Find the concordance in the back of your Bible and look under the word comfort. Chose one scripture that especially speaks to you, and write it out.

CHAPTER WRAP-UP

- Eve must bear the unimaginable grief of one of her sons murdering the other. She then must watch as God banishes the surviving son, Cain, to wander the earth. In one event she loses two sons.
- David and Bathsheba's son is struck by God and after seven days of illness dies. Bathsheba mourns alone as David lies prostrate in his room begging God to spare the child's life.
- As Jesus hangs dying on the cross, below him wait a group of women, one of whom is his mother. She must bear the unthinkable pain of watching her son die a slow torturous death. His final thoughts are for her well-being when he asks a disciple to take care of her.
- Everyone who mourns is unique, and yet there are some similarities or stages that each person goes through. The severity and length of each stage may be different. It's important to go through the process of mourning. There is also a promise that it will end.
- God is the source of all comfort. Through a personal relationship with him we can find the joy and peace that he has promised even though we face terrible loss.

- *The God of All Comfort*, Hannah Whitall Smith, Moody Press. Even though this is an older publication, the truth of the Gospel spans the generations and touches at the very heart of who God is.
- *To Help You Through the Hurting*, Marjorie Holmes, Doubleday. A collection of wonderful essays that are from Marjorie's heart. Any mother who mourns will be touched.
- *I'll Hold You in Heaven*, Jack Hayford, Regal Books. This is for those who have suffered a miscarriage, abortion, or death of a very young child. He answers some of the toughest questions.

Part Five

RECEIVING THE BLESSING

REVEREND FUN

"I can't really say I'm surprised."

16 THE BEST IS YET TO COME

WHAT'S IN THIS CHAPTER

- A Good Mother-in-Law
- A Godly Grandmother
- Storing Up Treasures in Heaven
- Reaping the Rewards

Here We Go

It's time to take our shoes off and put up our feet. We have prepared the soil, planted the seed, and harvested the crop. Now it's time to relax and enjoy the labor of our hands.

Of course, there are a couple of new roles to take on, but they'll be easy after weathering the terrible twos, adolescence, and the stormy teen years.

What's next? Being a loving mother-in-law and a doting grandmother. With the help of a few biblical role models, we can learn how to do it right.

At the end of our lives, we can take joy in Jesus saying, "Well done, good and faithful servant, well done."

A GOOD MOTHER-IN-LAW

THE BIG PICTURE

Ruth 1:1–5 When a famine hits the land, Elimelech moves his family from **Bethlehem** to **<u>Moab</u>** (see illustration, page 217). His wife is **Naomi** and his two sons are Mahlon and Kilion. Elimelech dies and leaves Naomi a widow with two sons. They marry Moabite women, Orpah and **<u>Ruth</u>**. After they have lived there for ten years, Mahlon and Kilion also die. Naomi is left without a husband and without her two sons.

☞ **GO TO:**

Genesis 36:35 (Moab)

Matthew 1:3, 5–6 (Ruth)

Bethlehem: *the place where David and the Messiah will be born*

Moab: *a country to the east of Israel inhabited by Baal worshipers*

Naomi: *"my joy"*

Ruth: *sounds like the Hebrew for "friendship"*

Refined by Suffering

Naomi had a rough life. First she and her family had to flee a famine and move to a foreign country thirty miles away that worshiped pagan Gods. While there, her husband dies, leaving her a widow.

She can take some comfort in the fact that she has her two sons to care for her. But they marry Moabite women, which isn't exactly forbidden, but *"no Moabite—or his sons to the tenth generation—was allowed to enter the* ***assembly of the Lord****"* (Deuteronomy 23:3).

After ten years of living among the Moabites, her sons die leaving her with absolutely no support and two daughters-in-law. She must have felt very lost and alone and wondering why God had allowed these horrible things to happen.

☞ **GO TO:**

Genesis 19:36–37 (Moabite)

assembly of the Lord: *any gathering for religious purposes*

Think About It

God had a plan that Naomi could not see. Notice that she made a plan to do something. Are you going through tough times? Maybe God has a plan for you, too. Maybe you need to make the first step and let God guide the next one.

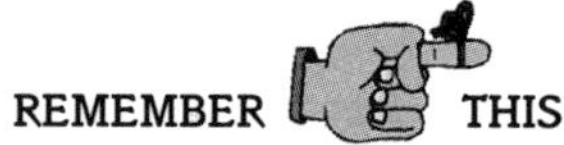

Widows had no way of earning a living. They were dependent upon their families to support them. When Naomi's husband died and then her two sons, there would have been no financial support for Naomi or her two daughters-in-law. Her only option was to return to Bethlehem and live off the kindness of relatives.

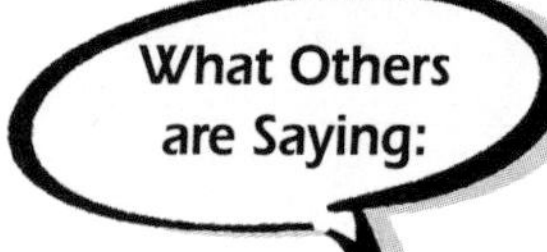

Margaret Wold: Conditions must have been extremely bad to make Elimelech and Naomi take their two sons, Mahlon and Chilion, to a foreign land, leaving behind the property that was their inheritance in their homeland.[1]

Erma Bombeck, *speaking to her daughter:* "I've never asked a lot of my children. Just that they get married and make me a mother-in-law and a grandmother . . . in that order."

"You wouldn't like it," [her daughter] said. "I hear being a mother-in-law is overrated. Trust me, she rides to the church in the front seat with her son and rides home in another car. She's in the front row at the wedding and in the kitchen at the reception. . . . And the only time she gets the grandchild is when it is contagious or they can't get a regular sitter."[2]

Ruth 1:6–14 When Naomi hears that the famine is over in Bethlehem, she and her two daughters-in-law prepare to leave Moab. On the road, Naomi urges her daughters-in-law to return to their mother's home and to find other husbands. They weep and beg to go with her. But Naomi says, "Return home, my daughters. Why would you come with me? Am I going to have any more sons, who could become your husbands? Return home, my daughters; I am too old to have another husband. Even if I thought there was still hope for me—even if I had a husband tonight and then gave birth to sons—would you wait for them? No, my daughters. It is more bitter for me than for you, because the LORD's hand has gone out against me." At this Orpah kisses her mother-in-law and says goodbye, but Ruth clings to her.

Oh, Naomi, You're Always Putting Others First!

Naomi is left with only bitterness, but she must've been a good mother-in-law for these two young, childless women beg to go with her to Bethlehem. You'd think they would have been anxious to return to their own people. Naomi has to almost push them away. Orpah finally agrees and turns around and says goodbye, but Ruth has formed such a strong bond with her mother-in-law that she cannot leave her.

The word mother-in-law has a negative connotation. But it doesn't have to be that way. Make friends with your sons- and daughters-in-law. Treat them as family, and don't interfere with their lives. Don't be critical of them, especially in front of their children and spouses. They will come to respect and love you.

Naomi alludes to the Israelite law that requires the childless widow to marry the brother of her husband. This law protected the widow and guaranteed the continuation of the family line.

☞ **GO TO:**

Deuteronomy 25:5–6; Mark 12:18–23 (widow)

> **Ruth 1:16–18** But Ruth replied, "Don't urge me to leave you or to turn back from you. Where you go I will go, and where you stay I will stay. Your people will be my people and your God my God. Where you die I will die, and there I will be buried. May the **Lord** deal with me, be it ever so severely, if anything but death separates you and me." When Naomi realized that Ruth was determined to go with her she stopped urging her.

Lord: *Yahweh instead of* Elohim, *the usual name which foreigners give to God*

Naomi's Example Turns Others to God

This verse is often quoted at weddings as an example of true love and devotion.

But Ruth was not speaking to her husband; she was speaking to her mother-in-law!

Naomi must have demonstrated her love for Ruth and her faith in God in practical everyday ways for Ruth to be willing to leave her home and set out for a foreign country. If Ruth had gone back to her parents, she would have been cared for, and eventually she would have found another husband. Instead, she begs to go with Naomi to a land where there is little chance for her, a Moabite woman, to find a husband. Since there is no man to take care of them, they will face poverty.

But such is her love for Naomi and her devotion to the God whom she has come to worship as her own. She is willing to risk everything.

KEY POINT

Joy in spite of great suffering can win others to Christ.

Think About It

How does your relationship with your son or daughter-in-law compare to Naomi and Ruth's? If there is tension, begin today to mend the hurts and show God's love to the newcomer who has entered your family.

What Others are Saying:

Jim and Sally Conway: The Apostle Paul said, *"I am still not all I should be but I am bringing all my energies to bear on this one thing: Forgetting the past and looking forward to what lies ahead. . . ."* [Philippians 3:13] Forget the failures of the past, forget the things you can't change. So you've made some bad choices, some things have happened in your life that you're ashamed of; you wish you could change some things, but you can't. Tell God—simply and directly in prayer. Ask him to forgive you; then walk away from it because he has forgiven you. Christ died to forgive you. Accept it![3]

Ruth 3:1–4:1 One day Naomi says to Ruth that it is time to find someone who will take care of her when she is gone. She advises Ruth to wash and perfume herself and to put on her best clothes and go to the **threshing floor** where Boaz will be winnowing barley [see illustration below]. When he lies down for the night, Naomi suggests that Ruth lie at his feet. Ruth follows Naomi's instructions.

When Boaz awakes in the middle of the night, he discovers Ruth keeping him warm. He is touched by her kindness and knows of her fine reputation. Since he is her kinsman-redeemer, he takes the necessary steps to marry her. She becomes his wife and gives birth to a son.

threshing floor: *a hard, smooth, open place on rock or clay*

GO TO:

Leviticus 25:23–28; Jeremiah 32:6–10 (kinsman-redeemer)

A Wise Adviser

Naomi is worried about her daughter-in-law, for she herself is getting older and she fears that she will die with no one to take care of Ruth. She sees an opportunity for Ruth in a marriage with Boaz.

Winnowing Grain

After the grain was threshed, it was winnowed—that is, cleaned by the wind. Men tossed the grain into the air, and the strong wind would blow away the straw and chaff.

She advises her daughter-in-law in what to do and because their relationship is so good, Ruth obeys her.

Boaz wakes to discover this beautiful, young widow at his feet and immediately is captivated by her. He takes the necessary steps and marries her, thus assuring a secure future for Ruth and Naomi.

God blesses this union by giving Boaz and Ruth a son and Naomi a grandson.

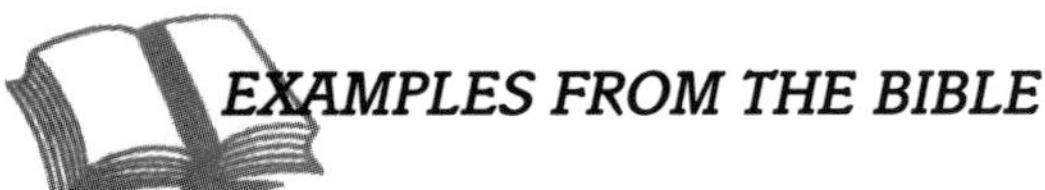

EXAMPLES FROM THE BIBLE

A kinsman-redeemer was a near relative and had the first option by law to buy any land owned by the tribe that was being sold, thus allowing it to be kept within the clan. Another duty was to marry the widow of a deceased kinsman.

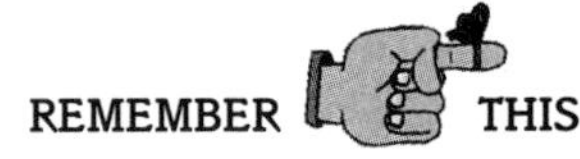

Harvesting grain in ancient Canaan took place in April and May (barley first, wheat a few weeks later). It involved the following steps:

1. Cutting the ripened standing grain with hand sickles—usually done by men
2. Binding the grain into sheaves—usually done by women
3. Gleaning, i.e., gathering stalks of grain left behind
4. Transporting the sheaves to the threshing floor—often by donkey, sometimes by cart
5. Threshing, i.e., loosening the grain from the straw—usually done by the treading of cattle, but sometimes by toothed threshing sledges
6. Winnowing—done by tossing the grain into the air with winnowing forks so that the wind, which usually came up for a few hours in the afternoon, blew away the straw and chaff, leaving the grain at the winnower's feet
7. Sifting the grain to remove the residual foreign matter
8. Bagging for transportation and storage

Think About It

In the New Testament, Jesus is described as our brother, who redeems us from the power of sin (Hebrews 2:11–12, 17). Have you accepted him as your redeemer? Have you asked him for forgiveness for your sins?

Ruth 4:14–17 The women said to Naomi: "Praise be to the LORD, who this day has not left you without a kinsman-redeemer. May he become famous throughout Israel! He will renew your life and sustain you in your old age. For your daughter-in-law, who loves you and who is better to you than seven sons, has given him birth."

Then Naomi took the child, laid him in her lap and cared for him.

Reaping the Rewards of Her Faithfulness

Naomi's faithfulness to God and to Ruth led her through a time of troubles and suffering into a time of happiness and peace. She thought all was lost when her husband and then her sons were taken from her. All she had left was a Moabite daughter-in-law. But God took what seemed like a burden and turned it into a blessing. Naomi was told that Ruth was better than seven sons!

KEY POINT

God can turn our sorrows into great rejoicing.

Are you going through hard times? Is your marriage struggling or your business failing? Do you have a rebellious son or daughter?

Whatever you are facing, God will use it to lead you into a better, richer life. Just be patient, stay close to him, and look for opportunities.

Naomi thought her family had perished in Moab, but the baby Obed lived to become the father of Jesse, and Jesse was the father of King David. Ruth is listed in Matthew's genealogy of Jesus, the Messiah himself. This would be a great honor for any woman, let alone a Moabite.

A GODLY GRANDMOTHER

2 Timothy 1:5 I have been reminded of your sincere faith, which first lived in your grandmother Lois and in your <u>mother</u> Eunice and, I am persuaded, now lives in you also.

☞ **GO TO:**

Acts 16:1 (mother)

Passing Your Faith Along

Paul is writing this letter to Timothy whom he loves so dearly that he calls him "my dear son." Then he goes on to give the credit for Timothy's sincere faith to his grandmother, Lois, and his mother, Eunice—a great compliment to these two women and an encouragement to all believing grandmothers that what they instill in their children may come to full fruition in their grandchildren.

☞ **GO TO:**

1 Corinthians 7:14; 2 Timothy 3:15 (godly parent)

EXAMPLES FROM THE BIBLE

Lois and Eunice were probably converted at Paul's first visit to Lystra (Acts 14:6–7). There is no sign that Timothy's father, who was Greek, was a believer. This demonstrates once again that the influence of one godly parent can overcome an ungodly one.

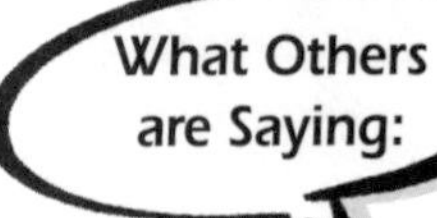

Paul D. Gardner: In an age when the "extended family" has almost ceased to exist in most Western countries, it is of great importance to see how influential a believing grandmother and mother could be in the life of a child, seeing him grow up to be a Christian. Such encouragement in the faith across the generations is often seen in Scripture. The fact that almost certainly Timothy had a nonbelieving father should give much hope to the many men and women who find themselves in similar positions today. Grandparents who are Christians and see grandchildren growing up without Christian teaching should recognize the significant impact they can often have as they teach Scriptures to their grandchildren.[4]

Titus 2:3–5 Likewise, teach the older women to be reverent in the way they live, not to be **slanderers** or addicted to much wine, but to teach what is good. Then they can train the younger women to love their husbands and children, to be self-controlled and pure, to be busy at home, to be kind, and to be subject to their husbands, so that no one will **malign** the word of God.

slanderers: *ones who make false accusations*

malign: *to speak evil of*

☞ **GO TO:**

Ephesians 5:25 (love their husbands)

Watch Your Tongue and Teach the Young

Older women in Titus' small group of converts were obviously causing problems with their slanderous talk, their irreverent behavior, and drunken ways. Paul instructs Titus to teach them to be reverent and to get up off their behinds and get to work showing the younger women how to be the kind of wives and mothers that would bring glory to God. This would especially apply to grandmothers who should be busy teaching their grandchildren.

KEY POINT

Grandmothers can play a key role in the spiritual lives of their grandchildren.

Today with both parents working, there is little time left over for the teaching of godly principles to children. Now would be a good time for you to step in and take on some of that responsibility.

Give your grandchildren Christian books, tapes, and music. Take them to church activities when their parents can't. Invite them to spend weekends with you so that they can see for themselves the work that God has done in your life.

Often, a grandparent can get through to a child when he or she is not open to listening to a parent.

Paul wrote this letter to Titus, who lived on Crete, the fourth largest island of the Mediterranean. In New Testament times Crete had sunk to a deplorable moral level. The Cretans were known for their dishonesty, **gluttony**, and laziness. Titus had the unenviable task of shepherding an unruly, rebellious flock of believers. Paul's letter gave him encouragement and also authority as he set about training his converts to live a new life.

GO TO:

Titus 1:12 (Cretans)

gluttony: *having concern only for the stomach*

> **Exodus 3:14–15** God said to Moses, "I AM WHO I AM. This is what you are to say to the Israelites: 'I AM has sent me to you.'" God also said to Moses, "Say to the Israelites, 'The LORD, the God of your fathers—the God of Abraham, the God of Isaac and the God of Jacob—has sent me to you.' This is my name forever, the name by which I am to be remembered from generation to generation."

GO TO:

Psalm 45:17; 72:17; 102:12 (generation)

Pass It On!

This is a great responsibility. We are charged with telling our children, their children, and even their children about God.

We cannot assume that they will hear it from any other source.

It's a challenge we should think about every day. We should ask ourselves how to communicate who God is, what he did for us on the cross, and what it will be like in heaven.

KEY POINT

Tell of the great things God has done in your life.

What a terrible loss if our love of the Lord is not passed on to our children and grandchildren, and ends when we die.

Grandchildren love to hear stories about famous people. Tell them the story of Jesus. Tell them of your conversion and what God has done in your life. Let them know how important your relationship with God has been to you. Don't assume they aren't interested.

A ten-year-old, under the tutelage of her grandmother, was becoming quite knowledgeable about the Bible. Then one day she floored her grandmother by asking, "Which Virgin was the mother of Jesus: the Virgin Mary or the King James Virgin?"

The Hebrew for LORD is Yahweh (often incorrectly spelled "Jehovah"). It means "He is" or "He will be" and is the third-person form of the verb translated "I am." When God speaks of himself he says, "I am" and when we speak of him we say, "He is."

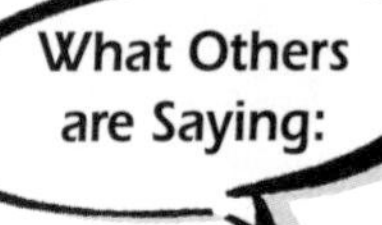

Dr. Deborah Newman: Are you making a difference in the world? Some people are remembered for generations. Perhaps they founded a nation, painted a masterpiece, or were the first to walk on the moon. The vast majority of us, though, will wither like the grass and go unremembered after we die. But we are each given 70 to 80 years, God willing, to make a difference in the lives of the people with whom we share our planet. . . . Our goal should be to leave this world a better place by virtue of the spiritual heritage we leave behind.[5]

FROM JUDY'S HEART

I grew up with a luxury few get to experience: a grandmother who lived within walking distance. Her name was Hannah Way. She immigrated to this country from Sweden and didn't learn to speak English until she went to school. As a young girl she played basketball and even went to college before she married my grandpa. Together they farmed a few acres of wheat land in northern Idaho and raised six children. Their only son was my dad.

She and Grandpa lived in a house behind ours. She seemed awfully old to me, but she probably wasn't as old as I thought. She was tall and as regal as any queen. I never saw her in anything other than a dress, even when she was gardening. Her hair was always the same, one large braid wound around the top of her head. In the evening she used to brush it out. She told us she had only cut it once.

She canned fruits and vegetables and made jams and jelly and her own soap. She washed her clothes in an old wringer washer. I used to want to help, but she wouldn't let me until I was old enough to remember not to put my hand through the wringer. By the time I was old enough she had gotten a real washer and dryer. She walked a mile to town every day to get the mail. Sometimes she'd let us go with her.

She never shared her faith openly, but every Sunday she went to church and often I'd burst into her house and find her reading her Bible. I'm sure she prayed for us all.

I can't remember ever seeing her getting upset about anything even though I'm sure we gave her much to be angry about. She never scolded us unless we were doing something dangerous like playing in the old barn or climbing the trees in her yard and even now I can't remember her being angry, just worried.

She didn't have an easy life. Her husband was a hard man or at least that's how I remember him. They never had much except lots of kids and grandkids.

She was my refuge. Whenever things got heavy at home or just boring I could run up there and visit. She would feed me tea and saltine crackers and her cookie jar was always full of raisin oatmeal cookies.

I didn't appreciate what I had until my children were born. They grew up in a city far away from their grandparents. They visited often, but that's not the same as having a grandparent who is part of your life, filling in the empty spaces when parents are too busy. They'll never know what they missed out on, but I will.

One thing Grandma Way did was to store up her treasure in heaven. All of my siblings are Christians as are many of my cousins. When we start entering those heavenly gates, she will be there to greet us. I like to think that she's up there, looking down, praying for me. I hope I'm making her proud.

> **Psalm 71:18** Even when I am old and gray, do not forsake me, O God, till I declare your power to the next generation, your might to all who are to come.

KEY POINT

If we don't tell our grandchildren about God, who will?

What's the Good Word?

The author of this psalm is asking God to stay with him so that he can tell the next generation about him. We should hold this goal in mind as our children begin to have children.

Have you experienced any miracles? How did God work through your trials? What great revelation did God give you that changed your life forever?

Answer these questions for yourself, then tell your children and grandchildren about them. The greatest disservice we can do to both God and our families is to keep quiet about the wonders God has performed in our own lives.

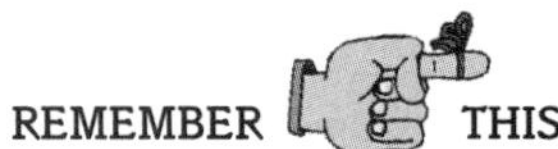

One of Satan's biggest lies is that our religious beliefs should be kept private. How will the next generation know of him personally as a God who affects people if all they hear is some abstract story in their Sunday school literature?

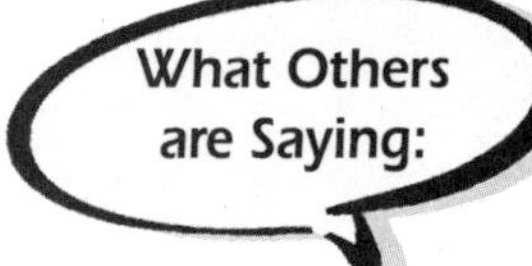

Cheri Fuller: Lord, I will not conceal Your goodness from my children or grandchildren but with Your grace will tell the generation to come the praises of the Lord. Help me to share with them Your strength and the wondrous work You have done.[6]

Grace H. Ketterman, M.D.: I made my mistakes raising my child. Now she's a mother. Forgive my errors and heal her heart so that she can mother well my grandchildren. Surround them with Your protecting angels. Give them Your wisdom, energy, and love. Most of all, bring them to that eternal life-giving commitment to Jesus Christ that will one day reunite us all in heaven.[7]

A grandmother was visiting with her grandson one day when he asked, "Grandma, do you know how you and God are alike?" Mentally polishing her halo, the grandmother replied, "No, how are we alike?" "You're both old," he said.

> **Psalm 102:18** Let this be written for a future generation, that a people not yet created may praise the LORD.

Write It Down

Have you thought about writing your life story down on paper? This would be a great way to pass along the history of your family, as well as the history of your spiritual journey.

What Others are Saying:

Cheri Fuller: To let her school-age grandchildren know she is praying for them, one grandmother writes the verse she's praying that week in calligraphy on a white card and then includes it in her letter to them.[8]

STORING UP TREASURES IN HEAVEN

> **Matthew 5:46–47** If you love <u>those who love you</u>, what reward will you get? Are not even the **tax collectors** doing that? And if you greet only your brothers, what are you doing more than others? Do not even pagans do that?

GO TO:

Luke 6:32 (those who love you)

tax collectors: *local men who were hated because they were employed by the Romans to collect often unreasonable taxes*

Love Even if You Don't Receive Love in Return

Jesus is calling us to a higher love.

It's easy to love the people we like; even the wicked do that.

What Jesus wants us to do is to love the unlovable. The difficult neighbor, the boss who is demanding, the drunk on the street, and even Uncle Joe, who ruins every Christmas.

As our children grow up, leave, and establish their own homes, it's awfully easy to feel ignored and unloved.

We can become resentful of the time they spend with other people. We also may not like the spouse our child has picked out or believe our grandchildren are spoiled and not fun to be around.

But God has called us to a higher way of living. He has called us to love even when we think our love is not returned.

Don't get caught up in petty grievances. If your grandchildren don't write thank-you notes, love them anyway. If they break a lamp or a window because they were being careless, forgive them. Make them feel welcome in your home. You can replace things; you can't replace their love.

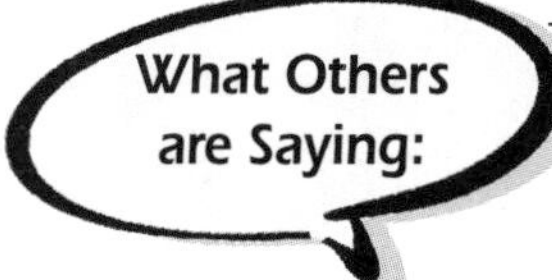

Barbara Johnson: Few people have clear enough sight to see their own faults. Conceit is a form of "I" strain that doctors can't cure. Yet, when it comes to spotting the faults of others, everybody seems to have 20-20 vision.[9]

acts of righteousness: *giving, praying, and fasting*

Matthew 6:1–4 "Be careful not to do your '**acts of righteousness**' before men, to be seen by them. If you do, you will have no reward from your Father in heaven. So when you give to the needy, do not announce it with trumpets, as the hypocrites do in the synagogues and on the streets, to be honored by men. I tell you the truth, they have received their reward in full. But when you give to the needy, do not let your left hand know what your right hand is doing, so that your giving may be in secret. Then your Father, who sees what is done in secret, will reward you."

☞ GO TO:

Colossians 3:23–24 (reward)

Getting Those Priorities Straight

Jesus is being critical of the Sadducees and Pharisees, who perform their acts of righteousness in front of others to show off their religion and to be praised by others. Jesus says that is all the reward they will receive and suggests instead that we should do our acts of righteousness in secret, and thus receive our reward in heaven.

Think About It

In this verse, Jesus is talking about acts of righteousness, but it can apply to being a grandmother too. Are you "doing" for others because you genuinely love them, or are you "doing" for others because you expect something in return?

Matthew 6:5–8 "And when you pray, do not be like the hypocrites, for they love to pray standing in the synagogues and on the street corners to be seen by men. I tell you the truth, they have received their reward in full. But when you pray, go into your room, close the door and pray to your Father, who is unseen. Then your Father, who sees what is done in secret, will reward you. And when you pray, do not keep on babbling like pagans, for they think they will be heard because of their many words. Do not be like them, for your Father knows what you need before you ask him."

If It's Sincere, God Will Hear

It's easy to slip into a pattern of praying only in church. Jesus is challenging us to spend time on our knees in secret praying for the needs of our children and grandchildren.

The prayers don't need to be full of religious language, and we don't need to go on and on. God knows the needs even before we pray them.

Think About It

With children living in other cities and states, there is a greater need to pray for them and our grandchildren. It's also a way of keeping in touch with their needs. Prayer keeps us involved in the daily lives of our children and interested in our grandchildren, and nothing is more important to them than to know that someone cares about them and is on their side.

Don't use prayer to disguise your nosiness. Learn to keep a respectful distance between you and your children, but don't stay away so much that you lose touch all together.

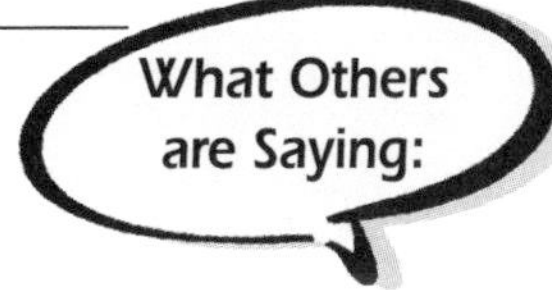

Cheri Fuller: Praying for our grandchildren grants us a special bonus. As we hold them up to the Lord in prayer, we draw closer to them and closer to Him as well. Praying for them is bonding. It strengthens our ties and gives them the very source of the strength of our own life—our relationship with the Lord.[10]

Matthew 6:16–18 "When you **fast**, do not look somber as the hypocrites do, for they disfigure their faces to show men they are fasting. I tell you the truth, they have received their reward in full. But when you fast, put oil on your head and wash your face, so that it will not be obvious to men that you are fasting, but only to your Father, who is unseen; and your Father, who sees what is done in secret, will reward you."

fast: *going without food or drink voluntarily, generally for religious purposes*

The Fast Is Going Okay, but I've Sure Had Better Hair Days

Jews put ashes on their heads to show that they were fasting. Putting oil on the head and washing the face were reserved for joyous occasions.

Think About It

If you've never fasted, now might be a good time to try it. Fasting can be done for any period of time. Usually it's sundown to sundown and might involve going without food only. Spend the day in prayer for your family. Pray for specific needs and future needs. Pray that God will direct you in the lives of your children and in his service.

What Others are Saying:

Chris Fabry: [To be an *ineffective* Christian] you must never fast. Fasting should be considered something weird people do. Think of fasting as an Old Testament phenomenon or something John the Baptist would do after a week of locust casserole.[11]

treasures: *wealth (literally or figuratively)*

> **Matthew 6:20** But store up for yourselves **treasures** in heaven, where moth and rust do not destroy, and where thieves do not break in and steal.

A Heavenly Investment

An investment of time and commitment can lead to the eternal treasure of our children and grandchildren going to heaven. What greater reward could any of us possibly want?

What Others are Saying:

Patsy Clairmont: If your home is like mine, you have several choices of Bibles. Let's not let them become museum pieces or dust collectors. Instead, let's daily invest ourselves in the pages that we might become true works of art at the hands of the Creator.[12]

forever: *for as long as it lasts*

> **Ecclesiastes 1:4** Generations come and generations go, but the earth remains **forever**.

Getting the Big Picture

The same course of events are repeated over and over without any permanent result or real progress. Events and people are forgotten but the earth remains unchanged. The author is implying that it is vanity to believe that anything we do will be remembered for very long.

It's easy to believe that we don't matter, that what we've accomplished on earth is for nothing because our life is so fleeting. The one thing we can do that will matter is to leave our descendants with the knowledge of Jesus Christ.

Think About It

As we grow older, it's easy to become bitter about our lives. Evaluate what you talk about when your children and grandchildren visit. Ask yourself, "Am I fun to be around or do I complain?"

What Others are Saying:

Laurie Beth Jones: Ten Ways to Grow Something besides Old

- Adopt a pet from your local animal shelter
- Become a child advocate
- Plan and take a trip with a friend
- Join a choir
- Start a walking club
- Take a course at your local community college
- Volunteer at a theater group
- Read to a child every day
- Plan a garden
- Dance[13]

KEY POINT

Be interested in others and they'll be interested in you.

REAPING THE REWARDS

Matthew 16:27 For the Son of Man is going to come in his Father's glory with his angels, and then he will reward each person according to what he has done.

☞ GO TO:

Matthew 8:20 (Son of Man)

1 Corinthians 16:12–14 (reward)

Wow, I Feel Like I've Died and Gone to Heaven!

Someday we will stand before Christ and account for our earthly actions (2 Corinthians 5:10). We will be rewarded for what we have done here on earth. If we have lived good lives and have done what Christ has asked, then we will look forward to that time. If, however, we have some things we have left undone, now is the time to begin to change and become all that God intended.

It's never too late to change and become all that God has called you to be. Shower your children and grandchildren with Christ's love. Treat each moment with them as something to be cherished.

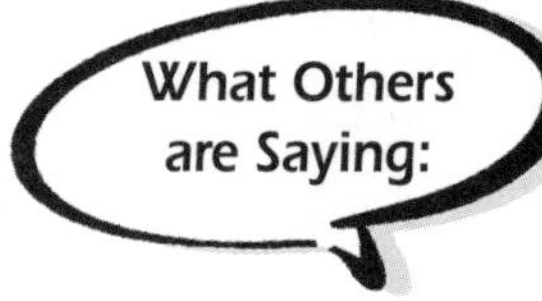

GO TO:

Luke 19:13 (servant)

> **Matthew 25:23** "His master replied, 'Well done, good and faithful servant! You have been faithful with a few things; I will put you in charge of many things. Come and share your master's happiness!'"

Well Done, Good and Faithful Servant

How proud this servant must have felt as his master said these words. We should long to hear these words from our Lord and master, too.

What Others are Saying:

Erma Bombeck: When I stand before God at the end of my life, I would hope that I would not have a single bit of talent left and could say, "I used everything you gave me."[14]

Study Questions

1. What were the circumstances surrounding Naomi's decision to return to Bethlehem?
2. Describe Naomi's attitude toward her daughters-in-law.
3. How did God reward Naomi for her faithfulness?
4. Why is it important to tell your grandchildren about what God has done for you?
5. What are "acts of righteousness"?
6. What treasures can you take to heaven?
7. At the end of your life, what would you like Christ to say to you?

CHAPTER WRAP-UP

- Naomi sets the biblical example of a loving relationship between a mother and daughter-in-law even in the face of terrible suffering. God rewarded her faithfulness by giving her a grandchild, thus assuring the continuation of her husband's lineage.

- Lois is highly praised by Paul because she passed along her faith to her grandson Timothy. He became one of the most beloved of Paul's friends because he demonstrated his faith in God. Grandmothers can influence their grandchildren even if the parents aren't godly.
- We are called to tell our grandchildren about the things of God. If we don't, who will?
- The most valuable treasures are the ones we can take to heaven. These consist of the people whom we love the most.
- The latter part of our lives should be spent developing our spiritual giving, prayer, and fasting. As God works in us, this will influence our grandchildren far more than preaching at them.
- At the end of our lives, we want to hear Jesus say, "Well done, good and faithful servant, well done."

JUDY'S BOOKSHELF

- *The Joyful Journey,* Patsy Clairmont, Barbara Johnson, Marilyn Meberg, and Luci Swindoll, Zondervan. Short stories that will make you laugh and inspire you to a closer walk with the Lord.
- *Only Angels Can Wing It,* Liz Curtis Higgs, Thomas Nelson. A humorous look at being a woman, wife, and parent.
- *The 77 Habits of Highly Ineffective Christians,* Chris Fabry, InterVarsity Press. A tongue-in-cheek collection of the ways we behave that turn others off to Christ and drain us of our spiritual fervor.
- *Women in Mid-life Crisis,* Jim and Sally Conway, Tyndale House. A careful and complete examination of the crisis that some women face during mid-life. Practical solutions are discussed.

APPENDIX A—THE ANSWERS

CHAPTER ONE

1. That they should both rule the earth on an equal basis. (Genesis 1:27–31)
2. The term "one flesh" means that two separate people join together to become one—marriage. (Genesis 2:23)
3. The engagement during biblical times involved an exchange of rings before witnesses and the paying of a bride-price. It could only be broken by death or divorce. Today engagements are promises to marry that can be signified with the giving of a ring by the man to the woman. Engagements can be broken at any time and for any reason. (Matthew 1:18–19)
4. Children were needed to carry on the family, for protection in old age, and as laborers.
5. It means to fear, obey, revere, and support them. (Psalm 127:3–5)
6. Migration and divorce. Migration because it scatters families and they lose the sense of heritage and belonging. Divorce because it undermines the family and hurts everyone who is touched by it. The family unit is torn apart and the pain can carry from generation to generation. (Pages 25–26)

CHAPTER TWO

1. Women have an unhealthy desire for their husbands. We look to our husbands to fill our needs.
2. Before the Fall, Eve was equally in charge of taking care of the Garden of Eden. She and Adam were to subdue it and rule over every living creature. They were also told to be fruitful and multiply (Genesis 1:28). After the Fall, woman's role changed. Eve was still an equal with Adam, but her role was relegated to taking care of the household.
3. Not only would woman experience pain while giving birth, but she would also suffer pains and discomfort in every aspect of her femaleness from menses to menopause.
4. When we have unrealistic expectations of an event like giving birth to a child we will be disappointed, because a child can't fill all of our needs. Only God can.
5. Memorize scripture verses, read reliable medical information, talk to your doctor or midwife, develop a friendship with another mother, and seek and find an older woman to mentor you.
6. Children were considered such a blessing that the loss of one was a tragedy for the entire family. (Exodus 21:22–26)

CHAPTER THREE

1. "If you will give me a son, I will give him to the Lord to serve all the days of his life and I will never use a razor on his head." (1 Samuel 1:11)
2. Sarah was ninety years old when she conceived Isaac. (Genesis 17:17)
3. Leah's need was for the love of her husband. She tried to have it fulfilled through the bearing of children. Rachel's need was for children. She tried to get it fulfilled by blaming her husband, using magic, and giving her husband her maidservant as a surrogate. (Genesis 29; 30:1–24)
4. Sarah (Sarai) was so desperate for a child that she gave her maidservant to her husband as a surrogate. The consequences were great unhappiness in her home. (Genesis 16; 21:8–20)
5. There was no apparent reason that Elizabeth was barren. (Luke 1:5–25)
6. In vitro fertilization is expensive and doesn't guarantee a positive outcome. Fertility drugs are less expensive, but the chance of a multiple birth is high. Adoption can also be expensive and in the case of older children, it may not work out as expected.
7. The blessing of seeing children growing up who would inherit not just your wealth but also your values. They teach you selflessness, forgiveness, and

love. They bring joy and pride and a sense of purpose into a world that is driven by consumerism. They are one of the "treasures" you can store in heaven. (Matthew 6:20)

8. A father gives a daughter a role model for picking out her future husband. He teaches his sons responsibility, and sets an example for them to follow. He builds into them self-discipline.

CHAPTER FOUR

1. It was part of the prophecy, and it also was a sign of purity. (Isaiah 7:14)
2. Joseph could have divorced her and she could have been stoned at the city gates. (Deuteronomy 22:13–19)
3. Joseph originally planned to divorce Mary quietly. He changed his mind after a visit from the angel Gabriel. (Matthew 1:18–25)
4. The one in Luke shows Mary's lineage, the one in Matthew Joseph's. (Luke 2:23–38; Matthew 1:1–17)
5. Every Hebrew maiden knew the prophesy about the Messiah and longed to be the chosen one. Also, Mary must've had a deep relationship with God so that she knew the truth when it was given to her.
6. Her first trip was early in her pregnancy when she visited her relative Elizabeth. It was a joyous occasion with much celebrating. The second trip was a three-day trip by donkey when she was nine months pregnant. She probably accompanied Joseph because, as a descendant of David, she needed to register in Bethlehem, too. That was a difficult trip.

CHAPTER FIVE

1. There is great anticipation while we wait for the birth of a child. There is also much preparation. We should look forward to Christ's coming with the same attitude. (Romans 8:22)
2. Labor is translated as hard work and that's what delivering a child is—hard work. Eve was told in Genesis that she would bear children in pain and her husband was told that he would toil all the days of his life. Both of these are considered "labor." (Genesis 2:16–19)
3. Cain and Abel. (Genesis 4:1–2)
4. Midwives, birthing stools, and swaddling clothes. Babies were wrapped tightly to limit the movement of the arms and legs in strips of cloth.
5. A manger is a feeding trough.
6. Bethlehem means "house of bread." Jesus was called the Bread of Life. (John 6:35, 48)

CHAPTER SIX

1. The shepherds were chosen because they would be believed by the citizens of Bethlehem, and they also were a symbol of Jesus being the good shepherd. (Luke 2:8–20)
2. All generations would call her blessed.
   God had performed a mighty deed.
   He had scattered the proud.
   He had brought down the rulers.
   He had filled the hungry with good things.
   He had been merciful to the Israelites.
   He had fulfilled his promise to Abraham for a Messiah. (Luke 1:46–55)
3. Circumcision was a symbol of God's covenant with the Hebrew nations. (Genesis 7:10ff)
4. Circumcision is not necessary for a Christian. God is more concerned with our inner transformation than an outer symbol. (Galatians 5:6)
5. I AM THAT I AM. (Exodus 3:14)
6. Jesus means "the Lord saves," and Mary and Joseph were told to name him that by the angels. (Matthew 1:18–21)
7. Abram — Abraham (Genesis 17:5)
   Sarai — Sarah (Genesis 17:5)
   Jacob — Israel (Genesis 32:28; 35:10)
   Saul — Paul (Acts 13:9)
   Levi — Matthew (Matthew 9:9; Luke 5:27)
   Simon — Peter (Matthew 16:18)

CHAPTER SEVEN

1. The firstborn male was to be consecrated to the Lord as a symbol of what God had done at the Passover.
2. The firstborn male inherited a double portion of his father's wealth, but he also was charged with taking care of his mother until her death, and his sisters until they married. He also was the spiritual head of the household.
3. They both were barren and they both had children dedicated before birth to serving the Lord.
4. Samson's mother was visited by an angel and told to raise the boy as a Nazirite. Hannah (Samuel's mother) made a vow to give her son over to the service of the Lord.
5. They serve as a sign that the children will be raised to know the Lord.
6. Churches practice infant baptism, first, because of the two cases recorded in Acts of entire households being baptized. Second, because Jesus asked that the children be brought to him for a blessing. Last, because it was practiced in the early church.

CHAPTER EIGHT

1. Laughter is contagious; it lifts our worries and eases the pain in our lives.
2. The fruit of the Spirit is love, joy, peace, patience, kindness, goodness, faithfulness, gentleness, and self-control. (Galatians 5:22–23)
3. Joy is a deep-down happiness that comes, not from our outer circumstances, but from our inner hearts.
4. You can build your faith through Bible study, prayer, obedience, giving, and love.
5. Faith takes care of a worried heart and gives it peace. (1 John 4:18)
6. Church, neighbors, family, friends, husband, and children. God wants us to be involved with one another, interdependent, so that we can support and love each other. Pride is a sin, because it's an attitude of "do it myself," which means you don't need God. (Matthew 28–30)
7. The second greatest commandment is to love your neighbor as yourself. (Matthew 22:39)

CHAPTER NINE

1. Parents are their children's greatest role models. They demonstrate through daily life what it means to be a Christian, to be loving, to be a wife or husband, and how to treat others. Everything the parents do, children will try to emulate.
2. Ask God for a thirst for his Word. Memorize "life" Scriptures to help with daily struggles. Spend time in prayer.
3. Love is patient, love is kind. It does not envy, it does not boast, it is not proud. It is not rude, it is not self-seeking, it is not easily angered, it keeps no record of wrongs. Love always protects, always trusts, always hopes, always perseveres (1 Corinthians 13:4–7). Love is an action, not a feeling.
4. The parents. Because we are their greatest role models.
5. It shows them that we love them. It gives them boundaries and teaches them to be selfless.
6. The Bible permits spanking. The world scorns it. That's because so many parents practiced it incorrectly. They used it out of anger and as punishment instead of with love and as instruction.

CHAPTER TEN

1. Jesus was pointing out to the rich, young ruler that the young man's riches meant more to him than following Christ. We must be willing to give everything up, even our wealth. (Luke 18:18–25)
2. The treasure that you can take to heaven includes your children, your husband, your friends, and good deeds.
3. Time, attention, respect, listening, love, and acceptance.
4. Answer is individual.
5. The greatest need our children have is for salvation.
6. Answer is individual.

CHAPTER ELEVEN

1. The Proverbs 31 woman and Lydia. (Proverbs 31 and Acts 16:14–15)
2. A nurse was a respected member of the family who nursed the baby and then helped raise the child. (Genesis 24:59)
3. Moses permitted divorce because of the hard-heartedness of men. (Matthew 19:4–9)
4. Answers can vary. Samuel may have been overly concerned with his work as a prophet and judge, like Eli. He, like Eli, may have been too "soft" on his sons.
5. Drinking too much can lead to debauchery, which means being controlled by sensual sins. (Ephesians 5:18)
6. Broken hearts, venereal disease, AIDS, emotional problems, abortion, pregnancy out of wedlock, financial problems.
7. Belt of truth, breastplate of righteousness, footgear of peace, shield of faith, helmet of salvation, sword of the Spirit. (Ephesians 6:13–17)
8. Examples: Ten minutes in the morning, during your lunch break, after you tuck them in bed at night, just after they leave for school.

CHAPTER TWELVE

1. It leads to discouragement. No matter what they do, they believe it will never be good enough, so they stop trying. (Colossians 3:21)
2. Lot's wife cared more about the things she was leaving behind (social position, luxuries, and society) than she did about the welfare of her family.
3. The consequence of Rebekah loving Jacob more than Esau was a home divided, which eventually led to her deceiving her husband, and losing her son. (Genesis 27)
4. When David failed to punish Amnon, hatred began to build in the heart of his other son Absalom. Absalom eventually killed Amnon. (2 Samuel 13:1–29)
5. Eli's greatest weakness was his inability to punish his sons for their evil. (1 Samuel 3)

6. Showing disrespect for your husband in front of your children can lead to confusion over roles, unhappiness, and even rebellion.
7. Possessiveness and vicariousness.

CHAPTER THIRTEEN

1. Abraham threw a feast to celebrate Isaac's weaning from the breast. (Genesis 21:8)
2. Jochebed and Hannah were forced to give up their children early. Jochebed's son Moses was in danger of being killed by the Egyptians, and so she placed him in a basket on the Nile River (Exodus 1:22ff). Hannah delivered her son Samuel to Eli as promised in return for God granting her the greatest desire of her heart which was to bear a son (1 Samuel 1:28ff).
3. Basic skills, humility, value of hard work, satisfaction of a job well done.
4. Jesus' response was, "Why were you searching for me? Didn't you know I had to be in my Father's house?" (Luke 2:41–52)
5. One father is Joseph, the other is God. (Luke 2:48–49)
6. Three attitudes which will help you survive your child's teen years are joy, patience, and prayer.
7. Daniel refused to eat the royal food and drink the royal wine because he knew it had been offered to pagan gods. (Daniel 1)

CHAPTER FOURTEEN

1. Mystique is an air or attitude of mystery or reverence. Things that you can do include taking a class, learning how to wear makeup, joining a book club, learning to ski.
2. The greatest commandment is to love the Lord with all our heart, mind, and spirit (Matthew 22:37–38). The reason is that when our love and attention is directed toward God and he is number one in our lives, then we will tend to choose the right paths and put sin behind us, because our focus changes from filling our own selfish needs to doing what God wants.
3. Prophesying, serving, teaching, encouraging, contributing to the needy, leadership, and mercy. (Romans 12:3–8)
4. A parent is the authority figure and tries to mold and shape their child's life. Parents tend to believe they know what is best for their child. A friend accepts the person for who he or she is, is a good listener, and only gives advice when asked.
5. Regret is a deep feeling of remorse over something that happened in the past. It may cause anguish, guilt, and sleepless nights. It can lead to living in the past or at least letting the past affect the present and future. It can strain relationships and even lead to depression. The solution is forgiveness, first from God and then from the person who was sinned against.

CHAPTER FIFTEEN

1. Abel's murder was particularly evil because Cain tricked him into coming out into the field so that he could murder him. (Genesis 4:8)
2. David mourned openly because he hoped to change God's mind, but once the baby had died, he knew there was nothing to be done except wait for the time he would be united with his son in the next world. (2 Samuel 12:13–23)
3. Answers may vary. He would be a great leader and rule over Israel. Everyone would adore him. He would live a long life.
4. Shock, disorganization, volatile emotions, guilt, loss and loneliness, relief.
5. Answers may vary. (Psalm 23; 119:50–82; Isaiah 61:2)

CHAPTER SIXTEEN

1. Naomi's husband and two sons died, leaving her destitute. Her only option was to return to her home and live off the kindness of relatives. (Ruth 1:1–5)
2. Naomi must have cared very much for her daughters-in-law. They were prepared to travel with her, but she thought of what they faced, foreigners in a foreign land, and told them to return to their parents. She thought of them instead of herself. (Ruth 1:6–14)
3. God blessed her through the marriage of Ruth and Boaz. They took her in and cared for her and then God gave her a grandchild thus assuring the name of her husband would never be forgotten. (Ruth 4:14–17)
4. It's important to tell our grandchildren what God has done for us so that he will be remembered from generation to generation. (Psalm 102:18)
5. "Acts of righteousness" are giving, praying, and fasting. (Matthew 6:1–18)
6. People are the treasures we can take to heaven.
7. "Well done, good and faithful servant." Answers may vary.

APPENDIX B—THE EXPERTS

Kay Arthur is a well-known Bible teacher and author. She and her husband, Jack, are the founders of Precept Ministries, which reaches thousands through its "Precept Upon Precept" Bible studies and the weekly radio and television program, "How Can I Live?"

Alan Beck is author and researcher in the field of ecology and health aspects of urban animals.

Erma Bombeck was a much-loved author of a humorous newspaper column and several humorous books. She died in 1996.

A. C. Bouquet is the author of *Everyday Life in New Testament Times*.

Helen Good Brenneman was born in Harrisonburg, Virginia, and always had an interest in writing. She has authored several books including a devotional for new mothers.

Ross Campbell, Ph.D., is a Christian psychologist whose books help parents raise godly children.

Oswald Chambers (1874–1917) was born in Scotland. The books that bear his name were compiled from the shorthand notes that his wife took of his talks.

Alice Chapin is the author of *Building Your Child's Faith*.

Evelyn Christenson is a well-known national speaker and author. Her latest title is *What Happens When Women Pray*.

Patsy Clairmont is a well-known speaker and author of such best-selling books as *God Uses Cracked Pots* and *Sportin' a Tude*.

Henry Cloud, Ph.D., is a popular speaker, radio host, and licensed psychologist. He is coauthor of the Gold Medallion–winning *Boundaries*.

F. Sessions Cole is professor of pediatrics and professor of cell biology and physiology at Washington University School of Medicine.

Dr. Charles Paul Conn is a pediatrician and the author of many books for the Christian market. His latest is *Believe!*.

Jim and Sally Conway are coauthors of several books and popular speakers.

Jim Cymbala is the best-selling author of *Fresh Wind, Fresh Fire* and has been the pastor of the Brooklyn Tabernacle in New York City for over twenty-five years.

James Dobson, Ph.D., is a psychologist, best-selling author, and founder and president of Focus on the Family. His nationally syndicated radio program is heard daily on more than 1,300 stations.

Henry E. Dosker was a professor of church history at the Presbyterian Theological Seminary and author of *The Dutch Anabaptist*.

Chris Fabry is the author of tongue-in-cheek books, *The 77 Habits of Highly Ineffective Christians* and *Away with the Manger: A Spiritually Correct Christmas Story*. Both are spoofs of popular secular books.

Harry Emerson Fosdick (1878–1969) was a liberal Protestant minister who founded the "National Vespers" radio program that aired from 1926–1946.

Cheri Fuller is an inspirational speaker and author of eighteen books. She's also a frequent guest on Focus on the Family radio program.

Paul D. Gardner was general editor and contributor to *The Complete Who's Who in the Bible*.

Ruth Bell Graham is the wife of evangelist Billy Graham. During his long absences she raised their five children to love him and the Lord. She is a poet, a mother, a grandmother, and a great-grandmother.

Alvin Vander Griend is director of HOPE, Houses of Prayer Everywhere. He is a member of the National Prayer Committee and serves as coordinator of the Denominational Prayer Leaders' Network.

Melissa Sexson Hanson has written two books on the heartbreak of losing an unborn child. They include *When Mourning Breaks* and *I Can't Find a Heartbeat*.

Jack Hayford is the senior pastor of The Church on the Way in Van Nuys, California. His ministry reaches around the world through television, radio, and the books and music he has written.

E. W. Heaton is the author of *Everyday Life in Old Testament Times*.

Liz Curtis Higgs is an author, speaker, and nationally knows humorist. She has a monthly column in *Today's Christian Woman* magazine.

Marjorie Holmes has been called America's favorite inspiration writer. She has been a columnist for *Woman's Day* magazine and the Washington *Star*. Other books include *Two from Galilee* and *Lord, Let Me Love*.

Wade Horn is the founder of the National Fatherhood Initiative and writes extensively on how to be a better father.

Todd Howard is president of the children's wear division of Tommy Hilfiger.

Michelle Howe is a book reviewer for *Publishers Weekly*, an author, a youth leader, and a mother.

Mary Howitt is a poet. Three of her most popular poems can be found on the CD, "The World's Best Poetry."

Barbara Johnson is the founder of Spatula Ministries and the author of ten best-selling books including *Mama, Get the Hammer! There's a Fly on Papa's Head*. She and her husband, Bill, have two sons on earth and two sons who are their "deposits in heaven."

Lady Bird Johnson served as first lady from 1963 to 1969. She was married to President Lyndon B. Johnson.

Laurie Beth Jones is the author of *Jesus CEO*, a controversial book that applies Biblical principles to modern business management.

Joseph Joubert (1754–1824) was French moralist and essayist.

Jay Kessler is a well-known author and national speaker. He coauthored the *NIV Teen Devotional Bible*.

Grace H. Ketterman, M.D., is author of over twenty-five books on parenting.

Ronald J. Knapp is a professor of sociology at Clemson University and teaches courses on the sociology of death.

Beverly LaHaye is founder of Christian Women of America, a national network of prayer and actions that aims to protect the rights of the family.

Ann Landers' column appears daily in newspapers across the country.

Laurie Lee (1914–1997) was an English poet, memoirist, and novelist, best known for his autobiographical trilogy *Cider with Rosie* (1959), *As I Walked Out One Midsummer Morning* (1969), and *A Moment of War* (1991).

C. S. Lewis (1898–1963) was a respected scholar and teacher at Oxford University for twenty-nine years. He also was a talented debater and prolific author.

Reverend Michael Lindvall is a writer and minister at the First Presbyterian Church in Ann Arbor, Michigan.

Herbert Lockyer is the author of the "All" series including *All the Women of the Bible*.

Max Lucado is a best-selling author and ministers to the Christians at the Oak Hills Church in San Antonio, Texas.

Jean Lush is an author, speaker, and frequent guest on Focus on the Family.

John MacArthur is a best-selling author and ministers at Grace Community Church in Sun Valley, California. He is also president of The Master's College and Seminary.

Gail MacDonald is an author, speaker, mother, and grandmother.

Karen Mains has written several best-selling books including *Open Heart, Open Home*, and *Friends and Strangers*. She has four adult children.

Mamie McCullough is one of the country's most popular motivational speakers. She once toured with Zig Ziglar. She currently publishes a quarterly newsletter, *The Encourager*, from her headquarters in Dallas, Texas.

Kathy McReynolds specializes in writing on Christian women and women in the Bible. She is a Ph.D. candidate at Biola University.

Marilyn Meberg is a captivating speaker and the author of *Choosing the Amusing*.

Kathy Collard Miller is the best-selling author of *God's Abundance* and the *God's Vitamin "C" for the Spirit* series. She writes and speaks about issues facing women, including how to heal and grow a marriage.

Dr. William Mitchell is an anthropologist and author who teaches at the University of Vermont.

Henry Vollam Morton (1892–1979), English journalist and travel writer. He was the author of the *In Search of . . .* series published during the 1950s. His earlier travel books include *The Heart of London* (1925), *In the Steps of the Master* (1934), *Through Lands of the Bible* (1938), and *Middle East* (1941). Later works include *This is Rome* (1960) and *H V Morton's England* (1975).

J. Alec Motyer is the former principal at Trinity Theological College, Bristol, England. He is presently retired.

Richard Nadler is editor of *K.C. Jones Monthly*, a Midwestern journal of opinion. He writes about education and his articles appear often in the *National Review*.

C. W. Neal is the author of *Your 30-Day Journey to Being a World Class Mother*, a practical self-help guide to improving your mothering skills.

Deborah Newman, Ph.D., is a popular conference speaker and frequent guest on both Christian and secular radio and television programs.

Sherwin B. Nuland teaches surgery and the history of medicine at Yale University.

Lance R. Odden teaches history at the University of Wisconsin.

Janette Oke has sold nearly fifteen million books. Her first work of fiction, *Love Comes Softly*, has sold more than one million copies.

Larry G. Peppers teaches courses at Clemson University on marriage and the family, aging, and psychology. He holds a doctorate in sociology from Oklahoma State University.

Pablo Picasso (1881–1973), famous Spanish artist.

Eugenia Price is an internationally known speaker and author of many books, including *God Speaks to Women Today*.

Jim Raburn is the founder of Young Life.

Larry Richards is the author of over 175 books about the Bible. They include books on Christian education, biblical theological study, devotion/enrichment, and study Bibles. Richards is the general editor on the entire *God's Word for the Biblically-Inept* series and *What's in the Bible for . . .* series.

Randy Rolfe is a family therapist, lawyer, and mother. Her parenting advice is considered practical and is highly recommended by *Library Journal* magazine.

Patricia H. Rushford has coauthored several books with Jean Lush. She is also the author of the popular Jenny McGrady mysteries for young adults. She and her husband live in Vancouver, Washington.

Melinda Sacks is a journalist who writes about family issues.

Laura Schlessinger, Ph.D., received her Ph.D. in physiology from Columbia University Medical School in New York, holds postdoctoral certification and licensing in marriage and family therapy, and hosts her own nationally syndicated radio show.

William Sears, M.D. and Martha Sears, R.N. are the parents of eight children and the coauthors of eighteen books on child care.

Gwen Shamblin is an author and registered dietitian who started Weigh Down Workshop, Inc. in 1986.

Luci Shaw is a popular speaker and author of *Water My Soul: Cultivating the Interior Life.*

Beth Spring holds a degree in journalism from Northwestern University. She is the winner of several awards from the Evangelical Press Association.

Hannah Whitall Smith (1832–1911) was an evangelist, reformer, suffragist, and author. She championed feminist causes and the right of young women to attend college. She cofounded Women's Christian Temperance Union.

R. C. Sproul, author and radio host, is considered the most articulate populizer of Calvinist theology today.

C. H. Spurgeon (1834–1892) has been called the world's greatest preacher. His sermons continue to speak to Christians today.

Sandra Stanley is married to Andy Stanley, son of internationally recognized pastor and best-selling author Charles Stanley. They are the parents of three children.

Chuck Swindoll serves as president of Dallas Theological Seminary. He is also president of Insight for Living, a radio broadcast ministry aired daily worldwide. He was senior pastor of the First Evangelical Free Church in Fullerton, California, for almost twenty-three years and has authored numerous books on Christian living.

Luci Swindoll is the former vice president of public relations at Insight for Living. She is a popular speaker and the author of six books.

Joni Earickson Tada is author of over twenty books. She serves as president of a Christian organization that advances Christ's kingdom among the world's 550 million people with disabilities.

Gigi Graham Tchividjian is an award-winning author and the daughter of Billy Graham.

Gary Thomas is a freelance author who lives in Bellingham, Washington.

John Townsend, Ph.D., is a popular speaker, author, and cohost of the nationally broadcast New Life radio program. He is coauthor of the Gold Medallion–winning *Boundaries.*

Anne Tyler was born in Minneapolis in 1941 but grew up in Raleigh, North Carolina. She graduated at nineteen from Duke University, and went on to do graduate work in Russian studies at Columbia University. Her eleventh novel, *Breathing Lessons*, was awarded the Pulitzer Prize in 1988.

Dave Veerman is a Christian writer and speaker. He is the coauthor of *From Dad with Love.*

Thelma Wells is an internationally known corporate keynote speaker, president of her own company, and author of *God Will Make a Way.*

Mary Whelchel is an author, popular speaker, and founder of the national radio program The Christian Working Woman.

Alexander Whyte (1836–1921) was a Scottish Presbyterian minister and teacher. Many of his sermons are available today. He was considered a man of great imagination and an expert at painting word pictures in his sermons.

Margaret Wold is the author of *Women of Faith & Spirit.*

Philip Yancey serves as editor-at-large for *Christianity Today* magazine. He has written eight Gold Medallion Award–winning books. Two of his books, *The Jesus I Never Knew* and *What's So Amazing About Grace*? were awarded the Book of the Year.

Joan H. Young is a freelance author whose articles have appeared in *Guideposts Magazine.*

Lin Yutang (1895–1976), Chinese writer and philologist, born in Changzhou. He devised a Chinese indexing system and helped formulate the official plan for romanizing the Chinese language. After 1928 he lived mainly in the United States. His many works, including *My Country and My People* (1935) and *The Importance of Living* (1937), attempt to bridge the cultural gap between East and West.

> NOTE: To the best of our knowledge, all of the above information is accurate and up to date. In some cases we were unable to obtain biographical information.
>
> —THE STARBURST EDITORS

ENDNOTES

Introduction

1. Charles Colson, "Why I Trust the Bible," *Practical Christianity* (Carmel, NY: Guideposts, 1987), 385.
2. Norman Geisler, "How Can We Know the Bible Is Reliable?" *Practical Christianity* (Carmel, NY: Guideposts, 1987), 385.
3. James Boice, "Study for Strength," *Practical Christianity* (Carmel, NY: Guideposts, 1987), 398.

Chapter One

1. Dr. Henry Cloud and Dr. John Townsend, *The Mom Factor* (Grand Rapids, MI: Zondervan, 1996), 7, 8.
2. Beverly LaHaye, *I Am a Woman by God's Design* (Old Tappan, NJ: Fleming H. Revell, 1980), 20.
3. Dr. Deborah Newman, *Then God Created Woman* (Colorado Springs: Focus on the Family, 1997), 1.
4. Henry E. Dosker, from *International Standard Bible Encyclopaedia* (Electronic Database, Biblesoft, 1996).
5. Mary Whelchel, *The Christian Working Woman* (Grand Rapids, MI: Fleming H. Revell, 1994), 13.
6. Herbert Lockyer, *All the Women of the Bible* (Grand Rapids, MI: Zondervan, 1998), 299.
7. William Sears, M.D. and Martha Sears, R.N., *Complete Book of Christian Parenting & Child Care* (Nashville: Broadman & Holman, 1997), 26.
8. Herbert Lockyer, *All the Women of the Bible,* 136.
9. T. J. Bach as quoted in *God's Little Instruction Book for Mom* (Tulsa, OK: Honor Books, Inc., 1994).
10. Alexander Whyte as quoted in *All the Women of the Bible* by Herbert Lockyer, 136.
11. Jill Maynard, editor, *Reader's Digest Illustrated Dictionary of Bible Life & Times* (Pleasantville, NY: Reader's Digest, 1997), 111.
12. Ibid., 226.
13. "Empty Nest," *1997 Information Please Almanac*, Annual 1997, 832.
14. Beth Spring, *The Infertile Couple* (Elgin, IL: David C. Cook, 1987), 12, 13.
15. John MacArthur, *Successful Christian Parenting* (Nashville: Word, 1998), 13.
16. Bill Cosby, *Kids Say the Darndest Things* (New York: Bantam Books, 1998), 33.
17. John MacArthur, *Successful Christian Parenting*, 3.
18. Ibid., 8.
19. Luci Shaw, "Biblical Metaphors Help Us Know God," in *Practical Christianity* (Carmel, NY: Guideposts, 1987), 124.
20. *Nelson's Illustrated Bible Dictionary*, Electronic Database © 1996, Biblesoft.
21. Diane Medved, *The Case Against Divorce* (New York: Ivy Books, 1989), 194.
22. Dave Veerman, "Undefiled Sex in Marriage," in *Practical Christianity*, 523.
23. Max Lucado, *God's Inspirational Promise Book* (Dallas: Word, 1996), 183.
24. R. C. Sproul, "Believing and Interpreting the Bible," in *Practical Christianity*, 391.
25. Bob Dyer, "Divorce Rate Ain't What It's Claimed." *Knight-Ridder/Tribune News Service*, May 2, 1995, 502.
26. John MacArthur, *Successful Christian Parenting*, 6.

Chapter Two

1. Liz Curtis Higgs, *Bad Girls of the Bible* (Colorado Springs, CO: Waterbrook Press, 1999), 25.
2. Eugenia Price, *Woman to Woman* (Grand Rapids, MI: Zondervan, 1979), 14, 15.
3. H. V. Morton as quoted in *All the Women of the Bible*, 58.
4. Kathy Collard Miller, *God's Word for the Biblically Inept: Women of the Bible* (Lancaster, PA: Starburst, 1999), 21.
5. Paula Mergenhagen DeWitt, "Breaking Up Is Hard to Do," *American Demographics,* October 1992, 52.
6. *NIV Study Bible* (Grand Rapids, MI: Zondervan, 1985), 11.
7. Paul D. Gardner, ed., *The Complete Who's Who in the Bible* (Grand Rapids, MI: Zondervan, 1995), 22.
8. Alison Bell, "Pregnant on Purpose," *Teen Magazine,* August 1997, 106.
9. Dr. Laura Schlessinger, *Ten Stupid Things Women Do to Mess Up Their Lives* (New York: HarperPerennial, 1994), 134.
10. Gwen Shamblin, *The Weigh Down Diet* (New York: Doubleday, 1997), v.
11. Anne Tyler as quoted in *God's Little Instruction Book for Mom.*
12. Janette Oke, *Janette Oke's Reflections on the Christmas Story* (Minneapolis: Bethany House, 1994), 42, 43.
13. Jean Lush, *Emotional Phases of a Woman's Life* (Old Tappan, NJ: Fleming H. Revell, 1987), 27.
14. Barbara Johnson, *Mama Get the Hammer! There's a Fly on Papa's Head* (Dallas: Word, 1994), 12.
15. Chandran Devanesen, *The Cross Is Lifted Up* (New York: Friendship Press, 1954), 33.
16. Melissa Sexson Hanson, *When Mourning Breaks* (Harrisburg, PA: Morehouse Publishing, 1998), viii.
17. Julie Sevrens, "Sexually Transmitted Diseases Are Rampant, Experts Say," *Knight-Ridder/Tribune News Service,* May 3, 1999, K6153.
18. Jean Lush, *Emotional Phases of a Woman's Life,* 175.

Chapter Three

1. Lin Yutang, as quoted in *God's Little Instruction Book for Mom.*
2. Kathy McReynolds, "Hannah," in *The Complete Who's Who in the Bible*, 229.
3. Cheri Fuller, *When Mothers Pray* (Sisters, OR: Multnomah, 1997), 22.
4. Kathy McReynolds, "Hannah," in *The Complete Who's Who in the Bible,* 228.
5. J. Alec Motyer, "Sarah/Sarai," in *The Complete Who's Who in the Bible,* 584, 585.
6. Janette Oke, "What Is Real Faith?" in *Practical Christianity*, 179, 178.
7. J. Alec Motyer, "Rachel," in *The Complete Who's Who in the Bible*, 564.
8. Joan H. Young, "Why Should I Pray if God Knows Everything?" in *Practical Christianity*, 437.
9. Beth Spring, *The Infertile Couple* (Elgin, IL: David C. Cook, 1987), 51.
10. Ibid., 104.
11. Christina Odone, "Barren in the Promised Land," *New Statesman,* May 16, 1997, 45.
12. Diane D. Aronson and Merrill Matthews, Jr., "Q: Should Health Insurers Be Forced to Pay for Infertility Treatments?" *Insight on the News,* February 8, 1999, 24.
13. Evelyn Christenson, "Learning in the Valley," in *Practical Christianity,* 326, 327.
14. Ruth Bell Graham and Gigi Graham Tchividjian, *Mothers Together* (Grand Rapids, MI: Baker Books, 1998), 12.
15. David L. Marcus, "Mothers with Another's Eggs," *U. S. News & World Report,* April 12, 1999, 42.
16. Ibid., 42.
17. "Adoption or Maladoption?" *Society*, March/April 1993, 2.
18. Ibid.
19. Scott Smith, "Some Couples Make Decision to go Childless," *Knight-Ridder/Tribune News Service*, May 5, 1998, 505.
20. Phillip J. Longman, "The Cost of Children," *U. S. News & World Report,* March 30, 1998, 50.
21. Mary Howitt as quoted in *God's Little Instruction Book for Mom.*
22. Wade Horn, Director, National Fatherhood Initiative, as reported in *Men's Health,* September 1999, 48.

Chapter Four

1. Jill Maynard, *Reader's Digest Illustrated Dictionary of Bible Life & Times*, 362.
2. Janette Oke, *Janette Oke's Reflections on the Christmas Story*, 68.
3. *NIV Study Bible*, 1441.
4. Kathy Collard Miller, *God's Word for the Biblically Inept: Women of the Bible*, 91.
5. Kathy MacReynolds, "Mary, the Mother of Jesus," in *The Complete Who's Who in the Bible*, 444.
6. *Nelson's Illustrated Bible Dictionary.*
7. Janette Oke, *Janette Oke's Reflections on the Christmas Story,* 71.
8. *Nelson's Illustrated Bible Dictionary.*
9. Helen Good Brenneman, *Meditations for the Expectant Mother* (Scottdale, PA: Herald Press, 1968), 35.
10. William Sears, M.D. and Martha Sears, R.N., *The Complete Book of Christian Parenting and Child Care,* 70.
11. Beverly LaHaye, *I Am a Woman by God's Design*, 31, 32.
12. Philip Yancey, *The Jesus I Never Knew* (Grand Rapids, MI: Zondervan, 1995), 58, 59.

Chapter Five

1. William Sears, M.D. and Norma Sears, R.N., *Complete Book of Christian Parenting & Child Care*, 57.
2. Joni Earickson Tada as quoted in *Families of Handicapped Children* (Elgin, IL: David C. Cook, 1988), 90.
3. Janette Oke, *Janette Oke's Reflections on the Christmas Story*, 110, 111.
4. David Heller, *Dear God, What Religion Were the Dinosaurs?* (New York: Doubleday, 1990), 113.
5. Ruth Bell Graham, *Mothers Together*, 15.
6. Chuck Swindoll, *Living Beyond the Daily Grind* (Dallas: Word, 1988), 96.
7. Gigi Graham Tchividjian, in *Prayers from a Mother's Heart* (Nashville: Thomas Nelson, 1999), 5.
8. William Sears, M.D. and Martha Sears, R.N., *Complete Book of Christian Parenting & Child Care,* 94.
9. Ibid., 73.
10. F. Sessions Cole, M.D. as quoted in "Saving Babies: Why C-section Is Not a Dirty Word," *Redbook*, October 1996, 102.
11. Jill Maynard, *Reader's Digest Illustrated Dictionary of Bible Life & Times*, 45.
12. Laurie Lee, as quoted in *Meditations for the Expectant Mother*, 71.
13. Helen Good Brenneman, *Meditations for the Expectant Mother,* 69.
14. A. C. Bouquet, *Everyday Life in New Testament Times* (New York: Charles Scribner, 1954), 146.
15. *Adam Clarke's Commentary*, Electronic Database. Copyright © 1996 by Biblesoft.
16. Philip Yancey, *The Jesus I Never Knew* (Grand Rapids, MI: Zondervan, 1995), 42.

Chapter Six

1. Janette Oke, *Janette Oke's Reflections on the Christmas Story,* 89.
2. Philip Yancey, *The Jesus I Never Knew,* 37.
3. Chuck Swindoll, *Living Beyond the Daily Grind,* 164.
4. David Heller, *Dear God, What Religion Were the Dinosaurs?,* 119.
5. Janette Oke, *Janette Oke's Reflection on the Christmas Story,* 91.
6. Jill Maynard, *Reader's Digest Illustrated Dictionary of Bible Life & Times,* 317, 318.
7. Patricia H. Rushford, *What Kids Need Most in a Mom* (Old Tappan, NJ: Fleming H. Revell, 1986), 179.
8. Janette Oke, *Janette Oke's Reflections on the Christmas Story,* 85, 86.
9. Christine Gorman, "Unkindest Cut?" *Time,* March 15, 1999, 100.
10. William Sears, M.D. and Martha Sears, R.N., *The Complete Book of Christian Parenting & Child Care,* 106.
11. *Nelson's Illustrated Bible Dictionary*.
12. E. W. Heaton, *Everday Life in Old Testament Times* (New York: Charles Scribner, 1956), 79.
13. *Nelson's Illustrated Bible Dictionary*.
14. Philip Yancey, *The Jesus I Never Knew,* 51.
15. Helen Good Brenneman, *Meditations for the Expectant Mother,* 61.

Chapter Seven

1. *NIV Study Bible*, 104.
2. *Nelson's Illustrated Bible Dictionary*.
3. C. S. Lewis, in the *The Quotable Lewis,* edited by Wayne Martindale and Jerry Rood (Wheaton, IL: Tyndale House, 1989), 513.

4. Alan Beck, "What Is a Boy?" as quoted in *Meditations for the Expectant Mother,* 72.
5. *Nelson's Illustrated Bible Dictionary*.
6. J. Alec Motyer, "Esau" in *The Complete Who's Who in the Bible,* 169.
7. Paul D. Gardner, *The Complete Who's Who in the Bible,* 323.
8. Kay Arthur, *As Silver Refined* (Colorado Springs: Water Brook, 1997), 72.
9. Margaret Wold, *Women of Faith & Spirit* (Minneapolis: Augsburg, 1987), 69.
10. Cheri Fuller, *When Mothers Pray*, 19.
11. Herbert Lockyer, *All The Women of the Bible*, 186.
12. David Heller, *Dear God What Religion Were the Dinosaurs?,* 83.
13. Reverend Michael Lindvall, "A Child Is Born," in *Chicken Soup for the Mother's Soul* (Deerfield Beach, FL: Health Communications, Inc., 1997), 31.
14. *Nelson Illustrated Bible Dictionary*.
15. Ibid.
16. Ibid.
17. T. Lewis, *International Standard Bible Encyclopedia*, Electronic Database, Biblesoft.

Chapter Eight

1. Patricia H. Rushford, *What Kids Need Most in a Mom*, 102.
2. Barbara Johnson, *Mama, Get the Hammer! There's a Fly on Papa's Head*, 19.
3. Liz Curtis Higgs, *Only Angels Can Wing It* (Nashville: Thomas Nelson, 1995), 167.
4. Randy Rolfe, *The 7 Secrets of Successful Parents* (Chicago: Contemporary Books, 1997), 251.
5. Chuck Swindoll, *Living Beyond the Daily Grind*, 176.
6. Dr. Henry Cloud and Dr. John Townsend, *Raising Great Kids* (Grand Rapids, MI: Zondervan, 1999), 165.
7. Cheri Fuller, *When Mothers Pray*, 19.
8. Karen Mains, *Parenting: Questions Women Ask* (Portland, OR: Multnomah, 1992), 66.
9. Charles Meigs as quoted in *God's Little Instruction Book for Mom.*
10. John MacArthur, *Successful Christian Parenting*, 23, 24.
11. Gigi Graham Tchividjian, in *Mothers Together*, 40.
12. William Sears, M.D. and Martha Sears, R.N., *The Complete Book of Christian Parenting & Child Care*, 250.
13. Alice Chapin, *Building Your Child's Faith* (San Bernardino, CA: Here's Life Publishers, Inc., 1983), 34.
14. Randy Rolfe, *The 7 Secrets of Successful Parents,* 186.
15. Dr. Henry Cloud and Dr. John Townsend, *Raising Great Kids,* 222.
16. Barbara Johnson, *Where Does a Mother Go to Resign?,* 153.
17. Margaret Wold, *Women of Faith & Spirit*, 95, 96.
18. C. W. Neal, *Your 30-Day Journey to Being a World Class Mother* (Nashville: Thomas Nelson, 1992), 9.
19. Mamie McCullough, *Get It Together and Remember Where You Put It* (Dallas: Word, 1990), 174.
20. A message from MOPS, as quoted in *Raising Great Kids*, 231.
21. John MacArthur, *Successful Christian Parenting,* 164.
22. *Adam Clarke's Commentary*, Electronic Database. Copyright © 1996 by Biblesoft.
23. Patricia H. Rushford, *What Kids Need Most in a Mom,* 132.
24. Dr. William Mitchell and Dr. Charles Paul Conn as quoted in *God's Little Instruction Book for Mom.*

Chapter Nine

1. William Sears, M.D. and Martha Sears, R.N., *The Complete Book of Christian Parenting & Child Care*, 329.
2. Liz Curtis Higgs, *Only Angels Can Wing It*, 23.
3. Dr. Deborah Newman, *Then God Created Woman*, 150.
4. Chris Fabry, *The 77 Habits of Highly Ineffective Christians* (Downers Grove, IL: InterVarsity Press, 1997), 21.
5. Alvin Vander Griend as quoted in *God's Little Instruction Book for Mom.*
6. Beverly LaHaye, *I Am a Woman by God's Design*, 41.
7. Joseph Joubert as quoted in *God's Little Instruction Book for Mom.*
8. Dr. James Dobson, *Emotions: Can You Trust Them?* (Ventura, CA: Regal, 1980), 57.
9. Max Lucado, *God's Inspirational Promise Book* (Dallas: Word, 1996), 89.
10. *Adam Clarke's Commentary*.
11. Dr. Henry Cloud and Dr. John Townsend, *Raising Great Kids,* 29, 30.
12. Jean Hodges as quoted in *God's Little Instruction Book for Mom.*
13. Jim Raburn, as quoted in "How Can I Keep My Child Interested in Church?" *Parenting: Questions Women Ask,* 73.
14. Alice Chapin, *Building Your Child's Faith*, 16.
15. Cheri Fuller, *When Mothers Pray*, 203.
16. Dr. Ross Campbell, *How to Really Love Your Child* (Wheaton, IL: Victor Books, 1977), 128.
17. *Nelson's Illustrated Bible Dictionary.*
18. *Nelson's Illustrated Bible Dictionary.*
19. Randy Rolfe, *The 7 Secrets of Successful Parents*, 291.
20. Barbara Johnson, "God's Kids," in *Joy Breaks* (Grand Rapids, MI: Zondervan, 1997), 206.
21. John MacArthur, *Successful Christian Parenting,* 32.
22. Dr. Henry Cloud and Dr. John Townsend, *Raising Great Kids,* 151.
23. C. H. Spurgeon as quoted in *God's Little Instruction Book for Mom.*
24. Dr. James Dobson, *Discipline with Love* (Wheaton, IL: Tyndale House, 1970), 10.
25. Dr. Ross Campbell, *How to Really Love Your Child*, 95, 96.
26. Patricia H. Rushford, *What Kids Need Most in a Mom*, 82.
27. David Heller, *Dear God, What Religion Were the Dinosaurs?,* 97.
28. Dr. James Dobson, *Parenting Isn't for Cowards* (Dallas: Word, 1997), 92, 93.

Chapter Ten

1. John MacArthur, *Successful Christian Parenting*, 117.
2. Kathy Collard Miller, *God's Word for the Biblically Inept: Women of the Bible*, 182.
3. Greg Gutfeld, "Kids on the Skids," *Prevention*, October 1992, 20.
4. Gwen Shamblin, *The Weigh Down Diet* (New York: Doubleday, 1997), x.
5. Mamie McCullough, *Get It Together and Remember Where You Put It*, 85.
6. Earline Steelberg as quoted in *God's Little Instruction Book for Mom.*
7. Philip Yancey, *The Jesus I Never Knew*, 93.
8. Randy Rolfe, *The 7 Secrets of Successful Parents*, 32.
9. William Sears, M.D. and Martha Sears, R.N. *The Complete Book of Christian Parenting & Child Care*, 321.

10. Dr. Henry Cloud and Dr. John Townsend, *Raising Great Kids*, 52–54.
11. Ruth Bell Graham and Gigi Graham Tchividjian, *Mothers Together*, 112.
12. Lady Bird Johnson as quoted in *God's Little Instruction Book for Mom*.
13. Joan Beck, as quoted in Kay Willis, *Are We Having Fun Yet?* (New York: Warner Books, 1997), 57.
14. Patricia H. Rushford, *What Kids Need Most in a Mom*, 77.
15. Sandra Stanley, "Loving Children as Individuals," in *Prayers from a Mother's Heart,* by Ruth Graham Bell (Nashville: Thomas Nelson, 1999), 15.
16. Pablo Picasso as quoted in *God's Little Instruction Book for Mom*.
17. Michelle Howe, *Going It Alone* (Peabody, MA: Hendrickson, 1999), 80.
18. Patricia H. Rushford, *What Kids Need Most in a Mom*, 103.
19. A. C. Bouquet, *Life in New Testament Times*, 186, 187.
20. John MacArthur, *Successful Christian Parenting*, 43.
21. Alice Chapin, *Building Your Child's Faith*, 9.

Chapter Eleven

1. Gail MacDonald, "How Can I Balance the Demands of Parenting, Marriage, and Work? in *Parenting: Questions Women Ask*, 97.
2. John MacArthur, *Successful Christian Parenting*, 193.
3. Herbert Lockyer, *All the Women of the Bible*, 85.
4. John MacArthur, *Successful Christian Parenting*, 192.
5. Mary Whelchel, *The Christian Working Woman: What You Need to Know* (Grand Rapids, MI: Fleming H. Revell, 1994), 159, 160.
6. Mildred B. Vermont as quoted in *God's Little Instruction Book for Mom*.
7. Ann Landers, *Wake Up and Smell the Coffee!* (New York: Villard, 1996), 14, 15.
8. Jay Kessler, "You're Not My Real Mom," *Today's Christian Woman,* September/October 1991.
9. Judy Bodmer, *When Love Dies: How to Save a Hopeless Marriage* (Nashville: Word, 1999), 12.
10. Gail MacDonald, "How Can I Win Over My Stepchildren?" in *Parenting: Questions Women Ask*, 119.
11. Herbert Lockyer, *All the Women of the Bible*, 176.
12. John MacArthur, *Successful Christian Parenting*, 20, 21.
13. Lance R. Odden, Headmaster, The Taft School, "Talk to Your Children About the Tough Stuff," *Vital Speeches*, March 1, 1999, 301.
14. Barbara Johnson, *Where Does a Mother Go to Resign?* (Minneapolis: Bethany House, 1979), 156.
15. Virginia Page Rohrer, "A Troubled Son," in *Prayers from a Mother's Heart*, 77.
16. Ruth Bell Graham, *Prayers from a Mother's Heart*, 49.
17. Melinda Sacks, "Parents May be Sending Contradictory Signals to Teens about Alcohol," *Knight-Ridder/Tribune News Service,* September 2, 1998, 902.
18. Lance R. Odden, *Vital Speeches*, 301.
19. Melinda Sacks, *Knight-Ridder/Tribune News Service*, 902..
20. Lance R. Odden, *Vital Speeches*, 301.
21. *Reader's Digest Illustrated Dictionary of Bible Life & Times*, 374.
22. Gary Thomas, "Where True Love Waits," *Christianity Today,* March 1, 1999, 40.
23. Richard Nadler, "Birds, Bees, and ABC's," *National Review,* September 13, 1999, 44.
24. Alison Bell, "Disordered Eating: Are You One of the Silent Majority?" *Teen Magazine,* February 1999, 66.
25. Adrienne Webb, "The Starvation Demons: The Fear of Becoming Fat Tortures Hundreds," *Maclean's*, May 2, 1994, 50.
26. Jim Cymbala, *Fresh Wind, Fresh Fire* (Grand Rapids, MI: Zondervan, 1997), 59–66.
27. Barbara Johnson, "A Remedy for the 'If Onlys'," *Joy Breaks* (Grand Rapids, MI: Zondervan, 1997), 242.
28. Cheri Fuller, *When Mothers Pray*, 42.
29. Ruth Bell Graham, "A Prayer for Hurting Mothers," in *Prayers from a Mother's Heart*, 63.

Chapter Twelve

1. Patricia H. Rushford, *What Kids Need Most in a Mom*, 72, 73.
2. Dr. Ross Campbell, *How to Really Love Your Child*, 105.
3. C. W. Neal, *Your 30-Day Journey to Being a World Class Mother*, 55.
4. Margaret Wold, *Women of Faith & Spirit*, 32.
5. Dr. James Dobson, *Parenting Isn't for Cowards*, 76.
6. John MacArthur, *Successful Christian Parenting*, 230.
7. Patricia H. Rushford, *What Kids Need Most in a Mom*, 86, 87.
8. Dr. James Dobson, *Parenting Isn't for Cowards*, 67, 68.
9. Dr. Ross Campbell, *How to Really Love Your Child*, 67, 68, 73.
10. Karen Mains, "How Do I Help My Child Develop Christian Sexual Morality?" in *Parenting: Questions Women Ask*, 68.
11. John MacArthur, *Successful Christian Parenting*, 186.
12. Randy Rolfe, *The 7 Secrets to Successful Parenting*, 195.
13. Dr. Henry Cloud and Dr. John Townsend, *Raising Great Kids*, 223, 224.

Chapter Thirteen

1. Randy Rolfe, *The 7 Secrets of Successful Parents*, 132.
2. William Sears, M.D. and Martha Sears, R.N., *The Complete Book of Christian Parenting & Child Care*, 282.
3. Ibid., 283.
4. Herbert Lockyer, *All the Women of the Bible*, 81.
5. Dr. James Dobson, *Parenting Isn't for Cowards*, 220.
6. Barbara Johnson, "God's Kids," *Joy Breaks*, 205.
7. Margaret Wold, *Women of Faith & Spirit*, 68.
8. John MacArthur, *Successful Christian Parenting*, 99, 100.
9. William Sears, M.D. and Martha Sears, R.N., *The Complete Book of Christian Parenting & Child Care*, 405.
10. Randy Rolfe, *The 7 Secrets of Successful Parents*, 136.
11. Todd Howard as quoted in the *Eastside Journal*, Sunday, September 12, 1999.
12. Liz Curtis Higgs, *Only Angels Can Wing It* (Nashville: Thomas Nelson, 1995), 186.
13. Cheri Fuller, *When Mothers Pray*, 98–100.
14. Dr. Henry Cloud and Dr. John Townsend, *Raising Great Kids*, 182.
15. Harry Emerson Fosdick as quoted in *When Mothers Pray*, 120.
16. Dr. James Dobson, *Parenting Isn't for Cowards*, 214.

Chapter Fourteen

1. Patricia H. Rushford, *What Kids Need Most in a Mom*, 182, 183.
2. Cheri Fuller, *When Mothers Pray*, 133.
3. Laurie Beth Jones, *Grow Something Besides Old* (New York: Simon & Schuster, 1998), 131.
4. Jean Lush, *Emotional Phases of a Woman's Life*, 172.
5. Liz Curtis Higgs, *Only Angels Can Wing It*, 11.

6. Dr. Deborah Newman, *Then God Created Woman*, 261, 262.
7. Thelma Wells, "The Main Line," in *Overjoyed* (Grand Rapids, MI: Zondervan, 1999), 88.
8. Marilyn Meberg, "Never Too Late," in *Overjoyed*, 107.
9. Oswald Chambers, *My Utmost for His Highest* (Westwood, NJ: Barbour and Company, 1935), 239.
10. Luci Swindoll, "Butcher, Baker, Candlestick Maker," in *Overjoyed*, 70.
11. Dr. James Dobson, *Parenting Isn't for Cowards*, 211.
12. Karen Mains, "How Do I Become Friends with My Adult Children?" in *Parenting: Questions Women Ask*, 141.
13. Patsy Clairmont, "Sistership," in *Joy Breaks*, 183.
14. Erma Bombeck, *Family: The Ties That Bind and Gag* (Boston: G. K. Hall & Co., 1987, lg. Print edition), 276.

Chapter Fifteen

1. Sherwin B. Nuland, *How We Die* (New York: Alfred A. Knopf, 1994), 131.
2. Sherwin B. Nuland, *How We Die*, 132, 133.
3. Herbert Lockyer, *All the Men of the Bible; All the Women of the Bible* (Grand Rapids, MI: Zondervan, 1996), 36.
4. Marjorie Holmes, *To Help You Through the Hurting*, 79.
5. Herbert Lockyer, *All the Men of the Bible; All the Women of the Bible* (Grand Rapids, MI: Zondervan, 1996), 36.
6. Larry G. Peppers, Ph.D. and Ronald J. Knapp, Ph.D., *How to Go on Living after the Death of a Baby* (Atlanta: Peachtree Publishers, 1985), 44.
7. *Nelson's Illustrated Bible Dictionary*, Thomas Nelson Publishers, 1986.
8. Marjorie Holmes, *To Help You Through the Hurting* (Garden City, NY: Doubleday & Company, 1983), 63.
9. *Barnes' Notes*, Electronic Database. Copyright © 1997 by Biblesoft.
10. Jack Hayford, *I'll Hold You in Heaven* (Ventura, CA: Regal Books, 1986, 1990), 66.
11. Philip Yancey, *The Jesus I Never Knew*, 202, 203.
12. Herbert Lockyer, *All the Men of the Bible; All the Women of the Bible*, 98.
13. Larry Richards, *God's Word for the Biblically-Inept* (Lancaster, PA: Starburst Publishers, 1998), 207, 208.
14. A. C. Bouquet, *Everyday Life in New Testament Times*, 149, 150.
15. Larry G. Peppers, Ph.D. and Ronald J. Knapp, Ph.D., *How to Go on Living After the Death of a Baby*, 36.
16. Ibid., 56.
17. Marjorie Holmes, *To Help You Through the Hurting*, 15.
18. Ibid., 108, 109.
19. Melissa Sexson Hanson, *When Mourning Breaks*, 37.
20. Hannah Whitall Smith, *The God of All Comfort* (Chicago: Moody Press, 1956), 45.

Chapter Sixteen

1. Margaret Wold, *Women of Faith & Spirit*, 55.
2. Erma Bombeck, *Family: The Ties That Bind and Gag*, 237.
3. Jim and Sally Conway, *Women in Mid-life Crisis* (Wheaton, IL: Tyndale House, 1984), 365.
4. Paul D. Gardner, *The Complete Who's Who in the Bible*, 413.
5. Dr. Deborah Newman, *Then God Created Woman*, 273.
6. Cheri Fuller, *When Mothers Pray*, 164.
7. Grace H. Ketterman, M.D., "Grandchildren," in *Prayers from a Mother's Heart*, 95.
8. Cheri Fuller, *When Mothers Pray*, 163.
9. Barbara Johnson, "Limited Visibility Ahead," in *The Joyful Journey*, 83.
10. Cheri Fuller, *When Mothers Pray*, 157.
11. Chris Fabry, *The 77 Habits of Highly Ineffective Christians*, 44.
12. Patsy Clairmont, "Masterpiece," in *Overjoyed*, 177.
13. Laurie Beth Jones, *Grow Something Besides Old*, 102.
14. Erma Bombeck as quoted in *Only Angels Can Wing It* by Liz Curtis Higgs, 211.

INDEX

Boldface numbers indicate defined (What?) terms in the sidebar.

D

Books by Starburst Publishers®

(Partial listing—full list available on request)

The ***What's in the Bible for . . .***™ series focuses its attention on making the Bible applicable to everyday life. Whether you're a teenager or senior citizen, this series has the book for you! Each title is equipped with the same reader-friendly icons, call-outs, tables, illustrations, questions, and chapter summaries that are used in the ***God's Word for the Biblically-Inept***™ series. It's another easy way to access God's Word!

What's in the Bible for . . .™ Mothers
Judy Bodmer
Is home schooling a good idea? Is it okay to work? At what age should I start treating my children like responsible adults? What is the most important thing I can teach my children? If you are asking these questions and need help answering them, *What's in the Bible for . . . Mothers* is especially for you! Simple and user-friendly, this motherhood manual offers hope and instruction for today's mothers by jumping into the lives of mothers in the Bible (e.g., Naomi, Elizabeth, and Mary) and by exploring biblical principles that are essential to being a nurturing mother.
(trade paper) ISBN 1892016265 $16.95

What's in the Bible for . . .™ Women
Georgia Curtis Ling
What does the Bible have to say to women? Women of all ages will find biblical insight on topics that are meaningful to them in four sections: Wisdom for the Journey; Family Ties; Bread, Breadwinners, and Bread Makers; and Fellowship and Community Involvement. This book uses illustrations, bullet points, chapter summaries, and icons to make understanding God's Word easier than ever!
(trade paper) ISBN 1892016109 $16.95

What's in the Bible for . . .™ Teens
Mark and Jeanette Littleton
This is a book that teens will love! *What's in the Bible for . . . Teens* contains topical Bible themes that parallel the challenges and pressures of today's adolescents. Learn about Bible prophecy, God's plan for relationships, and peer pressure in a conversational and fun tone. Helpful and eye-catching "WWJD?" icons, illustrations and sidebars included. (Available Fall 2000.)
(trade paper) ISBN 1892016052 $16.95

• **Learn more at www.biblicallyinept.com** •

The ***God's Word for the Biblically-Inept***™ series is already a best-seller with over 100,000 books sold! Designed to make reading the Bible easy, educational, and fun! This series of verse-by-verse Bible studies, topical studies, and overviews mixes scholarly information from experts with helpful icons, illustrations, sidebars, and time lines. It's the Bible made easy!

The Bible—God's Word for the Biblically-Inept™
Larry Richards
An excellent book to start learning the entire Bible. Get the basics or the in-depth information you are seeking with this user-friendly overview. From Creation to Christ to the Millennium, learning the Bible has never been easier.
(trade paper) ISBN 0914984551 $16.95

Revelation—God's Word for the Biblically-Inept™
Daymond R. Duck
End-Time Bible prophecy expert Daymond R. Duck leads us verse by verse through one of the Bible's most confusing books. Follow the experts as they forge their way through the captivating prophecies of Revelation!
(trade paper) ISBN 0914984985 $16.95

Daniel—God's Word for the Biblically-Inept™
Daymond R. Duck
Daniel is a book of prophecy and the key to understanding the mysteries of the Tribulation and End-Time events. This verse-by-verse commentary combines humor and scholarship to get at the essentials of Scripture. Perfect for those who want to know the truth about the Antichrist.
(trade paper) ISBN 0914984489 $16.95

Health & Nutrition—God's Word for the Biblically-Inept™
Kathleen O'Bannon Baldinger
The Bible is full of God's rules for good health! Baldinger reveals scientific evidence that proves the diet and health principles outlined in the Bible are the best for total health. Learn about the Bible Diet, the food pyramid, and fruits and vegetables from the Bible! Experts include Pamela Smith, Julian Whitaker, Kenneth Cooper, and T. D. Jakes.
(trade paper) ISBN 0914984055 $16.95

Life of Christ, Volume 1—God's Word for the Biblically-Inept™
Robert C. Girard
Girard takes the reader on an easy-to-understand journey through the gospels of Matthew, Mark, Luke, and John, tracing the story of Jesus from his virgin birth to his revolutionary ministry. Learn about Jesus' baptism, the Sermon on the Mount, and his miracles and parables.
(trade paper) ISBN 1892016230 $16.95

Men of the Bible—God's Word for the Biblically-Inept™
D. Larry Miller
Benefit from the life experiences of the powerful men of the Bible! Learn how the inspirational struggles of men such as Moses, Daniel, Paul, and David parallel the struggles of men today. It will inspire and build Christian character for any reader.
(trade paper) ISBN 1892016079 $16.95

Women of the Bible—God's Word for the Biblically-Inept™
Kathy Collard Miller
Finally, a Bible perspective just for women! Gain valuable insight from the successes and struggles of such women as Eve, Esther, Mary, Sarah, and Rebekah. Interesting icons like "Get Close to God," "Build Your Spirit," and "Grow Your Marriage" will make it easy to incorporate God's Word into your daily life.
(trade paper) ISBN 0914984063 $16.95

Genesis—God's Word for the Biblically-Inept™
Joyce L. Gibson
Genesis is written to make understanding and learning the Word of God simple and fun! Like the other books in this series, the author breaks the Bible down into bite-sized pieces making it easy to understand and incorporate into your life. Readers will learn about Creation, Adam and Eve, the Flood, Abraham and Isaac, and more.
(trade paper) ISBN 1892016125 $16.95

Prophecies of the Bible—God's Word for the Biblically-Inept™
Daymond R. Duck
God has a plan for this crazy planet, and now understanding it is easier than ever! Best-selling author and End-Time prophecy expert Daymond R. Duck explains the complicated prophecies of the Bible in plain English. Duck shows you all there is to know about the end of the age, the New World Order, the Second Coming, and the coming world government. Find out what prophecies have already been fulfilled and what's in store for the future!
(trade paper) ISBN 1892016222 $16.95

Romans—God's Word for the Biblically-Inept™
Gib Martin
The best-selling *God's Word for the Biblically-Inept™* series continues to grow! Learn about the apostle Paul, living a righteous life, and more with help from graphics, icons, and chapter summaries. (Available Summer 2000.)
(trade paper) ISBN 1892016273 $16.95

• **Learn more at www.biblicallyinept.com** •

The ***God Things Come in Small Packages*** series will make you want to blow the dust off your rose-colored glasses, open your eyes, and recount God's blessings! Join best-selling writers LeAnn Weiss, Susan Duke, Caron Loveless, and Judith Carden as they awaken your senses and open your mind to the "little" wonders of God in life's big picture!

God Things Come in Small Packages: Celebrating the Little Things in Life
Susan Duke, LeAnn Weiss, Caron Loveless, and Judith Carden
Enjoy touching reminders of God's simple yet generous gifts to brighten our days and gladden our hearts! Treasures like a sunset over a vast, sparkling ocean; a child's trust; or the crystalline dew on a spider's web come to life in this elegant compilation. Such occasions should be celebrated as if gift wrapped from God; they're his hallmarks! Personalized scripture is artfully combined with compelling stories and reflections.
(hard cover) ISBN 1892016281 $12.95

God Things Come in Small Packages for Moms: Rejoicing in the Simple Pleasures of Motherhood
Susan Duke, LeAnn Weiss, Caron Loveless, and Judith Carden
The "small" treasures God plants in mom's day shine in this delightful book. Savor priceless stories, which encourage you to value treasures like a shapeless, ceramic bowl presented with a toothy grin; a child's hand clinging to Mom's on a crowded bus; or a handful of wildflowers presented on a hectic day. Each story combines personalized Scripture with heartwarming vignettes and inspiring reflections.
(hard cover) ISBN 189201629X $12.95

God's Vitamin "C" for the Spirit™ of Women
Kathy Collard Miller
Subtitled: *"Tug-at-the-Heart" stories to Inspire and Delight Your Spirit*. A beautiful treasury of timeless stories, quotes, and poetry designed by and for women. Well-known Christian women like Liz Curtis Higgs, Patsy Clairmont, Naomi Rhode, and Elisabeth Elliott share from their hearts on subjects like marriage, motherhood, Christian living, faith, and friendship.
(trade paper) ISBN 0914984934 $12.95

God's Chewable Vitamin "C" for the Spirit™ of Moms

Delightful, insightful, and inspirational quotes combined with Scripture that uplifts and encourages women to succeed at the most important job in life—motherhood.
(trade paper) ISBN 0914984942 $6.95

The Weekly Feeder: A Revolutionary Shopping, Cooking, and Meal-Planning System

Cori Kirkpatrick

A revolutionary meal-planning system, here is a way to make preparing home-cooked dinners more convenient than ever. At the beginning of each week, simply choose one of the eight preplanned menus, tear out the corresponding grocery list, do your shopping, and whip up each fantastic meal in less than 45 minutes! The author's household management tips, equipment checklists, and nutrition information make this system a must for any busy family. Included with every recipe is a personal anecdote from the author emphasizing the importance of good food, a healthy family, and a well-balanced life.
(trade paper) ISBN 1892016095 $16.95

God Stories: They're So Amazing, Only God Could Make Them Happen

Donna I. Douglas

Famous individuals share their personal, true-life experiences with God in this beautiful new book! Find out how God has touched the lives of top recording artists, professional athletes, and other newsmakers like Jessi Colter, Deana Carter, Ben Vereen, Stephanie Zimbalist, Cindy Morgan, Sheila E., Joe Jacoby, Cheryl Landon, Brett Butler, Clifton Taulbert, Babbie Mason, Michael Medved, Sandi Patty, Charlie Daniels, and more! Their stories are intimate, poignant, and sure to inspire and motivate you as you listen for God's message in your own life!
(cloth) ISBN 1892016117 $18.95

Since Life Isn't a Game, These Are God's Rules: Finding Joy & Fulfillment in God's Ten Commandments

Kathy Collard Miller

Life is often referred to as a game, but God didn't create us because he was short on game pieces. To succeed in life, you'll need to know God's rules. In this book, Kathy Collard Miller explains the meaning of each of the Ten Commandments with fresh application for today. Each chapter includes Scripture and quotes from some of our most beloved Christian authors including Billy Graham, Patsy Clairmont, Liz Curtis Higgs, and more! Sure to renew your understanding of God's rules.
(cloth) ISBN 189201615X $16.95

God's Little Rule Book: Simple Rules to Bring Joy & Happiness to Your Life

Starburst Publishers

Let this little book of God's rules be your personal guide to a more joyful life. Brimming with easily applicable rules, this book is sure to inspire and motivate you! Each rule includes corresponding Scripture and a practical tip that will help to incorporate God's rules into everyday life. Simple enough to fit into a busy schedule, yet powerful enough to be life changing!
(trade paper) ISBN 1892016168 $6.95

Life's Little Rule Book: Simple Rules to Bring Joy & Happiness to Your Life

Starburst Publishers

Let this little book inspire you to live a happier life! The pages are filled with timeless rules such as, "Learn to cook, you'll always be in demand!" and "Help something grow." Each rule is combined with a reflective quote and a simple suggestion to help the reader incorporate the rule into everyday life.
(trade paper) ISBN 1892016176 $6.95

God's Abundance

Edited by Kathy Collard Miller

Over 50,000 sold! Learn to see the unexpected blessings in life. These individual essays describe experiences that seem negative on the surface but are something God has used for good in our lives or to benefit others. Witness God at work in our lives. Learn to trust God in action. Realize that we always have a choice to learn and benefit from these experiences by letting God prove His promise of turning all things for our good.
(cloth) ISBN 0914984977 $19.95

Promises of God's Abundance

Edited by Kathy Collard Miller

Subtitled: *For a More Meaningful Life.* The Bible is filled with God's promises for an abundant life. *Promises of God's Abundance* is written in the same way as the best-selling *God's Abundance.* It will help you discover these promises and show you how simple obedience is the key to an abundant life. Scripture, questions for growth, and a simple thought for the day will guide you to a more meaningful life.
(trade paper) ISBN 0914984098 $9.95

Stories of God's Abundance for a More Joyful Life

Compiled by Kathy Collard Miller

Like its successful predecessor, *God's Abundance* (100,000 sold), this book is filled with beautiful, inspirational, real life stories. Those telling their stories of God share Scriptures and insights that readers can

apply to their daily lives. Renew your faith in life's small miracles and challenge yourself to allow God to lead the way as you find the source of abundant living for all your relationships.
(trade paper) ISBN 1892016060 $12.95

More of Him, Less of Me
Jan Christiansen
Subtitled: *A Daybook of My Personal Insights, Inspirations & Meditations on the Weigh Down™ Diet.* The insight shared in this year long daybook of inspiration will encourage you on your weight-loss journey, bring you to a deeper relationship with God, and help you improve any facet of your life. Each page includes an essay, Scripture, and a tip-of-the-day that will encourage and uplift you as you trust God to help you achieve your proper weight. Perfect companion guide for anyone on the Weigh Down™ diet!
(cloth) ISBN 1892016001 $17.95

Desert Morsels: A Journal with Encouraging Tidbits from My Journey on the Weigh Down™ Diet
Jan Christiansen
When Jan Christiansen set out to lose weight on the Weigh Down™ diet she got more than she bargained for! In addition to *losing* over 35 pounds and *gaining* a closer relationship with God, Jan discovered a gift—her ability to entertain and comfort fellow dieters! Jan's inspiring website led to the release of her best-selling first book, *More of Him, Less of Me*. Now, Jan serves another helping of *her* wit and *His* wisdom in this lovely companion journal. Includes inspiring Scripture, insightful comments, stories from readers, room for the reader's personal reflection, and *Plenty of Attitude* (p-attitude).
(cloth) ISBN 1892016214 $16.95

Purchasing Information

www.starburstpublishers.com

Books are available from your favorite bookstore, either from current stock or special order. To assist bookstores in locating your selection, be sure to give title, author, and ISBN. If unable to purchase from a bookstore, you may order direct from STARBURST PUBLISHERS. When ordering please enclose full payment plus shipping and handling as follows:

Post Office (4th class)
$3.00 with a purchase of up to $20.00
$4.00 ($20.01–$50.00)
5% of purchase price for purchases of $50.01 and up

United Parcel Service (UPS)
$4.50 (up to $20.00)
$6.00 ($20.01–$50.00)
7% ($50.01 and up)

Canada
$5.00 (up to $35.00)
15% ($35.01 and up)

Overseas
$5.00 (up to $25.00)
20% ($25.01 and up)

Payment in U.S. funds only. Please allow two to three weeks minimum (longer overseas) for delivery. Make checks payable to and mail to:

Starburst Publishers® • P.O. Box 4123 • Lancaster, PA 17604

Credit card orders may be placed by calling 1-800-441-1456, Mon–Fri, 8:30 A.M. to 5:30 P.M. Eastern Standard Time. Prices are subject to change without notice. Catalogs are available for a 9 x 12 self-addressed envelope with four first-class stamps.

NOTES

NOTES

2/1 8:00

6:30 Thurs Fired up Rio Bravo

May 18-19 2001 Retreat + E.L. art fair